Major General
Israel Putnam

Major General Israel Putnam

Hero of the American Revolution

ROBERT ERNEST HUBBARD

McFarland & Company, Inc., Publishers
Jefferson, North Carolina

LIBRARY OF CONGRESS CATALOGUING-IN-PUBLICATION DATA

Names: Hubbard, Robert Ernest, author.
Title: Major General Israel Putnam : hero of the American Revolution / Robert Ernest Hubbard.
Other titles: Hero of the American Revolution
Description: Jefferson, North Carolina : McFarland & Company, Inc., Publishers, 2017 | Includes bibliographical references and index.
Identifiers: LCCN 2017012766 | ISBN 9781476664538 (softcover : acid free paper) ∞
Subjects: LCSH: Putnam, Israel, 1718–1790. | Generals—United States—Biography. | United States. Continental Army—Biography. | United States—History—Revolution, 1775–1783—Campaigns. | United States—History—French and Indian War, 1754–1763—Campaigns.
Classification: LCC E207.P9 H85 2017 | DDC 973.3/3092 [B] —dc23
LC record available at https://lccn.loc.gov/2017012766

BRITISH LIBRARY CATALOGUING DATA ARE AVAILABLE

ISBN (print) 978-1-4766-6453-8
ISBN (ebook) 978-1-4766-2783-0

© 2017 Robert Ernest Hubbard. All rights reserved

No part of this book may be reproduced or transmitted in any form or by any means, electronic or mechanical, including photocopying or recording, or by any information storage and retrieval system, without permission in writing from the publisher.

On the cover: *Major General Israel Putnam*, Dominique C. Fabronius, artist, Boston, ca. 1864 (Library of Congress)

Printed in the United States of America

McFarland & Company, Inc., Publishers
  Box 611, Jefferson, North Carolina 28640
    www.mcfarlandpub.com

Acknowledgments

I would like to thank the staff of the Connecticut State Archives for their generous assistance. I'm also grateful to Jennifer Busa, Melissa Traub, and Molly Woods at the Connecticut Historical Society's The Waterman Research Center.

Thanks to Nicholas Beams, MLS, at the Pomfret Public Library, for inviting me to present a talk on the life of Israel Putnam while I was working on this book.

A thank you to Martin Byster and Arleen Hamm at the Van Wyck Homestead Museum, Fishkill, New York, for information related to General Putnam's time in the Hudson Highlands. I also appreciate the help of Archivist Andrew Arpey of the New York State Archives.

I'm grateful to Sally Bretschger and Molly Kokoruda at the Greenwich, Connecticut, Putnam Cottage for the afternoon they spent showing me their wonderfully maintained site.

I have spoken with many other fine people in my research, but I would especially like to thank the following:

Candice Brashears, director of the Jonathan Trumbull Jr. House Museum in Lebanon, Connecticut.

Daniel Cruson, author of *Putnam's Revolutionary War Winter Encampment: The History and Archaeology of Putnam Memorial State Park*, for his insights into General Putnam's role in the Redding Connecticut encampment of 1778-1779.

Barbara Ducharme, for information on Israel Putnam's only surviving homestead.

The Rev. Francis H. Geer, rector of St. Philip's Church in the Highlands in Garrison, New York, was kind enough to point the author toward a couple of sources that were valuable in recreating Israel Putnam's time in Fishkill, New York.

Tina McEvoy, assistant director of the Lawrence Library in Pepperell, Massachusetts, for her help in researching the life of Pepperell's most famous resident—Israel Putnam's comrade-in-arms, Colonel William Prescott.

I would also like to recognize the staffs at the following historic sites: the Putnam Memorial State Park in Redding, Connecticut; the Bunker Hill Monument and the Battle of Bunker Hill Museum, which are part of the Boston National Historical Park; the Fort William Henry Museum in Lake George, New York; and the Crown Point State Historic Site.

Thanks also to the staff at the Webb-Deane-Stevens Museum in Wethersfield, Connecticut, and the staff at the Schuyler Mansion State Historic Site in Albany, New York, for answering detailed questions about General Schuyler and his house.

Also, I'm grateful to Beth Devlin at the reference department of the Wallingford Public Library and Denise Russo and her staff at the reference department of Middletown, Connecticut's Russell Library for their assistance.

Most of all, I'd like to thank my wife, Kathleen, for editing this book and providing many valuable suggestions.

Table of Contents

Acknowledgments	v
Preface	1
Introduction	3
ONE: THE NEW ENGLAND FARMER	7

    The Bamboo Cane • Salem Witch Trials and the Putnam Family • Growing Up in Massachusetts • The Connecticut Farm • The Wolf

TWO: FRENCH AND INDIAN WAR	19

    War Breaks Out • The Durkee Incident • Putnam Saves Robert Rogers' Life • Boat Attack on Lake George • Mission to Take a French Prisoner • Rescue of Captain Little • The Massacre at Fort William Henry • South Bay • Saving the Magazine • Failed British Attack on Fort Ticonderoga • The Three Choices • "Rogers always sent, but Putnam led his men to action" • A Prisoner • Jemima Howe, the Captive

THREE: BETWEEN THE WARS	45

    Expedition to the West Indies • Pontiac's War • Death of Hannah • Marriage to Deborah • Putnam's Appearance and Temperament • Tavern Owner • Preparation for War • 1773 Mississippi Expedition

FOUR: BLOODIEST BATTLE OF THE REVOLUTION	69

    Events Leading to the Battle • The Battle of Bunker Hill • Organization of an Army • Siege of Boston

FIVE: BATTLES IN NEW YORK 113
British Arrival at New York • Battle of Long Island • Retreat from Long Island • Battle of Kip's Bay • Battle of Harlem Heights • Battle of White Plains

SIX: WAR IN THE NORTH 132
Protection of Philadelphia • Battle of Princeton • Disease and Punishment • Hudson Highlands • Deborah Putnam Taken Ill • Deborah Putnam's Passing • The Recruiter • Cousin Rufus Putnam • Winter Encampment at Redding • The Horseneck Escape

SEVEN: PUTNAM'S LAST YEARS 171
The Last Command • After the War • Putnam's Death

EIGHT: THE LEGACY 186
People in Putnam's World • Putnam Remembered • Conclusion

Chapter Notes 205
Bibliography 235
Index 243

Preface

I was a teenager in 1967 when I met Medal of Honor recipient Captain Eddie Rickenbacker. It had been 50 years since he had achieved international fame as the "American Ace of Aces"—the United States fighter pilot who shot down the greatest number of enemy planes in World War I. As I shook his hand, I remembered that that hand had maneuvered primitive biplanes in combat and downed 26 enemy aircraft.

But Rickenbacker's World War I experiences weren't the only remarkable part of his life. Before the conflict, he had been one of America's most daring automobile racers, and in 1941 he almost died in an air crash. The following year, while on a World War II mission for the U.S. military, he again survived a plane crash—one which left him adrift on a rubber raft in the Pacific Ocean for 22 days.

Few people in United States history have willingly confronted such a number and variety of dangers as Rickenbacker. One of those few was an 18th century New England farmer named Israel Putnam.[1]

As a life-long resident of Connecticut, I had heard Israel Putnam's name mentioned countless times—the Town of Putnam in the northeast corner of the state is only about one-half hour away from my alma mater, the University of Connecticut. Also, many cities and towns have a Putnam Street or a Putnam Avenue, and the City of Meriden has an Israel Putnam Elementary School. But I didn't know much about the man behind the name.

In the 1990s, I discovered details of Putnam's incredible life and created a website, which included stories and pictures of the man and his accomplishments. I uploaded the first material to IsraelPutnam.com in

1996 and for the past 20 years I have added letters from visitors to the site, new links, and photographs of places Putnam lived, traveled, and fought.

In 2015, after having had five history books published, I was searching for a topic for another book. I didn't realize at first that the perfect topic was right on my website: Israel Putnam.

Introduction

In 1718 Jonathan Corwin, one of the last surviving judges of the Salem witch trials, died. It was also the year the English pirate Blackbeard (a.k.a. Edward Teach) was killed in battle. An old era was passing, and in the new one the old evils of witchcraft and piracy would take a back seat to the greater evils of political revolution and the first worldwide war in history.

In the first week of 1718, a baby was born a few miles from where the Salem witchcraft trials had been held 26 years earlier. His parents, Joseph and Elizabeth Putnam, had played a significant part in the witch hysteria—that is, in *opposing* it. At his baptism, the baby boy was given the name Israel. Despite having to compete with ten older brothers and sisters,[1] he would end up becoming a key player in nearly every major event in North America during the next 70 years.

I started my research on Putnam with Colonel David Humphreys's 40,000 word biography, *An Essay on the Life of the Honorable Major-General Israel Putnam*, published in 1788. I then collected every major biography of Israel Putnam, compared them, sifted through the stories and tall tales for the facts, and developed this first, modern full-length telling of his life story. Where there are discrepancies between past accounts (and there are many), I have tended to give the most credence to the Humphrey biographies—there were several editions published in the late 1700s and early 1800s.

The reasons for my preference for Humphreys's work is simple: it was based on interviews with Israel Putnam himself; it was written by a man who knew him well (Humphreys served as Putnam's aide-de-camp during the American Revolutionary War); and it was almost certainly edited by

George Washington, since Humphreys was a houseguest at Washington's Mount Vernon estate when he wrote the first edition. The 1788 edition was also the only biographical account of Putnam to be published during his life. One other distinction deserves mention: it was the first biography of an American written by an American author. Later, Humphreys wrote a biography of Washington, but he "cut his teeth" on the Putnam work.[2]

It's important to understand the background of David Humphreys.[3] After serving Putnam, he was appointed aide-de-camp to General Nathaniel Greene and, beginning in 1780, to George Washington. A wise and faithful right hand to these leaders, Humphreys rose to the rank of colonel. Later, he became the first minister appointed to a foreign country (Portugal) under the U.S. Constitution. Later, John Quincy Adams took over that position and Humphreys became minister to Spain.[4]

Humphreys also was responsible for enlisting the first African Americans in the American military forces. Although his work for Washington didn't allow him to command the soldiers in person, Humphreys formed and nominally led the all-black 2nd company of Connecticut's 4th regiment in October 1780. Composed of 48 black privates and non-commissioned officers, it served until November 1782.[5]

Of the dozen or so other biographies to follow Humphreys' 1788 work,[6] the most complete and accurate is William Farrand Livingston's 1901 *Israel Putnam Pioneer, Ranger, and Major-General 1718–1790*.[7] Livingston was an Episcopal minister, an assistant State Librarian of Maine, and a direct descendent of Israel Putnam.[8]

Today, many of the letters of key Colonial-era figures, including George Washington, John Adams, and Thomas Jefferson, are available on the Internet, allowing access to original source materials that earlier biographers couldn't possibly obtain. In addition, many 18th, 19th and 20th century books, journals, and newspaper articles are easily located and accessed online or through library microfilm archives.

I believe that before reading a biography, the reader should have a general impression of the subject. One of the best short descriptions that I've found is the following by historian Paul Lockhart:

> Israel Putnam was a fearless bull of a man, with a stocky pugilist's body surmounted by a great cube of a head and a face that was comically akin to a bulldog's. He was loud and brash and bellowing, but not a bully in any way. All who knew him loved him, and most who didn't know him loved him, too. Putnam didn't have an enemy worth mentioning. He exuded action; those who served under him would follow him anywhere. There was no pretense, nothing frivolous, about the man.[9]

Passenger, If thou art a Soldier, Drop a Tear over the dust of a Hero, Who Ever attentive to the lives and happiness of his Men, Dared to lead Where any Dared to follow.
—from Timothy Dwight's epitaph
on Israel Putnam's grave, 1790

One of the talismanic names of the Revolution, the very mention of which is like the sound of a trumpet.
—Washington Irving, 1856

ONE

The New England Farmer

The Bamboo Cane

There's a story associated with Israel Putnam's time on the island of Cuba, involving an African slave. It reveals much about his character.[1]

Toward the end of the French and Indian War, in 1762, British troops and their North American comrades attacked Spanish-controlled Cuba. As one of the commanders from the 13 American colonies, Putnam led a contingent of 1,000 Connecticut men. After the British side had consolidated its win, Putnam was walking alone down a Havana street. He came across a crowd of people gathered around an altercation. Putnam stepped up and saw a Spaniard beating a slave with a heavy bamboo cane.

Putnam rushed up to the man and, despite the jeers of the crowd, wrestled the cane from his grip. More Spaniards gathered around the ruckus and Putnam was barely able to escape. But he kept the cane.

To Putnam's surprise, the slave followed him back to his ship and pleaded to be taken aboard. Putnam took him onto the vessel and allowed him to accompany him back home. The man, named simply "Dick" in the records, was freed by Putnam and worked for him for the rest of the General's life.[2]

In 1786, in what was probably the last time he ventured outside of Connecticut, elderly Israel Putnam traveled to his birthplace in northeastern Massachusetts. Judge Samuel Putnam, said of his cousin:

> He rode on horseback from Brooklyn [Connecticut] to Danvers [Massachusetts] and paid his last visit to his friends there. At his way home he stopped at Cambridge at the [Harvard] College, where the governor of the College paid him much attention. It was in my junior year; he came into my room. His speech was much affected by palsy.[3]

On this final trip of his life, Putnam was accompanied by the man he had saved from a brutal beating in Havana 24 years earlier—his friend and servant, Dick.

Putnam kept the bamboo cane for the rest of his life. About seven months before his death, he dictated in a memorandum: "Walked out today supported by my Havana cane, which is a necessity in my present infirmity, and which I never carry without a remembrance of that day when I seized it."[4]

The General bequeathed the cane to Dick, who, then elderly himself, regularly used it about town and was always pleased to tell the story behind it.

Salem Witch Trials and the Putnam Family

Two of Putnam's great-grandfathers who lived in Massachusetts Colony's Salem Village were John Putnam, a village founder,[5] and William Hathorne, who was also novelist Nathaniel Hawthorne's ancestor.

In his preface to *The Scarlet Letter*, Nathaniel Hawthorne (1804–1864), described great-great-great-grandfather William as

> grave, bearded, sable-cloaked, and steeple-crowned progenitor,—who came so early, with his Bible and his sword, and trode the unworn street with such stately port, and made so large a figure, as a man of war and peace,—a stronger claim than for myself, whose name is seldom heard, and my face hardly known. He was a soldier, legislator, judge; he was a ruler in the church.[6]

More than one of these traits might be found in a description of great-grandson Israel Putnam's character as well.

Old William Hathorne, had a son, John Hathorne, who was a judge in one of the most infamous events of 17th century America: the Salem Witch trials. In fact, it is said that he was the only judge who did not later repudiate his role in the affair. Many think that writer Nathaniel added the "w" to his surname because he wished to distance himself from this witch trial judge, but others suspect that he discovered in his genealogical research that it had been spelled that way by his family before they moved to the American colonies[7]; No one knows for sure.

The Salem witch trials affected the Putnam family too. Thomas Putnam, the son of immigrant John Putnam, built a large colonial house near Hathorne Hill in 1648 and married widow Mary Veren in 1666. Later, in 1690, their son Joseph, who inherited the house, married Elizabeth Porter.

One. The New England Farmer 9

Two years later the couple found themselves on the dangerous end of the Salem witch trials.

It had started in January 1692, when Salem Village's minister, Samuel Parris's nine-year-old daughter, Elizabeth Parris, and his eleven-year-old niece, Abigail Williams, became ill. They experienced trances and underwent convulsive seizures during which they uttered blasphemies. The local physician diagnosed it as witchcraft and the Rev. Parris' slave, Tituba, was accused of being at the root of the problem. Witnesses claimed that the girls engaged in satanic ceremonies in the nearby woods with Tituba.

Local women, Sarah Goode and Sarah Osborne, along with Tituba, were put on trial. They were accused of placing spells on the Parris and Williams girls, as well as on 12-year-old Ann Putnam, a relative of yet-to-be-born Israel Putnam. Ann Putnam and General Israel Putnam were the grandchildren of Thomas Putnam. Ann by Thomas' first wife, Ann Holyoke, and Israel by his second wife, Mary Veren. Ann Putnam died in 1716, two years before Israel Putnam was born.

In all, about 150 people in Salem and nearby towns were accused of witchcraft and confined to prison, where several died. Between June and September 1692, 14 women and 5 men were found guilty and were executed by hanging. In addition, an eighty-one-year-old man was crushed to death in an attempt to force him to confess.

When the governor of Massachusetts Bay Province, William Phips, found his own wife was being accused of witchcraft, he stopped the trials and released the people who had been imprisoned.

While the Putnam family's reputation was badly sullied by the participation of Ann and her parents in the persecution and murder of innocent people, Israel Putnam's parents Joseph and Elizabeth helped redeem the family name by their courageous opposition to the persecutors—they were two of the most noticeable opponents of the witchcraft hysteria. In fact, during the months that the witch-hunts were in full swing, Joseph kept his musket loaded, and his best horse saddled, in case he and his wife were attacked for trying to stop the witch hunters. Hanson, in his 1848 history of Danvers, puts it this way: "Capt. Joseph Putnam, Israel's father, kept a horse in constant readiness several weeks, with the expectation that he would be accused on account of his opposition to the Great Delusion."[8]

Were it not for one later event, the Putnam couple would have gone down in history solely for their role as decent, courageous individuals who showed intelligence and compassion for their fellow human beings during a time of hysteria. But a quarter-century after the witch madness, Elizabeth gave birth to a child who was destined to provide an example of courage that would serve as an inspiration to millions. They named him Israel Thomas Putnam.

Growing Up in Massachusetts

Given the primitive state of transportation in early 18th century Colonial America, we may be inclined to assume that people were likely to spend their entire lives within their birth colony. Often, that was true. But in the case of Israel Putnam, wanderlust, ambition, and patriotism led to something different.

Born in Massachusetts on January 7, 1718,[9] and baptized on February 2, Israel was the eleventh of twelve children.[10] Until he reached the age of maturity, he lived in Salem Village (renamed Danvers in 1752), about 20 miles north of Boston. Then he purchased and operated a farm in the Connecticut colony—a farm he owned for the rest of his life. Although rooted in Connecticut, it has been said that in his military service and private expeditions Putnam may have traveled more widely throughout North America than any other person of his time.

It's interesting to investigate tales of his childhood, although such stories are often a mixture of fact and fiction. One anecdote of his youth in Massachusetts bears a similarity to the tale of the Havana cane, as well as to other stories that crop up throughout Putnam's life, underscoring his concern for the underdog.

One day near his home, young Israel came across a boy who was verbally abusing a neighbor's daughter because her parents were poor. He confronted the bully, who quickly ran away. The fact that Putnam as a teenager was strong enough to perform the farm work of an adult man may have influenced the other lad's reluctance to fight.[11]

In his Putnam biography, David Humphreys told the story of the first time Israel traveled to the metropolis of Boston. "He was insulted for his rusticity by a boy of twice his size and age; after bearing the sarcasms until his patience was worn out, he challenged, engaged and vanquished his unmannerly antagonist, to the great diversion of a crowd of spectators."[12] Not only is this story almost assuredly from Putnam himself, it is also one of only a handful of incidents in the life of young Israel that are recorded by Humphreys. Thus, one might conclude that it was an incident that Putnam personally considered significant.

Then there's a tale of young Putnam being sent to a pasture to bring

ONE. THE NEW ENGLAND FARMER 11

Putnam's birthplace in Danvers, Massachusetts, was built by his grandfather, Thomas Putnam, in 1648 (from William Farrand Livingston's *Israel Putnam Pioneer, Ranger, and Major-General 1718–1790*).

a bull back to his barn. As Israel entered the field, the animal charged. Immediately, Putnam returned to his house, put on spurs, and went back to the pasture. When the bull again chased him, Putnam jumped on his back, rode around a pasture as the beast tried to throw him off. The bull, eventually tired out, ended up in a swamp where he became trapped in the mud.[13] This tale doesn't have the pedigree of the Boston story, but it could well be based on truth.

These stories are similar to the tales of two figures in the following century: African American folk hero John Henry and giant lumberjack Paul Bunyan. However, there is one major different: the Putnam tales are tacked on to the real-life, fully-documented exploits of an already famous military hero.

In 1739, upon reaching the age of 21, Putnam received the inheritance that his father had left for him at his death 16 years earlier. This opened up a new chapter in young Putnam's life, beginning with his marriage and his investments.

On July 19, 1739, Israel wed 18-year-old Hannah Pope at a ceremony that took place at the home of Hannah's parents, Joseph and Mehitable Pope. The Popes, like Putnam's parents, were among the most affluent farmers of the area. In preparation for marriage, Putnam had built a small house on his Massachusetts' farm. The following year their first child was born, a son they named Israel.[14]

On March 15, 1739, using 1,920 pounds gained from the sale of land in Salem Village, which had been inherited from his father, 21-year-old Putnam teamed up with brother-in-law, Joseph Pope (also 21), to purchase 514 acres of raw land from Massachusetts governor Jonathan Belcher for 2,572 pounds.[15] The land, 75 miles southeast of Danvers, was in the Connecticut district of Mortlake, which 12 years later became part of Pomfret, and 35 years after that, part of Brooklyn. It sits about 12 miles southwest of the spot where Massachusetts, Rhode Island and Connecticut come together.

The following year, Israel brought his wife and young son to his Connecticut farm. He set about to the tasks of building a small house, constructing stone walls, growing crops, assembling livestock (primarily sheep and cattle), and clearing the fields of stones. New England farmers often said that no matter how well the edible crops thrived, the freezing and thawing of the ground always resulted in a new crop of stones each spring.[16]

Putnam achieved such success that within two years, between the profits from his farm and the sale of additional inherited land in Massachusetts, he was able to buy out his wife's brother and pay Gov. Belcher in full.

For the remainder of Israel's life, despite his many extended military missions, he would return to the town of Pomfret/Brooklyn—it was his home.[17]

The Connecticut Farm

From 1740 to 1755, Israel and Hannah lived the lives of prosperous Connecticut farmers. Israel aged from 21 to 37 in these years; Hannah from 19 to 35. David Humphrey's biography described the time as:

> Prosperity, at length, began to attend the agricultural affairs of Mr. Putnam. He was acknowledged to be a skillful and indefatigable manager. His fields were mostly enclosed with stone walls. His crops commonly succeeded, because the land was well tilled and manured. His pastures and meadows became luxuriant. His cattle were of the best breed and in good order. His garden and fruit-trees prolific. With the avails of the surplusage of his produce foreign articles were purchased. Within doors he found the compensation of his labors in the plenty of excellent provisions, as well as in the happiness of domestic society.[18]

Israel Putnam's great-grandson Lemuel Grosvenor described his ancestor's first Connecticut farm:

> This farm is situated on the summit of the high hill between the villages of Pomfret and Brooklyn; and the present line of separation between these townships, passes through this tract. It is nearly all fertile soil, admirably adapted to cultivation, being level or gently sloping. The first house he built, is not now standing [as of at least 1855], but the spot where it stood is pointed out. There still lie many of the stones of the old foundation—there is the first well he dug, but covered now with the modern invention of a platform, and a chain pump. There is an old pear tree, almost leafless and lifeless from old age, which it is said he planted. It stands about a hundred yards back of the house now occupied by Mr. Benj. Brown.[19]

In a 1919 agricultural magazine, an Arkansas farmer looked at Connecticut farming. His description could just as easily been of a farm in Israel Putnam's time. Writer Jay B. Iden observed:

> To clear a Connecticut hill farm means not only removing the brush and trees but the boulders as well. The thrifty farmer of other days cleared up and added to his tilled plots one acre of land a year. When the last stone that could possibly be moved was off the field there were others hidden beneath the surface. The damage they could do to a plowshare points out perhaps the real reason for the slow moving oxen which stop at the very moment of contact and start again very slowly.[20]

Warming up to the topic of Connecticut oxen, Iden goes on:

> In the use of oxen on a farm where much grass is grown one sees a very fine example of the Connecticut farmer's thriftiness. The grass not only furnishes grazing for the dairy cows and the young stock, but it is feed for the work team as well; for oxen can be worked all day and turned on grass at night greatly reducing the consumption of hay. A horse cannot work all day and spend the night harvesting feed for itself, a form of servitude under which oxen thrive.[21]

Lemuel Grosvenor also discusses Putnam's second farmhouse, which he built in about 1750 (and which is still standing today):

> About a quarter of a mile S.E. of this house is another which he built, and in it, is the long, narrow bed-room, ancient and comfortable in its appointments, in which he died. The main road from Pomfret to Brooklyn passes through the farm, and is planted on both sides, for a long distance, with very aged apple trees, which the old men in this neighborhood affirm were set out by the general. From the time of his arrival in Pomfret, even down to his death, he was as fond of the peaceful pursuits of agriculture and horticulture, as of the excitement of hair breadth escapes in the deadly breach, and by flood and field.

Putnam was well-known for his cultivation of fruit trees. Grosvenor mentions that "His neighbors give him the credit of introducing all the best varieties into Pomfret and Brooklyn, and especially, the famous winter apple, the Roxbury Russet, now so abundant here, he is said to have brought with him from Salem, when he first settled in Pomfret."[22]

The second home Israel Putnam built in Pomfret, Connecticut. The first one, which was much smaller, is no longer standing (author's collection).

Between 1740 and 1764, Israel and Hannah (1721–1765) had five sons and five daughters. They were spaced out by between 23 and 43 months.[23] They likely attended a school that had been built for the children of Governor Belcher's tenants. Sitting on Cooney Road, it was only about two miles from Israel's home and the only school in the area.[24]

Putnam's children had many offspring. Sixty-five years after the General's death, on October 25, 1855, at a meeting of his descendants, eight of his grandchildren were still alive: David Putnam of Marietta, Ohio, the son of Israel, Jr., William P. Tyler of Brooklyn, Connecticut, the son of Mehitable, L.P. Grosvenor of Pomfret Connecticut, the son of Eunice, Mrs. Harriet Grosvenor of Hartford and Mrs. Emily Brown of Brooklyn, the daughters of Daniel Putnam, and three sons of Peter Schuyler Putnam, who were living in New York and Ohio.[25]

During their early years in Connecticut, when Israel and Hannah were raising their children, only one event occurred that was out-of-the-ordinary. It was the first of many public acts of courage that would make Israel Putnam a "legend in his own lifetime."

The incident has been referred to as the "killing of the last wolf in Connecticut." Whether the animal in the story was the last wolf in the state is questionable to say the least, and the story has been embellished over the years, but the essential parts have been accepted by most historians as true.

The Wolf

In the Connecticut Colony's first century, wolves were such a serious threat to livestock that a substantial bounty was placed on them, as witnessed by the following law from March 1648: "It is agreed if any person do kill any wolfe or wolfs within the town of Nameaug [New London], he that kills the wolf shall have of everie familie in towne six pence conditionally that he bring the head and the skin to any two of the townsmen."[26]

Over the years, the wolves of Connecticut's Windham County, which borders New London County on the north, had gradually disappeared. Bayles in his county history relates that Indians Tom and Jeremy had "routed" them out of Plainfield and Killingly, and Pembascus [apparently also a Native American] had killed Woodstock's last wolf.[27] Ashford's last wolf was killed in 1735. Now, it was the winter of 1742-1743 and only one wolf appeared to be left to ravage livestock—the one that returned to Pomfret every year.

The Israel Putnam farm was noted for its cattle, sheep, goats, and poultry.[28] One night Israel found 70 of his sheep and goats dead, and many lambs and kids injured. The adult animals had been slain by the she-wolf that had been raiding local farms every fall and winter for several years. Sheep were a wolf's prey of choice since they were more docile than swine and smaller than cattle.

Each year, farmers had picked off predators that ravaged their herds, but the old timber wolf was too clever and resilient to be trapped. The wolf was said to have killed many more animals than it could possibly eat. Its taste for blood terrorized farm families who were fearful that the animal would attack their younger children. "Boys and girls feared to go to school or drive the cows home."[29]

The first full account of Putnam's role in the cornering of the wolf was told by David Humphreys in his biography of his friend and former commander. As his account came from the mouth of Putnam himself, this chapter is based primarily on this source, and supplemented with additional details from later biographies.

According to Humphreys, in 1742 Putnam teamed up with five other Pomfret area farmers to hunt down the wolf. They arranged to conduct a continuous hunt with two of them actively tracking the animal at any given time. They were aided by the fact that the wolf had distinctive paw prints—previously she had lost part of one foot to a steel trap.

By ten o'clock the next morning, their bloodhounds had cornered it in a den, which was only three miles north of the Putnam farm. Seventeen-

The Wolf Den in Pomfret, Connecticut, is virtually unchanged since the day when Putnam crawled its 41-foot length to confront a wolf that had killed 70 sheep (photograph by author).

year-old John Sharpe, running ahead of the hunters, was the first person to reach the den's opening—the long tunnel was set within massive granite boulders and difficult to navigate.

The farmers brought in dogs, but all that entered the tunnel returned frightened or, in several cases, injured by the wolf. They then tried to smoke her out. When that didn't work, they burned sulfur at the mouth of the den. That too was ineffective.

According to Ellen Larned, in her *History of Windham County*, Israel Putnam was not among the party that tracked the wolf that day. He was only summoned after someone mentioned that he owned one of the finest bloodhounds in the area.[30]

When Putnam arrived at the den, the other farmers were tired and frustrated. He attempted to get his dog to enter the tunnel. Failing at that, he tried to persuade his servant to crawl in with a gun and torch, and shoot the wolf. The man refused, as did all the other men who had gathered. The wolf had by now been cornered for 12 hours and Putnam cautioned that if they waited any longer the animal might find some crevice in the den and make its escape.

He fashioned a birch bark torch, removed his coat and waistcoat and tied a rope around his feet. As he crawled into the tunnel, men let out the rope, all the while being ready to pull it back out if Putnam gave it a tug.

What happened next was described by David Humphreys:

> He discovered the glaring eye-balls of the wolf, who was sitting at the extremity of the cavern. Startled at the sight of fire, she gnashed her teeth, and gave a sullen growl. As soon as he had made the necessary discovery, he kicked the rope as a signal for pulling him out. The people, at the mouth of the den, who had listened with painful anxiety, hearing the growling of the wolf, and supposing their friend to be in the most imminent danger, drew him forth with such celerity that his shirt was stripped over his head and his skin severely lacerated.[31]

Putnam loaded his musket with nine buckshot, and with a torch in one hand and the gun in the other, he crawled back into the den a second time. Humphreys continues:

> When he drew nearer than before, the wolf, assuming a still more fierce and terrible appearance, howling, rolling her eyes, snapping her teeth, and dropping her head between her legs, was evidently in the attitude and on the point of springing at him. At the critical instant he leveled and fired at her head. Stunned with the shock, and suffocated with the smoke, he immediately found himself drawn out of the cave. But having refreshed himself, and permitted the smoke to dissipate, he went down the third time. Once more he came within sight of the wolf, who appearing very passive, he applied the torch to her nose, and perceiving her dead, he took hold of her ears, and then kicking the rope, the people above, with no small exultation dragged them both out together.[32]

In celebration of the event, a torchlight procession ran through the rolling hills of Pomfret, with Israel Putnam being carried on a litter that was set on the shoulders of several farmers. Festivities ended at about midnight with a late night supper.

The wolf incident occurred when Putnam was 24 years old. The story of would follow him wherever he went for the rest of his life. In an era of a predominantly agrarian America, many people could relate to the dangers predators posed to their livestock and the bravery required of farmers on the rugged frontier—and in the 18th century many parts of New England were still wild.

While Putnam was risking his life in the Pomfret wolf den, ten-year-old George Washington was playing on his family's Virginia farm, and Thomas Jefferson wouldn't be born until the following spring. It would be another 33 years before the first shots of the American Revolution.

When Putnam went off to fight in the French and Indian War in 1755, his nicknames went with him—"Old Wolf Put" and "Wolf Putnam."[33] Later, through the 18th century, the story was handed down by elderly people who remembered the incident as children, or as young adults who were personally led to the wolf den by the aged hero. In the latter case, Putnam, with a voice partially slurred as a result of a paralytic stroke, would recount with clarity the details of his close encounter with the animal.

One such person was a young relative, Samuel Putnam who later became a judge on the Supreme Court of Massachusetts. In an 1834 letter he remembers, "I was once at [Israel Putnam's] house in Brooklyn, where he treated me with great hospitality. He showed me the place where he followed a wolf into a cave and shot it."[34]

Today, Putnam's wolf den sits intact within the 900-acre Mashamoquet Brook State Park. In 1899, the Daughters of the American Revolution, in their mission to safeguard places and possessions connected with the War of Independence, purchased the land containing the wolf den. Twenty-five years later the State of Connecticut bought it from them and added it to its Mashamoquet Brook land. One change has been made to the wolf den in recent years: over one-half of its length has been blocked off to keep visitors from getting stuck in the claustrophobic 40-foot-long tunnel.[35]

Two

French and Indian War

War Breaks Out

In 1755 Israel and Hannah Putnam were just one of many hardworking New England farm couples in their thirties. Other than the wolf den episode there was no indication that Israel had ambitions beyond his family and his farm. He apparently did not seek a leadership role in government or the church. He didn't pay for a pew in the meeting house, but attended services (sometimes lasting four hours long) sitting on a backless bench in the rear of the Congregational Church, which was the only organized religious body in the area.[1]

In the first Connecticut census, which was taken in 1756 (a year after Israel had left for war), his hometown of Pomfret numbered 1,677 white and 50 black residents. Native Americans were not included, but we know there were some, since Putnam gave a farm to one who was (or had been) his servant.[2]

Then came the French and Indian War and the Putnam family's idyllic farm life would never be the same. The Seven Years' War lasted from 1754 until 1763 (and was most intense in the seven years from 1756 through 1763) and involved Europe, North America, Central America, West Africa, India, and the Philippines. Great Britain and France were the main adversaries. In North America, the war was known as the French and Indian War.

By the 1750s both Britain and France laid claim to the Ohio River valley. When the French began actively constructing fortifications, the colonial governor of Virginia, Robert Dinwiddie, sent militia colonel George

Washington to demand that the French pull back their troops. When he was ignored, Dinwiddie sent a construction crew to build a British fort, with Washington's men as protection. Despite a small, early success by Washington, French forces fought and defeated him at Fort Necessity on July 3, 1754. Washington's surrendered to the French-Canadian commander Captain Louis Coulon de Villiers would mark the only time in his life that Washington surrendered to a military opponent.[3]

In 1755, 37-year-old Israel Putnam signed up with the Connecticut militia to fight in the French and Indian War. It's not known what his wife Hannah thought of his action. She probably agreed with the people of the nearby town of Ashford, which, like Pomfret, was asked to contribute men.

When in August 1755, a militia regiment was raised in Eastern Connecticut to attack the French at Crown Point, New York, Ashford passed a motion at a church meeting: "to keep a day of fasting and prayer one day in a month to Almighty God, in behalf of our friends that are gone and going to defend our land against an encroaching foe; that they may be preserved and have success." The same day, a town meeting passed a resolution stating: "That the town do concur with the church in keeping a day of fasting once a month."[4]

Volunteering to serve might have been a spur of the moment thing for Israel Putnam. His life was filled with impetuous actions and it would have been fully in his character to respond immediately when hearing of the need for men to fight for their country. It also didn't hurt that Putnam possessed incredible strength and stamina from 20 years of farm labor. That toughness came in handy during the next seven years as he trudged through the bitterly cold upper–New York State winters toting his supplies and an 11-pound, five-foot-long infantry musket.[5]

But what about his farm? Like the thousands of other ordinary people who served in the war, Putnam had to make arrangements. Undoubtedly, in the previous 15 years Putnam had built up a team of workers and servants who could handle the work of the farm. Also, Israel Jr., was 15 and Daniel was 13—they would do their share.

Israel's absence was mostly a problem for Hannah. She now had four little daughters (2, 6, 8, and 11) to raise, as well as another to be born in a few months (on January 10, 1756). Added to that, she now had final say on all matters affecting the management of a 500-acre farm. Apparently, she was up to the task as there is no record of any problems occurring during the many times Israel would be away from home during the next eight years.[6]

Two. French and Indian War

Putnam, starting as a private, was soon appointed to lead a company under Phineas Lyman, arguably the most able colonial commander in the French and Indian War. Born in Durham, Connecticut, in 1716,[7] Lyman graduated from Yale College at age 22 and after a few years as a tutor became a lawyer. He served as a member of the state's General Assembly until 1755 when he was appointed Major-General and Commander-in-Chief of the Connecticut forces.[8]

Putnam was charged with the task of raising men for the cause. As Humphreys states, Putnam's popularity made it easy for him to enlist recruits "from the most hardy, enterprising, and respectable young men of his neighborhood."[9]

Historian Francis Parkman described these fighting men well:

> The soldiers were no soldiers but farmers and farmers' sons who had volunteered for the summer campaign. One of the corps had a blue uniform faced with red. The rest wore their daily clothing. Blankets had been served out to them by the several provinces, but the greater part brought their own guns; some under the penalty of a fine if they came without them, and some under the inducement of a reward. They had no bayonets, but carried hatchets in their belts as a sort of substitute. At their sides were slung powder-horns, on which, in the leisure of the camp they carved quaint devices with the points of their jack-knives. They came chiefly from plain New England homesteads [with] capacious barns, rough fields of pumpkins and corn, and vast kitchen chimneys above which in winter hung squashes to keep them from frost, and guns to keep them from rust.[10]

General Lyman's regiment met up with the rest of the army on the west shore of Lake Champlain near Crown Point, New York. Perhaps the most important event of the first days in New York was a meeting between Putnam and Robert Rogers who at the time was a captain and later would command Rogers Rangers, probably the most famous unit of fighting men of the French and Indian War's North American theater. The Rogers Rangers units, known by their green uniforms, were assigned tasks no other units would or could perform.

A brave man and an unsurpassed pioneer in the development of frontier warfare, Rogers, as we shall see, did not possess the integrity or compassion of Putnam. One biographer stated of Rogers: "I do not introduce him here as a saint, for, as is well known, no quality of sanctity ever entered his composition; but rather, as the resolute commander of resolute men, in desperate encounters with a desperate foe; as a man eminently fitted for the rough work given him to do."[11]

Merrill's Marauders—known for their World War II commando missions in Southeast Asia behind Japanese lines—the U.S. Green Berets of the Vietnam War, and today's U.S. Army Rangers all claim direct descent from Robert Rogers' units. A version of the standing orders devised by Robert Rogers is used today by the Army Rangers.

Rogers' original 28 rules included such advice as:

- All Rangers are to be ... equipped, each with a fire-lock, sixty rounds of powder and ball, and a hatchet. (Rule 1)
- Whenever you are ordered out to the enemies [sic] forts or frontiers for discoveries, if your number be small, march in a single file, keeping at such a distance from each other as to prevent one shot from killing two men. (Rule 2)
- If you oblige the enemy to retreat, be careful, in your pursuit of them, to keep out your flanking parties and prevent them from gaining eminences, or rising grounds, in which case they would perhaps be able to rally and repulse you in their turn. (Rule 8)
- If you are to embark in canoes, battoes [bateaux: flat-bottomed riverboats], or otherwise, by water, chuse [sic] the evening for the time of your embarkation, as you will then have the whole night before you, to pass undiscovered by any parties of the enemy, on hills or other places, which command a prospect of the lake or river you are upon. (Rule 24)[12]

One rule would take on significance for Israel Putnam 20 years later when he commanded men at the Battle of Bunker Hill. Rule 13 states: "In general, when pushed upon by the enemy, reserve your fire till they approach very near, which will then put them into the greater surprise and consternation, and give you an opportunity of rushing upon them with your hatchets and cutlasses to the better advantage."

In the French and Indian War, Putnam and Rogers together carried out incredibly dangerous assignments involving "traversing the wilderness, reconnoitring [sic] the enemy's lines, gaining intelligence, and taking straggling prisoners, as well as in beating up the quarters and surprising the advanced pickets of their army."[13]

The Durkee Incident

Sometime in 1755, Putnam received orders to reconnoiter an enemy camp. He chose one man, Lieutenant Robert Durkee, to accompany him. Upon arriving in sight of the enemy campfires, the two men crawled up to what they expected was the edge of the encampment.[14]

Unknown to them, the configuration of the site was unlike anything they had experienced in British or American camps. The British and Colonials were used to having a camp, including their sentinels, surrounded by campfires. The French and their Indian allies customarily placed their fires in the center of the camp with the troops positioned outside and sentinels on the fringe. When Putnam and Durkee realized their error, they were already well within the circle of enemy soldiers. The sentinels spotted them, set off an alarm, and the two Americans jumped up and ran off.[15]

Durkee was wounded in the thigh by the pursuers, but not so badly that he couldn't run closely behind Putnam into the woods. In the pitch darkness, Putnam fell into a clay pit with Durkee tumbling in only seconds behind him. Thinking the figure who just joined him was an enemy soldier, Putnam pulled out his tomahawk and raised it to strike. Durkee, unaware of Putnam's intention, asked where Israel was hurt. Recognizing the man's voice, Putnam dropped his weapon. Both men jumped out of the hole and under a barrage of musket balls, ran to higher ground where they found shelter behind a large log.[16]

Before they settled in for the night, Putnam opened his canteen to share the rum he had packed away. To his disappointment it was empty— it had been riddled with enemy musket balls. The following day, Putnam counted 14 bullet holes in his blanket.[17]

Like Putnam, Durkee was to command troops two decades later in the American Revolutionary War. Commissioned on August 26, 1776, Captain Durkee led a company in New Jersey and Pennsylvania in 1777 and 1778, which included action at the battles of Brandywine and Germantown, and the hardships of Valley Forge. In the spring of 1778, Durkee resigned so he could go home to protect his family from Indian attacks. Like many other Connecticut natives, they had settled in Pennsylvania's Wyoming Valley.

A few weeks later, on July 3, 1778, their settlements were attacked by Iroquois Confederation warriors, along with British and Loyalist soldiers, who brutally massacred 360 settlers as they were fleeing or surrendering. It has become known as the Wyoming Massacre.[18] In his Putnam biography, Humphreys mentions that Robert Durkee was wounded and taken prisoner at the battle of Wyoming and "Having been condemned to be burnt, the Indians kept him in the flames with pitchforks, until he expired in the most excruciating torments."[19]

Putnam Saves Robert Rogers' Life

David Humphreys describes in detail an occasion in 1755 when Israel Putnam saved the life of Robert Rogers. The Colonials needed to ascertain the location and condition of French troops at Crown Point, New York. Due to the large number of French-aligned Indian warriors in the area, it was not possible to proceed to the enemy fort with their entire party. Rogers and Putnam left their men hidden at a distance and approached the fort in the evening. All night long they lay hidden and early in the morning obtained the information they needed.

Unfortunately, as they were leaving, Rogers was spotted by the enemy. A French soldier grabbed his flintlock with one hand and tried to grasp hold of him with the other, while alerting a nearby guard. Humphreys relates that "Putnam, perceiving the imminent danger of his friend, and that no time was to be lost or farther alarm given by firing, ran rapidly to them, while they were yet struggling, and with the butt-end of his piece laid the Frenchman dead at his feet." Putnam and Rogers reunited with their men and returned to camp.[20]

Rogers' October 22, 1755, official report, which was signed by Jonathan Butterfield[21] and Israel Putnam as well as himself, was sent to General William Johnson. It described the October 14 incident as:

> At length, a Frenchman came out of the fort towards us, with his gun, and came within fifteen rods of where we lay. Then I with another man ran up to him, in order to capture him—but he refused to take quarters—so we killed him, and took his scalp, in plain sight of the fort—then ran, and in plain view, about twenty rods, and made our escape.[22]

In his journal, published a decade later, Rogers entirely leaves out the fact another man assisted him:

> About 10 o'clock a single man marched out directly towards our ambush. When I perceived him within ten yards of me, I sprung over the log, and met him, and offered him quarters, which he refused, and made a pass at me with a dirk [a long dagger], which I avoided, and presented my fuse [a flintlock] to his breast; but notwithstanding, he still pushed on with resolution, and obliged me to dispatch him. This gave an alarm to the enemy, and made it necessary for us to hasten to the mountain.[23]

What was the reason for Rogers's omission of Putnam's name in the account? How could Rogers have refused to give credit to someone for an act of saving his life? Putnam biographer Livingston believed it was jealousy.

Boat Attack on Lake George

In the summer of 1755, 600 French and Indian combatants attacked British army baggage and provisions wagons at Half-Way Brook, so named because it was midway between Fort Edward and the south end of Lake George (about six miles from each location). After killing the oxen, they pillaged the wagons and left.

When General Webb heard of the attack, he ordered Israel Putnam and Robert Rogers to round up 100 volunteers and travel by boat part way down Lake George. They were told to take with them two cannon and two large-caliber blunderbusses. They were then to leave the boats with guards and go overland to try to intercept the 600 enemy troops at "the Narrows," which was a thin five-mile-long section of the lake that was filled with islands.

A half-an-hour after Putnam and Rogers took up position on the Lake George shoreline, they spotted the enemy boats. When the latter entered the Narrows, the Colonists fired, killing many of their oarsmen and sinking a number of boats. Only when the wind pushed the remaining boats into a wider part of the Lake and out of musket range, did the Putnam and Rogers rangers cease firing.

When the surviving French troops arrived at Fort Ticonderoga, they told of the ambush and a detachment was sent back to attack Putnam and Rogers, who were still 20 miles from where they left their boats.

By the next day, Putnam, Rogers and their men were back in their boats and heading home. Little did they know that the French troops had passed them in the night and were now directly in their path. When the opposing parties met, the French, overconfidently, rowed within pistol shot range of the British. The latter took out their blunderbusses and fired the cannon, which were mounted on railing of their boat. The French, surprised and frightened by the firepower, were battered as the American alternated between musket fire and the cannon and blunderbusses. It was soon over with the French and their Indian allies retreating.

After the French and Indians had left for Ticonderoga, the Americans surveyed the enemy losses: in one canoe of 20 warriors, 15 had been killed. In other boats, countless men had fallen overboard. Only one American had been killed and two "slightly" wounded.[24]

Mission to Take a French Prisoner

In 1755, soon after the episode at the Narrows, General Webb, in need of intelligence, gave Putnam another assignment: take five men and capture a French soldier. So, Putnam and his men went to the road between Fort Ticonderoga and the place the French baked their bread, known as "The Ovens." There, they hid in the woods and waited.

In time, Putnam's men became sure that they were safe and began to carelessly leave their hiding places. Putnam rebuked them, emphasizing the danger they were putting all of them in by their carelessness. In a short time, an Indian passed by, followed by a French soldier. Putnam jumped up and ordering his men to follow him.

Putnam ran about 500 feet, seized the French soldier by his shoulders and apparently had him under control. But the man looked behind Putnam and didn't see any supporting troops. Putnam's men had not followed him. Knowing his Indian compatriot would soon return to help him, the Frenchman violently resisted Putnam. Putnam let go of the man, stepped backward and aimed his musket at the solder's chest. It misfired.[25]

The Frenchman chased Putnam back through the woods. When he spotted Putnam's men standing up from the grass, he turned and fled. Humphreys relates that Putnam later "dismissed [his men] in disgrace" and completed the mission on his own by capturing another French soldier.

On November 25, 1755, Israel Putnam was made captain in charge of a company on winter duty at Fort Edward, while Rogers spent the winter at Fort William Henry. Five months later, Putnam returned home to Connecticut where he saw his daughter Eunice (born in January 1756) for the first time.

The Connecticut General Assembly passed the following on May 30, 1756:

> This Assembly grants to Capt. Israel Putnam the number of fifty Spanish mill'd dollars, and thirty such dollars unto Capt. Noah Grant,[26] as gratuity for their extraordinary services and good conduct in ranging and scouting the winter past for the annoyance of the enemy near Crown Point and discovery of their motions.[27]

In August 1756, the French captured Fort Oswego on New York's Lake Ontario. The fort had been recently reinforced by British General William Shirley. When it fell, over 1600 British soldiers were captured and more than 100 cannon confiscated.[28] The following year, the Connecticut General Assembly promoted Putnam to the rank of major.

Rescue of Captain Little

In 1757, General Lyman took over responsibility for Fort Edward.[29] On July 23,[30] he set 150 men to work in a swamp about 550 yards east of the fort cutting timber for fortifications. For their protection, Captain Little accompanied them with 50 British regulars.

One morning, one of the lookouts noticed several strange birds flying by. Soon an arrow struck a tree above his head and he realized that it wasn't

Two. French and Indian War

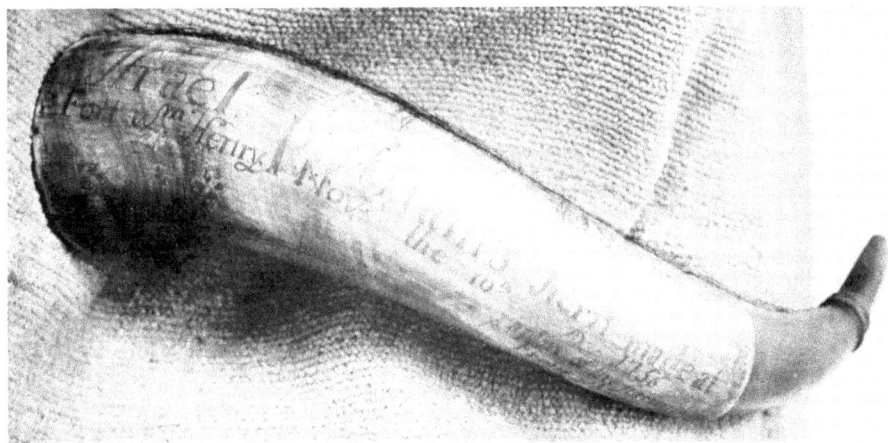

Israel Putnam's French and Indian War powder horn, dated 1756, is now in the collection of Historic Deerfield in Deerfield, Massachusetts (print from Livingston's biography).

birds that he had seen. Indians, hidden in the swamp, were attempting to silence him before he could call out an alarm.

He shouted to the workmen, who ran back toward the fort through a strip of dry land between the swamp and a stream. About 200 men, mostly Indians,[31] rose from their cover behind bushes in the swamp and, with tomahawks and muskets, began to slaughter the closest unarmed workmen.

Captain Little and his men rushed to aid the workers, succeeded in protecting them, and covered them until they reached the fort gates. Unfortunately, for fear of a general Indian assault, General Lyman had ordered the gates to be shut and secured.

Israel Putnam, who was with some of his rangers on a small island near the fort, heard the musket shots and was informed that Captain Little was in danger. Putnam jumped into the water, his men followed, and Putnam waded toward the fort. General Lyman spoke to Putnam from the parapet, commanding him to stop—insisting that it was futile for him and his rangers to risk their lives. Putnam responded that he was sorry that he must disobey the order and proceeded to lead his rangers past the fort toward the location of the fighting. Humphreys claims that "This is the only instance in the whole course of his military service, wherein he did not pay the strictest obedience to orders."[32]

Putnam, with his rangers, reached Captain Little and told him to take his men through the swamp, and then held back the Indian attackers. After fighting for about an hour, Putnam ordered his men to charge the enemy positions in the swamp. Having already lost a good number of men, the Indians ran and were chased by Putnam's rangers. Only one of Putnam's men died in the pursuit and his killer was immediate shot by a ranger.[33] In total, the British lost 13 men, with the ones killed before Putnam's Rangers arrived, being scalped. It was thought that many more warriors had been killed, but their bodies had been carried away by their comrades.

The Massacre at Fort William Henry

A major event of 1757 was the attack on Fort William Henry by the French and their Native American allies. Two years earlier, the British built the fort on the southern end of Lake George 60 miles north of Albany, New York. It was composed of a 30-foot-thick wall, which was constructed of pine log sides and filled with beach sand. Thirty-five miles to the north, at the other end of the lake, sat France's Fort Carillon (later renamed Fort Ticonderoga).

In 1757, the Marquis de Montcalm, Commander-in-Chief of the French in Canada, believed that the British forces in the area were at

> a dangerously weak level due to the troop demands of Lord Loudon at Louisburg in northeastern Nova Scotia. To take advantage of the situation, Montcalm created an army of almost 8,000 Indians, Canadians, and French soldiers who could be spared from Ticonderoga, Crown Point, and the other garrisons.[34]

The local British garrison at Fort William Henry, under the command of Lieutenant-Colonel George Monro, had less than 2,500 troops. Monro sent "express after express to Major General Daniel Webb, with an account of his situation and the most pressing solicitation for succour."[35]

General Webb, apparently more concerned with leaving the northern approaches to Albany under-protected, sent a return message to Monro in which he refused to send reinforcements. The messenger was intercepted and the message was delivered to General Montcalm who now knew he could attack the fort without the danger of additional British troops intervening.

Originally General Webb had about 4,000 troops at Fort Edward, which had been increased with General William Johnson's regulars and militia. Johnson was sent out to aid the men at William Henry. Included in his force were Provincials, Militia and Putnam's Rangers. After proceeding about three miles they were called back. An Indian ally of the French reported to French General Montcalm that he saw them return home.

David Humphreys relates that a few days before Fort William Henry was set upon by the French forces, Putnam and 200 men escorted General Webb to check on its defenses. Putnam planned to take a party of five men to scout out the forts in the area to ascertain the troop strength of the enemy. General Webb vetoed the plan but approved a second one whereby Putnam would take 18 volunteers and three whaleboats. When he spotted enemy troops on an island in Lake George, Putnam left two of his boats to stay near them until he returned. He took the remaining boat back to General Webb with troop information.

Upon returning to the two boats, Putnam spotted an army moving in the distance. Its likely destination was Fort William Henry. He himself was spotted and almost surrounded by canoes. Escaping from them in his whaleboats, Putnam returned to General Webb.

Display of French and Indian War cannonballs at the reconstructed Fort William Henry, Lake George, New York (photograph by author).

Webb ordered Putnam and his men to swear to remain silent about what they had seen. According to Humphreys's account, Putnam told General Webb that "he hoped his Excellency did not intend to neglect so fair an opportunity of giving battle, should the enemy presume to land." "What do you think we should do here?"[36] asked the General. The latter had already received the report that a French deserter had estimated the French army at 11,000 troops. Fearing they could smash through his forces, Webb sent only light reinforcements to William Henry.

The couple of thousand defenders at Fort William Henry were no match for the estimated 10,000 to 14,000 men under French commander Montcalm.[37] On August 8, 1757, after an intense bombardment by French artillery, the British garrison surrendered. The subjugation had only taken Montcalm and his French troops and Canadian and Indian allies four days.

On August 9, the day after the surrender, about 1600 of Montcalm's Native American allies entered the fort, took whatever British possessions they could find, and murdered and scalped the helpless wounded and sick British and Provincial soldiers.[38]

Arrangements were made for the fort's British soldiers to agree to not serve for the next 18 months and they were allowed to leave the fort unharmed, without ammunition, but with their muskets. However, as soon they exited the fort on August 10, under the escort of a few hundred French soldiers, they were set upon by Indian warriors who, beginning with the sick and injured, indiscriminately butchered or kidnapped hundreds in the caravan. This included children, women, African Americans, mulattoes, and Native Americans who were allies of the British.

Those who were able to escape ultimately arrived at Fort Edward to tell of the atrocities. Although the French apparently did little to intercede for the British during the slaughter, they later worked at getting back many of the 300 or so people who were captured and hauled away by the Native Americans. Immediately after the massacre, Montcalm ordered the fort to be burned to the ground.

The day after the fall of William Henry, Major Putnam with his rangers left Fort Edward to ascertain the state of the captured fort. They thought they knew what to expect—they had seen smoke from William Henry, which was 16 miles to the north. They found the fort and all its associated buildings entirely destroyed. All armaments and supplies which would prove valuable to the enemy had been taken. Putnam and his men were not prepared for what they saw amongst Fort William Henry's smoldering ruins.

Israel Putnam described the scene at William Henry:

> The fort was entirely demolished; the barracks, out-houses, and buildings were a heap of ruins; the cannon, stores, boats, and vessels were all carried away. The fires were still burning, the smoke and stench offensive and suffocating. Innumerable fragments, human skulls and bones, and carcasses half consumed, were still frying and broiling in the decaying fires. Dead bodies, mangled with scalping-knives and tomahawks in all the wantonness of Indian fierceness and barbarity, were every where [sic] to be seen. More than one hundred women, butchered and shockingly mangled, lay upon the ground, still weltering in their gore. Devastation, barbarity, and horror every where [sic] appeared, and the spectacle presented was too diabolical and awful either to be endured or described.[39]

Not satisfied with the scalps and clothing of the British prisoners, the Indians proceeded to dig up the bodies of soldiers in Fort William Henry's cemetery for their scalps, blankets, and uniforms. Unfortunately for them, many of the corpses were infected with smallpox. It was said that those Indians, in turn, infected their people back in Canada, as well as tribes all the way to the Mississippi River.[40]

The Fort William Henry massacre was later described by James Fenimore Cooper in his 1826 novel, *The Last of the Mohicans*. In later years, a pine grove covered the site of the fort and nothing was built there until the 1950s when a company of land developers reconstructed the entire fort from scratch. Today, it is operated as a living history museum.

South Bay

In the first edition of his Putnam biography, David Humphrey[41] mentions the time General James Abercrombie ordered Major Putnam to take 60 men to South Bay on Lake George to look for enemy troops. Reaching the destination, Putnam erected a stone wall, which he disguised with vegetation. The work took a long time and he was reduced to shooting game, something he rarely did in territory where enemy troops might hear the shots. He also needed to let 20 of his men, who had taken ill, return to the fort.

One evening, one of his soldiers informed Putnam of canoes loaded with men about to pass their location. Putnam assembled his troops behind the stone wall and waited. It was a full moon and the canoes filled with Native American warriors were clearly visible—and they far outnumbered Putnam's party. Just as they passed by, one of Putnam's men accidentally knocked his musket against a rock.

It became obvious that the men in the canoes heard the noise, as they gathered their men together. Putnam discharged his musket, which was the signal for his troops to begin firing. Things went well at first, but the Indians noticed that the shots were infrequent, revealing the size of Putnam's force. Putnam could tell that they were coming ashore.

In an effort to prevent an attack, Putnam sent 12 men under Lieutenant Durkee, 500 feet down the creek, and Lieutenant Parsons with a small party a short distance up the creek. Both parties were successful in preventing enemy landings.

All night Putnam's men held on, firing and hitting some of the attackers, but receiving little fire in return. By daylight, ammunition was running low and Putnam was told that another party was landing further down the creek. He immediately ordered a retreat up the creek and moved quickly enough that an attempt to surround him failed.

Casualties on the enemy side were high, but none of Putnam's troops were killed and only two, a Provincial and a British-allied Indian, were wounded. As the enemy approached, the wounded men told the rest of the small detachment to leave them and not risk their own lives. They did and, as Humphries relates, "The Provincial, whose thigh was broken by a ball, upon the approach of the Savages fired his piece and killed three of them; after which he was quickly hacked in pieces."[42] This was undoubtedly learned by Putnam when he later spoke with their Indian ally who was captured in the encounter. In addition, the man informed Putnam that their adversaries that day had amounted to 500 French and Indians troops.

Now reduced to only 40 men, Putnam journeyed through the wilderness until he again came under attack. To trick the enemy, who he guessed far outnumbered his force, he shouted out confidently for his troops to attack. Unknown to both parties, the attacking troops were also British. Fortunately, their commanding officer knew Putnam's voice and called for his men to cease fire, shouting "that they were all friends."

As the two parties came together, Putnam exclaimed to the other commander: "that friends or enemies, they all 'deserved to be hanged for not killing more when they had so fair a shot.'"[43]

One of Putnam's men had made it to the fort and General Lyman came with 500 men to protect Putnam's retreat. When Lyman reached him, Putnam was within a day's distance of the fort.

Saving the Magazine

In the winter of 1757, Colonel William Haviland was the commandant of Fort Edward when a fire started in the barracks that were connected to the northwest bastion of the fort. A magazine, only twelve feet from the barracks, contained 300 barrels of gunpowder. Haviland ordered his men to use heavy artillery to level the supports to the barracks to prevent the spread of the fire to the powder. It didn't work.

By the time Israel Putnam arrived from a post on a nearby island, the flames were approaching the gunpowder magazine. Fortunately, there was no shortage of water as they were on the banks of the Hudson River, and there was no lack of men to carry it to the fire. Immediately, the soldiers formed a chain to pass water by buckets to the barracks.

According to Humphreys, Putnam "mounted on a ladder to the eaves of the building, received and threw [the water] upon the flame." As he stood close to the raging fire, his "thick blanket mittens" were burnt from his hands. The other soldiers soaked a second pair in water and handed them up to him.[44]

Concerned for Putnam's life, Colonel Haviland told him to come down from his position. Putnam implored him to let him continue. The commander relented and ordered the other men to "redouble" their efforts, exclaiming "if we must be blown up, we will go altogether."

Only when the barracks appeared to be collapsing did Putnam descend to the ground. From that position, he continued to pour buckets of water on the magazine. By this time, the building's outside planks had already burned away. But Putnam, "still undaunted, covered with a cloud of cinders and scorched with the intensity of the heat, maintained his position until the fire subsided and the danger was wholly over."[45]

For an hour and a half Putnam had fought the fire, with the result that he suffered blisters over his face, arms, and lower body. When he removed the second set of mittens, the skin of his hands and fingers came off with them. It took Putnam a month before he was well enough to return to duty. Humphreys concludes his account by noting, "The Commandant ... could not stifle the emotions of gratitude, due to the man who had been so instrumental in preserving the Magazine, the Fort, and the Garrison."[46]

Failed British Attack on Fort Ticonderoga

The British Army planned three expeditions for 1758: General Jeffrey Amherst would attack Louisbourg (on today's Cape Breton Island, which is part of Canada's Nova Scotia province), Brigadier General John Forbes would hit Fort Duquesne (Pittsburgh, Pennsylvania now sits on the site of the fort), and General James Abercrombie would attack the fortifications at Crown Point, which was situated north of Fort Carillon (Fort Ticonderoga), on the southern end of Lake Champlain.

In early July 1758, British General James Abercrombie and Brigadier General Lord Howe, moved toward the French-occupied Fort Carillon (Fort Ticonderoga) with 16,000 British regulars and militia. Many of these were Connecticut men raised by General Lyman, and included Israel Putnam who was serving as a scout.

The Abercrombie force traveled up Lake George. Putnam was with Lord Howe, who was in front of the army's center column. They were met by about 500 French troops off to their left. According to Humphreys, this dialog took place between Howe and Putnam:

> HOWE: Putnam, what means that firing?
> PUTNAM: I know not, but, with your lordship's leave, will see.
> HOWE: I will accompany you.
> PUTNAM: My lord, if I am killed, the loss of my life will be of little consequence, but the preservation of yours is of infinite importance to this army.
> HOWE: Putnam, your life is as dear to you as mine is to me; I am determined to go.[47]

Lord Howe, Major Putnam, and about 200 men met the enemy. The first to fall was Howe, who died in Putnam's arms.[48] Robert Rogers then came with his rangers and the French were caught between him and Putnam's men.

Putnam, now joined by Captain James Dalzell and 20 men, maneuvered through the enemy and attacked their rear. They killed approximately 300 and captured half that number. Unfortunately, confusion reigned in another part of Abercrombie's force and his left wing, mistaking Putnam's men for the enemy, fired at them, killing several men. Finding no other way to prevent further friendly fire, Putnam personally raced through the hail of bullets to stop the firing.[49]

After the British won the battle, Putnam worked until darkness set in to round up the enemy wounded, placing them in one location where he gave them liquor and other refreshments and blankets. Humphreys describes how Putnam

> put three blankets under a French Sergeant who was badly wounded through the body, and placed him in an easy posture by the side of a tree—the poor fellow could only squeeze his hand with an expressive grasp. "Ah," said Major Putnam, "depend on it, my brave soldier, you shall be brought to the camp as soon as possible, and the same care shall be taken of you as if you were my brother."[50]

Humphreys relates what happened the next morning:

> Major [Robert] Rogers was sent to reconnoitre the field and to bring off the wounded prisoners—but finding the wounded unable to help themselves, in order to save trouble, he dispatched every one of them to the world of spirits. Putnam's was not the only heart that bled: The Provincial and British officers who became acquainted with the fact were struck with inexpressible horror.[51]

On July 8, Abercrombie stood before Ticonderoga and initiated a frontal attack on the fort. Although he didn't have cannon, he assumed his numerical superiority would be enough to defeat French general Montcalm, who only had about 4,000 troops. According to Humphreys, during the battle, Putnam "who acted as an aid in bringing the Provincial regiments successively to action, assisted in preserving order."[52]

The ruins of the British fort at Crown Point, New York, which was constructed under the supervision of Israel Putnam in 1759. The soldiers' barracks (right) still contain the original stone fireplaces and chimneys, while the officers' barracks (left) have had their more expensive brick fireplaces and chimneys removed and recycled (photograph by author).

The French death toll in the battle was about 100, while the British lost many hundreds of troops. The number of British soldiers killed has long been disputed, but was probably between 600 and 1,000. About 275 French soldiers were wounded, while the British suffered six times that number. It was said that most of the French who were killed suffered head wounds, as the walls of Ticonderoga provided protection for every other part of their bodies.

The battle was considered the bloodiest of the war. Ultimately, it led to the withdrawal of Abercrombie from his North American command, and the appointment of the far more competent General Jeffrey Amherst.

The French victory at Ticonderoga was offset by British successes in the other two major offensives of 1758: Generals Amherst and Wolfe captured Louisbourg, and General John Forbes took Fort Duquesne. In addition, Lt. Colonel John Bradstreet captured Fort Frontenac on the north shore of Lake Ontario.

The battle at Ticonderoga, afterward known as the Battle of Carillon, was an incredible French success, but unfortunately for the French forces, it was last major victory they would achieve during the war.

In 1759, Montcalm, with 15,000 troops, lost Quebec to Gen. James Wolfe's 8,500-man force in the Battle of the Plains of Abraham. It is said that the main reason for the loss was Montcalm's refusal to wait for reinforcements before confronting the enemy. Both Montcalm and Wolfe were mortally wounded in the 15-minute-long battle, with Wolfe dying immediately and Montcalm passing the following day. Montcalm was 47; Wolfe was 32.

While Wolfe's troops were winning in Quebec, General Amherst chose to build a new fort at the site of the French Fort Frederic at Crown Point, New York. Israel Putnam supervised much of the construction. According to archaeologist David R. Starbuck, the fortification complex was the "greatest British military installation ever raised in North America."[53]

The Three Choices

The closest date that Humphreys gives to the following story is "before the conclusion of the year" 1758. The place was the eastern shore of the Hudson near the Rapids, which were next to Fort Miller, which, in turn, was just south of Fort Edward. As Putnam and the five soldiers with him looked across the river, his men on the opposite bank signaled that large body of Native American warriors were at his rear and were approaching him."

In relating this story, Israel Putnam remembered that they had three choices: stay where they were and "be sacrificed"; attempt to cross the river and be shot; or take their single flat-bottomed boat and go down the falls [rapids], "with an almost absolute certainty of being drowned."[54]

Of course, Putnam chose the rapids. Unfortunately, one of his men had separated from the party and had to be left behind and ended up suffering option one.

The Indians were swift—they landed on the shore even before the Putnam rangers could leave. As soon as the rangers reached beyond musket range, they were faced with "prominent rocks, latent shelves, absorbing eddies, and abrupt descents, for a quarter of a mile."[55]

Taking the helm of his small vessel, Putnam navigated through the rapids; "at one moment the sides were exposed to the fury of the waves; then the stern, and next the bow."[56] To his men in the boat as well as to the Native Americans on shore, Putnam seemed calm as he successfully steered the boat. According to Humphreys, Putnam's escape from their musket balls as he was pushing off, and his unheard-of navigation of that stretch of water, contributed to an Indian legend that he was invulnerable. "They conceived it would be an affront against the Great Spirit, to attempt to kill this favored mortal with powder and ball, if they should ever see and know him again."[57]

"Rogers always sent, but Putnam led his men to action"

In August 1758, after hearing of French troops in the area, General Abercrombie ordered Robert Rogers to take several hundred men to South Bay, East Bay, and Fort Edward. Dividing the party, Rogers left half the troops with Israel Putnam at South Bay while he was stationed with the remainder 12 miles away.[58]

A few days later, when Rogers heard their locations were discovered by French scouts, he combined his two groups and headed toward Fort Edward. Again they divided—this time in three divisions—Rogers on the right, Captain Dalzell in the center, and Putnam on the left. The first night they encamped on the Clear River about a mile from Fort Anne, which was about 10 miles east of the southern part of Lake George.

The next morning, Rogers and British Lieutenant Irwin began firing their weapons at a target, even though they could not be certain the enemy was not within earshot. Putnam was incensed. Humphreys states: "Nothing could have been more repugnant to the military principles of Putnam than such conduct; or reprobated by him in more pointed terms."[59]

It turned out that the shots were heard by the enemy—a party of about 500 French soldiers and Native Americans under the French commander Marin. They prepared an ambush for the British troops. Meanwhile the latter moved their 530 men plus officers single file through the dense growth of brush, with Putnam and the provincials leading the way, Dalzell with the British regulars in the center, and Rogers and the rangers bringing up the rear.

After Putnam and his Connecticut men had gone about three-fourths of a mile, native cries filled the air and the enemy attacked. Putnam ordered return fire and sent word back for the other divisions to come up to support him.[60] Dalzell brought his men forward to help; Rogers did not, later saying that he ordered his men to guard the rear. This reinforced a saying of the British troops: "Rogers always sent, but Putnam led his men to action."

Unable to cross a creek, the Putnam party fought as best they could—in the open or from behind trees. As Putnam himself fought hand-to-hand with a warrior, he placed his musket against the chest of the man and it misfired. The warrior raised his hatchet, forced Putnam to surrender, and tied him to a tree.

A Prisoner

With Putnam taken prisoner, Dalzell and Harman took over command of his men and forced the Indians to retreat. An unwelcome result was that the fight now moved to the place where Putnam was tied up. For over an hour, musket balls repeatedly struck the tree to which he was tied, with some even passing through his clothing. Just when it seemed the situation couldn't get any worse, one of the young warriors decided to amuse himself by throwing his tomahawk at Putnam's head. Putnam assumed that he was attempting to see how close he could get without striking him.

After the man grew tired of his hatchet practice, a French officer attempted to shoot Putnam in the chest, but his musket misfired. He then repeatedly struck its muzzle against Putnam's chest and crushed Putnam's jaw with the gun's butt.

Ultimately Dalzell and Harman and their troops drove the enemy from the field. About 90 of the French-allied natives lay dead. (Five year later, Captain James Dalzell would not be as fortunate as he led troops in a battle against Chief Pontiac's forces at the Battle of Bloody Run on July 31, 1763. Though wounded twice himself, Dalzell turned back toward the enemy to rescue a wounded sergeant and was shot to death. The enemy scalped him, cut out his heart, and wiped the faces of their prisoners with the organ.)[61]

The retreating natives took Putnam with them. David Humphreys describes these events using information supplied by Putnam himself (in conversations in the 1770s and 1780s) and in Dr. Albigence Waldo's interviews of Putnam in the 1780s.

> Putnam was untied by the Indian who had made him prisoner, and whom he [Putnam] afterwards called master. Having been conducted for some distance from the place of action, he was stripped of his coat, vest, stockings and shoes; loaded with as many of the packs of the wounded as could be piled on him; strongly pinioned, and his wrists tied as closely together as they could be pulled with a cord. After he had marched,

through no pleasant paths, in this painful manner, for many a tedious mile, the party (who were excessively fatigued) halted to breathe. His hands were now immoderately swelled from the tightness of the ligature; and the pain had become intolerable...."[62]

Fortunately, a French officer took pity on Putnam and ordered that his hands be unbound and some of his load be removed. The Indian who had captured Putnam came up and gave him a pair of moccasins and "expressed great indignation at the unworthy treatment his prisoner had suffered."[63] After the man left, the others of the party (about 200 braves), headed on to where the night's encampment would be. They took along Putnam. It was during this forced march that they inflicted "a deep wound with a tomahawk, in the left cheek."[64]

Historian Abiel Holmes states in his 1826 *The Annals of America*: "A deep scar on the cheek of that veteran warrior is well remembered by the writer, who believes it was from the wound inflicted by the 'tomahawk.'"[65] It was only the most noticeable of the rumored 15 bullet and tomahawk wounds that covered Putnam's body by the end of his life.

Humphreys continues to the most horrific part of Putnam's capture:

> It was determined to roast him alive—For this purpose they led him into a dark forest, stripped him naked, bound him to a tree, and piled dry brush, with other fuel, at a small distance, in a circle round him. They accompanied their labors, as if for his funeral dirge, with screams and sounds inimitable but by savage voices. Then they set the piles on fire.[66]

Fortunately, a sudden shower put out the growing flame. Undeterred, the warriors started it again and tended it until it circled Putnam and the tree. His hands were tied in such a way that he could shift his body—which he did as the flames slapped him from different angles. In a thread that ran through his life, Putnam was not so much concerned with his own death—which he had faced so many times before. He thought rather of his home, his wife, and his children. Finally, according to Humphreys's account, he fixed his mind "on a happier state of existence, beyond the tortures he was beginning to endure."[67]

It was at this point that the French officer Molang rushed up to the fire, scattered the burning pieces of wood and untied the victim. Later Putnam found out that one of the Indians had told Molang what his tribesmen were doing. Molang kept Putnam with him until he could turn him over to the Native American warrior who had originally captured him.

Livingston mentions that there is a tradition among Freemasons that Putnam, "as a member of the secret order, gave in his great peril the sign of distress, which, on being recognized by a person present who belonged to the fraternity, led to his rescue."[68] Although no lodge existed near his home in Pomfret, Putnam's visits to Masonic lodges during his travels is well known.

Humphreys relates that Putnam was treated well by the warrior who had captured him. When he discovered Putnam could not chew the hard biscuits that he gave him because of the injuries sustained when the French solder smashed his jaw, the warrior soaked them in water and fed them to Putnam.

That night, in order to be sure Putnam did not escape, the Indians laid him in a spread-eagle position, with his arms and legs tied to four trees. In addition, they placed branches across his body and many Indians slept on each side of him. Recalling the discomfort of that night decades later, the elderly Putnam smiled when he thought of "this ludicrous group for a painter, of which he himself was the principal figure."[69]

The next day Putnam was marched to Fort Ticonderoga. This time, however, he did not receive any abuse from his captors, he was not required to carry a pack, and he was given some bear meat to suck on. At the fort he was turned over to the French troops.

In a 1834 letter to Colonel Perley Putnam of Salem, Massachusetts, Samuel Putnam, a native of Danvers and Judge of the Supreme Court of Massachusetts, relates what his famous cousin once told him:

Traditionally, this is the tree south of Crown Point, New York, to which Putnam was tied in August 1758 by Native American allies of the French Army. While the tree is long gone, a stone marker today rests near the site (print from Livingston's biography).

they lighted up the fire and danced and yelled around him.... General Putnam said that their gestures in the dance were so inexpressively ridiculous that he could not forbear laughing. I expressed some surprise that he could laugh under such circumstances, to which he mildly replied, that his composure had no merit—that it was constitutional—and then said that he had never felt any bodily fear.[70]

Israel Putnam's friend Yale president Timothy Dwight once wrote: "It is not known that the passion of fear ever found a place in his breast."[71] With his uncommon lack of fear, Putnam reminds one of the great British admiral, Lord Nelson, who when only a young boy asked his grandmother, "Fear, grandmama, I never saw fear—What is it?"

At the time Putnam was being tied to the tree in the New York wilderness, future comrades-in-arms Alexander Hamilton and the Marquis de Lafayette were only children. Hamilton was a toddler on the Caribbean island of Nevis, and Lafayette was an 11-month-old in central France. Two decades later would find all three playing key roles in the American Revolutionary War.

Jemima Howe, the Captive

Later in August 1758 Israel Putnam was taken by the French to General Montcalm at Fort Ticonderoga. From there Putnam was sent to Montreal, where he became friends with another prisoner of war, the wealthy New Jersey colonel, Peter Schuyler.

Schuyler had heard that a provincial major had been brought in and went to see him. He discovered that Putnam was "without coat, waistcoat or hose—the remnant of his clothing miserably dirty and ragged—his beard long and squalid—his legs torn by thorns and briars—his face gashed with wounds, and swollen with bruises."[72] He immediately saw to it that Putnam was given clothing and money.

Schuyler was concerned that Putnam's exchange might be denied if the French knew he was a "distinguished partisan." He also knew that there were other officers who had been prisoners of war longer. So Schuyler approached the governor with the argument:

> There is an old man here [although Putnam was only 40, he apparently didn't look his age], who is a Provincial Major and wishes to be at home with his wife and children. He can do no good here, or any where else: I believe your excellency had better keep some of the young men, who have no wife or children to care for, and let the old fellow go home with me.[73]

The governor agreed and let Putnam go. But first Putnam, Schuyler, and other officers were sent to Quebec. There Putnam lived as a prisoner in a private home with two other rangers.

Schuyler raised enough money to ransom himself and 116 captives, including Putnam and 25 women and children. One of the women, Jemima Howe (married three times, her full name at death was Jemima Sawtelle Phipps Howe Tute) was one of the most famous Indian captives in American history. She had lost her first two husbands to Indian attacks, and, in 1756, was taken captive in New Hampshire with her seven children. Although she suffered many deprivations, her main concern was always her sons and daughters who were split up among Native American families. Only her baby was allowed to stay with her. When the tribes selected husbands for two of her daughters, she convinced the French to allow the girls to live in a Canadian Catholic convent.[74]

Eventually she was ransomed to a senior British officer. An extraordinarily beautiful woman, Jemima found both the officer and his son attracted to her. One day the son attacked her and threatened to kill her with his knife if she didn't submit to him. Fortunately, she escaped and told the father, who arranged for her to sleep in his wife's room. Later, the Governor became aware of the situation and sent the son away on an assignment.

Afraid of what might happen upon his return, Jemima sought out Colonel Schuyler, who after hearing her story became her protector and arranged to pay her ransom. In addition, he worked to have her five sons returned to her. When Schuyler[75] was required to leave before the other captives, he left Jemima under the care of Israel Putnam. When the young French officer returned and continued to harass her, she was struck with fear again—until Putnam told the man he would protect Jemima at the risk of his life.

On the march of the captives to Albany, Putnam helped Jemima—by carrying her young sons over swampy terrain and by sharing his provisions with her and her sons.

Two years later, in 1760, after the British army had conquered Canada, Jemima Howe traveled to Quebec to find her daughters. One had married a French officer, the other was still in the convent and needed to be convinced to return with her mother to New England. Jemima Howe died in 1805 at age 82.[76]

Putnam never forgot the kindness of Colonel Peter Schuyler. In 1764, Israel and Hannah Putnam named their 10 and last child Peter Schuyler Putnam.

A year after the British defeated the French troops at the Battle of Quebec, they set their sights on the last French stronghold—Montreal. General

James Murray led 3,800 troops up the St. Lawrence River from Quebec, General William Haviland brought his 3,400 men up the Richelieu River from Lake Champlain, and General Jeffrey Amherst (who was commander of all the British forces in North America) came down the St. Lawrence from Lake Ontario with 11,000 soldiers. They were to meet outside Montreal.

Putnam, who was now a Lieutenant-Colonel, was with Amherst. His party, commanded by Brigadier General Thomas Gage,[77] was composed of provincials from New York, Connecticut, and New Jersey.

As they moved north toward Montreal, an armed French vessel prevented passage of the British, whose own ships had been delayed. However, Putnam with a thousand men and 50 small flat-bottomed boats were ready to confront the enemy vessels. Putnam decided to first attempt the type of maneuver that was characteristic of him. He approached General Amherst.

"General, that ship must be taken."

"Aye, I would give the world she was taken."

"I'll take her," said Putnam.

Amherst smiled and asked how that could be.

"Give me some wedges, a beetle (a large wood hammer), and a few men of my own choice."[78]

According to the 1775 edition of *Almon's Remembrance*:

> Amherst could not conceive how an armed vessel was to be taken by four or five men, a beetle, and wedges. However, he granted Putnam's request. When night came, Putnam, with his materials and men, went in a boat under the vessel's stern and in an instant drove in the wedges behind the rudder in the little cavity between the rudder and ship and left her. In the morning the sails were seen fluttering about; she was adrift in the middle of the lake, and being presently blown ashore was easily taken.[79]

Later, a second armed French ship appeared and was also captured.

The remaining obstacle was the fortress itself, which was well guarded by an abattis[80] of black ash, which projected over the water. Again, Putnam devised a method to defeat the French defenses: he fitted each British boat with moveable 20-foot-long planks. They were designed to smash up against the pointed poles and then be lowered to allow troops to walk over them.

According to Humphreys's account, just the sight of the modified vessels helped convince the French to surrender. The attack on Montreal was successful—and, best of all, it was accomplished without the loss of life.

The Indian village of Cochnawaga stood near Montreal. Here, Putnam found the Indian who two years earlier had captured him and later treated him well. Humphreys relates:

> That Indian was highly delighted to see his old acquaintance, whom he entertained in his own well-built stone house, with great friendship and hospitality; while his guest did not discover less satisfaction in an opportunity of shaking the brave Savage by the hand and proffering him protection in this reverse of his military fortunes.[81]

Three

Between the Wars

Expedition to the West Indies

Before 1762, British forces had captured several French Caribbean islands including Martinique, Guadeloupe, and St. Lucia. Now, their target and anticipated prize was the Spanish-controlled island of Cuba, which contained Spain's most important harbor in the Spanish West Indies—Havana. Their main contingent sailed from England in March 1762 and arrived off the coast of Cuba in early June. The fleet included about 40 ships of war and scores of lesser vessels. Admiral Sir George Pocock[1] was fleet commander and General the Earl of Albemarle was commander of an 11,000-man army.

Colonial forces, which were scheduled to join their British Army counterparts off Cuba, were composed of 1,000 men from Connecticut, 800 from New York, and 500 from New Jersey. General Phineas Lyman of Connecticut, as senior officer and leader of the largest contingent, was appointed overall commander. Putnam, who had been Lieutenant Colonel of the First Regiment, became acting colonel of all Connecticut troops.[2]

After leaving New York in June, they successfully reached the coast of Cuba when a storm erupted, wrecking the ship which held Putnam and 500 of his men on a "rift of craggy rocks." As the rest of the fleet rode out the "mountain-high" surf, Putnam directed his men to construct rafts with any material possible. Fortunately, "There happened to be on board a large quantity of strong cords (the same that are used in the whale fishery) which, being fastened to the rafts, after the first had with inconceivable hazard reached the shore, were of infinite service in preventing the others from driving out to sea."[3]

The rafts served them well and all men reached the shore safely. Without a break, Putnam had his men begin building fortifications. They stayed there until the storm passed several days later and were picked up by transports so they could be reunited with the other troops.

It was the end of July before the fresh, healthy Colonial soldiers joined the almost 30,000 British soldiers, sailors, and marines. The latter had been battling the Spanish troops at Morro Castle at the entrance to Havana Bay since June 7. Although the Spanish had less than half as many fighting men as the British, Morro was one of the strongest fortifications in the Western Hemisphere.

On July 30, fortified with the additional new troops, Albemarle stormed the Spanish fortress, losing only two officers and 30 enlisted men. The Spanish losses of killed and wounded were estimated at 500. There is no record of the details of Israel Putnam's actions in the battle, but if his earlier exploits and subsequent activities were any indication, he was probably in the thick of the action.

The strength and enthusiasm of the Connecticut, New York, and New Jersey men greatly contributed to the fall of the Spanish fort. Their fighting ability must have been a surprise to many in the British command. Those who noticed it would have done well to remember it, since, within 20 years, many of these North American militia fighters, from Maine to South Carolina, would seek independence for their colonies and become enemies of Britain.

After several weeks in the unfamiliar climate, the Colonial troops began succumbing to tropical diseases, especially Yellow Fever. The situation was most catastrophic in the regiment of 44-year-old Irish-born William Haviland. His 1,000 Irish veterans, who shortly before had successfully routed 500 Spaniards, were reduced to a mere 70 men. Haviland was no untested commander. In the French and Indian War, he had played a key part in the British conquest of Canada and the year before Havana, he had been second in command at the British capture of Martinique Island.[4]

After the fall of Morro Castle, the British advanced on Havana, spent 10 days constructing fortifications, and on August 11 began a bombardment with their 45 cannon. Several hours later, the Spanish surrendered and two days later the surrender documents were signed. British troops marched through Havana on August 14 and almost a thousand Spanish troops were captured, along with nine naval warships and four frigates.

In an orderly book, Colonel Putnam kept a record of orders he issued to the Colonial troops. The pages from August 25 to October 16, 1762, have survived. Among the entries is one for August 25, which includes this admonition (with spelling and grammar corrected) to respect those of a different religion, in particular Roman Catholicism. (Nearly all the Connecticut troops were Protestants of the Puritan tradition and probably were unused to the habits and customs of people of other religions.)

> Great decency is to be shown by the soldiers to all religious professors by stopping in the street and pulling their hats regularly and soberly. Will recommend the soldiers to the Earl of Albemarle[5] who would be sorry they should do anything to sully the good appearance he has of them.[6]

In October six transports took the Connecticut troops back to the Port of New York. Many men died of sickness on the trip. In all, nearly 400 of the 1,000 men in Colonel Putnam's command never made it back to Connecticut alive. The death toll percentage was similar for the New Jersey and New York regiments.[7]

After the Battle of Havana, Britain controlled Cuba for only six months. At the 1763 Treaty of Paris (which ended the Seven Years War and its French and Indian War component), Havana, as well as Manila in the Philippines, was restored to Spain in a global territory swap. Spain, in turn, would turn over Florida to Britain.

The treaty's massive global territory exchange also included the British acquisition of French territory east of the Mississippi River (with France only retaining fishing rights off Newfoundland),[8] and Spain's gain of French territory west of the Mississippi River plus the port of New Orleans. In exchange for these concessions, France was allowed to retain its holdings in Africa, India, and the Mediterranean, including islands of the latter that Britain had captured in the war.

Although on a map, Great Britain's winning of the French and Indian War paid off handsomely, there were disadvantages for the victor. The War dramatically increased Britain's debt, which resulted in calls in the British Parliament for the residents of the British Colonies to pay their "rightful" portion of the cost of defending their North American lands. Because the thirteen colonies were not represented in Parliament, cries of "taxation without representation" sprang up among the colonists. This led to the division of the three million-strong colonial population into two major groups: those opposed to British authority [patriots or rebels] and those still loyal to the mother country [loyalists or tories]. It also resulted in the King and Parliament sending additional soldiers to the North American colonies.

As tensions increased between the end of the French and Indian War in 1763 and the first armed combat in 1775, local patriotic organizations, termed Sons of Liberty,[9] sprang up. Perhaps the most influential leader of the Connecticut Colony's group was Israel Putnam. Behind him gathered hundreds of veterans of the last war who had served under him, as well as the people of Northeastern Connecticut who looked to him as their greatest local hero.

Pontiac's War

Pontiac (1720–1769)[10] was an Ottawa chief who emerged as a leader of a confederation of the Ottawa, Potawatomi, and Ojibwa tribes in the early 1760s. The tribes were united in opposing the British occupation of the French forts they had won in the recently ended French and Indian War. Over a period of many years, the French had nurtured good relations with the tribes, which wasn't too difficult considering that they were primarily interested in the fur trade, not in establishing settlements on Indian lands.

Now, the British not only demonstrated an interest in encroaching on the Indian territories, but they showed obvious hostility, condensation, and aggression.[11] They set up fortifications throughout the vast lands that were ceded to them by France, and even expelled the French Catholic priests.

In what was termed "Pontiac's Conspiracy," in 1762 and 1763, Pontiac arranged for tribes from Lake Superior to the Gulf of Mexico to attack the English forts closest to them in Maryland, Michigan, New York, Pennsylvania, and Virginia, and follow up with the destruction of nearby settlements. Eight of 12 targeted forts were eventually captured by Pontiac's allies and their garrisons slaughtered.[12] The forts that the British held onto included two major ones: Pitt and Niagara.

Pontiac chose to personally lead the attack on Fort Detroit. He laid a months-long siege to the fort and won the Battle of Bloody Run on July 31, 1762. By the fall of 1763, Pontiac and his associated tribes had killed or captured over 600 people.

When British General Thomas Gage took over command of the troops in North America, he sent a request to all colonial governments to supply him with troops with which to put down the Pontiac uprising. Connecticut colonial records for March 1764 state: "This Assembly doth appoint Israel Putnam, Esqr, to be Major of the forces now ordered to be raised in this Colony for his Majesty's service against the Indian nations who have been guilty of perfidious and cruel massacres of the English."[13]

In June 1764, Major General John Bradstreet, along with Major Putnam and his Connecticut soldiers headed west to Fort Niagara. They were supported by 600 Native American warriors, who were commanded by Britain's superintendent of the northern Indian tribes, William Johnson. One hundred of these men were natives of the Caughnawagas tribe whose leader was the chief who had captured Putnam a few years earlier.

An agreement was reached with the Indian confederation of tribes. This was followed by the construction of Fort Erie by Putnam's men. They continued on to reinforce Fort Detroit, which resulted in the withdrawal of Pontiac troops. Pontiac agreed to sign a peace treaty in 1766.

In 1769, Pontiac was murdered at a spot near St. Louis, Missouri by a Peoria Indian. Stories have implicated the British and/or other Native American tribes in the killing, but nothing was ever proven.

Death of Hannah

Israel's first wife, Hannah, died on April 6, 1765, at age 44. The upright double gravestone above her grave in Brooklyn, Connecticut's South Cemetery is shared with her 17-year-old daughter. It reads: "They both died in Faith Patience & Resignation to the will of God. Blessed are ye dead who die in ye Lord that they May rest From their Labours & their works do Follow them."

Hannah left behind seven living children. Israel was 25, daughters Hannah, Mehitable, Mary, and Eunice were respectively, 20, 15, 11, and 9, Daniel was five and Peter Schuyler was only three months old.

It's not thought that Putnam was much involved in organized religion before the death of Hannah. His biographer Increase N. Tarbox (1815–1888) notes that Putnam years earlier "lived in Mortlake, with whose inhabitants Pomfret had as little concern as possible. He was not a member of the church. School Committee, or Library Association. He was only a rough young farmer...."[14]

However, Putnam did attend church services, and when he was 35 years old he was admitted to the United Library Association and "paid sixteen pounds, old tenor."[15] Timothy Dwight, the future Yale College president who would someday create Putnam's epitaph, wrote: "During the gayest and most thoughtless period of his life he still regarded religion with profound reverence, and read the Scriptures with the deepest veneration."[16]

In 1765, with his wife gone and with children to raise, Putnam, now 47 years old, began thinking of his life and his family's future. He joined the Brooklyn Congregational Church. Dwight says: "On the public worship of God he was a regular and very respectful attendant. In the decline of life he publicly professed the religion of the Gospel."[17]

In a letter written in 1777 upon the death of Putnam's second wife Deborah, George Washington (who by that time had grown to know Putnam well, as he had been his commander for almost two and one-half years of war) wrote: "...I hope you will bear the misfortune, with that fortitude and complacency of mind, that become a man & a Christian."[18] In all the existing writings of Washington, this may be the only instance of him referring to an individual as a Christian.

A year after Hannah's death, Israel was involved in a church-related dispute. In 1766 Oxford-educated Godfrey Malbone, Jr., along with his wife and 21 slaves, came to Pomfret where overnight he became the wealthiest man in town.[19] Initially friendly with Israel Putnam despite their differences of politics—Malbone was a Loyalist and Putnam a rising leader of the opposition to Britain—things took a different turn when Malbone was about to be taxed for a new church.[20]

When Putnam and others supported a new Congregational Church in Pomfret to replace one with "shaky timbers, patched roof, and boarded windows,"[21] Malbone objected to the taxes he, the largest taxpayer in town, would be forced to pay.

In 1769 a final town meeting was held to decide the question. Malbone was "conveyed to the gathering on a sledge pulled by twelve streamer-bedecked oxen, and he was then carried into the meeting, apparently in a sedan chair, by his slaves." Apparently, the show did not impress the local leaders, who voted to replace the Congregational church.

The only way Malbone could escape paying the Congregational church tax would be if he belonged to another parish. Since there was none in the community, Malbone tried to start a church associated with the Church of England. He would save on taxes and he would establish a church for the local people who were still loyal to the mother country.

Town ended up with two churches: the new Congregational one championed by Putnam, which was constructed in 1771,[22] and the new Trinity Church started by Malbone. Both buildings survive to this day, two and a half centuries later, although in 1865 Trinity Church built a second church, constructed of brick, in downtown Brooklyn.

In 1772, the management of the new Congregational church was assigned to Israel Putnam, who was also voted in as ringer of the bell, a

Three. Between the Wars

The Congregational Church in Brooklyn, Connecticut, which Israel Putnam was instrumental in building. It is now a Unitarian Universalist church (photograph by author).

great honor at the time. When shortly afterwards, Putnam left on his trip to the Mississippi River, the Rev. Josiah Whitney replaced him in these duties. A lifelong friend and confident of Israel Putnam, Whitney would one day be a witness to Putnam's will and would conduct his funeral service.

Marriage to Deborah

A little over two years after the death of his wife Hannah, Israel Putnam married again. Life as a widower couldn't have been easy for Israel—he had been raising seven children alone, with the youngest being only three months old at the time of Hannah's death. The ceremony between Israel and Deborah Lothrop Avery Gardiner took place on June 3, 1767. The new bride had been widowed twice. Her previous husbands were a minister and a wealthy island owner.[23]

Deborah Lothrop was born in Norwich, Connecticut, on January 9, 1719, to Samuel and Deborah (Crow) Lothrop. Thus, she was one year and two days younger than Israel. Her parents were noted for their longevity: her father Samuel was born in 1685 and lived to age 82; her mother was born in 1691 and lived to age 104.[24]

Deborah's first husband had been the Rev. Ephraim Avery, the pastor of the Brooklyn, Connecticut's Congregational Church parish. They had married on September 21, 1738, when she was only 19. They had three daughters and six sons: John (born 1739), twins Samuel (who died in infancy) and Ephraim, Samuel (1742), Elisha (1744), Elizabeth (1746), Septimus (1749), Deborah (1751), and Ruth (1754).[25]

Israel Putnam had known Deborah Avery when her husband ministered to the people of Brooklyn. Deborah's husband and son Septimus passed away from malignant dysentery in 1754. Deborah was left alone with seven children to raise.

One year later, she married John Gardiner III (1714–1764), a widower and the fifth owner of Gardiner's Island, which is situated off the coast of eastern Long Island.[26] John's great-great-grandfather was Lion Gardiner (1599–1665) who had settled the island after received a grant from King Charles I (about 10 years before the king was executed). John's grandfather was John Gardiner I (1661–1738) who was best known as the recipient of Captain William Kidd's treasure.[27]

In 1699, Kidd landed on Gardiner's Island on his way to Boston. He gave Lady Gardiner a cloth of gold and desserts for her children. He then proceeded to bury a treasure of gold, silver, and jewels. He revealed the location of the treasure to John Gardiner I. Kidd then continued on to Boston where he was arrested by the Earl of Bellomont and sent to England for trial. Gardiner I gave the treasure from his island to Bellomont.[28]

Deborah's husband, John Gardiner III, was born 15 years after the Captain Kidd episode. He was a Yale College graduate, but it was said that "he was not a quarter as good a farmer as his father." When he inherited

Gardiner's Island at age 37, he and his first wife Elizabeth Munford already had five children. Although successful in retaining the family island, he lost heavily on bad investments.[29] John's first wife died in 1754.

In 1755, John Gardiner III married Deborah Lothrop Avery, and they had two children: a daughter, Hannah, who was born in 1757 and a son, Septimus, born in 1759.

John Gardiner III died on May 19, 1764, and was buried on his island. In his will, he left his "beloved Wife Deborah Gardiner one third part of all my Personal Estate." He left one-sixth shares of his "Personal Estate" to both Septimus (his son by Deborah) and John (his son by his first wife). He left the island to son David with the request that he provide for the younger children until they reach marriage or adulthood. Additional bequests were made to daughters Mary, Elizabeth, Jerusha, and Hannah.[30]

It was three years after Gardiner's death that Israel Putnam married Deborah. At the time, he was a 49-year-old prosperous farmer with possibly the most extensive (and certainly the most colorful) military background of anyone in the Connecticut colony. Deborah was a 48-year-old sophisticated woman who had raised a large family, served as a community leader as a minister's wife, and been the mistress of one of the largest privately-owned estates in the thirteen colonies.

It might have been at Deborah's suggestion that they moved from the Putnam farmhouse in Pomfret to the Avery house in Brooklyn, which had been left to Deborah by her first husband. Although Deborah had lived for years on Gardiner's Island, she was accustomed to circulating in refined society, and she probably found it boring to spend seven days a week on a remote farm.

Putnam's 27-year-old son Israel, with his wife Sarah Waldo, became manager of the family farm; Putnam's daughters Mehitable (17), Mary (14), and Eunice (11) sometimes lived on the farm and sometimes at their father's house in town. Sons seven-year-old Daniel and two-year-old Peter Schuyler Putnam lived with Israel and Deborah.[31]

Although it was only a few miles south of the farm, downtown Brooklyn was a different world. The Putnams were now living near the meetinghouse, commercial establishments and stagecoach routes. Soon they turned the former Avery house into the Gen. Wolfe Inn, named in honor of Putnam's former commander, James Wolfe, who had been killed in action at Quebec eight years earlier.[32]

It has been speculated that the many visits by friends and admirers to the war hero at his farm were very inconvenient, necessitating the family's relocation. Ellen D. Larned (1825–1912) writes in her *History of*

Windham County, Connecticut, that "A Virginian Jefferson would submit to such an invasion, though it made him bankrupt; a Yankee Putnam could contrive to turn it into profit or at least save himself from ruin."[33] It might be added that the "Yankee Deborah" probably had a hand in making the decision to open the inn.

At the time of Putnam's marriage to Deborah, he was one of the most famous men in New England, but with his limited education, he had never circulated in high society. Ellen D. Larned writes in her *History of Windham County, Connecticut,* that his second marriage brought Putnam "...into connection with many prominent families, and with that ecclesiastic element so potent in Connecticut at this period. Mrs. Putnam had a large circle of friends and much social experience."[34]

In Putnam she found a man in many respects the opposite of her second husband: Putnam was a "born farmer" who loved putting in a hard day's physical labor, and he was successful in most every business venture he had ever undertaken. Although Israel had received a substantial inheritance to start his career, in every other way he advanced through his own efforts. At a Putnam family gathering in 1855, great-grandson the Rev. L. Grosvenor stated: "Putnam was a 'self-made man,' so far as that appellation may be applied to any human being."[35]

Today, the site of Israel and Deborah Putnam's tavern is marked by a bronze plaque on a boulder across the street from the equestrian statue of the General. The boulder was moved from a farm owned by a great-grandson of Putnam; the plaque was unveiled during World War I, on August 9, 1918.[36]

Deborah Lothrop Avery Gardiner Putnam accompanied her husband to army headquarters in Cambridge, Massachusetts, in the winter of 1775-1776 and there became friends of General and Martha Washington. In the words of Thomas Jefferson, "Washington was only at ease in the circle of his friends, where he might be unreserved with safety, [there] he took a free share in conversation."[37]

Years later, Putnam biographer Tarbox relates son Daniel Putnam's words on the relationship between the Washingtons and the Putnams. Daniel, who was with his father during these months from the summer of 1775 until early 1776, stated:

> From the arrival of Washington at Cambridge till the enemy left Boston, his and Putnam's families [Washington's wife Martha and Putnam's wife Deborah were at Cambridge] were not only on the most friendly terms, but their intercourse was very frequent. Not a week passed but they dined together at the quarters of one or the other.[38]

Three. Between the Wars   55

Daniel Putnam mentions one dinner in September 1775, when Washington offered a toast for "a speedy and honorable peace." Several days later, Washington was at Putnam's headquarters. Israel Putnam recalled the toast and asked Washington if he could "drink one of rather a different character; I will give you, sir, 'A long and moderate war.'" According to Daniel,

> It has been truly said of Washington, that he seldom smiled and almost never laughed; but the sober and sententious manner in which Putnam delivered his sentiment, and its seeming contradiction to all his practice, came so unexpectedly upon Washington that he did laugh, more heartily than ever I remember to have seen him before or after; but presently he said, "You are the last man, General Putnam, from whom I should have expected such a toast; you, who are all the time urging vigorous measures, to plead now for a long and, what is still more extraordinary, a moderate war, seems strange indeed."[39]

Daniel continues:

> Putnam replied that "The measures he advised were calculated to prevent, not to hasten, a peace, which would only be a rotten thing, and last no longer than it divided us. I expect nothing but a long war, and I would have it a moderate one that we may hold out till the mother country becomes willing to cast us off forever." Washington did not soon forget this toast; for years after, and more than once, he reminded Putnam of it.[40]

Richard Frothingham in his *History of the Siege of Boston* brings up an incident that provoked General Putnam's anger at someone at the Cambridge Committee of Safety who treated Putnam's wife, Deborah, poorly. In a letter dated May 22, 1776, Putnam soundly came to his wife's defense by arguing:

> Pray did not I labor and toil night and day, through wet and cold, and venture my life in the high places of the field, for the safety of my country, and the town of Cambridge in particular? For it was thought we could never hold Cambridge; and that we had better quit it, and go back and fortify on the heights of Brookline. I always told them we must hold Cambridge; and pray did not I take possession of Prospect Hill the very night after the fight on Bunker Hill, without having any orders from any person? And was not I the only general officer that tarried there? The taking of said hill I never could obtain leave for before, which is allowed by the best judges was the salvation of Cambridge, if not of the country.[41]

In a response on June 18, 1776, the Committee of Safety wrote that General Putnam's conduct "while in Cambridge, in every respect, and more especially as a general, (without having it set forth,) we hold in the highest veneration, and ever shall." They continued,

> Nothing was ever aimed at treating you or yours unbecoming the many obligations that we are under for the extraordinary services you have done to this town, which

must always be acknowledged with the highest gratitude, not only by us, but by rising generations.⁴²

In his 1871 book *Old Cambridge and New*, Thomas C. Amory gives more information on the possible cause of the problem. The Putnam's headquarters were at a home that was abandoned by the Loyalist Inman family. Amory states:

> Mr. Inman left his house with all its costly plenishing, his stables amply provided with horses and handsome equipages. The general, in taking possession of the premises for his head-quarters, considered these not unnaturally as part of their appendages, and Mrs. Putnam took her airings in the family coach. The selectmen, provoked at this by them unwarranted appropriation of confiscated property, had the presumption, when she was some distance from home, to compel her to alight. The general was not of a temper to submit very meekly to such an affront, and his indignation was expressed with sufficient force to have become historical.⁴³

It's doubtful that Deborah Putnam was any more likely than Israel to take a slight lying down. After all, she worked for years alongside her first husband, a respected minister, in managing the affairs of a Congregationalist parish, and she had helped John Gardiner run one of the largest estates in the thirteen colonies.

Shortly before the Revolutionary War, Putnam was asked by a British officer "whether he did not seriously believe that a well-appointed British army of five thousand veterans could march through the whole continent of America."

In Putnam's response, we can detect something that Deborah might have said as well: "No doubt, if they behaved civilly and paid well for every thing they wanted—but"—after a moment's pause added—"if they should attempt it in a hostile manner (though the American men were out of the question) the women, with their ladles and broomsticks, would knock them all on the head before they had got half way through."⁴⁴

On May 8, 1895, a Deborah Avery Putnam chapter of the Daughters of the American Revolution was organized in Plainfield, Connecticut. In 1901, the Connecticut Daughters of the American Revolution published *Patron Saints*, a book of short American biographies. In it they said this of Deborah Putnam:

> Hers was a life of activity. Utterly discouraging indolence, she and her daughters spent much of their time spinning flax for the soldiers' shirts. At one time they were assisted by the daughter of a British Major, who had applied to General Putnam for protection. Mrs. Putnam had received her as a member of the family and treated her with the greatest kindness. In her letters home the young lady, though strongly objected to "working for the Yankee soldiers," did express great admiration for her hostess.⁴⁵

Putnam's Appearance and Temperament

In his widely-popular book, *1776*, historian David McCullough accurately pictures Israel Putnam as "Rough, 'thick-set,' 'all bones and muscles,' and leathery, with flowing gray locks and a head like a cannonball."[46] If a Hollywood studio were to cast a Putnam biography, it would need to find an actor who combined the personality of John Wayne and the appearance of John Goodman.

One hundred fifty years before McCullough wrote his book, Lemuel Grosvenor described his great-grandfather:

> Putnam, in personal appearance, was of medium height, of a strong athletic figure, and in the time of the revolutionary war, rather fleshy, weighing about 200 lbs. His hair was dark, his eyes light blue, his complexion a florid Saxon, and his broad, good-humored face, marked with deep scars, received in his encounters with the French and Indians. A portrait of him, taken in his younger days, when he was a provincial major, gives a rather slim but muscular figure, dressed in scarlet coat and breeches and a light vest, with buff gloves and black cravat. He is described by those now living, who frequently saw him in his old age, as being very large around the chest, showing what we should expect from his habits a great amount of the sanguine[47] vital temperament.[48]

Virtually every painting or sketch of Putnam depicts him as markedly overweight. However, he was not the largest man among Washington's generals. Henry Knox[49] held that distinction, and his wife was not far behind. In May of 1788, after dining with Henry and Lucy Knox, Abigail Adams Smith wrote to her mother, Abigail Adams: "The General is not half so fat as he was."[50] (Only three months later, on August 19, 1788, General Knox was 280 pounds when he was officially weighed at West Point.[51]) A month after Abigail Smith's observation, she wrote to her mother that General Knox's wife's "size is enormous; I am frightened when I look at her; I verily believe that her waist is as large as three of yours, at least."[52]

Putnam biographer Increase N. Tarbox, in his 1876 work, provides a lengthy quotation from Judge Judah Dana, a former United States Senator from Maine and a grandson of General Putnam.[53] While obviously a pro–Putnam piece, it is one of the most complete descriptions of Putnam in existence.

> In his person, for height about the middle size, very erect, thickset, muscular and firm in every part. His countenance was open, strong and animated; the features of his face large, well-proportioned to each other and to his whole frame; his teeth fair and sound till death. His organs and senses were all exactly fitted for a warrior; he heard quickly, saw to an immense distance, and though he sometimes stammered in conversation, his voice was remarkably heavy, strong and commanding. Though facetious and dispassionate in private, when animated in the heat of battle his countenance was

fierce and terrible and his voice like thunder. His whole manner was admirably adapted to inspire his soldiers with courage and confidence, and his enemies with terror.[54]

Although his formal education left much to be desired, Putnam's native intelligence was never in dispute. Judge Dana continues:

> The faculties of his mind were not inferior to those of his body; his penetration was acute; his decision rapid, yet remarkably correct; and the more desperate the situation the more collected and undaunted. With the courage of a lion he had a heart that melted at the sight of distress; he could never witness suffering in any human being without becoming a sufferer himself. Even the operation of a blood-letting has caused him to faint. In viewing a field of battle his distress was exquisite, until he had afforded friend and foe all the relief in his power. Once after a battle, on examining a bullet wound through the head of a favorite officer, Captain Whiting, who died upon the field, he fainted and was taken up for dead. Martial music roused him to the highest pitch, while solemn, sacred music sent him into tears. In his disposition he was open and generous almost to a fault; he never disguised; and in his social relations he was never excelled.[55]

Undoubtedly, Putnam followed the health and personal hygiene rules set forth in his orderly book for the 1777 Hudson Highland campaign:

> As Health & a respectable Appearance among Officers & Soldiers gives Strength & Dignity to an Army—and as their keeping themselves clean & neat, using proper diet well dress'd & not lying on the cold ground, & in the damp night air needlessly will contribute much to the Preservation of their Health & the Dignity of their Appearance. The Genl, expects that the Troops keep themselves clean & neat, their Hair cut decently short & comb'd & avoid using unwholesome Food or that is partially cook'd, when they have opportunity to cook it thoroughly. Also that they take Care not to lye upon the cold ground or in the damp night air when the Situation of the Army doth not make it necessary. And if any of the Officers should be so inattentive to the Preservation of their Health & Reputation as to neglect to observing these Regulations—the Genl requests the Officers to exert their Influence by Authority & by Example to compel & induce the Soldiers to a Compliance therewith & to inspire them with every Military Virtue.[56]

Putnam was also concerned with frequency with which military men of the time were resorting to the practice of dueling. It was opposed by many religious organizations including the Catholic Church and the Anglican Church. Benjamin Franklin famously wrote, "How can such miserable sinners as we are entertain so much pride, as to conceit that every offense against our imagined honor merits death?"[57]

Both Thomas Jefferson and George Washington opposed dueling, with the latter advising his officers to refuse to participate in the practice. In his 1885 book, "Schools and Masters of Fence from the Middle Ages to the Eighteenth Century," fencing expert Egerton Castle estimates that dueling "cost France in 180 years [the 1600s and 1700s] the useless loss of 40,000 valiant gentlemen, killed in single combats which arose generally on the most futile grounds."[58]

Interestingly, the most famous duel in American history occurred in 1804 between two men who were important to the career of Israel Putnam: his attentive aide-de-camp, Aaron Burr, and George Washington's aide-de-camp, Alexander Hamilton. Historians have not been kind to Burr, who at the time of the duel was Vice President of the United States; while they have often highly praised Hamilton, the first Secretary of the Treasury.

In his relations with Putnam, Burr was a loyal and respectful subordinate, while Hamilton was a man who was instrumental in damaging Putnam's military career. Most accounts of the duel paint Burr as the villain and there is substantial evidence that Burr might have been a traitor in later life.

It's significant, given this connection between these two men and dueling, that Putnam was a firm opponent of the practice. For Putnam there was nothing honorable about cold-blooded, premeditated killing. He had been known throughout his long military life as an officer who showed compassion for prisoners of war. If he took a life in battle it was in self-defense, to save either himself or a comrade. To deliberately avenge a verbal insult by aiming a loaded gun at another man and intentionally shooting him to death was repugnant to Putnam.

A story is told of Putnam insulting a British officer. Whether it is true or not will probably never be known, but it was widely repeated during the General's life. The time and location is uncertain, but was probably during the French and Indian War. Here we are using the account given in William Cutter's 1850 biography of Putnam.[59]

The offended officer demanded "reparation." Putnam agreed to meet him the next morning without seconds. At the designated time, the man showed up with a sword and pistols. Soon, Putnam appeared at the other end of the field, 30 rods [about 500 feet] away, holding a musket. Without waiting for a signal, he raised the gun, aimed at the officer, and shot. The man ran toward Putnam who was in the process of reloading. "What are you about to do? Is this the conduct of an American officer and a man of honor?"

"What am I about to do?" asked Putnam. "A pretty question to put to a man whom you intended to murder. I'm about to kill you. And if you don't beat a retreat in less time than would take old Heath to hang a Tory, you are a gone dog." Putnam finished loading the weapon and raised it to his shoulder. As he did so, the would-be duelist ran away as fast as he could.

Why, when so many other men would be fearful of appearing cowardly, did Putnam succeed with this ploy? Cutter editorializes, that while few men could afford to treat dueling with such "supreme contempt," Putnam could do just that, since his "courage was above suspicion."

This is not the only Putnam story to involve dueling. Another English officer is the challenger in the tale of the powder keg. The time period is probably the Revolutionary War. It seems that the officer was a prisoner on parole and Putnam had made a remark that he considered insulting to "the character of the British."[60]

Putnam accepted his challenge and agreed to meet the officer the following morning. Putnam had the right of choice of weapons and he agreed to bring them for both men. When the officer arrived, Putnam was in his tent calmly smoking a pipe. On the ground next to him was a powder keg. In the top of the keg Putnam had inserted two long wooden matches. After directing the man to a chair on the other side of the keg, Putnam lit the matches with his pipe and settled back, remarking that both of them had an equal chance of living. As the British officer nervously watched the matches burned down to the top of the gunpowder container, he looked at Putnam who wasn't even watching. Finally, the officer jumped up and quickly made for the exit.

"You are just as brave a man as I took you to be," said Putnam. "This is nothing but a barrel of onions with a few grains of powder on the head, to try you by."

It's likely that these were two of the stories that Putnam would tell visitors to his Brooklyn home and tavern. Biographer Livingston, after years of research, painted a picture of Putnam between the wars:

> It is easy to picture to ourselves Israel Putnam as the host of an old-time inn. Large and stout in figure, with round, good-natured face and hospitable manner, he was the typical landlord, heartily welcoming his guests and entertaining them with tales of his varied experiences, his numerous adventures on land and water, and hairbreadth escapes from fire and sword.[61]

Cutter remarks on two accidents that occurred before the American Revolution:

> During this short season of tranquility [sic], Putnam resumed his agricultural employments, which he pursued with his accustomed vigor, though slightly interrupted by two accidents, one of which deprived him of the first joint of the thumb of his right hand, while the other was attended with a compound fracture of his right thigh, which shortened that leg nearly an inch, and made him slightly lame for the remainder of his life.[62]

In addition to the scars acquired during the French and Indian War, the years of fighting in guerrilla fashion had a psychological impact on Putnam:

it was said that he always slept with one eye open.[63] (It's an intriguing piece of information, since it is common for some animals, such as dolphins, to sleep with one eye open,[64] but it is highly questionable that human beings do it too.)

Tavern Owner

A hint of Putnam's reputation for compassion was given in Utah's *Deseret News* in 1851: "It is stated of Gen. Putnam, that he planted in his native town in Windham county, Ct., a mile of apple trees in the highway, so that the poor might have apples as well as the rich. Let us have some in Salt Lake City."[65]

Whether this occurred before or after the French and Indian War, is not revealed, but as Putnam's farm was prosperous almost from the start, it could have been at almost any time in his life—from his early twenties until the year of his death.

On a tree in front of his new home and tavern in Brooklyn, Putnam placed a sign, which William Cutter described in his 1850 biography as follows:

> It represents General Wolfe, in full uniform, his eye fixed, in an expression of fiery earnestness, upon some distant object, and his right arm extended in emphatic gesture, as if charging on the foe, or directing some other important movement of his army.[66]

British commander Major General James Wolfe in 1759 led his forces to victory over the French at the Battle of the Plains of Abraham in Canada. Although he was killed in the battle, the success of his troops led to British control of Canada.[67] Putnam showed his respect for Wolfe by naming his tavern for him.

The General Wolfe sign showed on each side a full-length painting of red-coated British General James Wolfe. The buckshot holes in the sign were possibly added by American Patriots who, seeing a red-coated officer, didn't realize that the officer in the picture had died in action in the French and Indian War—years before colonists had even dreamt of seeking independence from Britain. Two hundred and fifty years after it was erected in front of Israel and Deborah's tavern, the sign was on permanent display at the Connecticut Historical Society Museum in Hartford, Connecticut.[68]

Livingston describes the Israel and Deborah Putnam tavern:

> This tavern, with its distinguished host and equally cordial hostess, became one of the best-known gathering-places in Eastern Connecticut, and was associated with many an interesting incident in Revolutionary days. Around the large hearthstone were discussed the vital questions of the colonial crisis that stirred the soul of every ardent

patriot. Putnam's tavern was a centre, also, for news of local interest; because here, as at other inns in the olden days, were posted notices of town meetings, of elections, of new laws, and notices of administration, as well as bills of sales, of auctions, and records of transfers. The inn was, indeed, an "original business exchange," and the genial Putnam found much social enjoyment in the intercourse with the neighbours and townspeople who flocked to the tavern for information in regard to local affairs as well as the matters of wider importance. The arrival and departure of the coaches loaded with travellers held a high place among the chief events in the village. Many a merry scene there was in the winter, too, when sleighs dashed up to the cheerful tavern entrance. Landlord and landlady were ready with their greeting, and soon all the new guests were in full enjoyment of the thrifty, homelike comforts.[69]

The position of innkeeper in Old New England was an honorable one in the late 18th century. In 1771, future United States president John Adams wrote of Enfield, Connecticut, landlord Pease: "I found he was the great Man of the Town—their Representative &c. as well as Tavern Keeper...."[70]

William Gordon, a contemporary of Putnam, says this of the Pomfret tavern owner:

> Col. Putnam served with the Connecticut troops under [General] Amherst in the last [French and Indian] war. By his courage and conduct he secured to himself a good share of reputation. When peace commenced he returned to the civil line of life. Of late he has occupied a tavern with a farm annexed to it. Such a junction is frequent in New England, and the occupation not at all inconsistent with a Roman character.[71]

There's evidence that Putnam also operated a brewery in connection with his tavern.[72] Some recent articles even claim he was one of the first brewers in America.

Among the many patrons of the Putnam tavern were his fellow comrades-in-arms from the French and Indian War. One of the most famous, a man who remembered Israel Putnam well, was Vermont's Seth Warner, who later gained fame by co-founding the Green Mountain Boys with Ethan Allen and winning a victory at the Revolutionary War's Battle of Bennington. In 1768, which was five years after the French and Indian War ended, Warner named his first-born son Israel Putnam Warner.

Young Israel Warner, showing the same spunk as his father and his namesake, served as a Green Mountain Boys scout and messenger in the Revolution starting at age nine. He was honorably discharged as a private at the War's end in 1783.[73]

Preparation for War

The Stamp Act, passed by the British parliament in 1765, required residents of the American colonies to pay a tax on paper items, including legal documents, licenses, newspapers, advertisements, almanacs, calendars, pamphlets, playing cards, etc. The money raised was to be used to fund the military troops who were stationed at the western reaches of the 13 colonies.

Many colonists strongly objected to the act, claiming that as British subjects, they should not be taxed by a legislative body, i.e., Parliament, that they had no role in electing. They insisted that only the colonial legislatures had the right to tax the colonists. In addition, the colonists feared the Stamp Act would set a precedent that would usher in other taxes by Parliament.

After the Stamp Act was passed on March 22, 1765, Putnam was one of three men who were most influential in stirring up opposition in Eastern Connecticut. Like Putnam, the other two had been British officers in the French and Indian War— Norwich's John Durkee (1728–1782) and Windham's Hugh Ledlie (c. 1724–1798). Putnam's counterparts in other states— people like orator Patrick Henry in Virginia and politician Samuel Adams in Massachusetts—would stir up opposition to the Act, while in the next decade Henry and Adams would be at the forefront of the movement to break away from Great Britain altogether.

In 1765, Putnam traversed the Eastern towns of Connecticut to ascertain what support existed for armed resistance. News of his activity spread to New York. Livingston quotes a British officer who was stationed there at the time:

> By advice from Connecticut, matters are arrived to greater lengths than in any other province, having already provided themselves with a magazine for Arms, Ammunition, &c., and 10,000 men at the shortest warning for opposing the Stamp Act, &c., all under the Command of a Connecticut man, called Col. Putnam, one that has received his Majesty's money, having been employ'd during the [French and Indian] War as a Provincial Colonel.[74]

Jared Ingersoll, Sr., had been sent to London by the Connecticut General Assembly to convince the British government not to pass the Stamp Act. Instead they convinced him of its fairness and sent him back as the official stamp agent for Connecticut. About 500 mounted men led by representatives of the Sons of Liberty met Ingersoll south of Hartford, and convinced him to resign his position as agent. Israel Putnam, who had helped found the Connecticut Sons of Liberty in 1765, was not with the rebels. It is possible that the farm accident that permanently damaged his right thigh prevented his participation.

However, Putnam was one of three representatives who was selected to convince Connecticut Governor Thomas Fitch (who served as governor from 1754–1766) not to enforce the Stamp Act. While copies of the Act were still in New York, Putnam visited Governor Fitch. The following words are quoted from Tarbox's Putnam biography:

> The Governor said to him, "What shall I do if the stamped paper should be sent to me by the King's authority?"
> "Lock it up," said Putnam, "until we [the Sons of Liberty] shall visit you again."
> "And what will you do with it then?"
> Putnam's reply was, "We shall expect you to give us the key of the room where it is deposited; and if you think fit, in order to screen yourself from blame, you may forewarn us upon our peril not to enter the room."
> "And," asked the Governor, "what will you do afterwards?"
> "Send it safely back again."
> "But," said he, "if I should refuse admission?"
> "Your house will be leveled with the dust in five minutes."[75]

Fortunately, before the stamped paper could be delivered to Connecticut from New York, the Stamp Act was repealed. Surprised by the hatred the bill had provoked, the British government felt it would be best to find other ways to accomplish the same goals and repealed it on March 18, 1766. Still, the act had given rise to feelings that would be impossible to completely suppress and within a decade they would fester and break out into history's first case of armed succession from the British Empire.

Israel Putnam wasn't only concerned with the Sons of Liberty business. He was a natural politician, who, as the most famous resident of Eastern Connecticut, could have won almost any public office that he wished. Back home he served as moderator of Pomfret town meetings, three times a selectman, and a deputy to the General Assembly. Ellen Larned in her *History of Windham County* states:

> He devised and laid out roads, he set out school-districts, he deliberated upon the great question whether to repair or pull down the meeting-house; nor did he disdain to 'hire the master,' seat the meeting-house, collect parish rates, nor even to receive crows' heads and pay out the bounty money.[76]

As a candidate who stood for colonial rights, Putnam was elected to the Connecticut General Assembly and served in the 1766 and 1767 sessions. Two centuries before modern technology would revolutionize political campaigning, the name Putnam became a household word primarily through word of mouth.

1773 Mississippi Expedition

After a decade in England trying to obtain a land grant from the government for provincial veterans of the French and Indian War, Putnam's former commander Phineas Lyman returned with news that the "King in Council" had approved the granting of lands by the governor of West Florida "in the same proportions as had been provided for His Majesty's regular troops."[77]

Although Lyman didn't return with written documentation, a meeting of veterans decided to pursue the matter and formed an "exploring committee" made up of Israel Putnam, Thaddeus Lyman, Roger Enos, and Israel's cousin Rufus Putnam. The latter's experience as a surveyor was the main reason for his inclusion.

On December 10, 1772, Rufus left his Massachusetts home for Pomfret, Connecticut, where he arrived the following day at Israel Putnam's house. After stocking up on provisions, he left on December 16 with Israel and Israel's 13-year-old son, Daniel.

Left behind were Israel's wife Deborah, his four daughters, Eunice, Mary, Mehitable, and Hannah, who ranged in age from 16 to 28, and Israel's youngest son, Peter Schuyler, who would be eight years old in three weeks. Also living with them were Deborah's children by second husband John Gardiner, 13-year-old Septimus and 15-year-old Hannah. Her children by her first husband were now adults. Israel's oldest child, Israel, Jr., was now 32.

Israel, Daniel, and Rufus took horses to Norwich and then a boat to New York City, where they arrived on December 20. They waited two weeks in New York, during which time (as Israel recorded in his diary) they went to church services; applied fresh paint to their ship, the *Mississippi*; and accumulated supplies for the voyage (including cattle and hogs).

After a relatively mild voyage down the Atlantic coast, the expedition arrived off Turks Islands north of Haiti on January 25, 1773. Five days later they reached the northwest coast of Haiti. The *Mississippi* joined about 80 other ships in the harbor as Putnam's party made several trips to shore for trading.

When they left Haiti, they headed west, passing Cuba on their right. It had been 10 years since Israel Putnam and fellow "military adventurer" Roger Enos had been shipwrecked off that island during the Havana expedition.

A few days later, on February 8, they were on Jamaica, where Israel had an encounter with a vicious dog. As the manager of a plantation was giving the New England men a tour, he was attacked by the animal. Putnam, in a struggle to subdue the dog, "tumbled into won [sic] of the vats that was full of Liquer to make rum of." Putnam, maintaining his usual good humor, changed his clothes and boarded the ship.

Using the Israel and Rufus Putnam diaries, Livingston details the journey[78]: Leaving Jamaica, the group headed northwest for about 500 miles to the Cape San Antonio, which is at the western tip of Cuba. There, they were welcomed by Spaniards, who approached their vessel in a canoe. Saying they had 20 tortoises to trade, they left to get them. When they were gone, a schooner approached. As the Putnam party suspected, it was a pirate vessel, and they continued onward, leaving the tortoises to the schooner's crew.[79]

Passing Cuba, Putnam headed toward Pensacola, Florida, which was a British haven on the Gulf of Mexico. Unfavorable weather resulted in the journey taking ten days. Putnam was pleased to find two friends from the French and Indian War at Pensacola: General Frederick Haldimand[80] and Major John Small.[81]

Unfortunately, no official documents granting lands to the Putnam party were waiting at Pensacola. Rufus Putnam described this as a "mortifying circumstance." However, given the likelihood that either the documents might arrive later or something else might be arranged, they decided to proceed with their survey of lands along the Mississippi River.[82]

The Putnam group encountered unfavorable winds and took the opportunity to replenish their supply of fresh meat. Putnam, in particular, enjoyed hunting and went ashore for deer. On March 22, the party reached the mouth of the Mississippi. Traveling up the river, Putnam and another man scouted out the country ahead in a whale boat. It was during one of these forays that Putnam shot three alligators. On March 28 he visited a French plantation owner who lived on the river. After this time, Putnam stopped keeping up with his journal, but Rufus continued with his. Two days later they reached New Orleans, where they spend over a week.

At New Orleans, Captain Goodrich decided not to proceed further with his vessel, so the Putnam party obtained a bateau and on April 8 went it alone. In three days, they traveled over 70 miles upriver to an Acadian settlement. Recently exiled by the British forces from Nova Scotia because of perceived French sympathies, the Acadians had established their homes in the remote area above New Orleans. The party spent a day there where they "were treated with hospitality, listening with interest to the stories of innumerable hardships and sad experiences which the exiles told."[83]

Continuing their journey up the Mississippi past French and Native American settlements, the Putnam party reached Fort Rosalie at Natchez on April 26. They were almost 400 miles north of the mouth of the Mississippi. Two days later they left for the Bayou Pierre, which was about 50 miles north of Natchez. Going another 17 miles northeast up the Bayou

Pierre, they reached the "Forks" where they marked a tree at the approximate location of the land that they believed would be granted to them.

They headed back down the Mississippi to the home of Indian trader Thomas James at Great Gulf. From there, Israel Putnam and Thaddeus Lyman, with a Choctaw Indian guide, took off on a nearly 60-mile-long expedition to Walnut Hills "which formed a portion of the great bluff bounding the valley of the Mississippi on the East." The rest of the Putnam party reached the same destination by water.

Under the date of Thursday, May 13, Rufus Putnam records:

> Colo. Putnam & Mr. Lymau & myself Set out by Land, more perticulerly to examin the high Lands, Stretching from the old French Station [on the Yazoo River], to the Walnut hills; we Steared our course as neer the hills as possible on account of the Cane brakes. Saw Several Small Streams issuing from the high Lands, & land very rich; in the afternoon we pursued one of these Streams to Some distence, when we were taken up by a mighty Cane Brake, here Colo. Putnam climbed a tree & discovered high Land at about 100 rods distent which we were two hours in gaining, on account of the difficulty of giting through the Cane ... we returned part of the way down the hill & Camped by a very fine Spring.[84]

Putnam and Lyman wanted to explore further toward the Big Black River, but their guide objected—for reasons that weren't clear given the man understood few English words. Later, Trader James spoke with the man, who explained that he had met two chiefs who warned that the Englishmen must not go further.

Characteristically, Israel Putnam didn't take "no" for an answer and, with Rufus and Lyman, began another excursion on May 17. Rufus noted in his diary: "Set out to explore the Lands on the Big Black.... Thursday May 20, we returned down the river to Mr. James' where we found the Second Chief of Chactau Nation [Mingo-oma or Snake-head] waiting for us."

The chief showed the Putnam party that Governor Chester had granted land rights to the region to the Choctaws. Mingo-oma explained, through interpreter Trader James, that no white people could settle above the Big Black River. He emphasized that it was "the only hunting ground they had left and that this was small."[85]

Faced with the strong claims of the Choctaws,[86] the Putnam party returned south, explored lands on the east side of the Mississippi, and arrived at Manchac on June 2. A few miles south of Manchac they found their boat and a month later arrived back in Pensacola. To their dismay, no land grant documents had arrived. Governor Chester and his Council did grant whatever rights were in their powers, and allowed the provincial veterans to settle on lands they had surveyed. On July 15, the Putnam party left for home. They arrived in New York City on August 6, 1773.

Rufus Putnam's diary contains the entries: "took passage in a sloop for Norwich, but on our way sprung the mast, and with some difficulty arrived at New London on Tuesday, the 10th"; "Wednesday August 11th—quit the sloop & took passag in a Row boate for Norwich"; and "Thursday August 12th—came on Horseback to Colo. Putnams & Friday 13th arrived at my own house in Brookfield."[87]

The Mississippi River expedition would prove to be the longest trip of Israel's life. His military adventures had taken him to Cuba, present day Michigan, and Montreal Canada, while his other non-military explorations now included visits to Haiti and Jamaica.

The Mississippi trip had been a great experience for the Putnams and their companions, but it was destined to prove fruitless. Political strife in the colonies was growing rapidly and both Israel and Rufus became more concerned with affairs back home. In a mere 20 months, the American Revolutionary War would began with the colonial militia and British troops battling each other in Massachusetts.

Four

Bloodiest Battle of the Revolution

Events Leading to the Battle

In about 1765, semi-secret Sons of Liberty groups sprang up in the British colonies in opposition to what they considered were increasingly unfair and oppressive measures enacted by the British government in London against British citizens in the thirteen North American colonies.

The most famous pre-war action by a Sons of Liberty organization was the December 16, 1773, Boston Tea Party, where activists destroyed a shipment of tea in Boston Harbor. It was in protest of a recently enacted tax on tea—a tax that was imposed by an elected body (the British Parliament) that did not include representatives of the people of the American colonies.

Colonial Williamsburg Foundation describes the state of military preparedness of the American colonies:

> The colonies required militia service, generally, of males between sixteen and sixty, excepting clergy, college students, slaves, and, often, free blacks. In Virginia, service by Catholics was forbidden. The militiamen came from the civilian ranks of tailors, mechanics, small farmers, bootmakers, smiths, gentry, common laborers, shopkeepers, clerks, lawyers, tutors, carpenters. The units roughly mirrored the laity of free white male colonial society.[1]

In one of its "Intolerable Acts,"[2] on March 25, 1774, Britain ordered the Port of Boston closed to trade until the East India Company was compensated for the loss of their merchandise in the Boston Tea Party. Throughout Massachusetts, Connecticut and elsewhere, towns and cities collected food and other supplies to be sent to the citizens of Boston who were harmed by the new measure.

In 1774, Israel Putnam led a Sons of Liberty Committee of Correspondence and was appointed lieutenant colonel of Connecticut's militia regiment. On August 11, 1774, he, along with fellow committee members Joseph Holland and Putnam's son-in-law, Daniel Tyler,[3] sent a letter to the people of Boston (addressed to patriot leader Samuel Adams) which began: "With our hearts deeply impressed with the feelings of humanity towards our near and dear brethren of Boston, who are now suffering under a ministerial, revengeful hand."[4]

The letter goes on to state that if peaceful means of protest do not work, "we are ready to march in the van, and to sprinkle the American altars with our heart's blood, if occasion should be."[5] Little did they suspect that the bloodiest battle of the American Revolution would take place a mere ten months later.

It was decided that Putnam would personally deliver the letter, along with a flock of 125 sheep, to the patriot leaders of Boston. After a 90 mile journey, he was warmly welcomed by the leading citizens of the beleaguered city and stayed as a houseguest of medical doctor Joseph Warren, who in the not too distant future would become the first martyr of the Revolution.

In an August 15, 1774, letter to Samuel Adams, Dr. Warren wrote "The celebrated Colonel Putnam is now in my house, having arrived, since I subscribed this letter, with a generous donation of sheep."[6]

Another patriot, Dr. Thomas Young (a member of the Boston Committee of Correspondence)[7] stated in an August 19 letter:

> The old hero, Putnam, arrived in town on Monday, bringing with him one hundred and thirty sheep from the little parish of Brooklyn. He cannot get away, he is so much caressed both by officers and citizens. He has had a long combat with Major Small, in the political way, much to the disadvantage of the latter. He looks fresh and hearty, and, on an emergency, would be as likely to do good business as ever.[8]

According to Ellen Larned in her *History of Windham County*:

> Putnam remained some days in Boston and was received with high honors. [Historian George] Bancroft reports him "Warren's guest and everyone's favorite." *The Boston Gazette*[9] informs its readers that "the town has had the satisfaction to be visited by the renowned Colonel Putnam, so well known throughout North America that no words are necessary to inform the public any further concerning him than that his generosity led him to Boston to cherish his oppressed brethren and support them by every means in his power. A fine drove of sheep was one article of comfort he was commissioned to present us with."[10]

The first military actions against the British took place at Lexington

Four. Bloodiest Battle of the Revolution

and Concord, Massachusetts, in April 1775. This was appropriate since that colony had been arguably the most vocal in its opposition to British misrule. The Boston area,[11] along with New York City and Philadelphia, had the most concentrated population. The entire population of the 13 colonies was only about 2.4 million people.[12]

On the night of April 18, 1775, British General Thomas Gage sent 700 soldiers from Boston toward Concord, Massachusetts, 20 miles to the west. Their objectives were to arrest Patriot leaders Samuel Adams and John Hancock at Lexington, and then continue on to Concord to confiscate military stores accumulated by the Colonial forces. The Patriots found out about the mission and sent silversmith Paul Revere[13] and tanner William Dawes[14] on horseback to warn the Colonials. Revere and Dawes reached Lexington in time to save Adams and Hancock. On the way to Concord they met medical doctor Samuel Prescott,[15] a noted member of the Sons of Liberty. A short time later Revere was captured by the British (and released) and Dawes was forced to return to Boston. Only Prescott was able to make it to Concord, where he warned the local militia of the impending British attack.

When at dawn on April 19 the British arrived at Lexington, they were confronted by about 70 militia soldiers. Although apparently the British commanders did not want a fight, someone released the first shot and it set off a full-scale attack by the British with musket shot and bayonets. Eight of the Colonial militia were killed and ten wounded. The British troops continued on to their objective—Concord. There they met between 300 and 400 militia that had been warned by Prescott, defeated them and burned whatever stores they could find. On their return march to Boston, the British troops were harassed by the militia all the way, as the latter shot at them from behind trees, buildings, and stone walls. The older colonial soldiers used guerrilla warfare tactics that they had learned from Native Americans during the French and Indian War (1755–1763). Although the British had accomplished one mission, i.e., the destruction of the Colonial military supplies, their losses were an incredible 300 casualties. The Colonials suffered only 95 killed and wounded.

The end result of Lexington and Concord was that a disagreement between the colonists and the mother country over economic issues had now become a bloody fight for political independence. Passions flared throughout New England and beyond, as thousands of colonial militia were activated. One of the men who cared the most was Israel Putnam, who upon hearing of the fighting in Massachusetts immediately set out on horseback to help.

After hearing Putnam's own narration of events, David Humphreys relates the following in the first edition of his biography:

> Putnam, who was ploughing when he heard the news [on April 20], left his plough in the middle of the field, unyoked his team, and without waiting to change his cloaths [clothes], set off for the theatre of action. But finding the British retreated to Boston and invested by a sufficient force to watch their movements, he came back to Connecticut, levied a regiment (under authority of the Legislature) and speedily returned to Cambridge.[16]

In his 1876 biography, Tarbox added: "Daniel Putnam his son, who certainly ought to know, as he was then in his sixteenth year, says, 'When this time came he loitered not, but left me, the driver of his team, to unyoke it in the furrow, and not many days after to follow him to camp.'"[17]

But when he left his plow, Putnam did not go directly to Massachusetts. In his 1901 biography, Livingston included many additional details.[18] Without changing his clothing, Putnam rode to Governor Jonathan Trumbull's Lebanon home. (Since it is over 20 miles southwest of Putnam's farm, and in the opposite direction of Cambridge, Putnam's ride consisted of many more miles than if he had gone directly to Massachusetts.) Trumbull directed Putnam to go to Boston.

While Putnam was consulting with the Governor, another rider reached Pomfret with news of the fighting at Concord, Massachusetts. Colonel Ebenezer Williams, one of Putnam's fellow Connecticut Committee of Safety members, sent out the message to neighboring towns alleging that about 40 militia had been killed by the British and requesting that "every man who is fit and willing" to assemble for a fight.[19]

At about 5:00 p.m., Putnam returned home to find hundreds of militiamen gathered on Brooklyn Green. He told them that he had arranged for militia officers to arrive soon to take charge. Then, without resting, Putnam took off for Cambridge. He arrived the next day, met with the Massachusetts Committee of Safety, and continued on to Concord. An entry in Massachusetts General Artemas Ward's Orderly Book for April 21 states: "This day, General Putnam, of Connecticut, attended the Council of War."[20] In 18 hours, Putnam had ridden at least 100 miles. He sent the following letter back to Colonel Williams.

Concord, April 21.

> To Colonel E. Williams. Sir—I have waited on the Committee of the Provincial Congress, and it is their Determination to have a standing Army of 22,000 men from the New-England Colonies, of which it is supposed the Colony of Connecticut must raise 6,000, and begs they would be at Cambridge as speedily as possible, with Conveniences; together with Provisions, and a Sufficiency of Ammunition for their own Use.

Bas-relief on the north side of Connecticut State Capitol building in Hartford. It depicts Putnam leaving his plow after learning about the first battle between British troops and colonial militia (photograph by author).

> The Battle here is much as has been represented at Pomfret, except that there is more killed and a Number more taken Prisoners.
> The Accounts at present are so confused that it is impossible to ascertain the number exact, but shall inform you of the Proceedings, from Time to Time, as we have new Occurrences; mean Time, I am,
> Sir, your humble servant,
> Israel Putnam.
> N.B. The troops of Horse are not expected to come until further notice.[21]

According to Humphreys, when Putnam found that the British had retreated to Boston, he returned to Connecticut, "levied a regiment (under authority of the legislature) and speedily returned to Cambridge. He was now promoted to be a Major-General on the Provincial Staff, by his Colony."[22]

On April 26, 1775, the Connecticut General Assembly appointed the following general officers of the Connecticut militia: David Wooster of New Haven a major general, Joseph Spencer of East Haddam, the First Brigadier General, and Israel Putnam the Second Brigadier General. Each of these three men also became the colonel of a regiment and the captain of a company (Putnam was appointed the colonel of the 3rd regiment and the captain of the 1st company of the regiment).

The General Assembly voted to raise 6,000 men, who were divided into six regiments, each with ten 100-man companies. In May, the Connecticut militia began their march toward Boston. Putnam's oldest son, Israel Jr., was captain of the 10th Company of his father's regiment. A few weeks later he was appointed his father's aide-de-camp.[23]

At the time Israel rode to Lexington, he had seven living children—ranging in age from 11 to 36. Israel, Jr., was the oldest at 36, followed by 31-year-old Hannah, three daughters in their 20s (Mehitable, Mary, and Eunice), Daniel (age 16) and Peter Schuyler (age 11). All of Deborah Putnam's children with the Rev. Avery were now in their 20s and 30s, and her two children with John Gardiner III, Hannah and Septimus, were 17 and 15, respectively.

Another Connecticut man who immediately went into action upon hearing the news of Lexington was Wethersfield's Samuel B. Webb, the stepson of American diplomat Silas Deane. When he heard of the fighting at Lexington, he volunteered as a private with Captain John Chester's light infantry company and marched to Boston. Only a few months later, Webb would become aide-de-camp to Israel Putnam.

Although we have the accounts of men like Putnam and Webb, who were the first to respond to their colony's request for aid after Lexington and Concord, and who were determined to fulfill their duty, others were fair-weather soldiers who deserted almost as soon as they signed up. The following notice appeared in the *Connecticut Courant* two days after the Battle of Bunker Hill. This man deserted a month after the Battle of Concord and a month before the Bunker Hill.

> Deserted from the 4th Regiment of Foot, raised for the defence of the colony of Connecticut, commanded by Col. Benjamin Hinman, and of my company, on the 24th of May, one Benjamin Buffington, about 5 feet 5 inches high, light complection, high forehead, thin foretop, brown hair, black eyes, a handsome sett of teeth, tall shoulders, and tolerably well proportioned; when he talks, stands stooping, and tells much of his honesty. Had on when he went away, a grey out side jacket, lappelled, green plush breeches and streaked trowsers, two hats, a new beaver or castor, and an old beaver, two or three pair of stockings, and two pair shoes. Whoever will take and secure said fellow, and return him to my company, or in any of the prisons in this colony, so as he may be in the service again, shall have five dollars reward, and all reasonable charges paid by Samuel Elmer, Major of the 4th Regiment.[24]

Although Putnam was not able to reach Lexington or Concord in time to participate, there was one lasting connection between the old Connecticut fighter and the engagements. Legend has it that British Army Major John Pitcairn fired one of a pair of finely-engraved metal Highlander Scottish officer pistols to signal his men to fire at the minutemen on Lexington Green. Often considered the first shot of the American Revolutionary War, it is sometimes referred to as the "shot heard around the world."

As Pitcairn retreated with his troops back to Boston, his horse was shot from under him and, in the confusion, his saddlebags, containing the two weapons were lost. As the story goes, they were later found by Minuteman John Scott of Winchester, Massachusetts. The pistols were presented to General Washington, who refused to accept them. Then, they were given to Israel Putnam who carried them at the Battle of Bunker Hill. Major Pitcairn was fatally wounded at that battle.[25]

Although it is not 100 percent certain that the pistols found after the Lexington skirmish were the ones owned by Pitcairn, there is little doubt they were the guns used by a British officer that day and that General Putnam owned them for the rest of his life. In 1879, Putnam's grandson John Putnam's widow donated the pistols to the Cary Library in Lexington, Massachusetts. Today, they reside in the Lexington Historical Society's Hancock-Clarke House. Along with the guns, Mrs. Putnam included a certificate of authenticity that her late husband had received from former Putnam aide-de-camp (and later U.S. Vice President) Aaron Burr. Sixty years after General Putnam had acquired the guns, Burr inspected them and certified they were the originals. Burr died the following year.[26]

After the Lexington and Concord fighting, Putnam was headquartered in Cambridge even though most of his troops were at Roxbury, Massachusetts. According to his son Daniel, it was to accommodate General Ward who wanted Putnam close by to lend advice as matters rapidly unfolded.[27] It was at the 1760 Apthorp House in Cambridge that Putnam worked out plans that would guide American militia at the Battle of Bunker Hill. Apthorp House is now the Master's Residence at Harvard University.[28]

Son Daniel remarked that his father's popularity:

> was not confined to Connecticut but pervaded the whole of the Massachusetts forces then before Boston; and there was not a soldier in their ranks but seemed ready to follow him, to fight for him, and if need be to die by his side. Even Warren, the accomplished gentleman, the daring patriot, and the future hope of the army, delighted, when the complicated duties of his station permitted, to spend an hour at Putnam's quarters. He would listen attentively to his tales of a former war, and make earnest and particular enquiries of him as to the relative power and influence of British and Provincial troops in that war. Putnam maintained that when the Provincial regiments were well officered, they were not inferior to the British. "Our men," he said, "would

always follow wherever their officers led—I know this to have been the case with mine, and have also seen it in other instances."[29]

According to Daniel Putnam, Dr. Warren asked his father, if 10,000 British troops should march out of Boston, what number of Americans should meet them? Putnam answered,

> Let me pick my officers, and I would not fear to meet them with half the number—not in a pitched battle to stop them at once, for no troops are better than the British, but I would fight on the retreat, and every stone-wall we passed should be lined with their dead—our men are lighter of foot, they understand our grounds and how to take advantage of them; and besides, we should only fall back on our reserve, while every step they advanced, the country would close on their flanks and rear.[30]

At the prodding of Putnam, Massachusetts and Connecticut troops were ordered to begin constructing fortifications at the town of Cambridge and at the base of Prospect Hill, which lay between Cambridge and the Charlestown peninsula. During this work, Putnam was described as being "constantly on horseback or on foot, working with his men or encouraging them."[31]

One day, Putnam discovered some of the Massachusetts men slacking off. According to one soldier, Caleb Haskell, Putnam asked them: "To what regiment do you belong?" "To Colonel Doolittle's," they replied. "Doolittle? Do nothing at all!" General Putnam answered.[32]

In addition to his belief in the value of strong defensive positions, Putnam was a great believer in keeping his men busy. His son Daniel recalled, "His experience had taught him that raw and undisciplined troops must be employed in some way or other, or they would soon become vicious and unmanageable. His maxim was, 'It is better to dig a ditch every morning and fill it up at evening than to have the men idle.'"[33]

Although many of the top American officers and civilian leaders felt the construction of defenses in the Cambridge area were too aggressive, one key leader agreed with Putnam—Massachusetts colonel William Prescott. Once, when Putnam was directing the construction operations, Prescott approached him, commenting "I wish, General, your men were digging nearer Boston." To which Putnam replied: "I wish so, too, and I hope we shall all be of one mind before long."[34]

Humphreys relates that the British Commander Gage, having learned that Israel Putnam, his personal friend from the time of the French and Indian War, was a leader in the army besieging Boston,

> found the means to convey a proposal privately to General Putnam that if he would relinquish the rebel party, he might rely upon being made a Major-General on the British establishment, and receiving a great pecuniary compensation for his services.

Four. Bloodiest Battle of the Revolution 77

General Putnam spurned at the offer; which, however, he thought prudent at that time to conceal from public notice.[35]

Similar proposals were made by Gage to other veterans of the French and Indian War, including New Hampshire's John Stark. None could be convinced to side with the British.

On May 13, in perhaps the boldest demonstration of defiance yet, Putnam led 2,200 of the troops at Cambridge over Bunker and Breed's hills and into Charlestown. The line extended for one and a half miles. They returned to Cambridge without a shot being fired.

In late May, the Americans (and at other times the British) collected hay and animals from Boston Harbor islands. In June 1775, A British paper, *Almon's Remembrancer*, published an article about a May 27 confrontation between the colonial militia and British soldiers at Boston's Hogg Island.

It stated that between 20 and 30 colonials who were driving livestock off of Hogg Island were challenged by a British schooner, a sloop and 40 marines. The newspaper related that the Americans drove off or killed a number of animals before the marines attacked. A fight ensued with the Americans killing three marines and driving off cattle, horses and over 300 sheep.

After removing the Hogg Island stock, the Americans called up 300 more men and two cannon. According to the article: "General Putnam went down and hailed the schooner and told the people that if they would submit they should have good quarters, which the schooner returned with two cannon shot; this was immediately answered with two cannon from the provincials."

The American shelling of the British schooner was so intense that the entire crew abandoned ship. Under fire from the British sloop, Americans removed the schooner's armaments, rigging, sails, and supplies and "burnt her to ashes." The British answered with cannon fire from Noddle's Island, and Putnam concentrated his fire of their sloop until it was disabled and many of its defenders killed.

The *Almon's Remembrancer* piece related: "Thus ended this long action without the loss of one Provincial and only four wounded, one of whom was wounded by the bursting of his own gun, and another only lost his little finger." The Americans estimated that British loses were "at least twenty killed and fifty wounded."[36]

Humphreys's account of this confrontation, likely from Putnam himself, ended with: "Thus ended this affair, in which several hundred sheep and some cattle were removed from under the muzzles of the enemy's cannon, and our men accustomed to stand fire, by being for many hours exposed to it without meeting with any loss."[37]

Putnam returned from this mission on Sunday morning, covered with mud below the waist, as his son Daniel wrote: "contracted by wading over the flats to burn the vessel." Before changing his clothes, Putnam met with Artemas Ward and James Warren at the Borland House to give them a personal account of the events. Putnam added,

> I wish we could have something of the kind to do every day; it would teach our men how little danger there is from cannon balls, for though they have sent a great many at us, nobody has been hurt by them. I would that Gage and his troops were within our reach, for we would be like hornets about their ears; as little birds follow and tease the eagle in his flight, we would every day contrive to make them uneasy.[38]

According to young Daniel Putnam,

> Warren smiled and said nothing, but General Ward replied, "As peace and reconciliation is what we seek for, would it not be better to act only on the defensive and give no unnecessary provocation?" Putnam turned to Warren and said with emphasis, "You know, Dr. Warren, we shall have no peace worth anything, till we gain it by the sword." Instead of any direct reply, Warren observed, "Your wet clothes must be uncomfortable, General, and we will take our leave that you may change them,"—and taking Putnam's hand he continued, "I admire your spirit and respect General Ward's prudence, both will be necessary for us, and one must temper the other."[39]

According to Humphreys, back home in Connecticut, "British troops were the Philistines, and Putnam, the American Samson, a chosen instrument to defeat the foe; and fortunately she [Connecticut] inspired her own confidence into all her sister states."[40]

The Noddle's Island affair was exactly the kind of fight at which Putnam excelled. As a member of Rogers Rangers during the French and Indian War, he had engaged in countless similar encounters with an enemy. There was probably no other person in the colonies who could pull off such a skirmish with such success.

This did not go unnoticed at the Continental Congress. They were about to choose Washington's major generals and Putnam's name was on everyone's lips. Roger Sherman, perhaps Connecticut's foremost leader and a member of the Congress, wrote in a letter on June 23, 1775, to David Wooster: "as General Putnam's fame was spread abroad and especially his successful enterprise at Noddle's Island, the account of which had just arrived, it gave him a preference in the opinion of the Delegates in general so that his appointment was unanimous among the colonies."[41]

It should be noted that Sherman wasn't much of a Putnam supporter.[42] In fact, the primary purpose of this letter to Wooster was to mollify Wooster and convince him to stay in the army even though he had been passed over by Putnam and only commissioned a brigadier general in the new Continental Army. In this same letter Sherman says:

> I am sensible that according to your former rank, you were entitled to the place of a Major General; and as one was to be appointed in Connecticut I heartily recommended you to the Congress. I informed them of the arrangement made by our Assembly, which I thought would be satisfactory, to have them continue in the same order.[43]

The following poem, using the letters of Putnam's name, appeared in newspapers of the time:

> **P**ure mass of courage, every soldier's wonder.
> **U**nto the Field he steps, enrobed with martial Thunder,
> **T**ares up the elements, and rends the Earth asunder.
> **N**ature designed him for the Field of Battle,
> **U**nused to Statesmen's wiles or courtier's prattle,
> **M**ars-like, his chief Delights, where thundering cannon rattle.[44]

The following lines come from the comic epic poem "M'Fingal," which poet John Trumbull (1750–1831) wrote during the Revolutionary War. Note: this John Trumbull should not be confused with his cousin, the painter John Trumbull, who was six years younger.[45]

> Nay, stern with rage, grim Putnam boiling,
> Plundered both Hogg and Noddle Island;
> Scared troops of Tories into town,
> Burned all their hay and houses down,
> And menaced Gage, unless he'd flee,
> To drive him headlong to the sea.[46]

Putnam is mentioned elsewhere in the poem. This section refers to General Gage and his reneging on his promise to let inhabitants leave Boston.

> So Gage of late agreed, you know,
> To let the Boston people go;
> Yet when he saw, 'gainst troops that braved him,
> They were the only guards that saved him.
> Kept off that satan of a Putnam
> From breaking in to maul and mutton him;
> He'd too much wit, such leagues t' observe,
> And shut them in again, to starve.[47]

On June 6, 1775, British and rebel forces met to exchange prisoners, which included some men captured at Lexington and Concord. Israel Putnam represented the American military forces, while Dr. Joseph Warren served as the representative of the civilian government. In its issue of June 8, the *Essex Gazette* stated that on the day of the exchange Warren and Putnam were accompanied by Captain Chester and his Wethersfield

Company. They brought several officers and enlisted men to Charlestown where they were handed over to British Major Moncrieff.[48]

According to Livingston, Major John Brooks, a future Governor of Massachusetts,[49] witnessed this meeting. Brooks used to relate how Moncrieff and Putnam, two comrades from the French and Indian War's Cuban campaign "ran into each other's arms and kissed each other to the great diversion and astonishment of the country people of the army."[50]

In 1901, in an address at a celebration of the 100th anniversary of the Putnam Masonic Lodge in Connecticut, the Rev. Eban Thompson discussed the life of its namesake and sheds light on this and similar episodes:

> After the battle of Concord and before that of Bunker Hill there were many communications between the officers of the British Army of occupation in Boston and those of the American troops in Cambridge under flags of truce. On one such occasion Putnam, the bearer of the communication, was noticed to have "embraced the two British officers, they putting their arms around him and kissing him." Of course we can well understand what took place but the uninstructed squad of soldiers reported only what they saw, and it is said that certain other officers laughed, while of late date an ignorant man named Dawson has referred to this and other things to show that Gen. Putnam was always a traitor and disloyal from the start. Some high authority charges that his sympathy for his prisoners was due to Tory sentiment.
>
> No, he had been very active in Masonry years before and had served and "sat with" these same British officers and we cannot doubt it was a severe trial to him as to Lafayette and Washington and other famous Masons to find himself opposed in deadly struggle to old friends and brothers.[51]

Ellen Chase in her *The Beginnings of the American Revolution*, states:

> The Wounded Privates were soon sent on board the *Lively*; but Major Moncrieff and the other officers, returned with Gen. Putnam and Dr. Warren, to the House of Dr. Foster, where an Entertainment was provided for them.
>
> About 3 o'clock a signal was made by the *Lively*, that they were ready to deliver up our Prisoners; upon which, Gen. Putnam and Major Moncrieff went to the Ferry, where they received Messrs. John Peck, James Hewes, James Brewer, and Daniel Preston of Boston; Messrs. Samuel Frost and Seth Russell of Cambridge; Mr. Joseph Bell of Danvers, Mr. Elijah Seaver of Roxbury; and Caesar Augustus, a negro servant to Mr. Tileston of Dorchester; who were conducted to the House of Captain Foster, and there refreshed; after which the Gen. and Major returned to their Company, and spent an Hour or two in a very agreeable manner. Between 5 and 6 o'clock Major Moncrieff, with the officers that had been delivered up to him, were conducted to the Ferry, where the *Lively*'s Barge received them; after which Gen. Putnam, with the Prisoners who had been delivered to him, &c., returned to Cambridge, escorted in the same manner as before.[52]

According to his son Daniel, Putnam returned from the prisoner exchange in "high spirits." Livingston relates:

> He said he had met again some of his old friends, but he appeared most gratified that Gage should have consented to an exchange of prisoners. "He may call us Rebels now,

Four. Bloodiest Battle of the Revolution

if he will, but why then don't he hang his prisoners instead of exchanging them? By this act he has virtually placed us on an equality, and acknowledged our right of resistance."[53]

Daniel recalls that on the following day (June 7)

there was quite a levee of officers at Putnam's quarters to talk about the exchange. He related to them all the particulars, and turning to Col. Prescott, said, "Colonel, I saw ground yesterday that may suit your purpose. I suppose you have not forgotten your remark of the other day about digging; but more of this another time." Prescott called in the evening and they walked out together; for several succeeding days he was at Putnam's quarters, and they were in private conversation.[54]

On about June 10, Putnam paraded his armed men around the Charlestown Common. Even his son, Daniel, who was among the troops, did not know the objective of the exercise. He stated: "I felt proud, to be numbered among what I then thought to be a mighty host destined for some great enterprise. We were marched to Charlestown, and I supposed it was intended to 'take Boston,' but after parading about on the high grounds awhile, we all returned in safety to our quarters at Cambridge."[55]

After this march, his son noticed that Putnam "appeared thoughtful and absent in his mind."[56] Daniel Putnam writes:

In such seasons of abstraction he was in the habit of giving an indistinct kind of utterance to his thoughts, or what may be termed "talking to one's self," and broken sentences such as follow escaped his lips—"We must go there"—"Think they will come out"—"Yes, yes, they must"—"I'll go with my regiment anyhow"—"We must go in the night"—"We'll carry our tools and have a trench before morning"—"He's a good fellow"—"He wants to go"—"Says he will go, if they'll let him"—"Lay still"—"Lay still, I say, till they come close"—"They won't hurt you"—"I know 'em of old, they fire without aim"—these and such like burstings of his mind continued several days, not in a regular chain as I have set them down, but breaking forth occasionally, and often accompanied with some significant gesture, which left no doubt but he was contemplating some important military operation. To me it was almost certain for I had all my life been accustomed to such sallies, but more especially after the alarm [of September 1774] up to the affair at Lexington, he had almost daily such like communings with himself.[57]

Putnam was not the only prominent American military commander to speak his thoughts out loud. In the Civil War, General William Tecumseh Sherman, after being promoted to command the Department of the Cumberland, often talked to himself while pacing, while Confederate General Stonewall Jackson was known for talking to himself on the battlefield.[58]

In early June 1775, the American military leaders had heated discussions on the next steps to take, especially as it related to Bunker Hill, the tallest piece of ground on Charlestown peninsula. Colonels Putnam, Prescott and Thomas Gardner[59] wanted a redoubt (a temporary fort consisting of earthworks) on Bunker Hill, General Ward and Dr. Warren opposed it. Ward argued: "We have no powder to spare and no battering cannon. It would be idle to make approaches on the town."[60]

Putnam's son Daniel details the proceedings, which demonstrate his father's ability to persuasively argue his positions.

> He [Putnam] told them they had entirely mistaken his views, that it was not for the purpose of battering the town, but to draw the enemy from it, where we might meet them on equal terms, and that Charlestown and Dorchester were the only points where this could be done, that the army wished to be employed and the country was growing dissatisfied at the inactivity of it.
>
> It was objected again that it might bring on a general battle and that in our position it was neither politic or safe to risk one.
>
> He replied, "2,000 men will be enough to risk, and with that number we will go on and defend ourselves as long and as well as we can and then give the ground."

When questioned about the possible difficulty of retreat, Putnam answered:

> "We will guard against that, and run when we can contend no longer with advantage; we can outrun them, and behind every wall rally and oppose their progress till we join our friends again. But suppose the worst, suppose us hemmed in and no retreat; we know what we are contending for; we will set our country an example of which it shall not be ashamed, and show those who seek to oppress us what men can do who are determined to live free or not live at all!"
>
> Warren, he [Putnam] said, rose and walked several times across the room, leaned a few moments over the back of a chair in a thoughtful attitude and said, "Almost thou persuadest me, General Putnam, but I must still think the project a rash one. Nevertheless, if it should ever be adopted and the strife becomes hard, you must not be surprised to find me with you in the midst of it."
>
> "'I hope not, Sir," said Putnam, "you are yet but a young man, and our country has much to hope from you both in council and in war. It is only a little brush we have been contemplating; let some of us who are older [Putnam was 23 years older than Warren] and can well enough be spared begin the fray; there will be time enough for you hereafter, for it will not soon be ended."[61]

One key Connecticut officer who didn't agree with the aggressive measures advocated by Putnam and Prescott was Captain Thomas Knowlton. He argued that with their naval support the British could land troops at the neck of the Charlestown peninsula and cut off ammunition and other supplies from any American troops that occupied the strip of land. However, like Dr. Warren, Knowlton agreed to wholeheartedly participate if the decision was reached to take Bunker Hill.[62]

In discussing the readiness of his troops for a Charlestown peninsula assault, Putnam used one of his favorite sayings: "The Americans are not

Four. Bloodiest Battle of the Revolution

at all afraid of their heads though very much afraid of their legs; if you cover these, they will fight forever."63

A Bunker Hill decision was reached by the American forces when they learned of the buildup of troops and the arrival of Generals William Howe, Henry Clinton, and John Burgoyne, as well as the planned takeover of Dorchester Heights in South Boston by General Gates on June 18. With the agreement of the Committee of Safety, the American commanders decided to fortify Bunker Hill without delay.64

When the decision to send troops to the Charlestown peninsula was made, almost one-half the American troops around Boston were stationed around General Ward's headquarters at Cambridge, which was conveniently close to the peninsula. They included fifteen Massachusetts regiments, a battalion of artillery, and Connecticut troops. Most of the latter were quartered at Tory Ralph Inman's estate. Inman was with the British forces in Boston, while his wife, still at home, was disturbed about the Colonial troops that were camped on their property.

To relieve the woman's anxieties, Putnam agreed to let his 16-year-old son, Daniel, stay with the Inman family. Daniel later wrote: "By direction of my father from about the middle of May, I lodged every night in her house. Young as I was, the family confided much in the protection afforded by General Putnam's son."65

On the evening of June 16, 1775, Colonial troops were ordered to parade on the Cambridge Common. These included three Massachusetts regiments: Prescott's, Colonel Ebenezer Bridge's and Colonel James Frye's. They were told "to furnish themselves with all the entrenching tools in the camp, with provisions for twenty-four hours, and with packs and blankets."66 Because implements for only about 1,000 men could be procured, only that number of soldiers was selected from the three regiments. These regiments were joined by Captain Thomas Knowlton and his 200 Connecticut troops, and Captain Samuel Gridley's artillery company, which possessed only two field-pieces. The whole party was put under the command of Colonel Prescott. The army's Chief Engineer, Richard Gridley,67 was directed to lay out the fortifications.

Daniel Putnam, an eyewitness to the comings and goings of the commanders, later remembered:

> I noticed an unusual stir among the troops at Cambridge. Putnam's regiment was under arms, and I was informed by the Adjutant that a detachment had been made from it for "secret service"; but what at the time impressed my mind most strongly was the preparation my father himself was making. With his own hands he prepared cartridges for his pistols, took out the old flints and put in the new. While he was doing

this, Col. Prescott came in and observing what he was about, said in a low tone, "I see, General, you are making preparation and we shall be ready at the time."[68]

While a great deal of effort went into the decision whether or not to move troops en masse onto the Charlestown peninsula, not enough attention was paid to the structure of the upper command. While General Ward assigned the task of constructing and manning the redoubt to Colonel Prescott, he never gave specific orders regarding the overall command of the operation. It wouldn't be Ward himself—illness would confine him to Cambridge. If a battle commenced, who would coordinate all elements of the defense and offense? Not just the soldiers at the redoubt, but those on Bunker Hill, on the peninsula's north shore, on its neck and elsewhere.[69]

It was a situation that probably didn't make Putnam unhappy. He was always ready to take charge. Ever since his fighting days in the 1750s he had been ready to volunteer for virtually any mission. Sometimes it lead to failure because a task was greater than he could handle, but most of the time his skills in leading men into battle were enough to bring some measure of success. For weeks, Israel Putnam had been the leading advocate of aggressive action against the British in Boston. Certainly, if one man might be expected to step into a leadership vacuum, it was he. And he would be more than happy to oblige.

There is no better source for an up-close look at Israel Putnam on the evening before the Battle of Bunker Hill than his 16-year-old son Daniel. In the evening, his father told him to go to the Inman home and stay there overnight and the following day. Daniel was told to stick with the family even if they left the house.

These orders, along with what he had seen during the day convinced Daniel that

> some military movement was going forward in which my father was to participate. I called to mind his abstraction and self-communing, the broken sentences that had escaped him, indicating battle and bloodshedding, and my imagination pictured him as mangled with wounds and none to help him. With earnest entreaty I asked leave to accompany him.
>
> "You, dear father," I said, "may need my assistance much more than Mrs. Inman; pray let me go where you are going."
>
> "No, no, Daniel, do as I have bid you," was the answer which he affected to give sternly, while his voice trembled and his eyes filled. Then, as if perfectly comprehending what had been passing in my mind, he added, "You can do little, my son, where I am going, and besides, there will be enough to take care of me."

As directed, Daniel went to the Inman house'

> but took no interest in the conversation of her nieces or the maternal kindness of their aunt; my mind was elsewhere and I retired early to bed, but not to sleep; the

night was as sleepless to me as to those who were toiling or watching on the confines of Boston. I had a strong suspicion that Charlestown was the spot to which the hostile movement was directed; and long before the first gun was fired I had risen and seated myself at the window of my chamber, anxiously looking thitherward.[70]

The Battle of Bunker Hill

The events took place north of the city of Boston on the Charlestown Peninsula, which projected toward the east from Cambridge, the site of Harvard College (now Harvard University). The neck of the peninsula was narrow in 1775, but in the succeeding two-plus centuries has been filled in, as has almost the entire coastline around Boston and Boston Harbor.

The Charlestown Peninsula featured two major hills: 110-foot-high Bunker Hill to the northwest and 62-foot-high Breed's Hill near the center. Beneath Breed's Hill, on the south shore of the peninsula was Charlestown, the only town on the peninsula. A third hill, Moulton's Hill, lay off to the east end of the peninsula. It was only 35-feet-high and of little importance to the battle.

Although the battle is traditionally known as the Battle of Bunker Hill (or in England as the Battle of Bunker's Hill), the fighting actually centered on Breed's Hill.

South of the peninsula was the west to east flowing Charles River, and south of that, the City of Boston. Copp's Hill, the highest land facing the peninsula from Boston, was 58 feet high.

On the evening of April 16, 1775, colonial forces at Cambridge were readied for what would become a major event in each of their lives: the first and, as it would turn out, the deadliest battle of the Revolutionary War. American spies had informed their commanders that the British were preparing an immediate assault on Charlestown. The Colonial militia could wait no longer.

The first troops assembled on Cambridge Common under the command of Colonel Prescott, and a prayer was offered by Samuel Langdon, president of Harvard College.[71]

A small party of men were dispatched south to guard Charlestown, while the main force, headed over to Bunker Hill. Connecticut private Josiah Cleveland remembered: "We marched in profound silence, General Putnam at our head."[72] Bringing little food and drink, the Americans marched, pulling carts loaded with picks and shovels with which to build dirt fortifications.

Completed in 1843, the Bunker Hill monument in Charlestown, Massachusetts, sits on the site of the Breed's Hill earthwork fortifications. Today it is part of the Boston National Historical Park (photograph by author).

Putnam rode ahead on horseback to the neck of the peninsula to await Prescott. There, they assembled together, and the officers explained the mission to the troops. According to Private Cleveland, Putnam gave the order for the soldiers to "load with two balls."[73]

Between Bunker Hill and Breed's Hill, the troops stopped. Putnam, another commander (Livingston thinks it likely was John Whitcomb; some think it was Colonel Prescott),[74] and Colonel Richard Gridley, the chief engineer, debated which hill they should fortify. For reasons that have been disputed in the centuries since, they decided to continue the short distance to Breed's Hill and built their dirt structure there. Breed's wasn't as tall as Bunker Hill but it was closer to the water and to the city of Boston. It would be possible, if necessary, to fire cannonballs from there that could hit Boston.

While they decided to build the redoubt on Breed's Hill, they also agreed that as soon as possible Bunker Hill should be fortified as well, since its position made its possession essential for a safe exit off the peninsula if a retreat became necessary.

Troops were told to be quiet as the commanders did not want to alert the British on their ships in Boston harbor that they were congregating en masse on the Charlestown peninsula. They had little time—as soon as the morning sun on April 17 rose above the water, their fortifications would be visible to the British.

Just before midnight, Gridley staked out the layout of the redoubt, the troops unloaded the picks and shovels, and over 1,000 men, as quietly as possible, began to work. Only four hours remained before the light of day would reveal their presence to the British on their ships and on the Boston shore. By candlelight, in dead quiet, the colonial soldiers created a redoubt eight rods [132 feet] square as well as a temporary wall that extended for one hundred yards.[75] (The redoubt was one-half the square footage of today's New York City Grand Central Station concourse, i.e., 17,000 versus 33,000 square feet.)

When the sun arose, the men on the British ship *Lively* were the first of the enemy to respond—at 4:00 a.m. they poured shot toward the colonial troops and their hours-old fortifications. Other ships, as well as the artillery positions on Boston's Copp's Hill, soon opened fire. Still, the Americans continued to fortify their positions. When Putnam heard the *Lively's* shots, he ordered a Lieutenant Clark to get a horse. However, by the time the officer returned, the ever-impatient Putnam was already mounted on another horse and riding off toward Charlestown peninsula to obtain reinforcements.

The four top officers of the day were Connecticut's Israel Putnam, William Prescott and Joseph Warren from Massachusetts, and New Hampshire's John Stark. With the ranking Massachusetts commander Artemas Ward too ill to lead troops into battle, Putnam and Prescott considered leadership to pass to Warren.

Joseph Warren was family physician to many of the most prominent families of Boston (including those of John Adams, John Hancock, and Samuel Adams). He was also the man who dispatched Paul Revere and William Dawes on their famous rides, the man who was seen by many in the anti–British movement as their leader, and the man who three days prior to the battle had been appointed a major general in the State of Massachusetts' militia. But now at the start of the battle he refused a military leadership position and chose instead to fight as a common soldier.

With Stark only a colonel, that left the leadership position to either Putnam or Prescott. There has been much controversy over the centuries about the "real" commander at the Battle of Bunker Hill. Perhaps the best way to describe their respective roles is to say that Prescott personally and heroically led the soldiers at the Breed's Hill redoubt, while Putnam was in overall command of the entire battle, including Breeds Hill, Bunker Hill, and other Charleston peninsula locations.

Livingston states:

> Putnam was all activity, riding up and down just behind the soldiers at the fence who rested their deadly weapons on the top rail and awaited with excited eagerness the order to fire. Says Reuben Kemp, one of this number: "General Putnam seemed to have the ordering of things. He charged the men not to fire until the enemy came close to the works, and then to take good aim, and make every shot kill a man, and he told one officer to see that this order was obeyed."[76]

Philip Johnson stated: "I distinctly heard him [Putnam] say, 'Men, you are all marksmen—don't one of you fire until you see the white of their eyes.'" Livingston contends that other words of Putnam were also repeated

> by Knowlton and Reed and Stark to the men whose fingers were so impatient to pull the waiting trigger: "Powder is scarce and must not be wasted." "Fire low." "Take aim at the waistbands." "You are all marksmen and could kill a squirrel at a hundred yards." "Reserve your fire and the enemy will all be destroyed." "Aim at the handsome coats." "Pick off the commanders."[77]

Soldier Henry Burbeck remembered that at one point, "General Putnam rode between Charlestown and Cambridge without a coat, in his shirtsleeves, and an old white felt hat on, to report to General Ward, and to consult upon further operations."[78]

The British did not respond in force until 3:00 in the afternoon. Then,

Four. Bloodiest Battle of the Revolution 89

they initiated a full-scale assault with 2,000 troops. Directing the operation was 45-year-old Major General William Howe, a well-connected upper class Englishman. General James Wolfe in 1758 stated: "Howe, is at the head of the best-trained battalion in all America."[79] He was proven right as Howe achieved a series of successes in the French and Indian War: in 1759 he had participated in the British Army's successful siege of Quebec, in 1760 he commanded forces that captured Montreal, and in 1762 he was part of the siege of Spanish Cuba. In recent years, he had served as a member of the British Parliament, and although personally doubtful of the wisdom of fighting the American colonists, he had agreed to command troops in the thirteen colonies. Now, at Bunker Hill, Howe was faced with probably the most important battle of his career.

Nineteen-year-old Joseph Spaulding was known as the first man to fire a shot at the Battle of Bunker Hill. Unfortunately, he did it before receiving the order to fire. It's recorded that he later said: "I fired ahead of time, and Putnam rushed up and struck at me for violating orders. I suppose I deserved it, but I was anxious to get another good shot at Gage's men ever since our affair at Concord. The blow from 'Old Put' hit me on the head, made a hole in my hat, and left this scar."[80] After hitting Spaulding, Putnam threatened to strike with his sword the next soldier who wasted a musket charge.[81]

According to Colonel Prescott, the first man to be killed on the American side was standing near him.

> The first man who fell in the battle of Bunker Hill, was killed by a cannon ball which struck his head. He was so near me that my clothes were besmeared with his blood and brains, which I wiped off, in some degree, with a handful of fresh earth. The sight was so shocking to many of the men, that they left their posts and ran to view him. I ordered them back, but in vain. I then ordered him to be buried instantly. A subaltern officer expressed surprise that I should allow him to be buried without having prayers said; I replied, "this is the first man that has been killed, and the only one that will be buried to day. I put him out of sight that the men may be kept in their places. God only knows who, or how many of us, will fall before it is over. To your post, my good fellow, and let each man do his duty."[82]

The soldier who was killed was thought to be Asa Pollard, a 39-year-old Billerica, Massachusetts, man. Pollard had served as one of Rogers Rangers during the French and Indian War and had participated in the clash with the British at Concord. The cannonball that beheaded him came from the British ship *Somerset*. According to a relative, Edward Pollard, when Asa was killed, General Putnam ran up from the rail fence and ordered the other men to fall back in line. Then, Prescott directed that the body be buried.[83]

Samuel B. Webb of Wethersfield, Connecticut, described his experience at Bunker Hill:

> For my part, I confess, when I was descending into the valley from Bunker's Hill, side by side of Capt. Chester[84] at the head of our Company, I had no more tho'ts of ever rising the Hill again, than I had of ascending to Heaven as Elijah did—soul and body together. But after we got engaged—to see the dead and wounded around me—I had no other feeling but that of Revenge. Four men were shot dead within five feet of me; but, thank Heaven, I escaped with only the graze of a musket ball on my head.[85]

The 1850 edition of Humphreys's biography states:

> The enemy were at eight rods [132 feet] distance, the deadly muskets were levelled, when Prescott commanded his men to take good aim, be sure of their mark, and fire. He was effectually obeyed. The whole front rank was swept away, and many a gallant officer laid low. They were, however, countrymen of those who gave the fire, and received it with the same cool courage with which it was given. Rank succeeded rank, and returned the fire, but the odds was fearful; the Americans were well protected by the works; the efforts and courage of the enemy were in vain, and with surly reluctance they were compelled to retreat. Warren animated and encouraged the men, and with the rest of the officers, set them an example with his musket; there was scarcely an officer of any grade, except Putnam and Prescott, without one.[86]

If General Howe still had any sympathy for the colonial cause it was not apparent on June 17 as he ordered the town of Charleston to be burnt. As the residents ran from their homes, the British troops were met with sniper bullets from American militia units.

People in Boston looked north toward the smoke and flames and watched as the buildings burned and the battle commenced. Even as far south as the town of Braintree on the other side of Boston, people gathered on hilltops to view the battle. Included there were the family of revolutionary leader, John Adams. His wife Abigail and their seven-year-old son John Quincy Adams had a clear if distant view of the burning of Charlestown and heard the sounds of the American and British guns.[87]

The day was still hot as the British troops marched up Breed's Hill toward where militia forces were crouched down behind earthworks and wooden rail fences. Having received the command "Don't fire until you see the whites of their eyes," they anxiously waited with their single shot muskets. Not only would premature shots from these notoriously inaccurate guns probably miss their targets, but it took time to load and ready the guns for the next shots; time during which the red-coated enemy could get dangerously close.

As soon as the British were close enough that the colonists could distinguish the whites of their eyes (about 150 feet away), the latter let loose

FOUR. BLOODIEST BATTLE OF THE REVOLUTION   91

of a hail of bullets. The smoke fogs over the field and the smell of gunpowder permeated the air for the rest of the afternoon.

As the British began to come closer, two Massachusetts militia captains, John Callender and Captain Gridley, who was the nephew Richard Gridley, the Army's chief engineer, were ordered to fire their cannon. When Captain Gridley tried, he had some difficulty and exclaimed that "nothing could be done with them." He left his post and most of his artillerymen followed him.[88]

One of the men who did not leave his post was Ezra Runnels. He later recalled:

> General Putnam came to one of the pieces near which I stood, and furiously inquired where our officers were. On being told our cartridges were too big and that the pieces could not be loaded, he swore, and said they could be loaded; taking a cartridge he broke it open, and loaded the pieces with a ladle, which were discharged; and assisted us in loading two or three times in that manner.[89]

According to Livingston, the cannon "were soon disabled" and were moved to the rear. Callender went with them. Reaching Bunker Hill, he ran into General Putnam. In testimony before a Massachusetts Provincial Congress committee, Putnam stated that he ordered Callender to "stop and go back." The captain protested that he had no cartridges. Putnam stepped down from his horse and opened the cartridge boxes. There were "a considerable number of" cartridges. Again, Putnam ordered Callender back to the front. He refused. Finally, Putnam threatened him with "immediate death" and Callender went back to the fight.[90]

In 1825, Samuel Swett interviewed soldiers who were present at Bunker Hill. These veterans told him that Captain Callender only stayed at his post a short time after Putnam threatened him and that Callender's men "were disgusted with a part of the service they did not understand, most of them had muskets and mingled with the infantry, the pieces were entirely deserted, and the captain relinquished them."[91] Swett relates:

> Putnam, on returning from Bunker Hill, whither he had gone to bring on some of the men who were intrenching [sic] there, came upon the abandoned cannon "at the foot of the hill." He demanded of the soldiers in the vicinity where the gunners were and was told that they had scattered.[92]

When Captain John Ford's company of Col. Ebenezer Bridge's regiment came by, Putnam ordered them to bring the cannon to the front. A member of the company stated,

> Our men utterly refused and said they had no knowledge of the use of artillery, and that they were ready to fight with their own arms. [34-year-old] Captain Ford [a tall and wiry man][93] then addressed the company in a very animated, patriotic and brave

strain, which is characteristic of the man; the company then seized the drag-ropes and soon drew them to the railfence, according to my recollection about half the distance from the redoubt on Breed's Hill to Mystic River.[94]

General Putnam personally took over the guns. "He pointed the cannon himself," writes Swett[95]; "The balls took effect on the enemy, and one case of canister made a lane through them. With wonderful courage, however, the enemy closed their ranks, and coolly marched on to the attack."[96]

After Washington arrived at Cambridge one of his first actions was to decide what to do about Callender. Washington wrote:

> It is with inexpressible concern that the General, upon his first arrival in the army, should find an officer sentenced by a General Court Martial to be cashiered for cowardice—a crime of all others, the most infamous in a soldier, the most injurious to an army, and the last to be forgiven.

Callender was stripped of his rank and drummed out of the army.[97] However, by the following year, Callender had reenlisted as a private and ended up at the Battle of Long Island, where he "so distinguished himself for personal valor that Washington publically revoked the sentence and restored him to his former rank."[98]

The report by the Massachusetts Provincial Congress committee ended with Putnam's opinion

> that the defeat of that day was owing to the ill-behaviour of those that conducted the artillery, and that one of these officers ought to be punished with death, and that unless some exemplary punishment was inflicted, he would assuredly leave the Army. That upon the defeat of the officers of the Train, the re-enforcements ordered up the hill could not be prevailed upon to go; the plea was, the Artillery was gone, and they stood no chance for their lives in such circumstances, declaring they had no officers to lead them.[99]

Putnam concluded that the only immediate action was to order the Massachusetts Committee of Safety to make out a new list of artillery officers and make sure that "no person unworthy of the office be appointed."[100]

At the Battle of Bunker Hill, twice the British attacked and twice they failed. For the third attack, they were reinforced by 400 more soldiers sent over from Boston. The militia units held out, but after the first volley of this last wave of the enemy, their ammunition began running out.

Putnam rode back to Bunker Hill to urge the men there to reinforce Prescott's troops. No amount of pressure was enough to force these men to Breed's Hill where they felt certain death awaited them. They knew the British were slaughtering men. In addition, fresh American troops on the other side of the neck toward Cambridge wouldn't cross out to the penin-

Four. Bloodiest Battle of the Revolution 93

sula. After the battle was over, Prescott asked Putnam why he had not brought in reinforcements. His reply was "I could not make the dogs go."[101]

The Colonists had lost many dedicated "sons of liberty" at the battle, but perhaps the greatest loss to the cause was Dr. Joseph Warren. At the very end of the battle, as the British troops were making their third and final assault on the Breed's Hill redoubt, he was fatally shot in the head. Prescott's troops retreated toward Cambridge, while Stark's men guarded their rear. One of the last to leave the fortifications was the best known Massachusetts rebel, Dr. James Warren. Before he could get far, he was killed by British bullets.

Humphreys describes the end of the battle as follows:

> the redoubt half filled with British Regulars, that the word was given to retire ... undisciplined [colonial militia] men, most of them without bayonets, disputing with the butt end of their muskets against the British bayonet and receding in sullen despair. Still the Light Infantry, on their left, would certainly have gained their rear and exterminated this gallant little corps, had not a body of four hundred Connecticut men, with the Captains Knoulton [Thomas Knowlton] and [John] Chester ... held the enemy at bay until the main body had relinquished the heights and then retreated across the neck with more regularity and less loss than could have been expected.[102]

Although Humphreys was not at Bunker Hill, he spoke with both Putnam and Washington. The latter undoubtedly absorbed every detail of the battle since he ended up commanding virtually all of its American survivors

Years later, many elderly veterans told of Putnam's actions at the Battle of Bunker Hill. In addition to Connecticut veterans, Massachusetts and New Hampshire soldiers who had seen Putnam "in the beginning, the middle and the end of the action." Grosvenor points out that

> Kemp of Stark's regiment, heard him charge the men not to fire till the enemy came close to the works. [Ebenezer] Bean, of Stark's regiment, deposed that he saw Putnam riding from one end of the line to the other, as far as he could see, giving orders.[103] [Amos] Barnes of Stark's regiment, heard him giving orders to Col. Stark, urging him forward with the principal part of his regiment.[104]

Putnam was observed assigning new arrivals to their locations as they arrived on the battlefield. "Others saw him in the action at the rail fence, at the breastwork, and behind the redoubt—they saw him on horseback amidst the flying balls, when they expected every moment to see him fall from his horse."[105]

Just like in the Trumbull painting, veterans remembered Putnam as the key officer leading the American militia to a successful retreat. "Lyman of Greenfield, Mass., saw Putnam directing the retreat. Miner of Massachusetts saw him during the retreat, riding through the lines, exhorting the men to form, and give the enemy one shot more before retreating."[106]

At the end of the fighting, engineer Colonel Richard Gridley had personally operated one of the American cannon and was wounded. As he was carried off in a buggy, he left the vehicle. As he walked away from it, it was "riddled with enemy shot" and the horse killed.[107] Gridley recovered and days later began the refortification of American defenses surrounding Boston. The Massachusetts Provincial Congress raised him to the rank of major general. In September 1775 General George Washington appointed Gridley as the first Chief Engineer of the Continental Army.[108]

The Colonial forces fought well—so well in fact that virtually everyone on both sides was surprised by their skill and endurance. Still, they were farmers, tradesmen, shopkeepers, etc. They weren't professional soldiers. When the going got rough, they realized their weaknesses and froze. Putnam was angry, and he made his "dogs" comment many times in later years; however he also knew from experience how men in these circumstances would react and he wasn't surprised.

After the battle there was a good deal of discussion about the conduct of the British, particularly some of the officers. The following is an excerpt from a letter by lawyer Benjamin Hichborn[109] to John Adams about six months after the Battle of Bunker Hill:

> As I find you are upon a Committee for collecting Evidence of the Hostilities committed by the British troops and Navy, I cannot omit the following anecdote, as a remarkable Instance of their Savage barbarity. One Drew, now a Lieutenant of the Scorpion or Viper, I am uncertain which, and Bruce, a private belonging to the Preston, landed on Bunkers Hill, soon after the battle of the 17th of June. Drew, after walking for some time over the bodies of the dead, with great fortitude, went up to one of our wounded Men, and very deliberately shot him through the Head. Bruce advanced further over the Hill, and meeting with a forlorn wretch, begging Mercy for Gods Sake! he advanced and with a "damn ye, you Bugger you! are you not dead yet?" instantly demolished him. In a day or two after, Drew went upon the Hill again opened the dirt that was thrown over Doctr: Warren, spit in his Face jump'd on his Stomach and at last cut off his Head and committed every act of violence upon his Body. I had this Story from two Gentlemen belonging to the Preston who were eye Witnesses of the facts. In justice to the officers in general I must add, that they despised Drew for his Conduct, the other was below their notice."[110]

However, that wasn't the end of the story for Warren's corpse. Ten months after its burial by the British, it was exhumed, with Paul Revere identifying the body by the false teeth he had made for him out of ivory and gold wire.[111] It was perhaps the first use of forensic dentistry in history. The remains were then reburied. In 1825, they were moved to a third location, and then in 1855 they were removed by a physician nephew of Warren

Four. Bloodiest Battle of the Revolution

to his home for a year. They were finally reburied in Roxbury Massachusetts the following year.

Although the British won a victory at the Battle of Bunker Hill, their staggering losses revealed their weaknesses, and they knew it. Eleven days after the battle, then Continental Army Brigadier General Nathanael Greene of Rhode Island wrote to his older brother Jacob: "I wish we could sell them another hill, at the same price."[112]

The casualties were far greater than probably anyone on either side had expected. Of the 1,500 American troops actively involved in the fighting, 140 were killed, 271 were wounded, and 30 were captured (of which maybe ⅔ died in confinement).

Of the estimated 2,500 to 3,000 British troops who were engaged, British losses amounted to 226 killed (35 officers and 191 soldiers) and 828 wounded (122 officers and 706 soldiers). Thus the total casualty count was British 1,054 and Americans 449, meaning 70 percent of the fighting men put out of action that day were British soldiers.[113]

Especially troubling for the British high command were the officer casualties. An astonishing 134 British officers were killed or wounded. Among the nineteen officers who were killed, were two majors and seven captains.[114]

When Putnam gave the order at the Battle of Bunker Hill to "Aim at the handsome coats, pick off the commanders," he meant it. His forces already were laboring under huge handicaps—in numbers and in experience. They couldn't afford to fight according to the British rules, no matter how ancient and supposedly honorable those rules were.

If the martyr at Breed's Hill had been Putnam rather than Warren, the most despicable of the British officers would have hated him just as much, and would, most likely, have desecrated his corpse. As Claremont Graduate School Professor of History John Niven described Putnam in his U.S. Bicentennial Putnam biography:

> The vision of the stout General on horseback, waving his curved sword and galloping up and down the line heedless of enemy fire would remain indelibly imprinted in many a veteran's recollections of that hot, chaotic, dreadful, yet somehow glorious day.[115]

Niven states that at the Battle of Bunker Hill,

> Putnam, who was acting as the entire staff—a messenger, an haranguer of the laggards, a prodder of General Ward, an entrencher of Bunker Hill, and a deployer of the regiments which were finally coming in to reinforce Prescott—seemed everywhere at once. The only mounted officer, his horse flecked with foam, he set an example of fearlessness ... he was in a large measure responsible for calming the nervous men and having them fire in unison on command, at point-blank range.[116]

One British officer, Lt. John Waller, who was Adjutant of the 1st Battalion of Marines, wrote in a letter four days after the Battle: "we gain'd Ground on the enemy but slowly, as the Rails Hedges & stone walls, broke [the ranks of the British] at every time we got over them and several Men were shot in the Act of climbing them."[117]

Lt. Waller stated in his letter: "when we enter'd [the colonist's redoubt] 'twas streaming with Blood & strew'd with dead & dying Men the Soldiers stabbing some and dashing out the Brains of others was a sight too dreadful for me to dwell any longer on."[118]

Before the battle, General Howe had issued the following order: "Genl Howe expects that all Officers will Exert themselves to prevent the Men from Straggling Quitting their Companys or platoons and on pain of Death no Man to be Guilty of the Shamefull and Infamous practice of pillaging and pilfering in the Deserted Houses."[119]

One of the most important lessons the British learned that day was a timeless one: never underestimate an enemy. Their commanders had made a relatively accurate assessment of the American rank in file—almost all were untrained, uncoordinated and, in some cases, unmanageable amateurs. Hardly the type of men to stand up to the career British soldiers. When not practicing maneuvers on New England village greens, they were planting corn and potatoes or they were selling dry goods to housewives or they were hammering out iron fittings in their blacksmith shops. The military experience of most consisted of "playing" soldier with their fellow townsmen.

But the British commanders forgot something they should have known—for many of them had served in the French and Indian War from 1755 through 1763. They forgot that this conglomeration of shopkeepers, farmers, and laborers were led by men who went through the same formative experiences they themselves had. They had "cut their teeth" in the forests of New York, Pennsylvania and Canada. The men on Breed's Hill were led by colony-appointed colonels who not only had learned well the tactics employed by the British Army, but had experienced firsthand the fighting techniques of the professional French soldiers, the Native American guerrilla fighters and even, to a lesser extent, Spanish troops.

At the American redoubt on Breed's Hill, the militia were commanded by the supremely competent Colonel William Prescott. Coming in with his men after the initial fortifications were constructed and making critical last minute decisions was the brilliant Colonel John Stark of New Hampshire. And overseeing every aspect of the preparations and fighting, seeming to many as if he was in two places at the same time, was arguably the toughest commander on either side—Israel Putnam.

Four. Bloodiest Battle of the Revolution 97

After the battle was over, the Americans made good use of the press. As historian Bernard Bailyn explains:

> The engraved "views" and maps of the battle and of Warren's death convey not so much the objective historical actuality as the contemporary sense of it. They also show the drift of images of the battle into popular iconography. Published reports and accounts show the use of the battle in what a later generation would call propaganda.[120]

Somewhat surprisingly, possibly the most persistent dispute to come out of the battle was not over strategy, tactics, great blunders, or a hundred live and death decisions. It was about the identity of the person who uttered the command, "Don't fire until you see the whites of their eyes." Some claimed Putnam, some Prescott and others (a tiny minority) someone else. It's possible that both Putnam and Prescott repeatedly yelled out these words, but which of them was first is a question that may never be known.

Historian Barbara Wertheim Tuchman (1912–1989) in a paper delivered in Greenwich, Connecticut, in 1979, on the 200th anniversary of Putnam's famous escape from the British, writes that the *Dictionary of Military Quotations* "assigns it to both officers on the inventive theory that Putnam transmitted an order already voiced by Prescott." Tuchman goes on to state, with perhaps a smile on her face, "As a Connecticut patriot, I reject any such measly solution. The phrase sounds like Putnam, and I will maintain his claim against any Massachusetts pretender."[121]

The following are excerpts from two remarkable letters by Adams' family witnesses—one written one day after the Battle of Bunker Hill and the other 71 years later.

The day after the battle, Abigail Adams wrote to her husband, patriot leader John Adams:

> I have just heard that our dear Friend Dr. Warren is no more but fell gloriously fighting for his Country—saying better to die honourably in the field than ignominiously hang upon the Gallows. Great is our Loss. He has distinguished himself in every engagement, by his courage and fortitude, by animating the Soldiers and leading them on by his own example ... the God of Israel is he that giveth strength and power unto his people. Trust in him at all times, ye people pour out your hearts before him. God is a refuge for us.—Charlstown [sic] is laid in ashes. The Battle began upon our intrenchments [sic] upon Bunkers Hill, a Saturday morning about 3 o clock and has not ceased yet and tis now 3 o'clock Sabbeth [sic] afternoon.[122]

In 1846, two years before he died, former U.S. President John Quincy Adams wrote in a letter to English Quaker and abolitionist Joseph Sturge,[123]

> ... on the 17th Of June lighted the fires of Charlestown—I saw with my own eyes those fires, and heard Britannia's thunders in the Battle of Bunker's hill and witnessed the

tears of my mother and mingled with them my own, at the fall of Warren a dear friend of my father, and a beloved Physician to me. He had been our family physician and surgeon, and had saved my fore finger from amputation under a very bad fracture.[124]

Over 100 of the Americans who fought at the Battle of Bunker Hill were either African American or Native American. By the end of the American Revolutionary War, the number of African Americans who served had risen to as many as 5,000.[125] These soldiers set a precedent that would be followed by the 180,000 black soldiers who served on the Union side in the American Civil War, the 400,000 who served in World War I (because of discrimination, primarily in support roles), and the approximately 1.2 million blacks who served in World War II.

One of the most celebrated African Americans at Bunker Hill was Salem Poor. A resident of Andover, Massachusetts, Poor was born a slave, purchased his freedom, and fought at Bunker Hill as a member of Capt. Ames Company of Col. Frye's regiment. Months after the battle, Colonel William Prescott and a dozen other officers signed a petition to the General Court of Massachusetts Bay Colony to "do in justice to the character of so brave a man," specifying that Salem Poor "behaved like an experienced officer, as well as an excellent soldier." Apparently, Poor was the only soldier, black, white or Native American who was singled out for such formal praise. Poor continued to serve after Bunker Hill, fighting at the battles of Saratoga and Monmouth.

Three of the best-known Native Americans at the Battle of Bunker Hill were Jonathan Occum and the Ashbow brothers, John and Samuel, all of whom served under Israel Putnam.

Fifty-year-old New London Connecticut Mohegan Jonathan Occum[126] was a veteran of the French and Indian War. He joined Putnam's regiment on May 10, 1775, and only a few weeks later found himself defending the rail fence on Breed's Hill against British troops, some of the most experienced professional soldiers in the world. Records show that he continued to fight throughout the Revolutionary War. In 1790 he was given 20 acres of land in Connecticut in recognition of his loyal military service.

After joining Capt. Durkee's company in Colonel Putnam's regiment, 29-year-old Samuel Ashbow and his 22-year-old brother John Ashbow[127] marched 76 miles from their home near Norwich, Connecticut, to Cambridge, Massachusetts. Sons of the Reverend Samuel Ashbow, they were members of the Mohegan tribe. They were stationed at the Breed's Hill rail fence where they fought back the British troops during the first two assaults. It's believed Samuel was killed during the third and final British attack. It's thought that his body was buried in a mass grave at the battle

FOUR. BLOODIEST BATTLE OF THE REVOLUTION   99

site with other patriots who died in action. Brother John continued serving until his tour of duty was up eight months later.

Although it would not be until a half-century after the Battle of Bunker Hill that photography would be invented, there is one accurate picture of Col. Israel Putnam at the battle. It was painted by a man who knew Putnam well and who was quite possibly the best American portrait artist of the time.

Connecticut painter John Trumbull (1756–1843) captured several key events of Bunker Hill in a single painting, *Death of General Joseph Warren at the Battle of Bunker's Hill, June 17, 1775*. To the far left of the picture, Israel Putnam is seen in a light blue and scarlet uniform waving his sword at the enemy troops. In his first (1788) edition of his Israel Putnam biography, David Humphreys compares this picture of Putnam with a stanza in the 1787 epic poem, *The Vision of Columbus*, by Connecticut writer Joel Barlow (1754–1812):

> There strides bold Putnam and from all the plains,
> Calls the tired host, the tardy rear sustains,
> And, mid the wizzing death's that fill the air,
> Waves back his sword and dares the foll'wing war.[128]
> There stood stern Putnam, seam'd with many a scar,
> The veteran honours of an earlier war;

In the biography, Humphreys mentions that he personally spoke with both Trumbull and Barlow about the similarity of the depictions of Putnam in their two works. These men were not ordinary artists: Trumbull had been an eyewitness to the Battle of Bunker Hill and an aide-de-camp to Washington during the Revolutionary War, and Barlow had fought at the Battle of Long Island under Putnam, and had been a chaplain in Washington's army for three years. Both Trumbull and Barlow were members of the Yale-affiliated literary group, the Connecticut Wits, AKA the Hartford Wits.[129]

One letter by an elderly veteran, written 68 years after the Battle of Bunker Hill appears in Cutter's 1850 biography of Putnam[130]:

> I, Sylvanus Conant, of Mansfield, in the County of Tolland and State of Connecticut, testify and say, that I am now in my ninety-second year; that I was a soldier in the Revolutionary War; that I was in the battle of Bunker's Hill, on the seventeenth day of June, 1775; that I was acquainted with General Israel Putnam, of Connecticut, and know that he was in the battle. Saw him at the commencement of the battle, riding about the hill, and giving orders to the troops, and heard him sharply reproving a soldier for cowardice, or neglect of duty; and was told by others, though this I did not see myself, that near the close of the battle, General Putnam, seeing a field piece deserted by the company, dismounted from his horse and fired the piece once or twice

with his own hands, and then remounted his horse, and rode off the hill with the retreating troops.

The last known survivor of the Battle of Bunker Hill was Ralph Farnham. The 18-year-old private in Capt. Philip Hubbard's company, Col. James Scamman's regiment, was present on the Charlestown peninsula on June 17, but apparently the entire regiment did not see fighting that day. However, Farnham's long service in the Revolutionary War included: serving under Putnam at Long Island, suffering through the winter at Valley Forge, and viewing British General Burgoyne's surrender at Saratoga.

A book published a few months before Farnham's 1860 death, *Biographical Sketch of the Life of Ralph Farnham of Acton, Maine*, quoted the then 104-year-old veteran saying of General Putnam: "Yes—old Putnam was rough and ready. He was afraid of nothing. He looked like a farmer; but he feared nothing, nor nobody."[131]

As the 50th anniversary of the great battle was approaching in 1825, plans were in place to erect a suitable monument on the battle site. The corner stone of a Bunker Hill monument was laid in 1826 on the 50th anniversary of the battle. Then funds dried up and the project languished for years. Finally, three people took on the cause: a Jewish businessman, a noted philanthropist, and the woman who was editor of the largest-circulation magazine in the United States.

American writer and magazine editor Sarah Josepha Hale (1788–1879), who created the nursery rhyme "Mary Had a Little Lamb" in 1830, was instrumental in raising money for the completion of the Bunker Hill Monument. Not only did she raise money from her subscribers, but at Boston's Faneuil Hall she hosted arguably the largest fundraiser (up to that time) in U.S. history.[132]

At about the same time Hale was doing her part, merchant and philanthropist Amos Lawrence promised to donate $10,000 if the remaining money could be found. The following year, Jewish businessman Judah Touro[133] of New Orleans anonymously matched Laurence's $10,000 with $10,000 of his own. Ironically, when his name was leaked to the public, people became aware for the first time of possibly the greatest American philanthropist of the first half of the 19th century.[134] The donation led to the following lines being read at the June 17, 1843, dedication of the Bunker Hill monument:

> Amos and Judah! venerated names!
> Patriarch and prophet press their equal claims;
> Like generous coursers, running neck and neck,
> Each aids the work by giving it a check.

Four. Bloodiest Battle of the Revolution

Christian and Jew, they carry out one plan;
For, though of different faiths, each is in heart a man.[135]

At the battle, the colonists had only four cannon. Two were captured by the British, the other two were hidden in a Dedham, Massachusetts, swamp. Nicknamed the Hancock and the Adams, the 500-pound brass cannon were placed at the Bunker Hill monument in the 1800s.[136]

On June 17, 1875, the celebration of the Bunker Hill Centennial attracted thousands of marchers. As the first marchers ended the six-mile-long route, one-half of the marchers hadn't even started yet.

In his 1876 Putnam biography,[137] Tarbox discusses the preceding year's Bunker Hill Centennial. While praising the people of Boston and Massachusetts for their efforts to include all the people of New England as well as those of other parts of the country, rather than to make it merely a local celebration, Tarbox recalls the efforts in the weeks before the event to push for recognition of Col. Prescott as the overall commander of the battle. He said some of the Boston newspapers had almost daily "droppings" of the idea that Prescott was the colonial leader that day—and not Putnam. Books and larger periodicals picked up on the same line. Apparently, it was much like a political party of the 21st century attempting to form public opinion with a barrage of television and radio advertisements.

It's not really very difficult to find reasons for this elevation of William Prescott to the supposed overall commander of the battle. He was, after all, a Massachusetts man through and through: born there, raised there, served in its wars, and was buried in its soil. Although Putnam was born and grew up in Danvers (Salem Village) Massachusetts, and he had made his life-long home barely 15 miles outside the Massachusetts' border, he was still considered a Connecticut man. Even a century after the Revolution, the old colonial loyalties still lived.

Tarbox, ever the Putnam partisan, notes with glee that one of the most famous army regiments, the New York Seventh,[138] paraded into Boston at the Bunker Hill Centennial singing a regimental song that they had composed for the occasion. Every one of its nine stanzas end with the chorus:

We won the victory at that fight,
We knew we should, for we were right;
Old Putnam led the men that night,
At Bunker Hill, at Bunker Hill.[139]

The guest list was headed by Henry Wilson, the Vice President of the United States (and a former U.S. senator from Massachusetts); two U.S. Supreme Court Justices; eight governors; and William Tecumseh Sherman, the Commanding General of the United States Army.[140] Sherman, who stated that he believed that Colonel Prescott was the "actual commander on Bunker Hill," went on to say that General Putnam "has ample honor without claiming this.... He was a glorious old soldier, and his services and examples are worth a dozen monuments like this on Bunker Hill, even if made of pure gold."[141]

Tarbox ends his Putnam biography with a salute to those he considered the main victors at the Battle of Bunker Hill: General Putnam, Colonel Stark, and Stark's New Hampshire fighters.[142]

> ... we have the full conviction that the time will come, when the whole nation will give the honors of the battle of Bunker Hill largely to the common soldiers of New Hampshire who, more than any other men, fought it; and to brave old General Putnam, who conceived the plan, and was chief commander on the field. The two hundred men from Connecticut performed extraordinary services, but they were few in number. Their heroic faithfulness has always been spoken of in terms of highest praise. The men at the redoubt who patiently endured and suffered to the end, are worthy of all honor. But the battle was fought chiefly by the soldiers of New Hampshire, whose muskets killed and wounded probably two out of three in that list of ten hundred and sixty-four, which General Gage reported to the home government.
>
> If a monument is to be erected upon that battle-ground to any Colonel, it should be to Colonel Stark of New Hampshire, whose services in the strife were more important than those of any other man bearing that title.[143]

Today the 221-foot-high the Bunker Hill Monument obelisk stands in the center of a square park on the top of Breed's Hill. The park is surrounded by dense upper-middle-class residential blocks. The park area is so small that if the obelisk were to fall toward any side of the park square, it would probably block a street.

The Bunker Hill Monument park is the only substantial area of green visible from ground level on Breed's Hill and it's very difficult to visualize the landscape as it was on the day of the battle. From the top of the Monument, there's a good view of downtown Boston and the Charles River, although the river is dramatically narrower what it was in 1775 due to centuries of landfill on both of its shores.

Organization of an Army

Early in July 1775, Washington arrived in Cambridge. In person, he was impressive. In the words of Thomas Jefferson: "His person ... was fine, his stature exactly what one would wish, his deportment easy, erect and noble; the best horseman of his age, and the most graceful figure that could be seen on horseback."[144]

Four. Bloodiest Battle of the Revolution

In October 1775, only months after Washington's became Commander-in-Chief of the Continental Army, patriot leader Dr. Benjamin Rush wrote the following to Thomas Ruston: "[Washington] has so much martial dignity in his deportment that you would distinguish him to be a general and a soldier from among ten thousand people. There is not a king in Europe that would not look like a *valet de chambre* by his side."[145]

There has been so much written about Washington in the last 250-plus years, it's difficult to choose a description. Perhaps one of the best is by a Jefferson, a fellow Virginian who knew him well. In 1814 in a letter to Dr. Walter Jones,[146] he wrote of Washington: "certainly no General ever planned his battles more judiciously. But if deranged during the course of the action, if any member of his plan was dislocated by sudden circumstances, he was slow in readjustment. The consequence was, that he often failed in the field, and rarely against an enemy in station, as at Boston and York."[147]

Thomas Jefferson had the most respect for the Commander-in-Chief's character:

> Perhaps the strongest feature in his character was prudence, never acting until every circumstance, every consideration, was maturely weighed; refraining if he saw a doubt, but, when once decided, going through with his purpose, whatever obstacles opposed." and "His integrity was most pure; his justice the most inflexible I have ever known, no motives of interest, or consanguinity, of friendship, or hatred, being able to bias his decision. He was, indeed, in every sense of the words, a wise, a good, and a great man.[148]

Another interesting observation by Jefferson: Washington's "temper was naturally irritable and high toned; but reflection and resolution had obtained a firm and habitual ascendency over it. If ever, however, it broke its bonds, he was most tremendous in his wrath."[149]

After taking command at Cambridge in 1775, Washington divided his army into three divisions with 12 regiments each, with General Artemas Ward commanding the right wing, General Charles Lee the left wing, and General Israel Putnam the reserve.

Congress on July 18, 1775, detailed the organization of the Continental Army. It provided that a company should have a captain, two lieutenants, an ensign, four sergeants, four corporals, a clerk, drummer, fifer and sixty-eight privates. The Connecticut Assembly at its October 1775 session made the same provision. Before this, it had specified that a state company would have one hundred men.[150]

Given the responsibilities shouldered by generals in the Revolution, it might be expected that their monetary compensation would be substantial. Looking at the pay scales of that war and comparing them with the

U.S. Army of the following century, we find that the pay of high-ranking officers, i.e., brigadier generals, colonels, and majors, was not that much different than the amounts received by major generals.[151]

On June 20, 1775, from Philadelphia, George Washington wrote to his younger brother John Augustine Washington (1736–1787):

> ... I am at liberty to inform you, that the Congress, in committee, have consented to a Continental currency, and have ordered two millions of dollars to be struck for payment of the troops and other purposes, and have voted fifteen thousand men as a Continental Army, which number will be augmented, as the strength of the British troops will be greater than was expected at the time of passing that vote.[152]

On June 20, 1775, Eliphalet Dyer wrote to Joseph Trumbull from the Congress in Philadelphia.[153] In his listing of the men who were to report to newly appointed army commander-in-chief Washington, he states:

> Brigdr Genll. Putnam is also appointed Majr Genll, the next in Command to Genll Lee. his [Putnam's] fame as a Warrior had been so far extended thro the Continent that it would be in Vain to urge any of our Genll officers in Competition with him and he Carried by Universal Voice.[154]

That same day, in his letter to his brother John, Washington wrote: "General Ward, General Lee, General Schuyler, and General Putnam are appointed Major Generals under me. The Brigadier Generals are not yet appointed...."[155]

On June 22, 1775, the brigadier generals were selected. (Horatio Gates had already been commissioned a brigadier general on June 17.) The delegates chose Seth Pomeroy of Massachusetts as the first ranking brigadier general and John Thomas of Massachusetts (a military surgeon) as the sixth brigadier general. Thomas complained, Pomeroy resigned because of age, and Thomas replaced him as the first ranking brigadier general.

Richard Montgomery of New York became the second brigadier general (he was an Ireland-born, former British soldier). David Wooster of Connecticut was the third (He had been in King George's War and the French and Indian War). William Heath of Massachusetts was the fourth, Joseph Spencer of Connecticut the fifth (He too had been in King George's War and the French and Indian War), John Sullivan of New Hampshire was the seventh, and Nathanael Greene of Rhode Island was the eighth brigadier general.

On June 26, the entire Connecticut delegation wrote to Connecticut Governor Jonathan Trumbull:

> ... In the arrangement of General officers, the Character of General Putnam commanded every Vote for his Major General Ship, an Honor peculiar to the Commander

in Chief and himself. We hope that his appointment will give no umbrage to General Wooster or General Spencer as they are honorably provided for.[156]

Wooster and Spencer at first refused to serve under Putnam because they claimed higher rank in the Connecticut colony forces. It's probable that lawyer and judge Joseph Spencer and Yale-educated Wooster also looked down on a man who only had three months formal education in his entire life. Neither the Continental Congress nor General Washington was impressed by Spencer's or Wooster's arguments and the Putnam appointment stood.

Connecticut Continental Congress delegate Roger Sherman wrote to Wooster after the vote on the appointments:

> I am sensible that according to your colonial rank, you were entitled to the place of major general; and as one was to be appointed from Connecticut, I heartily recommended you to the Congress. I informed them of the arrangements made by our Assembly, which I thought would be satisfactory to have them continue in the same order. But as Gen. Putnam's fame was spread abroad, and especially his successful enterprise at Noddle's Island, the account of which had just arrived, it gave him a preference in the opinion of the delegates in general, so that his appointment was unanimous among the colonies; but from your known ability and firm attachment to the American cause, we were very desirous of your continuance in the army, and hope you will accept the appointment made by Congress.[157]

Wooster's bitterness was transparent as he replied to Sherman:

> No man feels more sensibly for his distressed country, nor would more readily exert his utmost effort for its defense than myself. My life has been ever devoted to her service, from my youth up, though never before in a cause like this, a cause for which I would most cheerfully risk, nay lay down my life. Thirty years I have served as a soldier; my character was never impeached, nor called in question before. The Congress have seen fit, for what reason I know not, to point me out as the only officer among all that have been commissioned in the different colonies, who is unfit for the post assigned him. The subject is a very delicate one.[158]

In a July 5, 1775, letter to the Connecticut General Assembly, 49 of General Spencer's officers, including two who would soon distinguish themselves in military actions (Samuel H. Parsons and Return Jonathan Meigs), strongly criticized the Continental Congress's promotion of Putnam over Spencer, even stating that "with great reluctance our Troops at Roxbury [Massachusetts] could see their General superseded by an officer in previous lower command," and claiming that "the morals and good order and discipline of our Troops will be greatly endangered under the present arrangement."[159]

As a result of this letter, the Connecticut Assembly asked the governor to notify the Continental Congress of concerns about its military appointments. However, they also made a point to note "the singular merit of Gen. Putnam" and requested that "if practicable, to devise some method of obviating the difficulties apprehended."[160]

It might be noted that just like there were rivalries between colonies, there were allegiances and loyalties within the colonies. The officers who were under Spencer were primarily from Middlesex County, Connecticut, while Israel Putnam was a resident of Windham County.

The discontent of the two Connecticut officers provided the new Commander-in-Chief with a problem. In a July 10, 1775, letter to the Continental Congress, Washington stated:

> I am sorry to observe that the Appointments of the General Officers in the Province of Massachusetts Bay have by no Means corresponded with the Judgement & Wishes of either the civil or Military. The great Dissatisfaction expressed on this Subject & the apparent Danger of throwing the Army into the utmost Disorder, together with the strong Representations of the Provincial Congress, have induced me to retain the Commissions in my Hands untill [sic] the Pleasure of the Congress should be farther known (except General Putnam's which was given the Day I came into Camp and before I was apprized of these Uneasinesses).[161]

Washington goes on to make it clear that every general officer appointed was an "entire Stranger to me but from Character." And that "General Spencer was so much disgusted at the preference given to General Puttnam [sic] that he left the Army without visiting me, or making known his Intentions in any respect."[162]

According to Connecticut Congressional delegate Silas Deane, his fellow members disapproved of Spencer's actions after this Washington letter was read to them. Soon afterward (July 20, 1775), Deane wrote:

> Putnam's merit rung through this Continent; his fame still increases—and every day justifies the unanimous applause of the continent. Let it be remembered, he had every vote of the Congress; and his health has been the second or third at almost all our tables in this city. But it seems that he does not wear a large wig, nor screw his countenance into a form that belies the sentiments of his generous soul; he is no adept either at political or religious canting and cozening; he is no shake-hand body; he therefore is totally unfit for everything but fighting; that department I never heard that these intriguing gentry wanted to interfere with him in. I have scarce any patience. O Heaven! blast, I implore thee, every such low, narrow, selfish, envious manoeuvre in the land, nor let one such succeed far enough to stain the fair page of American patriotic politics.[163]

Apparently, the army officers in Massachusetts had as little sympathy for Spencer as the Philadelphia delegates. Deane's step-son, Lieutenant Samuel B. Webb wrote to Deane:

> You'll find the Generals Washington and Lee [Charles Lee had accompanied Washington from Philadelphia to Cambridge] are vastly fonder and think higher of Putnam

Four. Bloodiest Battle of the Revolution

than any man in the army; and he truly is the Hero of the day.... I find, the intention of Spencer was to get our [Connecticut] Assembly to remonstrate to the Continental Congress and beg a re-appointment; but little did he think that this could not be done without cashiering Putnam—as he is in possession of his commission; and better for us to lose four Spencers than half a Putnam.[164]

Ultimately, they didn't even lose one Spencer, as he returned to the army and accepted a brigadier general commission.

At the time of Washington's letter to his brother, Ward and Putnam were in Cambridge, Massachusetts, while Charles Lee and Philip Schuyler were in Philadelphia. Lee only arrived in the colonies 18 months earlier and until his appointment as Major General, he was a colonel in the British Army on half-pay.

All four newly-appointed major generals had held important commands in the French and Indian War, which had ended a dozen years earlier. Now, three were in their 40s—Schuyler 41, Lee 43, Ward 47—and Putnam was 57. In their quest to select military leaders equally from both the northern and the southern colonies, the Continental Congress had chosen well: the overall commander (Washington) and one of the four major generals (Lee) were from Virginia; the remaining three major generals were from Massachusetts, Connecticut, and New York.

Before the Second Continental Congress created the Continental Army on June 14, 1775, the main military force in the colonies was headed by a Massachusetts man. In a sense, commander Artemas Ward, leading an army of Massachusetts, Connecticut, New Hampshire, and Rhode Island troops was the new nation's first commander-in-chief. On June 14, 1775, when Congress appointed George Washington as the official commander-in-chief, Ward was relegated to the position as one of his four major generals.

Ward biographer Charles Martyn states: "Artemas Ward was "a man of medium height; clean shaven, of prominent features; too stout for his forty seven years and at the moment showing the effects of his recent illness, but well enough nevertheless to apply himself conscientiously to the duties to his hand."[165]

Born on November 26, 1727, in Shrewsbury, Massachusetts, Ward was a Harvard graduate and a long-time Massachusetts state legislator. His experience as a lieutenant colonel in the Massachusetts militia during the French and Indian War led to his appointment as a brigadier general by the provincial congress of Massachusetts on October 27, 1774, and commander in chief of the Massachusetts forces on May 19, 1775.[166] Although he was reluctant to take the decisive military action advocated by Putnam and Prescott that led to the Battle of Bunker Hill, Ward was a competent military man and a loyal and committed patriot.

Of Washington's first four major generals, Philip Schuyler is probably the least known today. It has been that way for quite some time— as one biographer wrote in 1860: "Of all the prominent men in public life in America during the last half of the eighteenth century, not one so really distinguished for important services as General Schuyler has received so little attention from the essayist, the historian, or the biographer, as he."[167] The same writer went on to, perhaps, give the reason: "General Schuyler's career was not brilliant but eminently useful."

Philip Schuyler was born in Albany, New York, on November 20, 1733. He served in the British army during the French and Indian War as a captain (from 1755 to 1757) and as a major (1758). He was appointed by the Continental Congress to be a Continental Army major general on June 17, 1775, and served as a member of the Congress much of this time as well. After resigning his commission in 1779, he became a New York state senator and a senator in the new federal government.[168]

An incident during the war illustrates the personal danger in which even the wealthiest and highest-ranking officers might be placed. In 1781, a group of Tories, British-allied Canadians, and Indians surrounded Schuyler's mansion in Albany, New York. The general moved his family to an upper room where he proceeded to fire at the party from a window, while making believe he was giving orders to nearby men. The ruse worked and the frightened family only suffered the loss of silverware.[169]

The fourth of Washington's major generals led a strange and varied life. Charles Lee was born in England on February 6, 1732, and thus was 16 days older than Washington. He served as a lieutenant colonel in the British Army during the French and Indian War, was wounded in an attack on Fort Ticonderoga, married the daughter of a Mohawk chief (a union Lee did not consider binding), commanded British troops at the Battle of Vila Velha in central Portugal at age 30, and was appointed a major general by King Stanislaus of Poland at age 37.

With his wealth of military experience, Lee moved from England to the Virginia colony, expecting to be selected to head the colonial army when war broke out—a rather ambitious goal considering he had been a colonist for only two years. However, the Continental Congress chose Washington instead. Lee had to settle with being one of his first four major generals, a situation he resented and which led to actions resulting in accusations of disobedience of orders and even treason. Three years after Bunker Hill, Washington would accuse Lee of "not attacking them [British forces at Battle of Monmouth] as you had been directed and in making an unnecessary, disorderly, and shameful retreat."[170] Ultimately, Lee was dismissed from the army.[171]

After meeting separately with Israel Putnam and Lee in October 1775, the Rev. Jeremy Belknap a preacher for Colonial troops, called Putnam "a rough, fiery genius" and Lee "a perfect original, a good scholar, and an odd genius, full of fire and passion, and but little good manners; a great sloven, wretchedly profane, and a great admirer of dogs." His Mohawk brethren had given Lee the name "Boiling Water" because of his quick temper.[172]

In addition to Washington and his first four major generals, there were a total of 82 additional Continental Army generals appointed during the American Revolutionary War.[173] Between December 1775 and October 1782, 25 brigadier generals were chosen who were later promoted to major general and between June 1775 and November 1783, 57 men were commissioned as brigadier generals but never promoted to become major generals.[174]

Of the 87 men who would become Revolutionary War generals between 1775 and 1783 their average age at the start of the war was 40 years old. Only five were older than Israel Putnam: Connecticut's David Wooster (8 years older) and Joseph Spencer (4 years older), and Massachusetts' Seth Pomeroy (12 years older) and Joseph Frye (7 years older), and Pennsylvania's John Armstrong (3 months older). Pomeroy, Wooster, and Spencer were appointed brigadier generals on June 22, 1775, and Frye and Armstrong in early 1776. Of the five, only Spencer would be promoted to Major General—in August of 1777.

Frye resigned at age 65, less than three months after his appointment, Armstrong resigned in 1777 at age 59, Pomeroy died in 1777 (age 70), as did Wooster, who was fatally wounded in battle when 66 years old. Spencer's resignation (at age 63 in January of 1778) left Putnam, at age 60, the oldest general in the Continental Army.

Siege of Boston

It was late June 1775, the Battle of Bunker Hill was over, the British held Boston and an American Army that was much larger than that which had just fought on the Charlestown peninsula now surrounded the city. As the British commanders discussed strategy, they also made attempts to win over the best of the American commanders. After all, most of the American leaders had been British officers about 15 years earlier.

British Colonel Small, whose life General Putnam saved at the Battle of Bunker Hill, asked to meet with Putnam.[175] Washington encouraged the meeting, and Small and Putnam met on neutral ground. Small stated:

> You must know, Putnam, that you can never ultimately succeed in your opposition. The power of Britain when it comes to be exerted, must crush you, and you'l [sic] be hanged for a Rebel. Your services in Canada the last War, are remembered—You are respected by the British Army, and I am authorized by Genl. Gage to say to you—If you will leave that Rebel service in which you are now ingaged [sic], and which must be but transient; and will join us in that which will be permanent, you shall have the same rank in the British Army as you now hold in the American. You have sons too—they also shall be provided for to your satisfaction.

Then laying his hand on the shoulder of the Genl. he said—"Putnam—you saved my life but yesterday as it were—I have a grateful heart, and wish henceforth to hail you as my friend, and never more to meet you as an enemy."[176]

Son Daniel related his father's answer to:

> "having embarked in the contest from a full conviction of the justice of the cause he should stand or fall with his Country—that it was only in defense of that country, that could ever meet Col Small as an enemy." These particulars were reported to Genl. Washington, & confidentially to his family at the time.[177]

Less than a month after Bunker Hill (July 11, 1775), Major Samuel Blachley Webb,[178] who was at Putnam's camp at Cambridge, wrote to his stepfather, Silas Deane:

Portrait of Israel Putnam published in London in 1775 by C. Shepherd. Many people in Britain were aware of Israel Putnam's role as a member of Rogers Rangers in the French and Indian War (print from Livingston's biography).

Dear Sir: Your several late letters I have received.... Gen. Putnam is a man highly esteemed by us. He has done me the Honor to appoint me his first Aid-de-Camp; since which, I have had the offer of being a Brigade Major from General Gates. They are both Honorable and agreeable Posts. I shall for the present, however, remain with Gen. Putnam. This post will cause me to lie continually with the best Company in camp; by which I hope to improve."[179]

On July 6, 1775, the Continental Congress had issued the "Declaration on the Causes and Necessity of Taking Up Arms." Twelve days later, all troops under Putnam's immediate command assembled in on Prospect Hill (which was a little northeast of Cambridge) for a public reading of it. After a patriotic address by the Rev. Abiel Leonard who was Chaplain to General Putnam's division, and a prayer, Putnam gave a signal and his men shouted "amen" with three cheers. Then a cannon was fired from the fort and a flag was displayed with "An Appeal to Heaven" on one side and "Qui transtulit sustinet" (He who transplanted sustains) on the other.[180]

In the weeks after Bunker Hill, tensions at Boston remained high. Word had it that the British government ordered General Gage to offer five thousand pounds to anyone who could bring him the head of Israel Putnam. Apparently, many of colonists in the Boston area who were loyal to Britain knew of the bounty.[181]

In September 1775, information came to American General Nathanael Greene that an encrypted letter had been found as it made its way to a British ship in Newport Harbor. Apparently, a traitor was providing information to the British and a woman was serving as an accomplice. General Putnam was assigned to ascertain their identities. The document was intercepted, and when the woman who had carried it was returning to Cambridge, she was personally arrested by General Putnam.

Shortly afterward, General Washington was looking out a window in his upstairs chamber at his Craigie House headquarters when he saw two figures on a horse galloping up to the building: Israel Putnam at the reins and an overweight woman uncomfortably positioned on the rear of the horse. It was rare for George Washington to laugh out loud, but in this case he couldn't help it.

Washington went to the top of the stairs and waited for the visitors to enter. Soon, the front door swung open and Putnam pulled the frightened woman in by her arm. Washington and Putnam demanded that she immediately confess under pain of corporal punishment. She revealed the traitorous actions of one of the most respected and committed patriots— medical doctor Benjamin Church, the first surgeon-general of the Continental Army, who had been a member of the Massachusetts Provisional Assembly and the Committee of Safety. He had given her the coded letter.

Dr. Church was arrested, tried before the Massachusetts Congress, and imprisoned in Connecticut. After months in prison, his health began to fail and he obtained permission to leave for exile in the West Indies. He departed from Boston, but apparently his ship sunk, since it was never heard from again.[182] Many years later, British General Gage's files revealed the extent of Church's spy activities.[183]

In the fall of 1775, one of Washington's colonels, 25-year-old Henry Knox, proposed retrieving cannon from New York's Fort Ticonderoga, which had been captured from the British, and transporting them by land to Boston. Incredibly, over six weeks, Knox and his men moved 60 cannon more than 300 miles in the middle of winter. In March 1776, General Washington placed the cannon on Dorchester Heights, which towered over Boston and the British fleet in Boston Harbor. With their forces now subject to attack, the British left Boston and the American troops occupied the city.

Five

Battles in New York

British Arrival at New York

In many areas of the 13 colonies, the persecution of Loyalists (those loyal to the King of England) by self-appointed patriots was epidemic. Punishments used by these vigilante-bullies included "tar and feathering," with the victim then paraded through the streets to show others what happens to "traitors." Other forms of humiliation included "liberty poles" and "riding the rails."

In New York of 1776, violence against Tories reached a fever pitch with tarring and feathering, destruction of Tory-owned printing facilities, and the burning of effigies. It also included placing victims on sharp rails with one leg on each side. Thomas Jones in his *History of New York* writes, "Each rail was carried upon the shoulders of two tall men, with a man on each side to keep the poor wretch straight and fixed in his seat. 'Numbers' were thus paraded through the streets, and at every corner loudly denounced as notorious 'Tories.'"[1]

According to Jones, General Putnam accidentally happened upon "one of the processions in the street, and shocked with its barbarity, attempted to put a stop to it." Jones states that General Washington gave "a very severe reprimand to General Putnam ... declaring that to discourage such proceedings was to injure the cause of liberty in which they were then engaged and that nobody would attempt it but an enemy to his country."[2]

"General Mifflin[3] and Putnam appealed to the Provincial Convention to stop the cruelty," wrote Jones, "But that body did not dare to condemn outright the course of the 'warm friends of liberty' and hence only disapproved of the transaction in a mild resolution."[4]

The Continental Congress minutes of June 12, 1776, state:

> Generals *Putnam* and *Mifflin* having complained to this Congress of the riotous and disorderly conduct of numbers of the inhabitants of this City, which had led this day to acts of violence towards some disaffected persons: It was therefore, *Resolved*, That this Congress by no means approve of the riots that have happened this day. They flatter themselves, however, that they have proceeded from a real regard to liberty, and a detestation of those persons who, by their language and conduct, have discovered themselves to be inimical to the cause of *America*. To urge the warm friends of liberty to decency and good order, this Congress assures the publick that effectual measures shall be taken to secure the enemies of *American* liberty in this Colony; and do require the good people of this City and Colony to desist from all riots, and leave the offenders against so good a cause to be dealt with by the constitutional Representatives of the Colony.[5]

Many states required "oaths of allegiance" and if someone refused to sign, they might be imprisoned, their property taken, sent into exile, lose they jobs, and sometimes even executed. The term lynching arose at this time. It is derived from the name of Charles Lynch (1736–1796), a Virginia justice of the peace who was noted for hunting down and punishing loyalists in his extra-legal court during the American Revolutionary War. The term "lynch law" is also derived from his name.

The year after Putnam's objection to the "railing" of civilians, his orderly book as commander of the Hudson Highland forces shows his strong opposition to any action by his soldiers that would harm civilians or their property. An order by the General on July 16, 1777, stated:

> The Genl having been informed of Damage being done to private property by the Soldiers destroying the Fences, &c. strictly forbid the Troops taking away or burning any Fence or rails to the Detriment of any particular Inclosure & expects that the Officers will take special care that this order is observed.[6]

Six days later, Putnam ordered General Parsons' brigade to take "particular care" that no individuals are injured under the pretense that they are enemies of the cause. He states there must be no complaints of soldiers of the brigade destroying fences or doing other damage.[7]

And a day after that:

> The Genl strictly forbids all persons robbing Gardens or taking any thing from the Inhabitants without leave of the Owner's or wasting or destroying private property of any kind, whereby the Inhabitants may be injured or distress'd on pain of severe punishment & all officers are strictly enjoined to see that this order is observed & complied with.[8]

Years later, at the end of the war, Tories faced problems adjusting to the new political system and living besides unforgiving neighbors. Many sold their homes and their lands and moved to England, British colonies in the Caribbean Sea, or Nova Scotia, Canada.

Battle of Long Island

After the British evacuated their troops from Boston, Washington assumed they were heading for New York City. However, they took their time, first sailing to Halifax, Nova Scotia. When they finally headed from there to New York, they joined up with a fleet of ships that had arrived directly from the British Isles.

While Washington was ordering most of his forces to converge on New York, the British moved their troops—the largest force they had ever assembled—to the shores of Brooklyn, New York. The land troops were under the command of General William Howe[9] and the naval forces were led by his brother Admiral Richard Howe.[10]

On March 29, 1776, General Washington ordered Israel Putnam to take command at New York City. The letter began:

> As there are the best reasons to believe that the Enemys Fleet & Army which left Nantasket Road last Wednesday Evening are bound to N.Y. to endeavour to Possess that Important Post & if Possible Secure the Communication By Hudsons River to Canada. it must be Our Care to prevent them their Designs.[11]

Washington ordered Putnam to assume overall command on arrival, fortify the city and secure the "Passes of the E. & N. Rivers."

Simultaneous with Putnam's movement, Washington arranged for Brigadier General Heath[12] with his riflemen and five battalions, General John Sullivan[13] and six battalions, and the rest of the available Continental Army to converge on New York City.

Washington showed every confidence in Putnam as he stated:

> Your Long Service and Experience will, better than any Particular directions at this Distance point out to you the Works most proper to be First rais'd & your Perseverance Activity & Zeal will lead you, without my recommending it to Exert every Nerve to disappoint the Enemys Designs.[14]

Putnam arrived at New York on April 3. Apparently, there was an amount of camaraderie among the American generals. General Anthony Wayne mentioned in a letter that he went fox hunting with Nathanael Greene, and was scheduled to participate in another hunt with General Israel Putnam and Colonel Thomas Mifflin.[15] Although 58 and overweight,

Putnam could still keep up with men like Wayne and Mifflin who were over a quarter century his juniors.

The television series *Liberty! The American Revolution* included an episode on the Battle of Long Island. It succulently described the arrival of the British forces: "30,000 troops. 10,000 sailors. 300 supply ships. 30 battleships with 1200 cannon. It is the largest seaborne attack ever attempted by England until the 20th century."[16] This is what Major General Israel Putnam faced with only 10,000 men and no sea support.

Livingston mentions a letter that was sent from Fort Ticonderoga by General Horatio Gates to Israel Putnam just before the Battle of Long Island. Gates humorously alludes to the fact that Putnam helped build the Crown Point fortifications during the French and Indian War. At the time this letter was written, Gates had abandoned the fort at Crown Point[17] and was strengthening his position just to the south at Fort Ticonderoga.[18]

> Tyconderoga, August 11, 1776.
>
> Dear Put: Every fond mother dotes upon her booby, be his imperfections ever so glaring, and his good qualities ever so few. Crown-Point was not indeed your own immediate offspring, but you had a capital hand in rearing the baby. You cut all the logs, which are now rotten as dirt, and tumbled in the dust. No matter for that. Why should you not be fond of Crown-Point? If I live to be as old as you I shall be as fond of Tyonderoga. I can assure you I fancy already that my booby is a great deal handsomer than yours, and has a thousand excellencies more than yours ever possessed. But don't be uneasy, the absurdities of your booby time will very soon obliterate; but mine will live for some future great engineer, like myself, to laugh at and despise.
>
> Joking apart: Have you blown up Staten Island? Have you burnt the enemy's fleet? Have you sent the two brothers [General Howe and Admiral Howe] to Hartford [American jail for British prisoners]? What have you and what have you not done? Sense, courage, honour, and abilities, you know to be the great outlines of a General. My friend Tom Mifflin [Brigadier-General Thomas Mifflin] has an uncommon share of all four. Present my affectionate compliments to him. I shall preserve your letter [probably Putnam's letter of July 26, 1776, about fire-ships and the chevaux-de-frise] for a winter evening's subject when we three meet again.
>
> Remember me affectionately, as you ought, and believe me, veteran, your sincere well-wisher and most obedient, humble servant,
>
> Horatio Gates

The American forces had fortifications in place on the southern tip of Manhattan Island; on 172-acre Governors Island, which is a little less than one-half a mile south of Manhattan; and on the western shore of Brooklyn. This part of Brooklyn consisted of fortifications at Red Hook to the south and Brooklyn Heights to the north.

As of July 1776, the British had landed thousands of troops on Staten Island and stayed there for eight weeks.

Major General Nathanael Greene led his troops through Rhode Island to New London, Connecticut, and from there sailed to New York. Upon arrival, he set up headquarters in Brooklyn. Washington had turned over to Greene the command of the entire force on Long Island while he stayed with the Manhattan forces.

Washington usually had an ability to accurately size up another person's capabilities. In the case of Greene, he judged well. As David McCullough states in *1776*: "Nathanael Greene was no ordinary man. He had a quick, inquiring mind and uncommon resolve. He was extremely hardworking, forthright, good-natured, and a born leader. His commitment to the Glorious Cause of America, as it was called, was total."[19]

When Greene became sick with a fever on August 20, just days before the battle, he was confined to bed in Manhattan to recover. On August 22, the British landed 15,000 troops. If they chose to go west instead of confronting Washington's Army, in about two days, they could reach Philadelphia, the largest city in the colonies and the home of the Continental Congress. But they didn't.

Four days before the Battle of Long Island (August 23), General Washington wrote to Congress: "I have been obliged to appoint Major General Sullivan to the command of the island, owing to General Greene's indisposition; he has been extremely ill for several days, and still continues bad."[20]

Washington, underestimating the number of British soldiers, only sent over from Manhattan about 1,500 additional men. On August 24, just three days before the battle, Washington replaced Sullivan with Putnam. Apparently, he felt that Putnam could pull off a victory just by force of his presence and legendary determination. Unfortunately, for the Americans much more was needed.

The same day that Putnam took over command, "Von Heister in command of the British auxiliaries, with Gen. Wilhelm von Knyphausen and two full brigades of Hessians,[21] landed at New Utrecht and advanced on the middle road towards Flatbush. The invading army on Long Island now numbered about twenty-one thousand well disciplined and experienced troops, supported by a large fleet in the bay."[22]

General Washington's instructions to Putnam included:

> form a proper line of defence, round your incampment and works, on the most advantageous grounds; Your guards which compose this are to be particularly instructed in their duty; & a Brigadier of the day to remain constantly upon the lines, that he may be upon the spot to command, & see that orders are executed. Field officers should also be appointed to go the rounds & report the situation of the guards; no person to be allowed to pass beyond the guards without special orders in writing.[23]

On August 26, Washington personally inspected and approved the Long Island fortifications. He also sent additional troops from Manhattan, including "Haslet's Delaware battalion, Smallwood's Marylanders,[24] two or three independent companies from Maryland, and one hundred picked men from Durkee's Connecticut Continentals, under the command of Lieut.-Colonel Thomas Knowlton." With these men, the American forces on Long Island rose to about 7,000 to 8,000."[25]

At the time of the battle, Putnam's aide-de-camp was Aaron Burr. Burr biographer James Parton relate that:

> He felt that he was formed to excel as a soldier. A mere stripling in appearance, with a stature of five feet six inches, a slender form, and a youthful face, he yet possessed a power of prolonged exertion, and a capacity for enduring privation, that were wonderful in a youth of nineteen. His courage was perfect—he never knew fear; even his nerves could not be startled by any kind of sudden horror.[26]

There were four passes through Brooklyn Heights. Three were guarded well by the American troops. The fourth, the easternmost one, Jamaica Pass, was left virtually unguarded.

On the evening of August 26, 10,000 British troops went through Jamaica Pass. At the same time, 69-year-old General Leopold Philip Von Heister[27] sent his Hessians against General Sullivan, while British General James Grant attacked General William Alexander (Lord Stirling). When Sullivan saw that the enemy was pouring though Jamaica Pass, he ordered his men to retreat to Brooklyn Heights. Stirling, seeing that he was being surrounded, ordered a retreat.

Only 400 Maryland men stood between the Continental Army and the British forces. It is said that without the protection provided by these men, the retreat would have failed, Washington's army would have been defeated, and the war would have been won by the British. Their heroism resulted in over 60 percent of the Maryland soldiers being killed or captured. Washington referred to their efforts to protect the retreating army as an "hour more precious to American liberty than any other."[28]

It's been said that Smallwood's Maryland regiment was a favorite of Greene's and when he was informed of their great casualties on his sickbed, he "burst into tears."[29]

On the 27, the Continentals lost about 1,000 men and Generals Sullivan and Sterling[30] were captured. In one of the small American victories on that day, Colonel Jedediah Huntington's Connecticut Regiment captured Battle Hill, which is Brooklyn's highest point, and, although outnumbered 6-to-1, held it through two British assaults. Battle Hill is now within the grounds of Green-Wood Cemetery, which opened in 1838.[31]

On the evening following the battle, British troops were eager to continue the fight and possibly destroy the American Army, which now had no means of retreat. Howe, ever the cautious commander, decided to wait.

Howe has been criticized by some who have claimed that it might have been an occasion when one more offensive thrust would have broken the Continental Army. However, there were strong reasons for calling it a day: Howe didn't have good intelligence on the size of the enemy force, he remembered what happened to his troops the previous year at Breed's Hill, his artillery was not in position, his troops did not have the implements needed to break through the American lines, the cornered enemy would fight with desperation, and Washington and Putnam were both personally commanding their forces on the ground. While Putnam was not at his best in the areas of strategy and tactics, in a desperate man-against-man fight there was no enemy leader the British less wanted to face than the Putnam of Bunker Hill and Rogers Rangers fame.[32]

Still the Battle of Long Island was another high point in General William Howe's career and an unusual one for a man who, as a member of Parliament just a few short years earlier, had serious doubts about the need for a war with the American colonists.

The Battle of Long Island was the first battle after the signing of the Declaration of Independence. It would also turn out to be the largest battle of the war in terms of the number of troops involved.

A few days after the battle (September 7, 1776), under General Putnam's direction, the first submarine attack in history took place in New York Harbor. Yale College graduate David Bushnell (1742–1824) had invented the first submarine to be used in warfare. In 1776, his one-man wooden "*Turtle*" (so named because of its resemblance to the reptile) was powered by a pedal-operated propeller. Its weapon was a gunpowder-filled mine that was designed to be screwed to the hull of a British ship. It would be set to explode at a set interval of time.

In his Putnam biography, David Humphreys gives a detailed description of the *Turtle*'s first use in New York Harbor during the Revolutionary War. Not being physically capable of rowing the submarine, inventor Bushnell taught his brother how to operate it. However, before the British fleet arrived, he took sick. At the last minute, a Connecticut sergeant was taught to operate the vessel. He navigated the *Turtle* against the 64-gun British warship, HMS *Eagle*. On board the ship was none other than Admiral Richard Howe.

Unfortunately for the Americans, the screw, which was designed to penetrate the ship's copper sheathing, struck the iron plates near the rudder. According to Humphreys, this problem, compounded by unexpected high tides and the inexperience of the sergeant, resulted in the operation taking much longer than anticipated. In fact, it took so long, that the first light of dawn caught the submarine still in the act of setting its charge.

Quickly, the sergeant terminated the mission, rose to the surface, and rowed back to land. Putnam saw the *Turtle* near Governor's Island and sent a whaleboat to retrieve it. Twenty minutes later the explosive charge detonated and sent a column of water high into the sky to the surprise of the British. Given that the operation had been kept secret from the Americans, as well as the British, Putnam's soldiers questioned whether the explosion was "produced by a bomb, a meteor, a water-spout or an earthquake."[33] Unfortunately, the *Turtle* did not get a second chance.

Although the *Turtle* and its one-man crew failed at its task of blowing up the British ship, the incident created anxiety among the British command, which was probably a major reason why they hesitated to advance up the East River. In the coming years, inventor Bushnell would test other variations of explosive devices that could be used against enemy vessels.

Three years after the *Eagle* episode, after David Bushnell had demonstrated his value to the American cause to Washington and Putnam, he was captured by Loyalist forces. The next day, May 7, 1779, Putnam wrote General Washington from his camp in Redding, Connecticut:

> Last night another party landed at Middlesex near Norwalk ... and the ingenious Doctor Bushnell fell into their [British] hands—As the last mentioned Gentleman [Bushnell], who was there in the prosecution of his unremitted endeavours to destroy the Enemies shipping, is personally known to very few People, it is possible he may not be discover'd by his real name or character & may be consider'd of less consequence than he actually is.[34]

As Putnam suspected, the British were not aware of Bushnell's importance to the Colonial war effort and exchanged him for British prisoners. Later, Washington assigned Bushnell to his corps of engineers.[35]

Retreat from Long Island

In testifying on the *Governors Island Preservation Act of 2001* at a hearing of the U.S. Senate Subcommittee on National Parks, former U.S. Senator Daniel Patrick Moynihan of New York spoke of Governors Island:

> If the island is little known, it is essentially because it has been a military base since the Revolutionary War and generally off limits to the public. This is no ordinary military

encampment. To the contrary, sir, it could be argued that we owe our national existence to the fortifications which General Israel Putnam threw up in April 1776 on the Buttermilk Channel side, which is just a baseball's throw from Brooklyn Heights.[36]

Senator Moynihan accurately described the immense forces facing the Americans and Putnam's role in the retreat from Long Island when he said:

> Lord Howe had arrived with the largest military force ever sent overseas by any Nation in the history of nations to put an end to this revolution then and there. There were 400 ships, 1,200 guns, 32,000 British, Scot and Hessian troops. They landed on Long Island and headed for George Washington and his army. He had to flee, and he made it just because Putnam's artillery firing on Brooklyn Heights, over the Buttermilk Channel, held Howe back just long enough for Washington to escape to Manhattan and for the Revolutionary War to proceed.[37]

On the night of August 29 through August 30, 9,000 of Washington's troops made it across the East River to Manhattan. It was said that Washington was the last man to leave Long Island.

A day after the Battle of Long Island ended, General Nathanael Greene wrote:

> Providence took me out of the way; I have been very sick for near three weeks; for several days there was a hard struggle between nature and the disorder. I am now a little better, though scarcely able to sit up an hour at a time. I have no strength or appetite, and my disorder, from its operation, appears to threaten me with long confinement. Gracious God! to be confined at such a time. And the misfortune is doubly great, as there was no general officer who had made himself acquainted with the ground as perfectly as I had. I have not the vanity to think the event would have been otherwise had I been there, yet I think I could have given the commanding general a great deal of necessary information. Great events sometimes depend upon very little causes.[38]

Writing to Connecticut Governor Jonathan Trumbull on September 12, 1776, Israel Putnam muses:

> General Howe is either our friend or no General. He had our whole army in his power on Long Island and yet suffered us to escape without the least interruption; not to escape but to bring off our wounded, our stores and our artillery. We are safe upon York Island [Manhattan] and the panic (which was at first universal) is nearly worn off. He is still with his army upon Long Island—his long stay there surprises us all. Had he instantly followed up his victory the consequence to the cause of liberty must have been dreadful.[39]

Battle of Kip's Bay

Sunday morning, September 15, 1776, General Putnam was preparing to evacuate his troops from Manhattan Island.[40] At about 11:00 a.m., he heard the sound of cannon in the distance—in the direction of Kip's Bay, an inlet of the East River about six blocks south of today's United Nations headquarters.[41]

On his way on horseback toward the sound of the gunfire, Putnam crossed the path of General Washington. Shortly before, Washington heard the noise and left his headquarters at the Morris mansion[42] in Harlem Heights (between West 160th and 162nd streets). Along with their officers, Washington and Putnam raced toward Kip's Bay. There, they discovered that the gunfire was the result of the bombardment of American positions on Manhattan Island by British General William Howe. When the firing ended, Howe landed about 4,000 British and Hessian troops at Kip's Bay.

Two militia brigades had been stationed in trenches along the East River at Kip's Bay. When Washington and Putnam arrived, they witnessed the troops in the process of a wild and embarrassing retreat. Putnam was especially disappointed since they were Connecticut men.

In an attempt to coax the fleeing troops to face the enemy, Putnam and Washington rode through them shouting commands. Washington yelling, "Take to the wall! Take to the cornfield!"[43] as he quickly rode in among the retreating men and tried to face them about. Frustrated with troops he deemed cowardly, the commanding general even resorted to using his cane to strike the men across their shoulders. It was all in vain as they had just seen the incredible number of British troops that were sweeping ashore.

General Israel Putnam from a painting by Alonzo Chappel (1828–1887). Although heavy and only 5 feet 6 inches tall, Putnam's physical strength and endurance were legendary (print from Livingston's biography).

Five. Battles in New York

Distracted even from concerns of his own safety, Washington ended up exposing himself to enemy fire. So great was the danger to him personally, that aides resorted to grabbing the bridle of his horse and directing the animal away from the heat of the battle.

As Putnam saw that the defense at Kip's Bay was hopeless, he thought of the men inland, including Gold Selleck Silliman's[44] militia brigade and [Henry] Knox's artillerymen who could be cut off from the rest of the American army by the British. Putnam raced back west to warn them off.

One man who witnessed Putnam's frantic ride was Hezekiah Munsell of Wadsworth's brigade. Coming up from his post at the bottom of East 23rd Street, he was retreating with the Army to Harlem Heights. Munsell recalled later:

> We soon reached the main road which our troops were traveling, and the first conspicuous person I met was Gen. Putnam. He was making his way towards New York, when all were going from it. Where he was going I could not conjecture, though I afterwards learned he was going after a small garrison of men in a crescent fortification, which he brought off safe. And when I passed him he was conversing with a field officer, who, as I judged from their conversation, was thinking it best to make a stand and face the enemy. This officer was crying, and I thought then, rather fuddled. Putnam in harsh language told him to "go along about his business."[45]

While Putnam was off investigating the gunfire at Kip's Bay, his aide-de-camp Aaron Burr saw that the British could cut Manhattan Island in two with one quick march westward from the East River to the Hudson River. With that in mind, he began moving his men north over the dirt roads and woods of the west side of the island. By the time Putnam caught up with them, they were struggling against heat and exhaustion. His arrival proved an inspiration and they redoubled their efforts.[46]

David Humphreys, who served as an Adjutant in the Second Connecticut Regiment of Militia on that day later wrote:

> I had frequent opportunities, that day, of beholding him [Putnam], for the purpose of issuing orders, and encouraging the troops, flying, on his horse covered with foam, wherever his presence was most necessary. Without his extraordinary exertions the guards must have been inevitably lost, and it is probable the entire corps would have been cut in pieces. When we were not far from Bloomingdale, an Aid-de-camp [Aaron Burr] came from him at full speed, to inform that a column of British infantry was descending upon our right. Our rear was soon fired upon, and the Colonel of our regiment [Jabez Thompson[47]], whose order was just communicated for the front to file off to the left, was killed on the spot. With no other loss we joined the army, after dark, on the Heights of Harlaem."[48]

Instead of commanding his troops to immediately cross the two-mile wide island, General Howe had waited until the arrival of a reinforcement of another 9,000 men. It was during that short period of time that Washington and Putnam moved their men up the shore of the Hudson River and consolidated them in Northern Manhattan.[49]

If Howe had continued west after the landing, the chances were excellent that he could have cut off Putnam's men in southern Manhattan from the rest of Washington's army on the northern end of the island. That could well have spelled the end of the revolution.

Why did Howe delay? Was it fear that he would repeat mistakes of the year before at the Battle on Bunker Hill? Was it overconfidence? Was it lack of intelligence regarding the number and distribution of American troops on Manhattan? There's a good chance it was all three.

However, another factor, perhaps the most intriguing of them all, was raised soon after the event. Was it because an American woman, who sympathizing with the Patriot cause, intentionally delayed Howe and his senior officers?

As Putnam's men were marching northward, two miles to the west, Howe and his principal officers stopped for rest and refreshment at the home of Robert and Mary Murray at the corner of Park Avenue and Thirty-Sixth Street.[50]

Army doctor James Thacher,[51] includes this story in his *Military Journal of the American Revolution*:

> Most fortunately, the British generals, seeing no prospect of engaging our troops, halted their own, and repaired to the house of Mr. Robert Murray, a Quaker and friend of our cause; Mrs. Murray treated them with cake and wine, and they were induced to tarry two hours or more, Governor [William] Tryon frequently joking [with] her about her American friends. By this happy incident, General Putnam, by continuing his march, escaped a rencounter [sic] with a greatly superior force, which must have proved fatal to his whole party. One half-hour, it is said, would have been sufficient for the enemy to have secured the road at the turn, and entirely cut off General Putnam's retreat. It has since become almost a common saying among our officers, that Mrs. Murray saved this part of the American army.[52]

Tarbox describes the British officers as "enraptured to find Mrs. Murray and her beautiful daughters ready to greet them with a warm welcome."[53] There's a story that Mary Murray stationed a maid at an upstairs window to watch until Putnam's troops were safely out of reach of the British forces.[54] Whatever the reasons for Howe's delay, it meant that Putnam's troops slipped by virtually under British noses.

The American troops marched up the west side of Manhattan for hours in grueling heat and thirst. According to David Humphreys, "few or none had canteens" and if they had been attacked on the march, they were almost too weak to resist.[55]

Fortunately, they did not need to fight again that day. The last southern Manhattan stationed troops arrived at Harlem Heights after dark. As David Humphrey's wrote in 1788: "Before our Brigades came in, we were given up for lost by all our friends."[56] There was wild cheering as each group of Americans arrived in the camp.

That night was not pleasant for the newly-arrived soldiers. In addition to the physical discomforts caused by a heavy rain, they knew that the following day might bring thousands of British troops from the south and perhaps the greatest battle of their lives.

Although General Howe missed a wonderful chance to cause a fatal blow to the Continental Army, it didn't much affect his reputation in the eyes of the King George and Parliament. They were impressed on his successes in pushing the American troops off Long Island and Manhattan Island. Ultimately his actions earned him a knighthood.

Today, in the median on Park Avenue at 37th Street, is a marker that reads:

> IN HONOR OF
> MARY LINDLEY MURRAY
> WIFE OF ROBERT MURRAY
> FOR SERVICES RENDERED HER COUNTRY
> DURING THE AMERICAN REVOLUTION,
> ENTERTAINING AT HER HOME, ON THIS SITE,
> GEN. HOWE AND HIS OFFICERS, UNTIL THE
> AMERICAN TROOPS UNDER GEN. PUTNAM ESCAPED.

Battle of Harlem Heights

By the morning of September 16, 1776, the British troops and their Hessian allies had gathered on rocky outcroppings of what is today the northern part of New York City's Central Park. Before them to the north lay the Harlem plains and, further still, the high ground where the American troops were waiting.

As soon as Washington was informed that the British troops had amassed to his south, he rode to his outposts to assess the situation. Shortly afterward, Lieutenant Colonel Thomas Knowlton and his volunteers raced back to camp after a skirmish with British soldiers. The redcoats were playing a tune on their bugles that was played after a fox hunt was over and the fox killed. Apparently meant as an insult to the American forces, it enraged Washington and his troops.

Washington sent Knowlton and Virginian Major Andrew Leitch out to circumnavigate the British and attack their rear. They were accompanied by three companies of Weedon's[57] Regiment of Virginian troops. Simultaneously, Washington sent 1,000 troops to attack the British head-on. The British, seeing what Washington was doing, sought protection behind fences and bushes, and commenced firing.

Inadvertently, Knowlton and Leitch confronted the enemy on their flank, rather than their rear. The British quickly changed direction and attacked them. Major Leitch was hit in his side by three musket balls and was carried off the field. He would die two weeks later.[58] Soon afterward, Colonel Knowlton was mortally wounded when he was shot in the back.

The troops of the two dying leaders continued on, but were in immediate danger of being overwhelmed. Seeing this, Washington ordered part of the Maryland Regiments of Colonels [Charles] Griffith and [William] Richardson,[59] and some Eastern troops to help. It was enough to cause a British retreat.

Two days later, in a letter to John Hancock from his headquarters at Colonel Roger Morris's House, Washington wrote: "These Troops charged the Enemy with great Intrepidity and drove them from the Wood into the plain, and were pushing them from thence, (having silenced their fire in a great measure)."[60]

To limit the British defeat, General Howe called up his "Reserve, with two field pieces, a battalion of Hessian Grenadiers and a company of Chasseurs."[61]

Knowing of the massive British forces to his south, Washington decided not to pursue the retreating redcoats. The total casualties in killed and wounded was roughly 100 British and 60 Americans. At the height of the battle, the American strength consisted of a little less than 2,000 troops, while the British had two-and-a-half times that number. As David Humphreys put it later, "our loss in killed, except of two valuable Officers, was very inconsiderable."[62]

However, the fact that the Americans were finally able to turn back the redcoats in an engagement meant the world to Washington's troops. Morale soared. The battle showed that the Americans could come back after their loss at the Battle of Long Island and their embarrassing retreat at Kip's Bay. It also was a sharp blow to British pride.

After having served as the American commander-in-chief for 15 months it was General Washington's first battlefield victory of the war.

Washington's general orders on the day after the battle paid tribute to "The gallant and brave Col. Knowlton, who would have been an Honor to any Country, having fallen yesterday, while gloriously fighting."[63]

Thomas Knowlton had been one of the most respected officers in the American army. Although a generation younger than Israel Putnam, Knowlton's background was very much like that of Putnam: both men had been born in Massachusetts, had become Connecticut farmers, had distinguished records in the French and Indian War as members of Rogers Rangers, and had fought with the British at the capture of Spanish Cuba (Knowlton had been in Putnam's company). In addition, both had large families: Knowlton had nine children; Putnam ten.[64]

Promoted to lieutenant colonel in early 1776, Knowlton formed Knowlton's Rangers which engaged in dangerous intelligence work for the Continental Army. The best known of Knowlton's spies was the 21-year-old Connecticut schoolteacher, Nathan Hale.

Perhaps the most well known phrase used in relation to Thomas Knowlton was "You cannot lead from behind." This was quite similar to a common phrase relating to Israel Putnam from the time of the French and Indian War: "Rogers always sent, but Putnam led his men to action."

Interestingly, Putnam's old commander from the French and Indian War, Robert Rogers, was instrumental in the death of Nathan Hale. After being denied a command in the Continental Army by Washington himself, Rogers, never one to abide by exalted principles, turned to the British. In late 1776, he was in New York drumming up recruits for his new pro–British commando force, the Queen's Rangers, when he met Hale. The young Yale graduate was no match for the wily ways of the amoral man-of-the-world Rogers. As James Hutson, chief of the Manuscript Division at the Library of Congress, states, such a ruse was perfectly in character for Rogers, who was once described by a comrade as "subtil & deep as hell itself."[65]

In 2003 a manuscript was donated to the Library of Congress that provided evidence that Rogers was instrumental in getting Nathan Hale apprehended and executed. According to its author, Loyalist Consider Tiffany, Rogers convinced the young Hale that he was also a spy for the Continental Army. The author of the manuscript, states that Rogers convinced Hale that "he had found a good friend, and one that could be trusted with the secrecy of the business he was engaged in; and after the Colonel's drinking a health to the Congress: informs Rogers of the business and intent."[66] Rogers then invited Hale to dinner where he was arrested by British soldiers on September 21, 1776. It was five days after the Battle of Harlem Heights.

Nathan Hale was hanged without trial the following day at an unknown location in New York City. Hale's last words, "I only regret that I have but one life to lose for my country," are some of the most famous and inspirational, in American history. After plying his trade with his Queen's Rangers, and later his King's Rangers, Robert Rogers left for England, where years later he died in obscurity.

One veteran of the Battle of Harlem Heights was future U.S. president James Monroe. A lieutenant in Col. Weedon's Virginia regiment, Harlem Heights was the first of several major battles in which he would participate.

Today, at least three markers in northern Manhattan commemorate the battle: a bronze plaque near Grant's Tomb at 121st Street and Riverside Drive,[67] a small stone marker on Broadway between 147th and 148th Streets,[68] and a plaque on the side of Columbia University's mathematics building at its Morningside campus.

One minor incident, which occurred around this time, gives an idea of what it was like to meet up with General Putnam if you were an unruly private. Joseph Plumb Martin in his 1830 memoir recalls that early one morning he was returning alone to his quarters from guard duty when he saw

> Gen. Putnam on horseback and alone, coming up the road in my rear. In my front, and nearer to me than I was to the General, was a high fence and a set of high and very heavy bars, composed of pretty large poles or young trees…. The General seeing me near the bars, bawled out, "Soldier, let down those bars." I was then at the bars, but seeing that the General was some distance off, I took down one bar, and slipped through, leaving him to let down the bars himself. He was apparently in a dreadful passion; drawing a pistol from his holsters, he came after me to the bars, with his usual exclamation—but I was where he could not see me, although I could see him, and hear him too—I was safe, and perhaps it was well for me that I was; for I verily believe the old fellow would have shot me, or endeavoured to have done it, if he could have got within reach of me.[69]

Battle of White Plains

In late October 1776, General William Howe and his British troops controlled New York City—it had been three months since they had landed on Staten Island and two months since they won the Battle of Long Island. The British had hope that they might take complete control of the Hudson River and physically split the 13 colonies in two. That could lead to the destruction of Washington's Continental Army.

In fighting on October 18 at Throg's Neck (in the southeastern Bronx where the East River meets Long Island Sound)[70] and Pell's Point in the

Bronx, Washington's soldiers delayed the British. On October 20 Washington sent Israel Putnam's cousin Rufus Putnam on a reconnaissance mission to ascertain the location of British troops. Based on his intelligence, the Commander-in-Chief began movement of the Army from Harlem toward White Plains in Westchester County, leaving only Nathanael Greene's troops to defend Fort Washington.[71] This would prevent a British effort to isolate Washington's entire force on Manhattan between the Hudson and East Rivers and break the Continental Army supply lines.

As the confrontation at White Plains began, each side numbered about 13,000 men. Participants included Continental Army soldiers from Delaware, Maryland, Connecticut, Pennsylvania, and New York, as well as numerous state militia, and some Native American allies. British forces included their regular troops, pro–British Loyalists, Hessian mercenaries, and Native Americans.

Washington sent Rufus Putnam to mark a line of defense on the hill. Rufus later stated:

> I had just arrived on Chatterton hill in order to throw up some works when they [the British] hove in sight. As soon as they discovered us, they commenced a severe cannonade, but without any effect of consequence. General McDougall about this time arriving with his brigade, from Burtis, & observing the British to be crossing the Bronx below in large bodies in order to attack us, our troops were posted to receive them in a very advantageous position. The British were twice repulsed in their advance. At length, however, their numbers were increased so that they were able to turn our right flank. We lost many men, but from information afterwards received, there was reason to believe they lost many more than we did.[72]

The British and Hessian troops stormed the American stronghold on Chatterson Hill near White Plains. After heavy fighting, they succeeded in driving the Americans off the hill. The last to leave were some of General McDougall's troops, who made an organized retreat. They were followed off the hill by the enemy, who only stopped when they were confronted by General Putnam's troops who, shooting from behind trees and fences, were covering the retreat.

Rufus then compares the battle with the Bunker Hill battle which took place almost 1½ years earlier: "The wall and stone fence behind which our troops were posted proved as fatal to the British as the rail fence and grass hung on it did at Charlestown the 17th of June 1775."[73]

Each side suffered approximately 300 casualties, including about 50 men killed in the action. When Washington ordered his troops to retreat, General Howe (as usual) delayed pursuing them, bad weather intervened, and the American forces escaped.

The 1850 edition of Humphreys's biography states:

> General Putnam was with the army at White-Plains, and took part in the action fought there the 28th of October. It was the position of Brigadier-General M'Dougal which was attacked, and Washington ordered a detachment of the army under Major-General Putnam to support him. Some days after this action, General Putnam was ordered to cross the Hudson, and provide against an irruption [sic] of the enemy into New Jersey. He was soon followed by Washington with part of his army, which took post in the vicinity of Fort Lee, and, after the fall of that Fort, General Putnam was constantly about his person during the whole retreat through New Jersey, and among the last of the fugitive army which crossed the Delaware....[74]

Instead of pursuing the Colonials after the Battle of White Plains, the British turned west. Washington was faced with a dilemma: were the British merely attempting to create a ruse whereby they would circle back and attack again, or were they headed toward Fort Washington on the Hudson or maybe even to the American capital of Philadelphia. Washington needed to cover all bases by sending out small parties to follow, and where possible hinder, the British troops. Howe later turned back south to attack Fort Washington.

Thirty-eight-year-old Colonel Robert Magaw, the American commander of Fort Washington, stated that he could hold out under siege until December, while engineer Rufus Putnam, who had supervised construction of the fort declared that it could withstand any attack. Confident of the strength of the fort and the ability of his troops to defend it, General Greene sent over substantial reinforcements.

On November 15, British General Howe presented Colonel Magaw with an ultimatum: surrender the fort or all of his men, upon its defeat, would be killed. Magaw replied that he doubted that Howe would follow through on a threat "so unworthy of himself and the British nation; but give me leave, to assure His Excellency that, actuated by the most glorious cause that mankind ever fought in, I am determined to defend this post to the very last extremity."[75]

On the evening of the 15, Nathanael Greene sent for General Washington, asking him to review the situation. Meanwhile Greene and General Putnam crossed the Hudson River and assured themselves that Fort Washington could resist an attack. On their way back to Fort Lee, at mid-river, they were met by Washington's boat. They assured the commander-in-chief that the fort's troops were in good spirits, and that they could defend the fort.[76]

On November 16 the British attacked Fort Washington. They were supported by Hessian troops that were personally led by General Wilhelm von Knyphausen.[77] In addition to superior numbers, they had the benefit of good intelligence—on November 2, Colonel Magaw's adjunct, William Demont headed south, crossed enemy lines, and gave British general Hugh

Percy the sketches of Fort Washington's defenses.[78] A competent commander, Percy immediately sent the information and the deserter to his superior, General Howe.[79]

Months earlier, General Putnam had had old ships sunk across the Hudson to prevent passage of British vessels. But they weren't enough to stop the British warships on November 16. British ships sailed up the Hudson River, slipped by Forts Washington and Lee, and avoided the sunken wrecks. British troops in the surrounding hills opened cannon fire on the fort and its outlying installations. Many Americans sought refuge in Fort Washington.

Three thousand Americans fought valiantly to defend the fort against about 8,000 Hessian and British troops. One notable hero was Margaret Corbin who served ammunition to her husband John, who was manning a cannon. When he was killed, she took over the cannon until she was badly wounded. She was taken across the river to Fort Lee where she received medical care, but she suffered from the effects of her wounds for the rest of her life.[80]

General Howe planned to attack the fort from the east, south and west and forced almost every colonial soldier to seek shelter within the fort's walls. The final blow was struck when Hessian troops scaled the north wall of the fort. There was not much Magaw could do at that point except surrender.

Fortunately, Howe did not follow through on his threat to murder all defenders of the fort, of which over 2,800 remained, including Colonel Magaw.[81] Unfortunately, most of them were headed to be abused as prisoners of war. They were marched to the Presbyterian and Reformed Dutch Churches in New York City where "through neglect, cold, famine, and disease they died in great numbers."[82] Many others ended up on the notorious British prison ships in New York harbor.

The battle ended with almost 60 Colonial soldiers dead. Slightly more British troops were killed and about 350 were wounded. Also, a great store of armaments and supplies fell to the enemy. The importance of the Hessian contributions to the critical success, was highlighted five days after the battle when Fort Washington was renamed Fort Knyphausen

With Fort Washington lost, its across-the-river sister, Fort Lee was ripe for the picking, Washington ordered the latter fort cleared of armaments and supplies that could be used by the enemy. Most were able to be removed before the Americans abandoned the fort to the British.

With the two important Hudson River forts lost, Washington's main objective was to protect Philadelphia and to that end he dispatched Israel Putnam.

Six

War in the North

Protection of Philadelphia

On December 9, 1776, Continental Congress President John Hancock[1] wrote to General Washington: "Under these Circumstances, the Security of Philadelphia should be our next Object...." He continued:

> In the mean time every Step should be taken to collect Force not only from Pennsylvania but from the most neighbourly States, if we can keep the Enemy from entering Philadelphia and keep the Communication by Water open, for Supplies, we may yet make a Stand, if the Country will come to our Assistance, till our new Levies can be collected.
>
> If the Measure of fortifying the City should be adopted, some Skillful person should immediately view the Grounds and begin to trace out the Lines and Works. I am informed there is a French Engineer [Tadeusz Kosciuszko, who was Polish, but had studied in France] of eminence in Philadelphia at this time. If so he will be the most proper.
>
> I have just recd the inclosed from Genl Heath. Genl Mifflin is this Moment come up and tells me that all the Military Stores yet remain in Philadelphia. This makes the immediate fortifying of the City so necessary that I have desired Genl Mifflin to return to take Charge of the Stores, and have ordered Major Genl Putnam immediately down to superintend the Works and give the necessary Directions.[2]

The residents of Philadelphia were concerned about their safety, as well as their property, should the city turn into a battleground. The supporters of Washington's army among them were especially worried about what a British takeover would mean for them.

Putnam's main task was now to defend the city of Philadelphia from the British, while satisfying the demands of the Continental Congress, as well as those of Commander-in-Chief Washington. He was encouraged to take the proactive measures that he preferred. On December 11, the Continental Congress passed the motion

> That General Putnam be directed to order parties of active, spirited men, with proper guides, to cross from this city into Jersey; and, under the conduct of good officers, to act as harassing parties, and get the best intelligence of the motions and situation of the enemy, directing them to send frequent daily intelligence thro' him to Congress, of the discoveries they be able to make of the enemies movements and situation.[3]

These assignments must have brought Putnam's thoughts back to his time two decades earlier when he fought with Rogers Rangers. Now, although only about a year before he would turn sixty, Putnam probably would have been more at home personally leading such missions than he would be dealing with politicians.

On December 12, 1776, Congress resolved: "That General Putnam be authorized to employ all the private armed vessels in this harbour, for the defence and security of the city. And that he take the most effectual measures for manning them, and putting them in fit condition for the above purpose."[4]

On the same day, the Congress passed this measure:

> That General Putnam, or the commanding officer in Philadelphia, be desired to appoint suitable persons to make proper provision of combustibles, for burning such of the frigates and other continental vessels as may be in imminent danger of falling into the enemies' possession should this city come into their hands.

Congress was especially concerned with the 32-gun frigate, *Randolph*:

> But when it shall happen that the General has no further occasion for the use of the frigate, *Randolph*, for the defence of this city, if the same should fall into the enemies hands, should Captain [Nicholas] Biddle in that case carry the said frigate safely to sea, and thereby save her from falling into the enemies hands, this Congress will reward him and his people with a present of 10,000 dollars.[5]

With the 26-year-old Biddle commanding, *The Randolph* successfully left Philadelphia for sea in February 1777. On March 7, 1778, as the *Randolph* was escorting a merchant convoy in the Caribbean (about 150 miles east of Barbados), it engaged battle with the British ship *HMS Yarmouth*, which outgunned it two to one. A shot from the *Yarmouth* exploded gunpowder on the *Randolph's* deck, killing all but four of the 315 crew members, including Captain Biddle.[6] It would be over 160 years before an American military ship would suffer a greater loss of life—at World War II's Pearl Harbor.

Humphreys describes Putnam's command in the colonial capital:

> While the hostile forces ... had been pursuing the wretched remnants of a disbanded army to the banks of the Delaware, General Putnam was diligently employed in

fortifying Philadelphia, the capture of which appeared indubitably to be their principal object. Here, by authority and example, he strove to conciliate contending factions, and to excite the citizens to uncommon efforts in defence of every thing interesting to Freemen. His personal industry was unparalleled. His Orders with respect to extinguishing accidental fires, advancing the public works, as well as in regard to other important objects, were perfectly military and proper. But his health was, for a while, impaired by his unrelaxed exertions.[7]

From his headquarters in Philadelphia on December 14, 1776, Putnam issues the following orders:

> Colonel Griffin is appointed Adjutant General to the troops in and about this city. All Orders from the General [Putnam], through him, either written or verbal, are to be strictly attended to and punctually obeyed.
>
> In case of an alarm of fire, the city guards and patroles are to suffer the inhabitants to pass unmolested at any hour of the night; and the good people of Philadelphia are earnestly requested and desired to give every assistance in their power, with engines and buckets, to extinguish the fire. And, as the Congress have ordered the City to be defended to the last extremity, the General hopes that no person will refuse to give every assistance possible to complete the Fortifications that are to be erected in and about the City.[8]

Putnam described the situation in Philadelphia in a letter to Washington:

> All things in this city remain in confusion, for want of men to put them in order. The citizens are generally with you. The Continental recruits are clothing and arming as fast as possible, and are employed on guard and fatigue duty, for which there is scarce a relief. A party are now going to the Jerseys, to bring off all the craft out of the creeks.... The Council of Safety have this day issued orders for every able-bodied man to be enrolled and put to work in throwing up the lines. I have reconnoitred the ground round the city, in company with General Mifflin, and the French Engineers, who are preparing a draft of the lines, which we are to begin to-morrow. The principal stores are removed to Christiana Bridge.[9]

On December 12, Putnam established martial law in Philadelphia via this general order:

> The late advances by the enemy towards this place oblige the General to request the inhabitants of this city not to appear in the streets after ten o'clock at night, as he has given orders to the piquet-guard to arrest and confine all persons who may be found in the streets after that hour. Physicians and others having essential business, are directed to call at Head-quarters for passes.[10]

In consequence of a rumor that Philadelphia was to be burned by the Patriots to prevent the city's possible capture by the British, Putnam issued the following on December 13, 1776:

> The General has been informed that some weak or wicked men have maliciously reported that it is the design and wish of the officers and men in the Continental Army to burn and destroy the city of Philadelphia. To counteract such a false and scandalous

report, he thinks it necessary to inform the inhabitants who propose to remain in the city, that he has received positive orders from the honourable Continental Congress, and from his Excellency General Washington, to secure and protect the city of Philadelphia against all invaders and enemies. The General will consider every attempt to burn the city of Philadelphia as a crime of the blackest dye, and will, without ceremony, punish capitally any incendiary who shall have the hardness and cruelty to attempt it.[11]

Putnam enlisted the citizens of the city in military service, reluctantly exempting Quakers. Though he did not press the issue, he spoke with contempt for the Quaker belief in nonviolence. Putnam had never before lived in a society where Quakers composed as large a portion of the population as they did in Pennsylvania. One Quaker he had worked closely with, General Nathanael Greene, hadn't followed the tenets of his faith that dealt with nonviolence.

Perhaps most of the American generals harbored some anti–Quaker resentment. Even, Washington, who prided himself on encouraging toleration of oppressed religious minorities like the Jewish people, stated in a 1789 letter to a Quaker meeting:

Your principles & conduct are well known to me—and it is doing the People called Quakers no more than Justice to say, that (except their declining to share with others the burthen [burden] of the common defence) there is no Denomination among us who are more exemplary and useful Citizens.[12]

In his 1898 *Memorial History of the City of Philadelphia*, John Young states:

The course pursued by the Philadelphia Tories, and especially the rich Quakers, during the first two years of the war, was more detrimental to the cause of independence than the royal armies under Sir John Burgoyne and Sir William Howe. Refusing to take the Continental money, or even the depreciated paper currency of the province, the disaffected merchants bought salt and provisions with the coin they had in hand, until the greatest scarcity prevailed. Prices rose enormously.[13]

Young states: "Salt rose from two to twenty-five shillings a bushel, and the cost of all the necessaries of life was doubled and tripled."[14]

Putnam's work in Philadelphia was not easy. Many residents seriously considered the British offer of amnesty. On the other hand, supporters of the Patriot cause needed to be encouraged to defend the city. Sometimes Putnam's orders appeared harsh. For instance, the Continental Congress had issued too much currency causing it to rapidly depreciate. The only way Putnam could achieve some measure of control was to dictate that it would be a criminal offense to refuse to accept it at its face value.[15]

In mid–December, upon the recommendation of Putnam and General Mifflin, Congress voted to move to Baltimore, Maryland. At the same time, according to a letter by Connecticut delegate Oliver Wolcott, Congress ordered Putnam to defend Philadelphia "to the last extremity, and God grant that he may be successful in his exertions."[16]

Apparently, the efforts to move Congress and defend the city from both British invaders, as well as Tories from within, took a toll on Putnam's health. It wasn't until the end of the month that he was able to write Washington to assure him he was on the mend.[17]

On Christmas Eve 1776, Putnam was presented with one of the biggest secrets of the war. Adjutant-General [Joseph] Reed[18] arrived at his headquarters with news that the Commander-in-Chief was about to attack the Hessian mercenaries at Trenton, New Jersey. Reed inquired about the possibility of Putnam providing troops for a diversion into New Jersey.[19]

The next day, Reed wrote to a fellow commander:

> General Putnam has determined to cross the river with as many men as he can collect, which he says will be about 500; he is now mustering them and endeavouring to get Proctor's company of artillery to go with them. I wait to know what success he meets with, and the progress he makes; but at all events I shall be with you this afternoon.[20]

But it was not to be. Putnam had received intelligence that the Philadelphia Tories were set to take over the city as soon as he left. Consequently, he decided to withhold the troops.

In December 1776, Washington made his legendary crossing of the icy Delaware River and went on to surprise a garrison of Hessian soldiers at Trenton, winning the most perfect victory of the War: capturing 1,000 enemy soldiers and suffering no deaths and only six injuries. Interestingly, one of those six was an 18-year-old lieutenant named James Monroe who would 40 years later be elected the fifth president of the United States and become the only president besides Washington who would be a veteran of the Continental Army in the Revolutionary War.[21]

The Hessians captured at Trenton were brought to Philadelphia where they were marched through the streets along with their flags. Soldiers were moved from their barracks to make room for the new prisoners. On New Year's Day, the Hessian officers were taken to Putnam's headquarters where they were invited to partake of a glass of wine. One Hessian later wrote: "He shook hands with each of us, and we all had to drink a glass of Madeira with him. This old gray-beard may be a good, honest man, but nobody but the rebels would have made him a general."[22] Even some of the city's prim and proper elite spoke disparagingly of Putnam. Livingston remarks that "certain fastidious Philadelphians had expressed great surprise that the unpolished Yankee fighter was ever made a general."[23]

Many of Washington's generals were vain and prideful men and would have taken great offense at the Hessian's remark. However, if Putnam could have known that more than two centuries later, the brief comment was still being quoted, he likely would have had a good laugh.

Immediately after the Trenton victory, Washington wrote Putnam to inform him that his sources had revealed that the British would be moving against Philadelphia as soon as the Delaware River was iced up enough to allow the transport of their artillery. Concerned for the defense of the city, he suggested to Putnam that militia colonel David Forman,[24] be sent in to head the efforts.[25] Forman, who a few months later became a brigadier general in the New Jersey militia, was nicknamed "Devil David" because of his obsession with hunting down Loyalists.[26]

One incident associated with Israel Putnam's time in Philadelphia relates to the development of the first American flag. According to one legend, Putnam asked for seamstress Betsy Ross's help in creating the flag.

Twenty-four years old in 1776, Betsy Ross was running her own upholstery shop in Philadelphia.[27] In one story, she was approached by George Washington and other members of a Continental Congress committee, with the request to sew a new American flag. Washington presented her with a version of today's stars and stripes, but with six-pointed stars. Betsy Ross asked why he had not made them five-pointed, to which he replied, it was too difficult to manufacture stars with five points. Ross was said to pick up a pair of scissors and demonstrate that it could easily be done, and Washington changed his mind.

A second version of this story is basically the same, except it has Putnam as the person who met with Ross and proposed the six-pointed stars. Either way, the following year, 1777, the Continental Congress adopted the stars and stripes as the first flag of the new nation.[28]

The main argument for Putnam's involvement with the new flag stems from a letter he received from Washington on May 28, 1776. Washington's postscript stated: "I desire you'l speak to the Several Colonls & Hurry them to get their Colours done."[29] Did this charge to Putnam lead to a meeting between Putnam and Betsy Ross? Unless some new documentation is found, it is unanswerable.

Battle of Princeton

After the Continental Army's Trenton victory in December 1776, British General Cornwallis sent a force of 8,000 men to intercept Washington before he could escape the area. Washington did escape, and in the process engaged one of the enemy detachments, killing 275 British soldiers and only suffering the loss of 40 American troops.

On January 3, 1777, about 200 British soldiers were occupying the College of New Jersey's Nassau Hall (now Princeton University). American General John Sullivan ordered a cannon brought to high ground. One cannonball hit the two-foot-thick sandstone wall of Nassau Hall, where its mark is visible today. Another shot traveled through the faculty room and destroyed a painting of King George II. Later the frame was used to hold a painting of George Washington. The story goes that the cannon ball was fired by Alexander Hamilton.[30]

One often-repeated description of Hamilton at that time is revealing of the impression he made on other people. An observer remarked:

> Well do I recollect the day, when Hamilton's company marched into Princeton. It was a model of discipline; at its head was a boy, and I wondered at his youth; but what was my surprise, when struck with his diminutive figure, he was pointed out to me as that Hamilton of whom we had already heard so much.[31]

Humphreys tells an interesting story of a Captain John McPherson, who Putnam found seriously wounded after the Battle of Princeton. Almost assuredly repeating what Putnam told him, Humphreys states:

> Captain McPherson, of the 17th British Regiment, a very worthy Scotchman, was desperately wounded in the lungs and left with the dead. Upon General Putnam's arrival there, he found him languishing in extreme distress, without a surgeon, without a single accommodation, and without a friend to solace the sinking spirit in the gloomy hour of death. He visited and immediately caused every possible comfort to be administered to him.[32]

While apparently dying, McPherson asked if Putnam would allow a friend in the British Army to visit to help him prepare his last will and testament. Putnam was just the kind of man to approve such a request—he had the ability to separate the demands of war from the need to show compassion to other human beings. However, in this case it would be difficult to comply since a visitor could easily detect that Putnam's command was depleted—in fact, at the time, he only had 50 men in camp.

Under a flag of truce, one of Putnam's men left for the British camp. He made a point to return with McPherson's friend after dark. Meanwhile, Putnam ordered candles lit in scores of windows through the camp and the town. Humphreys relates: "During the whole night, the fifty men, sometimes altogether, and sometimes in small detachments, were marched from different quarters, by the house in which McPherson lay." Later, it was learned that the visitor reported back to his superiors that Putnam's forces "could not consist of less than four or five thousand men."[33]

Six. War in the North

Captain McPherson survived his wounds. Sometimes afterward, he was speaking with Putnam and asked his captor:

> "Pray, Sir, what countryman are you?"
> "An American," answered the latter.
> "Not a Yankee?" said the other.
> "A full-blooded one," replied the General.
> "By G—d, I am sorry for that," rejoined McPherson, "I did not think there could be so much goodness and generosity in an American, or, indeed, in anybody but a Scotchman."[34]

That winter Putnam encamped with his troops in Princeton, where he directed his men on against British foraging parties. They captured almost 1,000 prisoners and "more than 120 baggage wagons and large quantities of provisions and other booty."[35] With Putnam at Princeton, Washington's troops spent the winter (January 6, 1777, to May 28, 1777) at Morristown, New Jersey, which was about 40 miles north of Princeton.

It may seem unusual today, but in the 18th century it was common for armies in cold climates to cease all major fighting during the winter months. During the Revolutionary War, Washington would carefully scout out locations where his troops could camp from approximately December until the spring thaw. The most famous (and infamous) of the American winter encampments was the following year's Valley Forge. Located about 20 miles from Philadelphia, Pennsylvania, it was a place where over 2,000 American soldiers died of disease, starvation and exposure.

Disease and Punishment

The problem of disease in a Revolutionary War camp was never ending. At the beginning of the war, Washington gave orders that the troops not be inoculated from smallpox. He knew that a certain percentage of the people inoculated would die of the disease (in the 18th Century maybe as high at 2 or 3 percent), even though the others would become immune to it. He also was aware that it would take weeks for the inoculated soldiers to recover, and if the British army struck during those times, battles could be lost. On the other hand, if his soldiers were not immune and the British made a large-scale attack at the height of an epidemic, the result could be at least as catastrophic.

In 1776, a doctor in Washington's Army named Azor Betts was imprisoned for giving several officers smallpox inoculations. Later, Betts defected to the British and served them as an officer and physician.[36]

At the beginning of 1777, Washington reversed himself and ordered a smallpox inoculation program.[37] Significantly, most British troops had already been inoculated from smallpox.

After two years of war, John Adams wrote to his wife Abigail on April 13, 1777:

> I took a walk into the [Philadelphia] Potter's field, a burying ground between the new stone prison and the hospital ... during the course of the last summer fall and winter dead of the small pox and camp diseases are enough to make the heart of stone to melt away. The sexton told me that upwards of two thousand soldiers had been buried there and by the appearance of the graves and trenches it is most probable to me he speaks within bounds.... Disease has destroyed ten men for us, where the sword of the enemy has killed one.[38]

This entry in Israel Putnam's orderly book for July 6, 1777, shows his concern for smallpox and the seriousness of violating quarantine:

> The Genl is resolved to prevent the small Pox from spreading among the Troops or Militia who are arriving. For this Purpose all Officers & Soldiers who appear to be infected shall be immediately removed to the small pox Hospital, & nowhere else. He expects the Officers will exert themselves for the exact Observance of this Order & he assures them that every infected Person who presumes to go more than a Hundred Yards from the small Pox Hospital without a Certificate from the Surgeon, that he is sufficiently cleans'd, shall be treated [as] a Common Enemy, be the Consequences ever so fatal.[39]

This orderly book gives numerous examples of cases of misconduct that range from the most minor offenses to treason. One man was tried on September 4, 1777, at a court-martial for

> fireing his gun at a party of fatigue men as they was Coming from Work and uncaping another Cartradg to fire again are found Guilty of the Charge But are of Appinan that the Prisoner Ment to fire at one Barns Who had thretned to kill his wife the Court therfore Sentance the Prisoner to set upon the gallos half an hour with A halter Round his neck and then to receave 50 Lashes on his naked Back at the gallos the generl aproves the Sentance and orders it to be Put in Execution tomorrow at 9 oclock.[40]

Given Putnam's less than perfect spelling and punctuation skills, this was most likely written by the General himself.

With hundreds or thousands of men in camp, and without any jails or prisons nearby, swift corporal punishment was often the only practical means of maintaining law and order. Whether an offence was spying for the enemy or just being lazy, it was the direct concern of the General. Here's an entry in Putnam's orderly book for August 19, 1777:

> the general takes notice that the greatest Loads Drawn in Carts and Wagons are of hearty & well men Whereby the Teams are greatly Woryed he orders that no Soldier Ride in Carts or Wagons Except the Drivers and Sick Who are ordered to be Carryd on Pain of Being Whipt 20 Lashes on the naked Back.[41]

The following entries in Putnam's orderly book for July 7, 1777, relates the results of the most recent court-martial that the General had ordered. It gives a good indication of the type and severity of punishment that was meted out.

> Wm. Ross of Capt. [James] Eldridge's Comy late Col. [Jedidiah] Huntington's Regiment, for attempting to desert to the Enemy. The Court sentence the Prisoner to receive one Hundred Lashes upon the naked back.
> John Wilds of Capt. [Martin] Kirtland's Company, late Col. [William] Douglass's Regt, for desertion the second time. The Court having no proof before it of the First Desertion; but for the Crime against the Prisoner of Desertion the second time, sentence Prisoner to receive one Hundred Lashes on his bare back.
> John Thompson of Capt [John] Mills Comy, Col. Charles Webb's Regiment, tryed for deserting from & inlisting into three Different Regts. and taking Continental Bounty [money given for enlisting]. The Court considering the Circumstances of the Prisoner being an old and worthless person, sentence him to receive one hundred lashes and then to be drum'd out of Camp with a Halter about his Neck as a Rogue and Rascall.[42]

The orderly book included any and all orders, from items lost and found to capital punishment cases, as seen in these entries from July 15, 1777:

> At a Genl Court Martial held at Phillipsburgh on Sunday, July 13th, 1777, by order of Philip Van Cortlandt.
> Thomas Powall private in Capt. [Charles] Graham's Co Col. Cortlandt's Regt, was tried for Deserting to the Enemy returning & deserting again & persuading other Soldiers to desert with him, found guilty & sentenced to be shot to Death. The Genl approves the Sentence, & orders it to be executed on Monday next the 21st of this Instant between the Hours of ten & Eleven in the Morning.
> B. Genl Parson's Brigade hath Liberty to discharge their Pieces at Retreat Beating this Evening under the Directions of their Officers.
> The Bridge Guard to be augmented to 30 privates.
> Lost on the Road from White Plains the day before yesterday, a large leather pocket Book, Saml Brown wrote on it, two 30 Dollr Bills, three [?] York Bills, one 6d Do a number of papers—if the Pocket Book should be found, it is ordered to be bro't to Head Quarters.[43]

One of the capital cases at this time has gone down in the history books because of Putnam's response to the British Governor of New York. Brigade Orders of July 18, 1777, noted:

> Edmund Palmer that Noted Tory a Robber Was taken Prisoner & Confined in ye Provost Guard for Robing the Inhabitence & Leving war Against his Country: is to have his Tryal Next Tuesday at 9 o'clock in the Morning by A General Court Marshel all Parsons that Can give Evidence Against sd Palmer are Requested & Required to Attend the Trial.[44]

The orderly book five days later stated:

Edmund Palmer was arraigned & tried upon a Charge of Plundering, robbing & carrying off Cattle, Goods, &c. from the well-affected Inhabitants & for being a Spy for the Enemy. The Court finds him guilty of the whole Charge alledged against him, & sentence him to suffer the Pains of Death. The Genl approves the Sentence & orders it to be put in Execution on Fryday, the 1st. of next August ensuing between the Hours of 9 & 11 in the Morning—by hanging him up by the Neck till he is dead, dead, dead.[45]

According to David Humphreys, British Governor Tryon heard that Palmer had been taken prisoner by Putnam's forces, and claiming him to be a British officer, wrote to Putnam threatening vengeance if he was executed. Putnam replied to Tryon[46]:

Sir,
Nathan Palmer, a Lieutenant in your King's service, was taken in my Camp as a Spy—he was tried as a Spy—he was condemned as a Spy—and you may rest assured, Sir, he shall be hanged as a Spy.
I have the honor to be, &c.
Israel Putnam
P.S. Afternoon.
He is hanged.[47]

The Orderly Book entry for July 22, 1777, is robust:

Henry Hercules Hoff, private in Col. [Henry B.] Livingston's Regt tried at the above Court for Desertion, found guilty & sentenced to receive one Hundred Lashes on his naked back.
Saml Fosdick of Col. Livingston's Regt tried by sd Court for Desertion, found guilty, & sentenced to receive 50 Lashes on his naked back.
Thos Doyle tried by sd Court for Desertion, found guilty & sentenced to receive 100 Lashes on his naked back.
Thos Colvill of Col. Saml B. Webb's Regt, tried by sd Court for Desertion, found guilty & sentenced to receive 50 Lashes on his naked back.
Edward Murphey of Lt Col. [Jeremiah] Olney's Detachment tried for Desertion found guilty & sentenced to receive 100 Lashes on his naked back.
Henry Williams of Col. [Heman] Swift's Regt, tried for perswading Soldiers to desert, found guilty & sentenced to receive 100 Lashes on his naked Back.
The Genl approves the several Sentences & orders them to be executed to-morrow morning at Guard Mounting on the grand parade.
The Genl is sorry that he is so frequently put to the disagreeable Necessity of ordering Punishments to be inflicted owing to the great Frequency of Crimes, the Perpetration of which renders punishments absolutely necessary for the Reformation of Offenders, & to deter others in order to maintain that Subordination, Order & Regularity which is necessary for the well-being of an Army—earnestly recommends it to all the Soldiers to take Warning by the Sufferings of others: for tho his Eye pities their Sufferings, his justice will not spare their Crimes, & so to behave as to give as little Occasion for the disagreeable Employment of inflicting punishment as possible & to prevent what he imagines to be one principle cause of such irregular Conduct, vizt [] drinking spirituous Liquors to Excess, he strictly forbids the Soldiers frequenting taverns, Tippling Houses, or Sutler's Shops where spirituous Liquors are sold & their drinking spirituous Liquors to excess.[48]

The major entry of the day, however, concerns a private:

Amos Rose, private in Col. Saml B. Webb's Regt, tried for firing a gun loaded with a Ball at Lt. [Elisha] Brewster, found guilty & sentenced to suffer the Pains of Death.

The Genl approves the Sentence & orders that said Rose be shot to Death on Friday the first of next August between the Hours of Ten & Eleven in the Morning.

Rose's life was later spared when Putnam asked the Court Martial to pardon him.

On September 26, 1777, the British moved into Philadelphia. Many anti–British activists feared what might happen to them and their property. One item fresh in their minds was the Paoli Massacre, which occurred about 30 miles northwest of Philadelphia. On September 20, 1777, British Major General Charles Grey surprised General Anthony Wayne's American troops, who were sleeping.

Before the confrontation, General Grey had ordered his light infantry to remove the flints from their weapons so they could not be fired and alert the sleeping enemy soldiers. It worked—the Americans were totally surprised. As they ran around in confusion, the British bayonetted them. As the wounded Americans lay on the ground, the British set fire to the camp and called in their light dragoons who began slashing everyone with their swords, including the wounded, the sick and those who surrendered.[49]

According to historian Benson Lossing,

A Hessian sergeant, boasting of the exploits of that night, exultingly exclaimed, "What a running about, barefoot, and half clothed, and in the light of their own fires! These showed us where to chase them, while they could not see us. We killed three hundred of the rebels with the bayonet. I stuck them myself like so many pigs, one after another, until the blood ran out of the touch-hole of my musket."[50]

General Grey used the same tactics almost exactly a year later (September 28, 1778) in New Jersey in what has become known as the Baylor Massacre,[51] where he ordered his troops to bayonet sleeping American soldiers in Northeastern New Jersey. Charles Grey was later knighted for his service to his king.[52]

The British stayed in Philadelphia almost nine months—until June 18, 1778—at which time they moved to New York City.

Hudson Highlands

On August 16, 1777, Washington wrote the following to Putnam regarding Daniel Morgan's riflemen.

> The people in the Northern [American] army seem so intimidated by the Indians, that I have determined to send up Colonel Morgan's corps of riflemen, who will fight them in their own way. They will march from Trenton tomorrow morning, and reach Peekskill with all expedition. You will please to have sloops ready to transport them, and provisions laid in, that they may not wait a moment. The corps consists of five hundred men.[53]

Born in New Jersey in 1736, Welshman Daniel Morgan, like Putnam, received virtually no formal education. During the French and Indian War, when he was about 20, he drove supply wagons for British forces. On one occasion, an officer hit him with the side of his sword. After Morgan knocked the man out with one punch, he was court-martialed, found guilty and sentenced to receive 500 lashes. In later years, Morgan claimed that he was "only" given 499 lashes. With his characteristic humor, Morgan would say, "While the drummer was laying them on my back, I heard him miscount one. I was counting after him at the time. I did not think it worthwhile to tell him of his mistake, and let it go."[54]

For the rest of Morgan's life, his back bore scars from the lashes, but those marks weren't as noticeable as the scar on his cheek that he received later in the same war from an Indian bullet's exit wound. The entry wound was on the back of his neck. Now, in the Revolution, Morgan was considered one of America's most capable commanders.[55]

A few weeks after Washington's letter to Putnam, approximately 150 miles north of the latter's Fishkill headquarters, one of the most important confrontations of the entire war was taking place. At Saratoga, approximately 14,000 American troops under Major General Horatio Gates were opposing about 6,000 British, German, Canadian and Native American soldiers commanded by Major General John Burgoyne. The fighting at Freeman's Farm had taken place on September 19, 1777, and the lines separating the enemies remained in place for three weeks. General Burgoyne (1722–1792) was in a tenuous position at Saratoga. He hoped to receive aid from the British forces in New York City. It was not to be.

Humphreys, who was with Putnam at the time, recounts the following. He obviously desired to be loyal to both Putnam and George Washington as he tried to reconcile their accounts:

> Important transactions soon occurred. Not long after the two Brigades had marched from Peeks Kill, to Pennsylvania, a [British] reinforcement arrived at New York from Europe. Appearances indicated that offensive operations would follow. General Putnam, having been reduced in force to a single Brigade in the field, and a single Regiment in garrison at Fort Montgomery, repeatedly informed the Commander-in-Chief, that the posts committed to his charge must in all probability be lost, in case an attempt should be made upon them; and that, circumstanced as he was, he could not

be responsible for the consequences. His situation was certainly to be lamented, but it was not in the power of the Commander-in-Chief to alter it, except by authorizing him to call upon the militia for aid—an aid always precarious; and often so tardy, as when obtained to be of no utility.[56]

On October 6, 1777, instead of heading north to relieve Burgoyne, Gen. Henry Clinton (1738–1795)[57] headed toward the west bank of the Hudson River and attacked two installations built the previous year south of West Point: Forts Clinton and Montgomery. Fort Montgomery was just to the north of Fort Clinton, which was at the foot of Bear Mountain.

General Clinton apparently felt the attack on the forts would pull American troops south and away from Burgoyne. In addition, he wanted to demolish a massive iron chain that Washington had instructed Captain Thomas Machin to stretch across the Hudson River from Fort Montgomery in an effort to prevent the passage of British ships. Completed in April 1777, the chain spanned 1800 feet over water that was up to 120 feet deep. So far, it had been successful in preventing British ships from passing up the river.

Because all available Colonial troops had been sent north to fight Burgoyne, Forts Montgomery and Clinton had a combined force of only about 600 American soldiers. They were under the command, respectively, of two brothers, General George Clinton (1739–1812), who in July had been elected the first Patriot governor of the state of New York[58] and General James Clinton (1736–1812). In addition to the two American commanders being named Clinton, their British opponent bore the name Clinton as well—Henry Clinton. This coincidence led to the attack on the two forts being called "the Battle of the Clintons."

On October 5, General Henry Clinton landed a small number of troops at the town of Verplanck on the east side of the Hudson, across the river and somewhat north of Stony Point. The maneuver was designed to convince Putnam that the British would be attacking the Peekskill area. It worked, as Putnam directed his attention and his troops to the east side of the river.

Clinton returned down the Hudson River to Stoney Point, disembarked his main force, and marched inland to the rear of Forts Clinton and Montgomery. A little less than half his men circled around the west side of Bear Mountain to attack the rear of Fort Montgomery, while the remainder traveled north along the river shoreline to attack Fort Clinton.

Governor Clinton send a messenger to Putnam with the request for assistance, but Putnam never received it. Putnam rode to King's Ferry with General Parsons and Colonel Root to assess the situation. Meanwhile, the

American garrisons had no chance against the superior British forces. But fortunately all of their officers and men were able to escape in the confusion and darkness.

It seemed, at that point, that the British victors might, with the Hudson River clear of obstructions, head north to rendezvous with General Burgoyne at Saratoga. But the British at Forts Montgomery and Clinton decided to return to New York City.

However, before they left, British General John Vaughan (1731–1795) took a detachment and burned town of Esopus on October 13, 1777. Esopus, also known as Kingston, was about 50 miles north of Forts Montgomery and Clinton. Just a few months before its burning, it had been designated the capital of the new independent State of New York.

In the defense of Fort Clinton, American general James Clinton was seriously wounded by a bayonet, but he survived by fleeing to the mountains.[59] His brother George, escaped from Fort Montgomery by taking a boat to the east side of the Hudson. There is a story that he slid down the steep bank from the fort "on the seat of his pants."[60] By midnight, George was in General Putnam's camp, while his brother James had gone over the mountains to his home in New Windsor, New York, which is about 15 miles upriver.[61]

In addition to destroying both forts, the British burned two American frigates and demolished the massive chain across the Hudson. Although the British had about 3,000 British, Tory, and Hessian troops to oppose the 600 Americans, the battle casualties were comparable. About 40 British soldiers were killed and 150 wounded. American casualties were 300, of which 227 were captured.

Unfortunately for the British, the attack on the forts did not help Burgoyne who, hopelessly trapped by Colonial troops, including recent militia arrivals from New England, was forced to surrender his army on October 17, 1777. Without question, the victory over the British at Saratoga was the key American battle of the year.

Even in the Hudson Highlands, the loss of the two Hudson River forts did not lead to serious consequences and the troops in Pennsylvania still held back the British. Also, Putnam's troops didn't stop offensive actions. Humphreys relates:

> When the enemy fell back to New-York by water, we followed them a part of the way by land. Colonel Meigs,[62] with a detachment from the several regiments in General Parsons' Brigade, having made a forced march from Crompond [which is just east of Peekskill] to West-Chester, surprised and broke up for a time the band of freebooters, of whom he brought off fifty, together with many Cattle and Horses which they had recently stolen.[63]

Six. War in the North 147

In his Putnam biography, David Humphreys adds his personal account of the day Forts Clinton and Montgomery fell:

> The Author of these Memoirs, then Major of Brigade to the first Connecticut Brigade, was alone at Head-Quarters when the firing began. He hastened to Colonel Wyllys,[64] the senior officer in camp and advised him to despatch all the men not on duty to Fort Montgomery, without waiting for orders. About five hundred men marched instantly under Colonel Meigs; and the author, with Doctor Beardsley, a Surgeon in the Brigade, rode at full speed through a bye-path, to let the garrison know, that a re-enforcement was on its march. Notwithstanding all the haste these officers made to and over the river, the Fort was so completely invested, on their arrival, that it was impossible to enter.[65]

Washington didn't blame Putnam very much for the loss of Forts Montgomery and Clinton, because he had reduced Putnam's troop strength to a minimum. He had on several occasions taken Putnam's veteran troops, forcing him to replace them with inexperienced militia.[66] Livingston quotes Washington as saying earlier, "the situation of our affairs this way [Philadelphia] has obliged us to draw off so large a part of our force from Peekskill, that what now remains there may perhaps prove inadequate to the defence of it."[67]

A Court of Inquiry investigated the causes of the Fort Montgomery loss[68]: Composed of Major General [Alexander] McDougall, Brigadier General [Jedediah] Huntington[69] and Colonel [Edward] Wigglesworth, the Court of Enquiry into the loss of Fort Montgomery sat in the spring of 1778. It found that the loss of Forts Montgomery and Clinton were "not from any fault, misconduct, or negligence of the commanding officers, but solely through the want of an adequate force under their command to maintain and defend them."[70]

During the investigation, as was standard procedure, Putnam had been relieved of duty. When the Continental Congress approved the Court of Enquiry's report, Washington assigned Putnam command of the right wing of the Army. In the winter of 1778-1779, Putnam's troops went into winter quarters at Redding, Connecticut.

One final result of the Battle of Forts Montgomery and Clinton bears mention. According to Putnam biographer William Cutter, the British had given "to their own killed a decent soldier's burial, while the Americans left upon the bloody field were thrown in heaps, like so much carrion, into a pool in the rear of the fort."[71]

Dr. Timothy Dwight, a chaplain in General Parsons's brigade and later Yale president for 22 years, visited the location in May 1778, seven months after the battle, and describes what he saw[72]:

> The first object, which met our eyes, after we had left our barge and ascended the bank, was the remains of a fire, kindled by the cottagers of this solitude, for the purpose of consuming the bones of some of the Americans, who had fallen at this place, and had been left unburied. Some of these bones were lying, partially consumed, round the spot, where the fire had been kindled; and some had, evidently, been converted into ashes. As we went onward, we were distressed by the foetor of decayed human bodies. To me this was a novelty; and more overwhelming, and dispiriting, than I am able to describe.
>
> As we were attempting to discover the source, from which it proceeded; we found, at a small distance from Fort Montgomery, a pond of a moderate size, in which we saw the bodies of several men, who had been killed in the assault upon the fort. They were thrown into this pond, the preceding autumn, by the British; when, probably, the water was sufficiently deep to cover them. Some of them were covered at this time; but at a depth, so small, as to leave them distinctly visible. Others had an arm, a leg, or a part of the body, above the surface. The clothes, which they wore, when they were killed, were still on them; and proved, that they were militia; being the ordinary dress of farmers. Their faces were bloated, and monstrous; their postures were uncouth, distorted, and in the highest degree afflictive. My companions were accustomed to the horrors of war; and sustained the prospect with some degree of firmness. To me, a novice in scenes of this nature, it was overwhelming. I surveyed it for a moment: and hastened away.

Since 2002, the site of Fort Montgomery has been a State Historic Site, with the fort's ruins open for inspection. Archeological excavations have unearthed stone foundations of its gunpowder magazine, barracks and walls. Unfortunately, the site of Fort Clinton was destroyed in the 1920s with the construction of the U.S. Route 9W highway.

One interesting relic of the time that is on display today is a length of chain from West Point. In 1778, engineer, and by now veteran chain-builder, Captain Thomas Machin was put to work fortifying the chain that stretched 1,500 feet across the river at West Point. Every winter it was taken down when the river froze and returned to its position in the spring. On a bill of expenses that were incurred during 1777 and 1778 on the Hudson chains, Machin identifies himself as the "Engineer and Superintendent of the works for Obstructing the Navigation of Hudson River under the Direction of Bd Genl George Clinton and by Order of Maj. Gen. Putnam."[73] Lasting to the end of the war, the West Point chain was never breached by the British.

Today, a segment of the "Great West Point Chain," with its twelve 100-plus pound, two-foot-long links, can be seen on the grounds of the United States Military Academy at West Point, New York, where they have been on display since 1857.

The only structure still standing from Putnam's Fishkill Supply Depot is the Van Wyck Homestead, a Dutch Colonial farmhouse. Farmer and surveyor Cornelius Van Wyck (1694–1761) constructed it on almost 1,000 acres of land that he had purchased. The oldest portion, the east wing, dates back to 1732. The west part of the building was added in approximately 1757. In 1776, it was requisitioned by the Continental Army and used as the headquarters of General Putnam. In addition it was the location of military trials and a quartermaster's office. It's thought that the Van Wyck Homestead was the setting of James Fenimore Cooper's 1821 novel, *The Spy*, a historical romance set at the time of the American Revolution.[74]

Deborah Putnam Taken Ill

In 1777, as hostilities settled down somewhat, Israel arranged for his wife Deborah and his 17-year-old stepson Septimus Gardiner to join him at the Peekskill, New York, headquarters. It was a relatively relaxing time for the General. Septimus was scheduled to replace Aaron Burr as the Putnam's aide-de-camp.[75] They stayed with Israel in the home of Beverly Robinson, which had been seized by the Colonial Army. Robinson, a wealthy New York Tory, commanded a regiment of loyalists who fought Washington's Continental Army.[76]

Then things took a turn for the worse. Shortly after arriving in New York, Septimus became sick. He died on June 1, 1777.[77] It was too much for Deborah whose health immediately began failing. Although Israel wanted to stay with her, the British excursions up the Hudson following the fall of Forts Clinton and Montgomery necessitated his presence with his troops at Fishkill.

Apparently, in order to better provide for her, Mrs. Putnam's attendants moved her to the Mandeville House in Garrison, New York, where she died on October 14, 1777. It is not known whether Israel Putnam had time to reach her bedside before she passed. There is even some doubt that he was in attendance at her burial. Accounts relate that she was buried in Beverly Robinson's family vault or in the churchyard of St. Philip's Church in Garrison, New York.

In a letter to Israel Putnam dated five days after Deborah's death, General Washington stated: "I am extremely sorry for the death of Mrs Putnam & sympathise with you upon the occasion. Remembering that All must die, and that she had lived to an honourable age...."[78]

Washington was obviously in an optimistic mood after the American defeat of British General Burgoyne's forces at Saratoga 12 days earlier. He writes: "Should providence be pleased to crown our Arms in the course of the Campaign with one more fortunate stroke I think we shall have no great cause for anxiety respecting the future designs of Britain...."[79]

Still, Washington was cognizant of the fact that the British were a powerful enemy and he needed to constantly be concerned with the big picture. A few days later, on October 30, 1777, Washington sent a letter to Alexander Hamilton stating:

> It having been judged expedient by the Members of a Council of War held yesterday, that one of the Gentlemen of my family should be sent to Genl Gates in order to lay before him the State of this Army; and the Situation of the Enemy and to point out to him the many happy Consequences that will accrue from an immediate reinforcement being sent from the Northern Army.[80]

Washington needed those reinforcements from Gates to give him the strength in New Jersey to foil British General Howe's plans to open communications between Philadelphia and British ships. Washington's letter then reads:

> I have under stood that Genl Gates has already detached Nixons & Glovers Brigades to join Genl Putnam, and Genl Dickinson informs me Sr: Henry Clinton has come down the River with his whole force. If this be a fact, you are to desire Genl Putnam to send the two Brigades forward with the greatest expedition, as there can be no occasion for them there.[81]

Hamilton immediately started off for Albany in a quest to find General Gates and deliver his message. On the way, he stopped at Putnam's headquarters on the Hudson River and told him he must forward on the required troops that would shortly be coming from the north.

Days later, after discovering that General Putnam had not sent troops south to Washington, Hamilton wrote a scathing letter to Putnam and the following day one to Washington complaining "on my arrival here [New Windsor], I find everything has been neglected and deranged by General Putnam, and that the two brigades. Poor's and Learned's, still remained here and on the other side the river at Fishkill."[82]

In one of the greatest mistakes of his military career, Putnam did not immediately send the troops to Washington. Sure, the young Hamilton was arrogant, but it was the Commander-in-Chief who was the source of the request.

Putnam had hesitated to send the troops because he felt he needed them to launch an offensive against New York City which had been discussed and approved by Washington in the past. However, he did not recognize the situation had changed for the rest of the American forces, and there were more important uses for the men in the current situation. Putnam was also concerned that the enlistment periods of many of his men were coming up soon, and that he would not have the forces to replace them unless he used some of the men coming down from Gates's northern army.

After hearing Hamilton's complaint, Washington wrote Putnam a stinging rebuke: "I cannot but say there has been more delay in the March of the Troops than I think necessary and I could wish that in future my orders may be immediately complied with without arguing upon the propriety of them."[83] Putnam immediately sent the required troops south.

Questions remain. Washington's urgency to pull in support from the North was clear, but did Hamilton deliver the message completely and accurately? It must be remembered that the Hamilton of 1777 was merely a 22-year-old aide on Washington's staff—he was not yet the middle-aged founding father who would create the country's financial system.

Hamilton biographer Christopher James Riethmüller quotes a man who saw Hamilton ten months earlier: "I noticed," he says, speaking of the retreat through the Jerseys,

> a youth, a mere stripling, small, slender, almost delicate in frame, marching beside a piece of artillery, with a cocked hat pulled down over his eyes, apparently lost in thought, with his hand resting on the cannon, and every now and then patting it as he mused, as if it were a favourite horse, or a pet plaything.[84]

The man described here probably did not fit Putnam's idea of the ideal soldier. Still, would a dislike for Hamilton have been reason enough for him to be so obstinate in a bad decision. After all, Putnam had employed his future biographer David Humphreys as his aide-de-camp when he was only 25. And his aide-de-camps, Samuel Webb and Aaron Burr, had been only 22 and 20, respectively.

As George Canning Hill stated in his 1903 Putnam biography:

> Washington was unacquainted with the exact state of matters in the highlands, just at that time; there was a mutinous spirit among a large portion of the troops, who threatened to desert altogether unless they could be paid; and this Hamilton himself knew; and Hamilton was evidently hasty, if not impetuous, and used language, for a young man of twenty, in his letter, such as no man of his years should employ towards a scarred veteran of sixty.[85]

However, was there another reason for Putnam's failure to act reasonably? Could there have been something so horrifying that even a man like General Putnam could lose control of his common sense. Remember, in his old age, when discussing the occasion when he was almost roasted alive, Putnam had told his young cousin, Samuel Putnam, that he "had never felt any bodily fear." Thus, it would need to be something worse than being almost burned alive while tied to a tree. And something worse than having your ship sink beneath you in a vicious Caribbean storm. Is it possible that in making arrangements for the movement of his wife's body to their Pomfret home Putnam discovered something shocking?

In the end, it was fortunate for the American forces that Putnam's delay in forwarding the troops did not have an effect on the war. Washington received his reinforcements, and Putnam managed fine without them. Several weeks after the Putnam–Hamilton conflict, on December 19, 1777, Washington's troops would enter into their winter and spring quarters at Valley Forge, Pennsylvania. The men would be there for up to six months and suffer some of the worst living conditions of the war.

Deborah Putnam's Passing

Perhaps a reason for Israel Putnam's emotional state in the Fall of 1777 was revealed 127 years later—in 1904. It was then that Stuyvesant Fish, president of the Illinois Central Railroad and one of New York's most powerful people, received a letter from J.S.C. Hamilton, a Civil War Colonel and great-grandson of Alexander Hamilton. What Hamilton revealed was astonishing[86]:

> An old acquaintance of mine, Michael Lee by name, who for many years had been the trusted employee of the late Henry R. Worthington,[87] informed me that when he first arrived at Castle Garden from Ireland, he was employed by a contractor and taken up the river to Garrison; the first work allotted him was to take up the remains of a considerable number of persons buried in a very old churchyard, the object being to grade up the grounds preparatory to the erection of some other building; [footnote: "Undoubtedly the new church in 1861"] in the course of this work he opened a vault situated in the side of the bank, and took out a casket containing the remains of the wife of Major-General Putnam; upon opening the same it was found that she had been prematurely buried, as the remains were face downward, and that the hair was not only in a perfect state of preservation, but had grown until it had covered nearly all the interior of the casket.

Except for the possible superstitious interpretation of the word "grown," there is nothing here that is not plausible. The state of the hair might be the result of a person in a state of hysteria pulling it out and spreading it around the coffin. The author of the book, *Buried Alive: The Terrifying History of Our Most Primal Fear*, tells of a conversation with an old grave-digger who claimed to have exhumed coffins containing the remains of women who had been buried alive. Some had pulled out their long hair which he found wound around their fingers.[88]

The above Deborah Putnam story appeared in a *New York Times* article on January 10, 1904.[89] The entire passage can be found in the 1912 book, *History of St. Philip's Church in the Highlands, Garrison, New York*.[90] where the author states: "Upon further pursuing his investigation Colonel Hamilton found a brother-in-law of the contractor, who testified that the remains, with others, were re-interred immediately in the rear of the present church."

Was Deborah Putnam buried alive? And if so, did Israel find out? There is a story that he had exhumed her body in order to have it moved to Pomfret, but returned it to the ground in New York.

Surely, if Israel found Deborah was buried alive, even a man as strong as he was would be emotionally affected. Perhaps more than any other person of his time, with the exception of physicians, he had seen death up close many times. During his seven years of service in the French and Indian War, as well as at Bunker Hill, he had seen countless men seriously injured and many others die violent deaths, he had helped care for them in their last moments, and, yes, he had had to make quick decisions on their chances for survival and, after battles, verify they were dead before burial.

Years after Deborah Putnam's death, Edgar Allan Poe described well the horror of premature burial in his story by the same name:

> It may be asserted, without hesitation, that no event is so terribly well adapted to inspire the supremeness of bodily and of mental distress, as is burial before death. The unendurable oppression of the lungs—the stifling fumes of the damp earth—the clinging to the death garments—the rigid embrace of the narrow house—the blackness of the absolute Night—the silence like a sea that overwhelms—the unseen but palpable presence of the Conqueror Worm—these things, with thoughts of the air and grass above, with memory of dear friends who would fly to save us if but informed of our fate, and with consciousness that of this fate they can never be informed—that our hopeless portion is that of the really dead—these considerations, I say, carry into the heart, which still palpitates, a degree of appalling and intolerable horror from which the most daring imagination must recoil.[91]

One final thought regarding the possibility of Deborah Putnam being buried alive: if Israel Putnam had found that it had happened, would he have told anyone? Might he have confided in his commander, George Washington? Washington was known as a person who could keep confidences, and it would be characteristic of him not to reveal even the most interesting morsels of gossip. One thing is known: on his death bed, in the last minutes of the last day of his life, Washington was worried about one thing above all else—the possibility of being buried alive.

Washington's personal secretary, Tobias Lear, wrote this in his journal:

> About 10 o'clock he made several efforts to speak to me before he could affect it, at length he said, "I am just going! Have me decently buried; and do not let my body to

be put into the vault less than three days after I am dead." I bowed assent, for I could not speak. He then looked at me again and said, "Do you understand me?" I replied "Yes!" "'Tis well!' said he.

Those were Washington's last words.[92]

The Recruiter

From April through May of 1778, Putnam had made so much progress in obtaining new recruits in Connecticut, that he anxiously asked Washington for another assignment. Uncertain where best to use him, Washington, in a May 29 letter from Valley Forge to Gouverneur Morris of the Continental Congress,[93] included the following plea:

> What am I to do with Putnam? If Congress mean to lay him aside decently, I wish they would devise the mode—He wanted some time ago to visit his family; I gave him leave, & requested him to superintend the forwarding of the Connecticut recruits—This service he says is at an end, & is now applying for orders—If he comes to this army he must be in high command (being next in rank to Lee)—if he goes to the North River he must command Gates, or serve under a junior officer —The sooner these embarrassments could be removed the better—If they are not to be removed, I wish to know it, that I may govern myself accordingly; indecision & suspense in the military line, are hurtful in the extreme.[94]

The top army command had changed recently: Horatio Gates had replaced Alexander McDougall in the Hudson Highlands and General Charles Lee was back in action, having been exchanged for a British general in early May. As mentioned, with the retirement of Spencer four months previously, Putnam had become the oldest general in the Continental Army, as well as the one with the most seniority. And he showed no signs of slowing down.

However, three weeks after Washington's letter to Morris, on June 18, 1778, the British evacuated Philadelphia, and on June 28 Washington's troops won the Battle of Monmouth. The "misconduct" of General Lee at the battle resulted in his arrest and court-martial. General Putnam was called to the Hudson to fill the void. He was given the brigades of Pennsylvania's Peter Muhlenberg, and Virginia's William Woodford and Charles Scott along with the order to guard West Point.

Upon arriving at their temporary hospital, Putnam met with surgeon James Thacker, who in his Military Journal of September 8 noted that the General was accompanied by a division of Virginia and Maryland troops, which were camping on the river banks. Brigadier generals Woodford and Muhlenburg were given rooms in the hospital.

This was the first time Dr. Thacker had met Putnam. He recorded his impressions of the "celebrated hero" as follows:

> In his person he is corpulent and clumsy, but carries a bold, undaunted front. He exhibits little of the refinements of the well-educated gentleman, but much of the character of the veteran soldier. He appears to be advanced to the age of about sixty years [he was exactly 60 years old], and it is famed of him that he has in many instances, proved himself as brave as Caesar.[95]

Dr. Thacker records that Putnam visited the hospital and

> inquired with much solicitude into the condition of our patients; observing a considerable number of men who were infected with the ground itch, generated by laying on the ground, he inquired why they were not cured. I answered, "because we have no hog's lard to make ointment." "Did you never," says the General, "cure the itch with tar and brimstone?" "No, Sir." "Then," replied he good humoredly, "you are not fit for a doctor."[96]

Dr. Thacher's entry two months later (November 3) noted that General Muhlenburg, who occupied a room in the hospital, was playing host to "forty-one respectable officers" at tables furnished with 14 different dishes. The doctor continues:

> After dinner, Major General Putnam was requested to preside, and he displayed no less urbanity at the head of the table, than bravery at the head of his division. A number of toasts were pronounced accompanied with humorous and merry songs. In the evening we were cheered with military music and dancing, which continued till a late hour in the night.[97]

Apparently, Putnam's subordinate, General Peter Muhlenberg, was his kind of soldier. As Dr. Thacher goes on to narrate, Muhlenburg was

> a minister of a parish in Virginia, but participating in the spirit of the times, exchanged his clerical profession for that of a soldier.[98] Having in his pulpit inculcated the principles of liberty, and the cause of his country, he found no difficulty in enlisting a regiment of soldiers, and he was appointed their commander. He entered his pulpit with his sword and cockade, preached his farewell sermon, and the next day marched at the head of his regiment to join the army, and he does honor to the military profession.[99]

The main part of Washington's army was stationed north of British-held New York City. This part of the Continental Army consisted of four divisions: Putnam's (1st Division) near West Point, Baron de Kalb's (2nd Division) at Fishkill, Lord Stirling's (3rd Division) near Fredericksburg, and Gates' (4th Division) at Danbury, Connecticut.[100]

Given the criticism of Putnam's actions in the previous couple of years, Washington probably was already considering ways to move Putnam out of the New York command. In fact, Washington mentioned in a September 26, 1778, letter to General Gates that New York dislikes "General

Putnam, and not reposing confidence in him, they will be uneasy if he should be left to command."[101]

During late 1778, Putnam successfully repelled several incursions by British troops north into his territory. On September 24, 1778, he wrote to Washington, who after more than three years working closely with Putnam was well aware that he probably was the worst speller of any of his generals—in the following letter, a third of the words are spelled incorrectly. A keen judge of character, Washington knew well the value of a man of Putnam's loyalty and integrity over that of a Charles Lee, a Swiss military school graduate who was proficient in six languages.[102]

> Pickskill, ye 24 Sept 1778.
> Dear GINROL,—Larst night I received a Leator [letter] from Collo Spencor informing me that the Enimy had Landed at the English Naborwhod [neighbourhood] and ware on thar March to hackensack. I immedat called the ginrol ofesors together to consult what was beast to be don it was concluded to Exammin the mens gons and Cartridges && and to have them ready for a March at the shortest notis when it shuld be thought beast or on receaving your Orders. I waited som tim for further Intelleganc but hearing non I rod down to Kings fary and on my way met 4 men with thar horses loded with bagig going back into the contry which said thay cam from within 2 milds [miles] of tarytown who said the Enimy had com out of New York in 3 larg Colloms won [one] by the way of Maranack and won by taritown and won had gon into the jarsys [Jerseys] Just as I had got to the farry I meat won Capt Jonston with a leator from Collo hay [Col. Hay] which informed me that the Enemy had got as fur as Sovalingboro church and was incamped thare and it was said thay war [were] waiteng for a wind to bring up the ships: the Enimy are colecting all the catel sheap and hogs thay can in this setuation shuld be glad of your Excelanceys ordors what to do
> I am Sir with the gratest Estem
> your humbel Sarveant
> Israel Putnam[103]

In his biography of Israel Putnam, history professor John Niven charitably noted, "... his spelling, strictly phonetic, imparted strange and wonderful results to the few letters in his own hand that still exist."[104] With his sense of humor, Putnam would have undoubtedly appreciated the 19th century quip (attributed, probably incorrectly, to Mark Twain): "I have no respect for a man who can spell a word only one way."

Still, Washington was always ready to overlook the poor written communication skills of his general. Perhaps it was partly because he too had a less than complete education. While most of the founding fathers had received college degrees, many from Ivy League schools, Washington had not.[105] As Thomas Jefferson wrote: "for [Washington's] education was merely reading, writing and common arithmetic, to which he added surveying at a later day. His time was employed in action chiefly, reading little, and that only in agriculture and English history."[106]

Also, Washington had much in common with Putnam: both were French and Indian War officers, both belonged to the Masonic fraternity, both had an incredible knowledge of and interest in agriculture, and both were noted for their apparent lack of fear.

Thomas Jefferson wrote that Washington was "incapable of fear, meeting personal dangers with the calmest unconcern."[107] We have seen how Yale president Timothy Dwight and Judge Samuel Putnam described Israel Putnam in similar terms. But perhaps most important of all, both Washington and Putnam were men of integrity and honesty—and each of them saw the same virtues in the other man.

This doesn't mean that Washington would overlook Putnam's weaknesses if it might mean possible harm to the cause. But it does mean that if Putnam did not perform as Washington had expected, and the Commander-in-Chief was frustrated and angry, he would find some way to "soften the blow" by finding another position for which Putnam was better suited—whether it be guarding the northern border of New York City, undertaking special missions, protecting the capital city of Philadelphia, recruiting new replacements, etc. And Putnam was constantly busy with assignments equal to his rank—right up to the day he physically couldn't serve anymore.

Cousin Rufus Putnam

While there is no doubt about the most famous Putnam family member in the history of the United States, there are several candidates for the second best known. Is it Anne Putnam, a key figure in the Salem witch trials? Or G.P. Putnam who in the early 19th century founded what is today the publishing giant, G.P. Putnam's Sons? Or maybe World War I fighter pilot David Endicott Putnam?

However, if we are limiting our search to Israel's lifetime, then there is no question about the second most prominent. Without a doubt it's Rufus Putnam who, although having been overshadowed in the history books by his larger-than-life distant cousin, was one of the most heroic and influential men of 18th century America.

Although many sources simply call Israel and Rufus "cousins," they were not first cousins. Israel's father Joseph and Rufus' grandfather Edward were half-brothers.[108]

Born in Sutton, Massachusetts, on April 9, 1738, Rufus was almost exactly 20 years younger than his kinsman. Although brought up in a different branch of the family than Israel Putnam, Rufus shared the same lack of education. (Israel is said to have only had three months of formal schooling; Rufus had only three weeks.) Throughout their lives, both Putnam's were notorious for their lack of spelling and grammatical skills.[109]

After active service in the French and Indian War, Rufus spent the years between the wars working as a farmer and a millwright. In addition, like many men of the day, he practiced the profession of surveying. Three years before the Revolutionary War, Rufus joined Israel in a nine-month-long land hunting expedition up the mouth of the Mississippi River. It was an adventure neither man ever forgot although neither received any financial benefits from it.

When Rufus Putnam joined the Continental Army it was as a Lieutenant Colonel. He was chosen by Washington himself to construct the Boston fortifications. During the New York campaigns of 1776–1777 Rufus was in charge of many construction efforts. But at the Battle of Saratoga in October 1777 he was placed in command of a regiment in what was the greatest victory yet achieved by American forces.

In 1778 Rufus Putnam worked at fortifying West Point and ended his career at the end of the war as a brigadier general. Today, a plaque at West Point's Fort Putnam states: "Fort Putnam Built in 1778 by Colonel Rufus Putnam's Regiment of Massachusetts Infantry Rebuilt and Enlarged 1794 Restored 1909."

Winter Encampment at Redding

As the British remained in New York City, Washington, planning for the winter of 1778-1779, stationed his army as follows: Three brigades under Israel Putnam (Connecticut, New Hampshire and Hazen's regiment) to Danbury, Connecticut; Alexander McDougall's forces to the Hudson Highlands[110]; and Washington's headquarters' troops to Middlebrook, New Jersey.

Like Putnam, General McDougall had been an early patriot; before the war, he had been one of the most active members of the Sons of Liberty. When McDougall was arrested for a handbill considered libelous against the government, he refused bail and was jailed. He had so many visitors to his cell that he published a card stating his visiting hours were between three and six.[111]

It took Putnam a three-day trip east to reach the Danbury-Redding area. At the beginning of December 1778, he established his headquarters

The base on the west side of the 42-foot tall granite obelisk in Putnam Memorial State Park (Redding, Connecticut) reads: "Erected to commemorate the Winter Quarters of Putnam's Division of the Continental Army November 7th 1778. May 25th 1779" (photograph by author).

in a farmhouse in Redding, Connecticut. With him were his sons, 38-year-old Israel and 19-year-old Daniel, as well as his new aide-de-camp, 26-year-old David Humphreys. Later, Humphreys, who would go on to serve generals Washington and Greene, was to write about himself:

> With what high Chiefs I play'd my early part,
> With Parsons first, whose eye, with piercing ken,
> Reads through the hearts the characters of men;
> Then how I aided, in the foll'wing scene,
> Death-daring Putnam—then immortal Greene—
> Then how great Washington my youth approv'd,
> In rank preferred, and as a parent lov'd.[112]

The Putnam camp in Redding was to serve several military objectives in the winter of 1778-1779. First, it would discourage the British from making another raid on the American supply depot at Danbury, as they had done in April 1777. Also, it would provide a pool of about 3,000 troops that could be used to guard against and counter any raids that the British army or Loyalists might make along the New York–Connecticut border, along the Connecticut coastline, or on the Connecticut River.

The Redding encampment was divided into three brigades. The 1st Brigade, which consisted of Brigadier General Samuel Parsons 3rd, 4th, 6th and 8th Connecticut Regiments, camped the furthest west, in West Redding; The 2nd Brigade commanded by Brigadier General Jedediah Huntington held the 1st, 2nd, 5th and 7th Connecticut Regiments and camped about a mile and a half east of the 1st Brigade. The 3rd Brigade consisting of New Hampshire's three regiments under Brigadier General Enoch Poor, and one regiment (the 2nd Canadian Volunteers) under Colonel Moses Hazen. This 3rd Brigade, camped about one and a half miles east of the 2nd Brigade in the location now covered by Putnam Memorial State Park.

All Brigade commanders reported directly to Major General Israel Putnam who established his headquarters in a farmhouse about a mile south of the 1st Brigade's camp. The physical layouts of all three camps were based upon Baron von Steuben's plan for the Valley Forge, Pennsylvania encampment of the previous winter.

Charles B. Todd's 1890 "Guide to Putnam Memorial Camp" at Redding gives some information regarding the food and other items that were furnished to the soldiers:

> 90 marquees or officer's tents, 500 private tents, cloth for 48 tents, and for 500 tents, 1,092 iron pots of 10 quarts each—if not pots then tin kettles: 1,098 pails, 2 brass kettles of 10 gallons each for each company, 2,500 wooden bowls, 4 frying pans per company, 6,000 quart runlets [alcohol], 60 drums, 120 fifes, 1 standard for each regiment,

Six. War in the North 161

a medicine chest and apparatus not to exceed £40 in cost, a set of surgical instruments for the corps, 70 books in quarto of one quire each, 2 reams of writing paper, 10 of cartridge paper, 1 cart for each company, etc.[113]

Todd notes:

> The Continental soldier had to furnish himself with a good musket, carrying an ounce ball, a bayonet, steel ramrod, worm [used to clean the barrels of muskets], priming wire and brush, cutting sword or tomahawk, cartridge box containing twenty-three rounds of cartridges, twelve flints and a knapsack. Each man was also to provide himself with one pound good powder and four pounds of balls. The rations of the militia were also sufficiently liberal, provided they could have secured them—¾ pound of pork, or one pound beef, 1 pound bread or flour, 3 pints beer Friday, beef fresh two days in the week, ½ pint rice or pint of meal, 6 ounces butter, 3 pints peas per week, a gill of rum per day when on fatigue, and no other time. Milk, molasses, candles, soap, vinegar, coffee, chocolate, sugar, tobacco, onions in season, and vegetables at the discretion of the field-officers are mentioned.[114]

And:

> The musket prescribed by Connecticut [enlisted men] must have a barrel 3 feet 10 inches long, ¾ inch bore, bayonet blade 14 inches long, iron ramrod, good lock and stock well mounted with brass, and the name of the maker on it. 1s 6d [1 shilling and 6 pence] was given each man who supplied himself with 3 pounds of balls, 3s for a pound of powder, and 3d for six flints; otherwise they were supplied out of the Colony stock.[115]

Although ready at any moment to be called away on guard duty to Danbury or the Connecticut coast, the soldiers stationed at Redding were usually busy with such mundane tasks as local guard duty, drills on the camp parade grounds and a hundred other tasks designed to keep the camp clean and the troops healthy and fit. Undoubtedly, all officers were given what we have seen was one of Putnam's favorite orders: "It is better to dig a ditch every morning and fill it up at evening than to have the men idle."[116]

Still, the cramped winter quarters (12 enlisted men shared each 12 foot by 16 foot log hut) and the poor financial support by the colonial governments, led to serious discontent. The following is David Humphreys's account (1788 edition) of the attempted mutiny that occurred on December 30, 1778. Humphreys personally witnessed the event.[117]

> The troops who had been badly fed, badly cloathed and worse paid, by brooding over their grievances in the leisure and inactivity of winter-quarters began to think them intolerable. The Connecticut Brigades[118] formed the design of marching to Hartford, where the General Assembly was then in Session, and of demanding redress at the point of the Bayonet. Word having been brought to General Putnam that the second Brigade was under arms for this purpose, he mounted his horse, galloped to the Cantonment and thus addressed them:

"My brave lads, whither are you going? Do you intend to desert your Officers and to invite the enemy to follow you into the country? Whose cause have you been fighting and suffering so long in, is it not your own? Have you no property, no parents, wives or children? You have behaved like men so far—all the world is full of your praises—and posterity will stand astonished at your deeds: but not if you spoil all at last. Don't you consider how much the country is distressed by the war, and that your officers have not been any better paid than yourselves? But we all expect better times and that the Country will do us ample justice. Let us all stand by one another then and fight it out like brave Soldiers. Think what a shame it would be for Connecticut-men to run away from their Officers."[119]

In the words of eyewitness Humphreys:

After the several Regiments had received the General as he rode along the line *with drums beating and presented arms*; the Sergeants, who had then the command, brought the men *to an Order*, in which position they continued while he was speaking. When he had done, he directed the acting Major of Brigade to give the word for them to shoulder, march to their Regimental parades, and lodge arms. All which they executed with promtitude and apparent good humor. One Soldier only, who had been the most active, was confined in the quarter-guard: from whence, at night, he attempted to make his escape. But the centinel [sic], who had also been in the mutiny, shot him dead on the spot, and thus the affair subsided.[120]

One of the causes of malcontent was the soldiers' pay and the delayed payments. Todd gives the pay scale:

The pay of officers and men was as follows: Major General, £20 per month; Brigadier General, £17 ; Colonel, £15; Lieutenant-Colonel, £12; Major, £10; Chaplain, £6; Lieutenant, £4; Ensign,£3 ; Adjutant, £5, 10s. Quarter master, £3; Surgeon, £7 10s; Surgeon's mate, £4; Sergeant, £2, 8s; Corporal, £2, 4s; fifer and drummer, £2, 4s; private £2. If they found their own arms £10 for use of the latter.[121]

Six days after the attempted mutiny, on January 5, 1779, Putnam wrote to General Washington. (Given the letter's normal spelling, the letter was obviously proofread by his aides): "... Nothing new has happened since I had the honor to address you on the subject of the disturbances in General Huntington's Brigade, which I am happy to inform you has not been repeated, or attended with any farther ill consequences."[122]

Putnam relates that the "chief instigators & ringleaders" are being held under guard. In this letter, Putnam asks for Washington's advice regarding punishments. Putnam doesn't want to set a "dangerous example, of suffering such proceedings to pass with impunity," but he describes the prisoners as "sober, spirited, ambitious Young fellows of good families & educations, who have signalized themselves in action, & acquired the best reputations as Soldiers."[123]

On January 18, 1779, General Washington, then at his headquarters in Philadelphia, responded to Putnam: "The mutiny of the Soldiers in Huntington's brigade was on its first appearance of a very alarming nature, but I am in hopes from the success with which your spirited exertions were attended in dispersing them, that there is no danger of farther commotion."[124]

Washington proceeds to recommend immediate action in such cases of insubordination. Regarding the current prisoners, he views it as: "so dangerous a tendency as to call for the exercise of wholesome Severity." He leaves the details to Putnam, but concludes: "If the same causes should unluckily give birth to any future mutiny—the conduct abovementioned must be pursued—the severest and most summary example must be made of the Leaders."[125]

In the 1904 Putnam biography, *Old Put The Patriot*, author Frederick A. Ober praises Putnam's role in aborting the mutiny in the strongest possible terms[126]:

> In or near the camp preserved within the park, General Israel Putnam once performed a deed which some have called his greatest act. "Greatest if measured by results, and most typical of him. Who is not thrilled with the poem of Sheridan's ride—turning a panic-stricken army, and snatching victory from defeat; and here, near a century before, Putnam rode after a deserting army and brought them back to victory ... a victory over themselves.[127]

Months later, before the Redding encampment broke up, Putnam was faced with two soldiers, Edward Jones and John Smith, who had deserted to the British and allegedly became spies. Seemingly, taking Washington's stern advice, Putnam made examples of both solders by immediately arranging for a trial and quickly executing them. Livingston gives James Olmstead's account of the affair, which was published in the *Danbury News*. He received it from his father, who was an eyewitness.

> My father, being an officer himself and well known to some of the officers on duty, was one of the few who were admitted within the enclosure formed by the troops around the place of execution, and able to witness all that there took place. After prayer by the Rev. Mr. Bartlett, the younger prisoner, Smith, was first brought forward to his doom. After he had been placed in position and his death warrant read, a file of soldiers was drawn up in a line with loaded muskets and the word of command given. The firing was simultaneous and he fell dead on the spot. After the smoke had cleared away it was found that his outer garment, a sort of frock or blouse, had been set on fire by the discharge, and it was extinguished by a soldier who had fired.

Olmstead's father was within a few feet of the scaffold when, "pale and haggard" looking, Edward Jones, the second condemned man, had his death warrant read. "He seemed to recognize some few of his old friends, but said very little except to bid farewell to all, and his last words were, 'God knows I'm not guilty,' and he was hurried into eternity."[128]

Native American Tom Warrups was one of Putnam's most important scouts and guides in the years 1778 and 1779. Because of his value to the army, his drunkenness was often overlooked. One day after the officer of the day found him badly inebriated, he ordered him ridden out of the camp on a wooden rail. He was placed on the pole and it was lifted onto the shoulders of four men. As they proceeded to march Warrups out of the camp, they came across General Putnam who said "Tom, how's this? Aren't you ashamed to be seen riding out of camp in this way?"

Tom replied, "Yes, Tom is ashamed, very much ashamed, to see poor Indian ride and the General he go afoot."[129]

Daniel Cruson's book on the Redding encampment mentions Putnam's concern for the gambling by enlisted men. In his General Orders of May 19, 1779, the General warns, "Especially Card playing and gaming of every species is prohibited ... all who are possessed of playing Cards are to bring them forth together & make a Burnt Offering of them this evening at Retreat Beating."[130]

Between March 25 and March 30, Colonel Hazen's Canadian regiment left the camp for Springfield, Massachusetts.[131] The New Hampshire troops began leaving camp for the Hudson Highlands at the end of March, the last of the men departing on April 11.[132] The last troops to leave Redding were the Connecticut regiments. Parson's men were ordered out on May 29 and arrived near Fishkill, New York, two days later.[133]

The Redding encampment location would eventually become the first state park in Connecticut. It has also been remembered in the world of music: American composer Charles Ives's[134] pre–World War I composition, "Three Places in New England" includes a movement entitled "Putnam's Camp, Redding, Connecticut."[135]

While Putnam's troops were at Redding, from November 30, 1778, to June 3, 1779, Washington's portion of the Continental Army encamped at Middlebrook, New Jersey.

The Horseneck Escape

At 11:00 p.m. February 25, 1779, British Governor William Tryon left Kingsbridge, New York, with 1,500 troops to raid the town of Horseneck (today a part of Greenwich, Connecticut) and destroy a key American salt works.[136] American Captain Titus Hosmer discovered the plan and with 30 men followed the British. Upon being discovered, the Americans made a stand, but were overwhelmed and barely escaped with their lives.

Putnam Cottage in Greenwich, Connecticut. One of the possible locations where Putnam was staying when he became aware of the British raid on the Horseneck section of Greenwich (photograph by author).

Hosmer and his men had just warned the Horseneck troops when the full British force appeared at 9:00 a.m. Meanwhile, Putnam, the commander of all Connecticut forces, was staying nearby. Several competing stories describe where he was at the time he discovered that the British were approaching.

One story has Putnam at the home of Captain John Hobby, which was close to the meetinghouse. The approaching British saw Putnam with his coat slung over his arm. He mounted his horse and galloped toward his troops. The second story has Putnam at Israel Knapp's tavern, which was also near the meetinghouse.

The last scenario has Putnam at the home of General Ebenezer Meade,[137] a member of the Committee of Safety. Putnam was in a front room shaving when in his mirror he saw red-coated men advancing from the west. With shaving cream still on his face, he grabbed his sword and rushed from the house. He mounted his horse and at full gallop headed for meetinghouse hill, a half mile away.

According to all three accounts, Putnam proceeded to rally his troops next to the meetinghouse, preparing them to meet the British. In his official report a week later, Putnam wrote to Connecticut Governor Trumbull, "As I was there myself to see the situation of the guards, I had the troops formed on a hill by the meeting-house, ready to receive the enemy as they advanced."[138]

Putnam possessed 150 men and two iron field pieces. But he didn't have the horses to move the cannon. Even if he had, it would not have done any good since he didn't have ropes strong enough to pull them.

In the Trumbull report, Putnam described the events:

> They came on briskly, and I soon discovered that their design was to turn our flanks and possess themselves of a defile in our rear, which would effectually prevent our retreat. I therefore ordered parties out on both flanks, with direction to give me information of their approach, that we might retire in season. In the mean time [sic] a column advanced up the main road, where the remainder of the troops (amounting only to sixty) were posted.[139]

Putnam was able to direct his men to position the cannon on a hill near the meeting house. As the British approached, the Americans fired off several shots. Seeing they were vastly outnumbered by British infantry and cavalry, Putnam ordered his men into the nearby swamp; a marsh so dense that the enemy horses wouldn't be able to follow.

Perhaps at this time Putnam was remembering his old French and Indian War commander's rules. Robert Rogers' tenth rule had advised:

> If the enemy is so superior that you are in danger of being surrounded by them, let the whole body disperse, and every one take a different road to the place of rendezvous appointed for that evening, which must every morning be altered and fixed for the evening ensuing in order to bring the whole party, or as many of them as possible together, after any separation that may happen in the day....

After ordering his men to leave him behind and ride out of danger, Putnam turned around to see how close the enemy was getting. British soldiers were nearly within a "sword length" behind him. In front of him, Putnam looked down upon 70 wide stone steps set into the hill at near a 90-degree angle. They had been placed there to facilitate foot traffic from the low ground to the meetinghouse.

Without hesitation, Putnam pushed his horse down the steps at a full gallop. The danger this posed to Putnam is evidenced by the fact none of the British dragoons dared to follow him. As Putnam descended the hill, the British attempted to stop him with musket fire. One bullet pierced his beaver hat. Legend has it that when he reached the base of the hill, Putnam

The plaque on the hilltop granite monument reads: "This marks the spot where on February 28, 1779, General Israel Putnam, cut off from his soldiers and pursued by British cavalry, galloped down this rocky steep and escaped, daring to lead where not one of many hundred foes dared to follow" (photograph by author).

turned around, looked up at the enemy, and swore as loud as he could while shaking his fist.[140]

By the time the enemy took a less dangerous route around the hill, Putnam was a safe distance away. Apparently so safe that he was able to stop for a moment. Biographer William Farrand Livingston relates:

> On that eventful day in Putnam's career, it appears that, in a farmhouse situated about half a mile below the hill, a mother, busy over her milk-pans, heard the rapid beat of horse-hoofs coming down the road which led past the house. She rushed to the door to look for her four little girls, who had been playing outside and who might be in danger of being trampled upon. The hatless General, his long hair blowing about his round, kindly face, dashed up in front of the house and drew up his horse so suddenly as to pull him back on his haunches. "For God's sake, take your children in," Putnam called to the mother. "The British are upon us." After this momentary halt—an act of thoughtfulness, like that of a personal friend, to warn the mother to find a hiding-place for her family—the General put spurs to his horse and sped on towards Stamford.[141]

Statue commemorating Putnam's daring Horseneck escape, created by sculptor Anna Hyatt Huntington. At its 1969 unveiling, Albert D. Putnam, a descendent of General Putnam, gave the main speech, stating that his famous ancestor "rode down the hill to everlasting fame and into the heart of Mrs. Huntington" (photograph by author).

Reaching Stamford, the General engaged reinforcements, and returned to confront Tryon. Although Putnam's force was far smaller, they forced a British retreat, capturing 50 of the redcoats in the process. The following day, the British were exchanged for American prisoners of war. Because of Putnam's compassion for his prisoners, Governor Tryon made Putnam a gift of a suit of clothes that included a new hat to replace the one damaged by the musket ball.[142]

Perhaps the last surviving American witness of Putnam's plunge down the Horseneck steps was William Knapp who died in Stamford on January 31, 1844, in his 88th year.[143]

Over the almost two-and-a-half centuries since Putnam made his heroic escape, the residents of Greenwich have never forgotten the event, and have maintained the term "Put's Hill." On June 16, 1900, the Daughters of the American Revolution erected a memorial stone with a bronze plaque

Six. War in the North

inscribed with: "This marks the spot where on February 28, 1779 General Israel Putnam, cut off from his soldiers and pursued by British cavalry, galloped down this rocky steep and escaped, daring to lead where not one of many hundred foes dared to follow."

Among the speakers at the unveiling[144] were two men who earned the Medal of Honor for bravery during the Civil War: Generals O.O. Howard and Nelson A. Miles.[145]

The great slope of the hill has been dramatically reduced over the centuries to accommodate buggy, and later motor vehicle, traffic. Greenwich resident, historian Barbara Wertheim Tuchman, remembered that during her childhood it was a "favorite pastime" of Greenwich residents to watch heavy trucks try and fail to ascend the hill.[146]

Nearby is the Knapp Tavern, now commonly referred to as the Putnam Cottage, which was built about 90 years before Putnam's ride. Lovingly preserved by the Daughters of the American Revolution, it looks today much like it did in Putnam's day.

The most impressive memorial to Putnam's escape from the British troops is a bronze equestrian statue at Putnam Memorial State Park in Redding, Connecticut. The most ubiquitous markers are the Greenwich, Connecticut, town seals, which depict Putnam making his descent.

There's another Putnam tale that takes place at Horseneck, but it has far less veracity than the story of the escape from Tryon's troops. It appeared in newspapers across the United States (in California, Connecticut, Kansas, Michigan, etc.) in the 1850s. The version in the November 24, 1854, *Hartford Daily Courant* titled "Anecdote of General Putnam," reads as follows:

> At the time a stronghold, called Horse Neck, some miles from New York, was in possession of the British, Putnam, with a few sturdy patriots, was lurking in its vicinity, bent on driving them from the place. Tired of lying in ambush, the men became impatient and importuned the General with questions, as to when they were going to have a 'bout with the foe. One morning he made a speech to the following effect, which convinced them something was in the wind.
>
> "Fellers, you've been idle too long, and so have I. I'm going down to Bush's, at Horse Neck, with an ox team and a load of corn. If I should not return, let them have it by the hockey!"
>
> He shortly after mounted his ox-cart dressed as one of the commonest order of Yankee farmers, and was soon at Bush's tavern, which was in possession of the British troop. No sooner did the officers espy him, than they began to question him as to his whereabout, and finding him a complete simpleton, (as they thought,) they began to quiz him, and threatened to seize the corn and fodder.
>
> "How much do you ask for your whole concern?" asked they.
>
> "For mercy's sake, gentlemen," replied the mock clodhopper, with the most deplorable look of entreaty, "only let me off, and you shall have my hull team and load for

nothing; and, if that won't dew, I'll return to-morrow and pay you heartily for your kindness and condescension."

"Well," said they, "we'll take you at your word; leave the team and provinder with us, and we won't require any bail for your appearance."

Putnam gave up the team and sauntered about for an hour or so, gaining all the information he wished; he then returned to his men and told them of his foe and his plan of attack.

The morning came and with it sallied out the gallant band. The British were handled with rough hands and when they surrendered to Gen. Putnam, the clodhopper, he sarcastically replied: "Gentlemen, I have kept my word. I told you I would call and pay you for your kindness and condescension!"[147]

Although this tale is likely imaginary, certain aspects of it ring true, such as Putnam's brand of humor. Also, he was always on the lookout for "outside the box" solutions to problems, whether it be chains across rivers to impede enemy travel, the device to overcome the British abattis at Montreal or a submarine to attach charges to the bottom of ships.

Seven

Putnam's Last Years

The Last Command

In the fall of 1779, Putnam commanded "the Maryland line posted at Butter-milk Falls [it's now New York's Village of Highland Falls]," which was about two miles south of West Point and on the west bank of the Hudson River. With Putnam were his two aides-de-camp: his second-oldest son, Daniel, and David Humphreys. As Humphreys wrote in his biography nine years later: "This campaign, principally spent in strengthening the works of West Point, was only signalized for the storm of Stony-Point, by the Light Infantry under the conduct of General Wayne, and the surprise of the post of Powles-Hook, by the Corps under the command of Colonel Henry Lee."[1]

While the army consolidated at its winter headquarters at Morristown, New Jersey, Putnam, along with his son and Humphreys, left for a few weeks to visit the General's home in Pomfret, Connecticut. Meanwhile, Washington's troops settled in for their second winter at Morristown (they would stay this time until June 1780). It would prove to be America's worst winter of the 18th century. However, Israel Putnam would never make it to the winter camp.

In December 1779, Putnam left Pomfret on his return journey to Morristown to rejoin his troops. As he approached Hartford, he

> felt an unusual torpor slowly pervading his right hand and foot. This heaviness crept gradually on, and until it had deprived him of the use of his limbs on that side, in a considerable degree, before he reached the house of his friend Colonel Wadsworth. Still he was unwilling to consider his disorder of the paralytic kind and endeavored to shake it off by exertion. Having found that impossible, a temporary dejection, disguised

however, under a veil of assumed cheerfulness, succeeded. But reason, philosophy, and religion soon reconciled him to his fate.[2]

The partially paralyzed Putnam returned home where he was cared for by his daughters 30-year-old Mehitable (wife of Daniel Tyler), 26-year-old Mary (wife of Samuel Waldo), and 23-year-old Eunice (wife of Elisha Avery and the future wife of Lemuel Grosvenor). That winter Israel's sons, 39-year-old Israel Jr., and 20-year-old Daniel stayed nearby to help their father.[3]

From New Haven a few months later (April 1780), Humphreys wrote "A Letter to a Young Lady in Boston" in which he related in verse a recent journey, which included a visit to General Putnam's home. It includes the lines:

> The sun, to our new world now present,
> Brought on the day benign and pleasant;
> The day by milder fates attended,
> Our plagues at Gen'ral Putnam's ended.
> That chief, though ill, receiv'd our party
> With joy, and gave us welcome hearty;
> The good old man, of death not fearful,
> Retain'd his mind and temper cheerful;
> Retain'd (with palsey sorely smitten)
> His love of country, pique for Britain;
> He told of many a deed and skirmish,
> That basis for romance might furnish;
> The story of his wars and woes
> Which I shall write in humble prose,
> Should heav'n (that fondest schemes can mar)
> Protract my years beyond this war.[4]

In his Putnam biography eight years later, Humphreys stresses that in the year after the stroke, the General's "strength of memory and all the faculties of his mind" had been unaffected. Also, his "relish for enjoyment" and "love of pleasantry" had been unimpaired. However, physical impairments remained.

In 1855 at a Putnam family gathering in Putnam, Connecticut, the General's great-grandson, the Rev. Lemuel Grosvenor, relayed memories of people who had known the General toward the end of his life and who were still alive 65 years after Putnam's death. Grosvenor stated: "Even after his final return from the wars, when one side of him was so paralyzed that his right arm clung close and useless to his side, and he had to be assisted to mount his horse, he rode almost every day on horseback, 'sitting up as straight as a boy.'"[5]

Israel Putnam's disability came along exactly at the time the war was shifting to the southern colonies. Up until mid–1778 Massachusetts, New York, New Jersey, and Pennsylvania had taken the brunt of the fighting. Now, there would be no more major northern battles.

Just months before Putnam suffered his crippling stroke, Savannah, Georgia was captured by the British. Soon, all talk would center on the Siege of Charleston, and the Carolinas and Virginia would experience the remaining, and decisive, last battles of the American Revolutionary War. Francis Marion, Thomas Sumter, the brilliant field commander Daniel Morgan, and man who brought it all together, Major General Nathanael Greene, would, under the direction of Washington, take center stage, finish the war, and win the final victory.

After the War

In September 1780, only nine months after his stroke, Putnam traveled to the army camp in Tappan, New York, on the west side of the Hudson River. At the time of the visit, Major General Nathanael Greene wrote his wife Catharine: "General Putnam is here talking as usual, and telling his old stories, which prevents my writing more. The old gentleman, notwithstanding the late paralytic shock, is very cheerful and social."[6]

Israel had always been an extrovert. With a quick sense of humor and a generous nature, he had many friends and few enemies. For seven years between the wars, Putnam and his wife, Deborah, had owned and operated their tavern and inn in Pomfret. Connecticut, where the General had swapped stories with veterans of the French and Indian War and where countless members of the public had gone to meet one of the great legends of the time.

It was while the 62-year-old Putnam was at Tappan, that the Benedict Arnold conspiracy was discovered. Details of the escape of Arnold and the capture of his confederate, British Major John André, were "on everyone's lips."[7]

Decades after Putnam's death, his detractors used Greene's phrase "telling his old stories" to support their contention that Putnam's reputation was in large part a result of his oft-repeated yarns about his own exploits. Taking a revisionist approach, these detractors published their theories after most of the veterans of the battles were dead.

One of the great men of New England, U.S. District Court Judge Elijah Paine, dispelled the notion that Putnam was a braggart; and as Putnam's neighbor for thirty years, he knew the General well. Judge Paine stated of

Putnam: "he was a modest, unassuming man, and had nothing of the braggadocio about him.... Universally considered, by all his neighbors, a man of the strictest truth and veracity." Judge Paine was born in Brooklyn, Connecticut, in 1757, served in the Continental Army and became a lawyer after graduating from Harvard. After one term as a U.S. Senator from Vermont, he was nominated by President John Adams to a seat on the United States District Court of Vermont, on which he served for 41 years (1801–1842).[8]

Even with the disabilities that resulted from his paralytic stroke, Putnam enjoyed life to the fullest. Always a man who enjoyed good food, good drink, and good company, he received both old comrades in arms as well as members of the public at his Pomfret home.

A June 18, 1776, letter written by Captain Caleb Gibbs,[9] the commander of Washington's Guard (the Continental Army headquarters security staff), notes that General Putnam was taken sick that day at a dinner given to Washington by the Provincial Congress of New York. Gibbs remarked that the General was missed because there was not "a chap in the camp who can lead him in the *Maggie Lauder* song."[10]

Portrait of Israel Putnam by John Trumbull. It was said that by the end of Putnam's life, his body had the visible scars of more than a dozen tomahawk and bullet wounds (print from Livingston's biography).

This genuineness and openness illustrates why Putnam was considered a soldier's general. His troops appreciated the fact that his high rank was achieved entirely by reason of his battlefield accomplishments. This meant a great deal to the inexperienced soldiers who knew that their very lives depended on the competence of their commanders. They wanted leaders who would personally lead them in a fight and would expose themselves to enemy bullets to the same extent that they allowed them to be exposed.

Like World War II General Omar Bradley, who

was often called "The Soldier's General," Putnam was known as an officer who cared for his soldiers and who was not using them to seek advancement through the type of political maneuvering engaged in by so many of his peers.

An "Original Revolutionary Anecdote" in the Army and Navy Chronicle in 1837 is revealing:

> When the American army was stationed in Putnam County, during the Revolutionary war, one of the soldiers saw a boat approaching, and he cried out, there comes "old Put," a name familiarly applied to the gallant General Putnam.
> A young upstart officer hearing this caused him to be put under arrest for speaking disrespectfully of the General.
> On the arrival of General Putnam on shore, he inquired what that man was sent away for.
> The officer said, "he has spoken disrespectfully of your Excellency."
> "What did he say?" inquired the General.
> "He called you 'old Put.'"
> "So I am old Put," said he; "release him instantly."[11]

Another reason for Putnam's favorability rating among the rank-in-file may be his education, or rather, lack thereof. Military leaders with a great deal of education were suspect—was their commission the result only of their formal education? Was their education paid for by well-to-do fathers? Were they leading their men into life and death situations using tactics copied out of a military academy's freshman course textbook?

In the case of Putnam, not only had he had extensive combat experience in the French and Indian War, but he himself had developed or refined battlefield tactics that he passed on to an entire generation of colonial militiamen. To use the idiomatic phrase, "School of Hard Knocks," which was coined by writer Elbert Hubbard long afterward, Putnam's military expertise was derived from his real-life experiences.

This is not to say that Putnam did not suffer from his nearly complete lack of formal education. At a time when the mechanics of written communication were not yet standardized, Putnam's spelling, punctuation, and grammar stood out as among the worst of the army officers'. While it would be impossible for a man of Putnam's lack of formal schooling to rise within the 21st Century's U.S. armed services, late Colonial America was a different world. A great many successful and influential people in all walks of life had little or no education. In fact, to become a doctor or a lawyer, a person's key training consisted of apprenticeship with another person who was established in the profession.[12]

General Putnam's friend, Yale College president Timothy Dwight, noted in 1823 that Putnam

In his manners, though somewhat more direct and blunt than most persons who have received an early polished education, he was gentlemanly and very agreeable.... His intellect was vigorous, and his wit pungent, yet pleasant and sportive. The principal part of his improvements was, however, derived from his own observation and his correspondence with the affairs of men.[13]

Putnam never seemed to labor under inferiority complexes, even in the presence of such people as the internationally-experienced, multilingual general, Charles Lee. But the fact that Putnam was not familiar with the latest European military strategy and tactics was woefully evident when it came to managing the deployment of large numbers of troops against the British. Washington, while not having any more experience in that realm than Putnam, and with a formal education that was less than might be desired, read extensively and made it a top priority to make up for whatever was lacking in his childhood schooling.

Putnam, on the other hand, didn't even attempt to improve upon his writing. Even after serving over three years as a major general under Washington, the letters in his own hand still reflected his lack of basic spelling, punctuation and grammar skills. It doesn't take a graphologist to detect whether a document was penned by aides Webb, Burr, or Humphreys, or by Putnam himself. Still, the ideas behind the General's words were still lucid, creative, and even brilliant.

In October 1781, the decisive victory of the war was won at Yorktown, Virginia by the Americans and their French allies. After completing his official report of the victory, Washington entrusted the captured flags of the British and German forces, as well as his report to Continental Congress, to future Putnam biographer David Humphreys for delivery from Yorktown to the Congress in Philadelphia. Humphreys arrived at Philadelphia on November 3, 1781, was paraded through the city while displaying the colors of the United States and France, and made his presentation before the Congress and the citizens of Philadelphia.

Along with the flags, Washington sent along the following letter to Congress: "My present dispatches being important I have committed them to the care of Colonel Humphreys, one of my aide-de-camps, whom for his fidelity, and good services I beg leave to recommend to Congress and your Excellency."[14]

Humphreys was further honored later when he and fellow Washington aide-de-camp Tench Tilghman[15] were the only individuals allowed to accompany their Commander-in-Chief when he appeared before the Continental Congress to resign his commission.

Now six years later, Washington had fulfilled even the most optimistic

Seven. Putnam's Last Years

expectations. He had held his patchwork militia units together and maneuvered his way through battle after battle against the most powerful European nation. And he won. Never again would an American leader be so respected by the American people. Oh, some would come close—Pershing returning from World War I, Dwight Eisenhower and Douglas MacArthur coming home as World War II victors, John F. Kennedy after his 1963 assassination, and the closest of all: Abraham Lincoln in April 1865 after the Surrender of Robert E. Lee's army at Appomattox, effectively ending the American Civil War. Five days later, Lincoln was murdered. None of these great men could equal George Washington, and even now over two centuries after his death, only Lincoln is a contender for the title "Greatest American."[16]

At the end of the Revolutionary War, 24 men remained as major generals. Although he was permanently disabled, Israel Putnam was still on the active list—the only major general, except for Washington who was appointed to the rank as early as the year 1775.[17]

In 1783, the year that saw the signing of the treaty that ended the American Revolutionary War, also witnessed the founding of Society of the Cincinnati by the Revolution's American and French officers. Today, it is the oldest patriotic organization in the United States. Spearheaded by Major General Henry Knox, the Society's original aims were

> to perpetuate the memory of the War for Independence, maintain the fraternal bonds between the officers, promote the ideals of the Revolution, support members and their families in need, distinguish its members as men of honor, and advocate for the compensation promised to the officers by Congress.[18]

The Society is named for Roman military hero and statesman Lucius Quinctius Cincinnatus. Interestingly, part of the ancient Roman's life story resembles that of Israel Putnam. A former general, Cincinnatus retired to his small farm outside of Rome. When messengers came to inform him of an eminent attack on Rome by the Aequians tribe and ask him to lead them, he was in the act of plowing his field. Without hesitation, he dropped his plow in the furrow and left to lead his people to victory over the enemy.

British traveler John Bernard, who toured America for years, beginning in 1797, wrote of Putnam:

> Most of the native leaders were of the family of Cincinnatus, but no one so strikingly akin to that celebrity as the patriarchal Putnam, whose whole life was such an alternation between fighting and farming that one would suppose he could scarcely have had time to bend his sword into a sickle before he was required to thump it straight again.[19]

The Society of the Cincinnati's first president general was George Washington, and upon his death in 1799, Alexander Hamilton. Society founders included almost all of the surviving top commanders of the war: Nathanael Greene, Daniel Morgan, Baron von Steuben, Horatio Gates, the Marquis de La Fayette, Philip Schuyler, and Anthony Wayne. In addition, 23 of the 56 signers of the United States Constitution would become Society members.[20]

David Humphreys was one of the Society's most active members. In fact, the first edition of David Humphreys's biography of Israel Putnam was addressed to "the State Society of the Cincinnati in Connecticut," with a forward to the state society's president, Col. Jeremiah Wadsworth.

When on May 20, 1783, Putnam wrote a letter to Washington from his home in Pomfret,[21] the preliminary articles for a peace treaty ending the American Revolutionary War, establishing British recognition of American independence, and establishing the borders of the new country had been signed six months earlier. (The official Treaty of Paris would not be signed until September 3, 1783, with ratification by Congress occurring on January 14, 1784.)

Putnam began the letter:

> I take this opportunity to congratulate your Excellency on the Establishment of peace after a long tedious & Glorious Struggle, conducted under your Excellencys auspiceous [sic] Command, against the whole power of Britain, with that Wisdom & fortitude which finally convinced them of the necessity of puting [sic] a final period to the War."[22]

He continues with questions regarding payments the Continental Congress had promised him and other officers who had fought in the Revolutionary War.

Two weeks later, Washington responded:

> Your favor of the 20th of May I received with much pleasure—For I can assure you, that, among the many worthy & meritorious Officers, with whom I have had the happiness to be connected in Service, through the Course of this War, and from whose chearfull [sic] Assistance & Advice I have received much support & Confidence in the various & trying Vicissitudes of a Complicated Contest, the Name of a Putnam is not forgotten; nor will it be, but with that Stroke of Time which shall obliterate from my Mind, the Remembrance of all those Toils & Fatigues, through which we have struggled for the preservation & Establishment of the Rights, Liberties & Independance [sic] of our Country.[23]

Regarding payments for Putnam's war service, Washington doesn't hold out any false hopes, noting that "Republics in particular have ever been famed" for ingratitude. Washington then relates that he queried both the Secretary at War and the Paymaster General regarding Putnam's retirement pay and they both agreed that Putnam has "ever been considered as entituled [sic] to full pay, since your Absence from the field, & that you will be still considered in that Light till the Close of the War—at which period, you will be equally entituled [sic] to the same Emoluments of half pay or Commutation, as other Officers of your Rank."[24]

Washington had much to be proud of—he had accomplished so much with small and inexperienced forces. The Veterans Administration (VA) estimates that there were between 184,000 and 250,000 people in the armed services on the American side during the American Revolutionary War. This includes both state militia members as well as soldiers serving in the Continental Army. At any given time, the number in active service was far less than this since many were enlistments of one year or less.

The VA also states that 2,213,363 served on the Union side in the American Civil War. Thus, there were approximately ten times as many individuals who served in the Civil War as in the Revolutionary War less than 90 years earlier.[25]

Putnam cousin, Judge Samuel Putnam, wrote a letter on July 10, 1834, to Colonel Perley Putnam of Salem, Massachusetts, stating:

> Some of the family have distinguished themselves in war. General Israel Putnam, is known to the world, certainly as a soldier of great bravery. I was once at his house in Brooklyn, where he treated me with great hospitality. He showed me the place where he followed a wolf into a cave and shot it. And he gave me a great many anecdotes of the war in which he had been engaged before the Revolution, tracing the places of remarkable events upon a map.[26]

Throughout the 1780s, even though still afflicted with the effects of his paralytic stroke, Israel Putnam actively participated in activities at his local Congregational Church. In addition to Sunday worship services, he attended evening prayer meetings and gave public religious testimony.

A story was told about one member of Putnam's congregation who remarked that he doubted that God granted "irresistible grace" to someone who had been addicted to using profanity. Many members of the congregation probably glanced at Putnam, since tales of his swearing during his 14 years at war were well known. When the man finished, Putnam rose and admitted that he had long been afflicted with the vice, but that he had overcome it. Then, "with a twinkle in his eye," he added, "It was enough to make an angel swear at Bunker Hill to see the rascals run away from the British!"[27]

Putnam's interest in community affairs did not cease with his paralysis and retirement. The following letter was sent to the Windham County Court on February 18, 1782, in which he opposes the licensing of more than one tavern in his town.

> GENTLEMEN—Being an enemy to Idleness, Dissipation, and Intemperance, I would object against any measures which may be conducive thereto; and the multiplying of public houses, where the public good does not require it, has a direct tendency to

ruin the morals of youth, and promote idleness and intemperance among all ranks of people.... As I kept a public house here myself a number of years before the war.... I hope your Honours will consult the good of this parish, so as to license only one of the two houses....[28]

In 1784, Hartford's *Connecticut Courant and Weekly Intelligencer* featured a piece on Putnam that must have brought a good laugh to the good-natured retiree. Apparently, some writer had given the Putnam wolf story a bear theme. It read:

> We read that David slew a lion and a bear, and afterwards that Saul trusted him to fight Goliath. In Pomfret lived Col. Israel Putnam, who slew a she-bear and her two cubs with a billet of wood. The bravery of this action brought him into public notice; and, it seems, he is one of Fortune's favorites. The story is as follows: In 1754, a large she bear came in the night from her den, which was three miles from Mr Putnam's house, and took a sow out of a pen of his. The sow, by her squeaking, awoke Mr. Putnam, who hastily run in his shirt to the poor creature's relief; but before he could reach the pen, the bear had left it, and was trotting away with the sow in her mouth. Mr. Putnam took up a billet of wood, and followed the screamings of the sow, till he came to the foot of a mountain where the den was. Dauntless he entered the horrid cavern, and after walking and crawling upon his hands and knees for fifty yards, came to a roomy cell, where the bear met him with great fury. He saw nothing but the fire of her eyes; but that was sufficient for our hero; he accordingly directed his blow, which at once proved fatal to the bear, and saved his own life at a most critical moment. Putnam then discovered and killed two cubs; and having, though in Egyptian darkness, dragged them and the dead sow, one by one, out of the cave, he went home, and calmly reported to his family what had happened. The neighbors declared, on viewing the place by torch light, that his exploit exceeded those of Sampson or David.[29]

Toward the end of his life, Israel Putnam continued to show an interest in the affairs of his hometown. In 1786, Brooklyn, Connecticut, was established as a separate town. Israel Putnam was selected to chair its first town meeting on June 26. (At the time his son-in-law Daniel Tyler, Jr., was chosen as one of Brooklyn's selectmen.) Items discussed and decided upon at the meeting included the finalization of town lines and various appropriations bills.[30]

On October 25, 1855, great-grandson Lemuel Grosvenor, delivering an address on the life of Putnam at a family gathering, stated:

> Many anecdotes are related of his energy and perseverance in the days of his bodily feebleness. Those who are old now, but boys then, remember, and tell with delight, about the general's spirited bay mare, and the perfect mastery which he maintained over her, bringing her at any time to a dead halt, by shaking the head of his ivory headed cane. He was frequently seen at the houses of his sons and daughters in Brooklyn and Pomfret, and at the raisings and other gatherings and merry makings in the neighborhood. There, seated in some arm chair, promptly brought forward by the young men for his comfort, he leaning like another old patriarch, on the top of his staff, surrounded by a crowd of children and grandchildren, and friends and neighbors,

related abundant anecdotes of the olden time, while his happy audience greeted with loud laughter, the outflowings of his ready wit and his kindly and genial humor.[31]

Sometime after 1785, Israel's son, Israel, Jr., and his family accompanied cousin Rufus Putnam to Ohio. It surely brought back memories to General Putnam of the experiences he and Rufus had shared in the French and Indian and American Revolutionary wars. It had also only been a dozen years since their expedition together to the Caribbean and lower Mississippi River. At the time Israel, Jr., left with Rufus, Daniel had been married to Catherine Hutchinson for about three years and had his own farm. About the same time, the General's youngest son Peter Schuyler Putnam, along with his new bride, Lucy Frink, moved in with Israel and took over management of the old farm.[32]

Putnam lived to see two history-making events of the late 18th century. On April 30, 1789, his old commander-in-chief Washington was sworn in as the first President of the United States, and on July 14, 1789, the French Revolution begin in earnest with the storming of the Bastille prison and fortress by revolutionaries.

On April 19, 1951—over a century and a half after General Putnam's death—General Douglas MacArthur made one of the most memorable retirement speeches in American history, broadcast to the nation on television. He ended it with the words:

I still remember the refrain of one of the most popular barrack ballads of that day which proclaimed most proudly that "old soldiers never die, they just fade away." And like the old soldier of that ballad, I now close my military career and just fade away—an old soldier who tried to do his duty as God gave him the light to see that duty. Good-bye.[33]

Television viewers with a knowledge of American history might have been reminded of another old soldier, who also just faded away. Like MacArthur, Israel Putnam had had an amazing military career and was one of the most respected people in the United States. Both had achieved fame in two major wars and had become legends in their own lifetimes. Also, like his successor, Putnam had ended his career on a down note. MacArthur had been fired over disagreements with President Harry Truman; Putnam had been given lesser assignments after defeats in New York. But in victory and in defeat, both "old soldiers" were totally devoted to their country and set examples of courage that still inspire millions.

Putnam's Death

In Newport, Rhode Island, at 5:20 p.m. on Saturday, May 29, 1790, delegates at the Convention of the State of Rhode Island voted to ratify the United States Constitution. The state was the last of the original 13 colonies to vote for ratification; the vote couldn't have been much closer—34 in favor, 32 opposed.

On that same day, 60 miles to the northwest, the 72-year-old hero of the Battle of Bunker Hill, whose exploits in the two major North American wars of the century were known to every citizen of the new country, died in bed on his farm in Pomfret, Connecticut.

While dining with his son Daniel, two days earlier, Israel was taken sick and carried to an adjoining room in the farmhouse that he had built decades before.[34] He passed away of an inflammatory disease.[35] Up to the day of his death his mind had been sharp, although his body still labored under the after-effects of his career-ending stroke a decade earlier. Curiously, over the years most biographers mistakenly gave the date of death as May 19 instead of May 29 even though the original marble marker over Putnam's grave and the new equestrian monument correctly had May 29.[36]

Six of Putnam's children survived him: 50-year-old Israel, Jr., 45-year-old Hannah, 37-year-old Mary, 34-year-old Eunice, 30-year-old Daniel, and 25-year-old Peter Schuyler Putnam. Forty-one-year-old Mehitable had died six months earlier.

Putnam's pastor the Rev. Josiah Whitney (1731–1824)[37] conducted the funeral service. A longtime friend and spiritual mentor of Israel, Whitney touched upon Putnam's admirable qualities: his patriotism, compassion, and family-centered priorities:

> He was eminently a person of a public spirit—an unshaken friend to liberty; and was proof against attempts to induce him to betray and desert his country; the baits to do so were rejected with the utmost abhorrence. He was of a kind, benevolent disposition—pitiful to the distressed—charitable to the needy—ready to assist all who wanted his help. In his family—he was the tender, affectionate husband—the provident father—an example of industry and close application to business.

As might be expected Whitney spoke of Putnam's religious faith. Although Putnam in his early years wasn't too concerned with organized religion, the Putnam of middle age had a change of heart. Whitney says:

> He was a constant attendant upon the public worship of God, from his youth up. He brought his family with him, when he came to worship the Lord, He was not ashamed of family religion—his house was a house of prayer. For many years he was a professor of religion. In the last years of his life he often expressed a great regard for God and the things of God.

Whitney acknowledges that Putnam confided in him when he states:

> There is one at least to whom he freely disclosed the workings of his mind—his conviction of sin—grief for it—dependence on God through the Redeemer, for pardon—

Seven. Putnam's Last Years

Karl Gerhardt's statue of General Putnam stands above his grave in Brooklyn, Connecticut. At its 1888 dedication, the main speaker, former Hartford Mayor Henry C. Robinson, spoke of Putnam's legacy: "The inspiration of Colonists, the hate of Frenchmen, the fear of Englishmen, and the awe of Indians" (photograph by author).

and hope of a happy future existence whenever his heart and strength should fail him. This one makes mention hereof for the satisfaction and comfort of his children and friends; and can add, that being with the General a little before he died, asked him whether his hope of future happiness (as formerly expressed) now attended him? His answer was in the affirmative, with a declaration of his resignation to the will of God and willingness even then to die."[38]

The Rev. Whitney closed with a passage from Ecclesiastes 7:2, "That is the end of all men; and the living will lay it to his heart."

The following obituary appeared in the June 7, 1790, issue of the *Connecticut Courant and Weekly Intelligencer*:

On Saturday the 29th of May last, died at Brooklyn of a Fever, in the 73d year of his age, that justly celebrated Hero, Patriot and Philanthropist, ISRAEL PUTNAM, Esq. Major-General in the late Continental Army. He enjoyed his reason to the last moments of his life, and with remarkable cheerfulness, and solid satisfaction, left *this* for the everlasting rewards of a *better* and more *glorious country*; and on Tuesday following his Funeral was attended by the largest and most respectable collection of the inhabitants, ever known there on the like occasion—After a well adapted Sermon, delivered by the Rev. Josiah Whitney, the procession moved to the Burying ground in the following order:

Company of Grenadiers.
Militia of the Town with reversed Arms.
Music.
Company of Artillery.
The Masons, in the Badges of their Order.
The CORPSE.
Mourners.
The Clergy.
The Church of Brooklyn.
Military Officers.
Inhabitants.

When the procession had arrived at the burying ground, the troops, opening to the right and left, the Masons passed on to the grave, and after performing their accustomed ancient ceremonies, and pronouncing a brief Eulogium on the Character of the deceased, the Grenadiers advanced and fired three platoons, which was succeeded by a discharge of Artillery. The whole was conducted with that order and decorum, which the love and respect of the inhabitants inspired.[39]

The following eulogium was pronounced at the grave of Israel Putnam by the General's friend and neighbor, surgeon Albigence Waldo (1750–1794).[40] Three years earlier, Dr. Waldo had collected stories on Israel's life, which he gave to David Humphreys for his Putnam biography.[41] Dr. Waldo was a surgeon to Colonial troops during the Revolutionary War, including at the Battle of Monmouth and during the 1777-1778 winter at Valley Forge. At the latter encampment, he kept a diary that was published in 1861. He was especially known for his success in inoculating troops there for smallpox.[42] The Waldo eulogy came from a man who knew Putnam well:

> Those venerable relics! once delighted in the endearing domestic virtues, which constitute the excellent neighbour—husband—parent—and worthy brother! liberal and substantial in his friendship;—unsuspicious—open—and generous;—just and sincere in dealing; a benevolent citizen of the world—he concentrated in his bosom, the noble qualities of an HONEST MAN.
>
> Born a hero—whom nature taught and cherished in the lap of innumerable toils and dangers, he was terrible in battle! But, from the amiableness of his heart—when carnage ceased, his humanity spread over the field, like the refreshing zephyrs of a summer's evening!—The prisoner—the wounded—the sick—the forlorn—experienced the delicate sympathy of this SOLDIER'S PILLOW—the poor, and the needy, of every description, received the charitable bounties of this CHRISTIAN SOLDIER.
>
> He pitied littleness—loved goodness—admired greatness, and ever aspired to its glorious summit! The friend, the servant, and almost unparalleled lover of his country;—worn with honourable age, and the former toils of war—PUTNAM! "Rests from his labours."

Seven. Putnam's Last Years

Till mouldering worlds and tumbling systems burst!
When the last trump shall renovate his dust—
Still by the mandate of eternal truth,
His soul will "flourish in immortal youth!"
This all who knew him know;—this all who loved him, tell.[43]

On February 25, 1782, eight years before his death, Israel Putnam prepared his Last Will and Testament. At the beginning of it, Putnam stated, "First I commend my Soul to God that gave it and my Body to be buried with a decent Christian burial. And such Worldly Estate as God hath been pleased to give me in this life I give and bequeath in the following manner."[44]

Putnam's peaceful last days and his simple humility was a far cry from fellow major general Charles Lee, who, in his Last Will and Testament, vented his bitterness, writing "I desire most earnestly that I may not be buried in any church or church yard or within a mile of any Presbyterian or Anabaptist meeting house for since I have resided in this country I have kept so much bad company when living that I do not chose to continue it when dead."[45]

Eight

The Legacy

People in Putnam's World

In the opinion of most historians, the most important person of the American Revolutionary War was George Washington. Often called the "indispensable man," he was just that, for without him the Colonial Army would have lost the war on any number of occasions. Those people who have compared Washington and Putnam and their respective roles and actions to Dwight Eisenhower and George Patton have not been far off the mark.

Washington and Eisenhower were the military leaders "for all seasons"—able to devise strategy and tactics that would win battles and then actively implement them, all the while working with politicians who could be stubborn and obstructionist. Putnam and Patton were the fighting men who made sure the troops were in top shape and that when battles were engaged, they were won—men who always preferred to go on the offensive. However, their lack of tack and diplomatic skills often limited their effectiveness.

In addition to his military leadership, Washington's actions as the first president of the new country cannot be praised too highly. When told by American painter Benjamin West that Washington was going to voluntarily step down from the United States presidency after only eight years, King George III of England, his adversary in the War, stated: "If he does that, he will be the greatest man in the world."

In 1799—less than three years after leaving the Presidency and retiring to his Virginia farm, and 18 days before the turn of the century—Washington took ill and died within two days, probably from a combination of an infection and severe blood-letting by his physicians. He was 67.

The key figure in the French and Indian War for Israel Putnam was Robert Rogers. The incredible military prowess exhibited by both men undoubtedly played a part in their good relationship during the war; each man respected and valued the other as a loyal and trustworthy comrade-in-arms. Rogers would have died on at least one occasion but for the actions of Putnam, while Putnam's survival in countless battles, skirmishes and dangerous missions owed much to the instruction and example of Rogers.

But while their professional military life stories told one tale, their beliefs and personal characteristics revealed quite a different story. From a young age Putnam had consistently adhered to high moral standards, displaying a compassion for other people that extended even to his enemies. Rogers, on the other hand, was known for his brutality and ruthlessness. Just the fact that he deliberately murdered helpless prisoners of war provides examples of conduct that cannot be excused by any civilized human beings.

A hint of the fragile state of the two men's relationship can be seen in Rogers's memoirs — he gives Putnam little credit for his military exploits, including even the time when Putnam saved his life. General Washington rejected Rogers but relied upon Putnam. Rogers, at the end of his life reduced by debt and alcoholism to poverty, understandably was jealous of Putnam, who lived comfortably on his prosperous Connecticut farm surrounded by a large and loving family.

Things weren't always so bleak for Rogers. After the French and Indian War, he was hailed as a hero, a man who more than almost any other fighter had won the war. However, his reputation took a different turn when, at the start of the American Revolution, his request for a military command was turned down by General Washington, who suspected he might be a spy and who, at one point, stated that Rogers was "the only man I was ever afraid of."

In an act of revenge against an America that he felt didn't appreciate him — an act which verified Washington's opinion of him — Rogers joined the British forces, formed a new rangers organization, and fought against the Americans. In retrospect, it's possible that the American Commander-in-Chief had short circuited a second Benedict Arnold. After the war Rogers returned to England where he died in 1795 at age 63.[1]

A century and a half later, the exploits of Robert Rogers and his original rangers were brought back to public attention with the 1940 film

Northwest Passage, which starred Spencer Tracy as Rogers. It was not surprising, given Hollywood's usual lack of concern for historical accuracy, that the producers replaced real-life Rangers, Israel Putnam and his fellow Bunker Hill hero, John Stark, with fictional characters.

Of the great leaders at Bunker Hill who survived the battle, Putnam and John Stark[2] went on to further fame, while William Prescott[3] somewhat faded away.

Unlike Washington, who at any given time had several aides, Putnam usually had one aide-de-camp (with sometimes his son, Daniel, assisting too). After his time as aide-de-camp to Putnam, Samuel Blachley Webb went on to become one of General Washington's most trusted aides. Webb arranged the meeting between Washington and Rochambeau at Wethersfield, Connecticut, in May 1781—a meeting where plans would be made that would lead to the winning of the war at Yorktown, Virginia in October. Webb died on December 3, 1807, at age 53 and was buried at the Dutch Reform Church near his home in Claverack, New York.

Of all of Putnam's associates from the Revolutionary War era, the most controversial was his aide-de-camp Aaron Burr. After almost two years with Putnam, he received his commission as a lieutenant colonel and commanded his own regiment. Leaving the Army at age 23, Burr became successively a theology student, a practicing attorney, New York's attorney general, and, from 1791 to 1797, a U.S. Senator. In the U.S. Presidential Election of 1800, he tied Thomas Jefferson with 73 electoral votes. It took the House of Representatives 36 ballots before it elected Jefferson. As the runner-up, Burr became Vice President. Three years later Burr killed former Treasury Secretary Alexander Hamilton in a duel. Indicted for murder in both New York State and New Jersey, he was never brought to trial and eventually finished his term as Vice President. In 1807, Burr apparently attempted to create a separate nation in the American Southwest for which he was tried for treason but was acquitted. He died on Staten Island at age 80.[4]

As mentioned, another Putnam aide, his son Daniel, in later years provided unique firsthand information on his father's Revolutionary War years, and long after Israel's death vigorously defended his reputation. Born in 1760, Daniel married Catherine Hutchinson in 1782 and the following year joined his wife's Episcopal church. He died in 1831 and Catherine died in 1844.[5]

After Putnam's stroke, David Humphreys served as aide-de-camp to Nathanael Greene and George Washington. After the war he was appointed secretary to a trade delegation composed of Benjamin Franklin, John Adams, and Thomas Jefferson. Humphreys later became minister to Portugal and Spain under Washington and Adams. Born in 1752 in Derby, Connecticut, Humphreys passed away in 1818.

One of the first four Continental Army major generals, along with Ward, Lee, and Putnam, Philip Schuyler died on November 18, 1804, at age 70 only months after the death of his son-in-law Alexander Hamilton.[6] General Schuyler's daughter Elizabeth had married Hamilton in 1780. Their first child, the General's grandson, Philip Schuyler Hamilton, was killed in a duel at age 18 (1801) at almost exactly the same spot in New Jersey where his father would be killed in his own duel three years later. In later years, widow Elizabeth Schuyler would team up with friend Dolly Madison to raise money for charities, although Elizabeth was nearly impoverished herself. Another passion in her life was collecting and preserving the writings of her late husband. She died at age 97 in 1854, one of the last participants of the American Revolutionary era.

Major General Artemas Ward resigned from the army in 1777 because of ill health. In later years he was a delegate to the Continental Congress (1780–1781) and U.S. congressman (1791–1795). He died on October 28, 1800, at age 72.[7]

Major General Charles Lee died in poverty and disgrace. After being reprimanded by the Continental Congress for insubordination, Lee proceeded to verbally attack Washington. This led to him being challenged to duel by Major General Anthony Wayne. Lee was unable to oblige since before the scheduled day he was wounded in the side in another duel—with Colonel John Laurens. Lee was dismissed from the Continental Army in 1780 and died of natural causes two years later.

Less than two years after he complained about Putnam being appointed over him, General David Wooster was wounded on April 27, 1777, Battle of Ridgefield [Connecticut] as he was leading troops against the British. He died five days later. He was the highest-ranking officer to die in the American Revolutionary War. The speaker at the 1854 ceremony marking the completion of the Wooster Monument in Danbury, Connecticut, stated: "… second to Putnam, and to Putnam alone, in the length, variety and hardship of his martial labors; superior even to him, in the glory of his final exit, and the obscurity of his grave."[8]

Wooster Square in New Haven is named for David Wooster. He had owned a warehouse on a nearby street—Wooster Street. An Italian-American neighborhood since the late 19th century, Wooster Street is now nationally known for its family-owned pizza restaurants.

In the years after the Revolutionary War, Israel Putnam's cousin, fellow general and "military adventurer" to Mississippi, Rufus Putnam, became one of the most influential leaders of the Northwest Territory and played a part putting down Shays' Rebellion. John W. Campbell, Judge of the U.S. Court for the District of Ohio said of him:

> In the month of January 1787, the insurrection headed by Shays, and other factious spirits, broke out. To restore order and tranquility [sic], General Lincoln was placed at the head of an army composed of between four and five thousand militia. On this occasion, General [Rufus] Putnam was his volunteer aid, and continued with him until the insurgents were dispersed, at Petersham and insubordination quelled.[9]

In 1788 Rufus led the Ohio Company of Associates, a small group of settlers that founded Marietta, Ohio, the "first white settlement in the Northwest Territory." On March 9, 1792, Washington provided a brief evaluation of several of his key officers. Of Rufus Putnam, he says: "Possesses a strong mind, and is a discreet man. No question has ever been made (that has come to my knowledge) of his want of firmness. In short, there is nothing conspicuous in his character. And he is but little known out of his own State, and a narrow circle."[10]

Later, Washington appointed Rufus a judge of the Northwest Territory, and, in 1796, he became surveyor general of the United States, serving from 1796 to 1803. Later in life, Rufus was influential in preventing the legalization of slavery in Ohio. He died in Marietta, Ohio on May 4, 1824, at age 86. In a publication 14 years after Rufus Putnam's death, Judge Campbell describes him: "In person he was tall, and of commanding appearance; muscular, bony, and athletic; eminently fitted for the hardships and trials of war. His mind, though not brilliant, was solid, penetrating, and comprehensive, seldom erring in conclusions."[11]

Israel Putnam faced General William Howe's troops in most of the Revolutionary War's early battles. In 1775, General Howe commanded the left wing of the British forces as they attacked the Colonial militia units on Breed's Hill. The next year, he rose to overall command of British troops in the war and made the decision to move his forces from Boston to New York City.

Although he appeared to be heading toward success with the victories at the Battle of Long Island and the 1777 Battles of Brandywine and Germantown, General Howe failed to destroy Washington's forces at Valley Forge and he neglected to support General Burgoyne in upper New York State. The result was the defeat of Burgoyne's forces at the Battle of Saratoga. This led to criticism in Britain and Howe's ultimate resignation. Never holding an important military command after the 1777 campaign, he died in 1814 at age 84.[12]

Although Israel Putnam never came within 3,000 miles of British King George III, the monarch's actions had a strong influence on Putnam's military career. In the latter part of the French and Indian War (after 1760), Israel Putnam served George III, the British king, as a major in Britain's North American army. In 1775, Putnam was directly opposing him as a major general of the American anti–British forces.

The long-reigning George III not only brought the French and Indian War to a conclusion (one which was very favorable to his realm), but he also oversaw the end of the American Revolutionary War, and as well as the full range of the Napoleonic wars. George ultimately lived to see his commander, the Duke of Wellington, defeat Napoleon Bonaparte at Waterloo in 1815.[13]

Putnam Remembered

During the 19th and early 20th centuries a remarkable number of laudatory Israel Putnam biographies were published. An exception was that of General Henry Dearborn, who had been a 25-year-old New Hampshire captain at the Battle of Bunker Hill, and who 43 years after the battle, and 28 years after Putnam's death, criticized Putnam's role in that battle. Although there had been questions for years about the overall command of the Colonial troops at the Battle of Bunker Hill, and the respective roles of Putnam, Warren and Prescott, the Dearborn write-up was so obviously filled with rancor that people were shocked.

Dearborn attracted an inordinate amount of attention because at the time of his attack on Putnam, he was in the midst of a battle of his own—for the governorship of Massachusetts and for his own reputation—a few years previously he had been relieved of one of the top commands during the war of 1812 because of his mistakes.[14] In addition, in 1815 he had been nominated to the post of Secretary of War by President Monroe, but was rejected by the U.S. Senate. It was the first time in history that the Senate voted against confirming a presidential cabinet choice.[15]

Whatever Dearborn's motivations, the reaction by people devoted to the late general was swift and sure. The most forceful response came from Putnam's 58-year-old son, Daniel. As a 16-year-old volunteer soldier at the very outbreak (May 1775) of the Revolutionary War and later his father's aide-de-camp for three years, Daniel knew Israel Putnam better than any person alive.[16] He knew the man Dearborn had castigated was not the Putnam he had known for the first 30 years of his life.[17]

Of the many famous people who came to the defense of the long-deceased general were John and Abigail Adams. Abigail Adams, arguably the most influential woman in Colonial America, explained it well when she said that "... Gen'll Dearbourn too must Disturb the ashes of the dead, and do honour neither to himself or his Country."[18] Abigail Adams first became aware of Daniel Putnam's quest to support his father by a letter he wrote on May 21, 1818, to her husband, former President John Adams.

On June 5, 1818, John Adams wrote to Daniel Putnam:

> this I do Say without reserve that I never heard the least insinuation of dissatisfaction with the Conduct of General Putnam through his whole Life. And had the Characters of General Green, General Lincoln, General Knox, General La Fayette or even General Warren, General Montgomery or General Mercer been called in question it would not have Surprised me more.[19]

Ultimately, Dearborn and his followers ran out of steam as the voices of historians and highly-respected men like John Trumbull,[20] Washington Irving, and Daniel Webster[21] condemned the attacks on Putnam's reputation.

In 1893, family member Alfred P. Putnam wrote, *A Sketch of General Israel Putnam*. Toward the end of his piece, he describes well one of Israel's most attractive features—one that even most critics would agree with—while many, if not most, of the top generals in Washington's army were engaged in backbiting, libel, slander, intrigue and other associated evils, Putnam, by all accounts, was never counted as one of them.

Alfred Putnam states:

> General Putnam, however he has himself been maligned or wronged, never by word or act betrayed any such feeling of jealousy, hatred, or revenge towards others.... He never sought to undermine the good reputation or the fair fame of those who deserved well of their country. He was not troubled at their popularity or promotions, and as little did he seek by unworthy means or with a selfish spirit his own advantage or distinction.... He wore no masks, but was frank, open and honest, and as transparent as the day. His was no dark, sinister, tricky or deceitful nature.[22]

Timothy Dwight, Revolutionary War chaplain and, beginning in 1895, president of Yale College, wrote regarding Putnam: "In his disposition he was sincere, tender-hearted, generous and noble.... His word was regarded as an ample security for anything for which it was pledged, and his uprightness commanded absolute confidence...."[23]

One of the great writers of 19th Century America, James Fenimore Cooper, helped keep alive the story of Putnam. A larger-than-life Putnam provided inspiration for Cooper's *The Last of the Mohicans*. Cooper's biographer Wayne Franklin observes "Cooper was impressed with Putnam and

Eight. The Legacy

J.Q.A. Ward's statue of Israel Putnam in Bushnell Park, Hartford, is just north of the Connecticut State Capitol building (photograph by author).

made the hero of *Lionel Lincoln* a fan of the Connecticut soldier."[24] It is undeniable that Cooper was strongly influenced by the Israel Putnam biography written by David Humphreys.

Paragraphs in 1825 novel *Lionel Lincoln* that refer directly to Putnam follow:

> But the name which in secret possessed the greatest charm for the ear of the young British soldier, was that of Putnam, a yeoman of the neighboring colony of Connecticut, who, as the uproar of the alarm whirled by him, literally deserted his plough, and mounting a beast from its team, made an early halt, after a forced march of a hundred miles, in the foremost ranks of his countrymen.[25]
>
> By these grave veterans, who should know him best, the name of Putnam was always mentioned with strong and romantic affection; and when the notable scheme of detaching him, by the promise of office and wealth, from the cause of the colonists was proposed by the cringing counsellors who surrounded the commander-in-chief, it was listened to with a contemptuous incredulity by the former associates of the old partisan, that the result of the plan fully justified. Similar inducements were offered to others among the Americans, whose talents were thought worthy of purchase; but so deep root had the principles of the day taken, that not a man was found to listen to the proposition.[26]

There is no doubt of the identity of the "old partisan of the woods" at Bunker Hill in this paragraph by Cooper:

> Including men of all ages and conditions, there might have been two thousand of them; but, as the day advanced, small bodies of their countrymen, taking counsel of their feelings, and animated by the example of the old partisan of the woods, who crossed and recrossed the neck, loudly scoffing at the danger, broke through the fire of the shipping in time to join in the closing and bloody business of the hour.[27]

Interestingly, in early 19th-century Northeastern Connecticut, tavern owner Israel Putnam's name was used to promote temperance. Perhaps it's not too surprising when considered in light of his already quoted 1782 letter to the Windham County Court: "the multiplying of public houses, where the public good does not require it, has a direct tendency to ruin the morals of youth, and promote idleness and intemperance among all ranks of people."[28]

In 1829, Brooklyn minister John Marsh's lecture on abstinence from alcohol was titled "Putnam and the Monster Destroyed." After summarizing the Putnam wolf story, he stated that they must hunt "a more terrible monster, and whose destruction will require Putnam courage."[29] According to local historian Susan Jewett Griggs, the term "Putnam Courage" became the slogan of the temperance societies.[30] In 1840, Putnam's old hometown of Pomfret prohibited the sale of alcohol, a prohibition that would last for over a century.

It's interesting that decades after Putnam's death, his name was associated with the word "courage" much like in the 20th century the name of Mother Teresa of Calcutta would invoke the word "compassion" and Albert Einstein's name would be synonymous with "genius."

On August 5, 1844, the dramatic play "Putnam, or the Iron Son of '76" debuted in New York City. Written by Delaware-born playwright Nathaniel Bannister, it ran for 78 consecutive nights (an amazing run for the time) and was revived annually thereafter. In addition to Putnam, the characters included: Washington, Greene, Cornwallis, and Putnam's horse.[31] In a performance in May 1851, the actor who played Putnam suffered a broken arm and his horse was killed when he was riding over scaffolding.[32]

In the late 1850s, Washington Irving wrote his "Life of George Washington." It included his description of Putnam, a description that was repeated many times in the literature of the day:

> A yeoman warrior fresh from the plough, in the garb of rural labor; a patriot brave and generous, but rough and ready, who thought not of himself in time of danger, but was ready to serve in any way, and to sacrifice official rank and self-glorification to the good of the cause. He was eminently a soldier for the occasion. His name has long

been a favorite one with young and old; one of the talismanic names of the Revolution, the very mention of which is like the sound of a trumpet. Such names are the precious jewels of our history, to be garnered up among the treasures of the nation, and kept immaculate from the tarnishing breath of the cynic and the doubter.[33]

In 1859, popular 19th century American poet Lydia Huntley Sigourney (1791–1865) wrote the following poem, entitled "General Putnam":

GREAT Soul, and brave, 'tis good to think of thee,
And with a filial reverence raise the veil
From patriot valor, that ne'er sought of Fame
Her clarion-payment.
         See we not again,
The unfinished furrow, the forsaken home,
The flying steed, urg'd by thy sleepless heart
That throbb'd indignant o'er a smother'd found,
The cry of Lexington?
         That echoed cry
Rous'd a young nation from its lingering sleep
To rush against the force of tyrant power,
Time-consecrated, and with fling and stone
Defy the giant.
         Bunker Hill records
Thy stern o'ermastery of the battle-storm,
The deep memorial of thy dauntless deeds
That bore the spirit of a trampled land,
Through this red preface of her liberty.

Hark!—from the heaving of yon burial sods
Where sleep our Country's champions, comes a voice
Demanding for thy name its just reward
Too long withheld.—Of History it demands
That lingering truth should light her lettered scroll,
And summons tardy man to set thy fame
In sculptured marble, that recording stars
May read it clearly from their silver thrones,
And lisping children from its tablet learn
What patriot virtue means.[34]

In 1874, Israel Putnam's home state of Connecticut honored his memory with a larger-than-life bronze statue in Hartford's Bushnell Park. It was created by J.Q.A. (John Quincy Adams) Ward (1830–1910), whose many works included statues of Washington and Shakespeare in New York City.[35]

Today, the Revolutionary War era is kept alive through the efforts of the many reenactment groups throughout the United States. Members research the lives of people of the time, and dress, eat, and speak as those colonists once did. Then, they share what they learned with members of the public for purposes of entertainment and education.

One of the predecessors of modern military "reenactment" groups was the Putnam Phalanx. Founded in 1858, its members wore Revolutionary War uniforms at events and kept alive the memories of the patriots of the war that freed America from the control of the British Empire. As one might guess, the perpetuation of the memory of its namesake, Israel Putnam, was high on its list of priorities. Its main function was to provide ceremonial guard for public events.

In the 1930s, the Putnam Phalanx merged with Connecticut National Guard units. All activity by the group ended in the first years of the 21st century.

By the late 1800s, relic hunters and the weather had so damaged Putnam's table-top tomb in Brooklyn, Connecticut's South Cemetery that the State of Connecticut stepped in to prevent further damage.[36] In 1886, the General Assembly set aside funds for the erection of a burial monument in the center of Brooklyn, Connecticut. Sculptor Karl Gerhardt (1853–1940), who had recently completed the statue of Nathan Hale at the Connecticut State Capitol, was chosen to create a statue of Putnam on his warhorse.

Original plans called for the placement of the monument over Putnam's grave in the South Cemetery, but it proved to be impractical since it was closely surrounded by numerous other graves. Then, Putnam descendants offered to pay for the cost of moving the General's remains if another suitable place could be found. The spot finally chosen was just south of the church building in which Putnam worshiped, just west of the field where he dropped his plow before answering the call of Lexington, and just yards southwest of the site of his tavern. In fact, at the time of the 1888 monument dedication, the tree that had held the sign with General Wolfe's image during Putnam's life was sprouting its summer leaves across the road.

Livingston's 1901 biography states that "The dust of Putnam was removed from the cemetery, where he was originally buried, and placed in a sarcophagus which was built into the foundation of the monument."[37]

The descriptions of the exhumation appearing in Bayles' History of Windham County, Connecticut, in 1889 and a *New York Times* article in 1894 are much more detailed. Bayles states:

> Previous to the erection of the bronze statue, the bones of Putnam were removed from their previous resting place to a new grave beneath the pedestal. When the remains were taken up the large bones were found well preserved, especially the hip bones, by which the body was additionally identified by a relative. A piece of the shroud was found. The coffin was much decayed.[38] A large stone that had been cemented directly over the body is supposed to have kept off the surface water and assisted in preserving the bones. The remains, the bit of shroud and pieces of coffin were placed in a metallic casket five feet long and reinterred in the new grave. The large stone that had lain over

them since 1790, was also replaced in a like position in the new location and cemented down. Then the grave was graded down ready for the statue pedestal.[39]

The 1894 *New York Times* article relates:

> A few years ago, a famous monument was raised to him in the very yard of the hotel in Brooklyn, his bones were dug up and redeposited under the nobler stone. The graves of his family were left undisturbed in the neglected corner of the burying ground, where they had reposed over a century. It is related that, in the digging, the skeleton of the general was found nearly intact, but the coffin had disappeared save for a fine line of a darker color in the mold around the bottom of the grave. Some hand-hammered wrought-iron nails and a brass hinge or two were found, and these are treasured in Brooklyn to-day as relics of the greatest value.[40]

Putnam's remains faired far better than those of his fellow commander, General Anthony Wayne. Acquiring the nickname "Mad Anthony" because of his reputation as one of Washington's most accomplished "fighting generals," Wayne followed up Revolutionary War successes with a defeat of powerful Native American forces at the 1794 Battle of Fallen Timbers. When Wayne died of gout two years later at Fort Presque Isle (at today's Erie, Pennsylvania), he was buried next to a flagstaff. In 1809, his son Isaac, accompanied by a surgeon friend of his father's, came with a two-wheeled buggy to retrieve Wayne's remains. When found, the old General's body was almost perfectly intact and wouldn't fit in the small vehicle. So, the surgeon boiled the flesh from the body, placed it in the grave, and boxed up the bones. The story goes that on the 400-mile trip to bury the bones in a suburb of Philadelphia, many of the bones accidentally fell off the carriage, leaving few to be ultimately buried.[41]

On June 14, 1888, Brooklyn, Connecticut, was visited by thousands of people who had come for the dedication of the equestrian statue that was to be placed above General Israel Putnam's new tomb.

Governor Phineas C. Lounsbury represented the state of Connecticut, while Royal C. Taft, attended in his official capacity as governor of Rhode Island.[42] As the two governors were escorted to the stand, a governor's salute was fired from the spot in the field across the road where Putnam had dropped his plow when he rushed to help at Lexington and Concord 113 years earlier.

A prayer was read by Yale University president Timothy Dwight V, whose grandfather, Timothy Dwight IV, had been the eighth president of Yale. The latter had written the epitaph which appeared on the General's original gravestone and was now inscribed on the sides of the new 25-foot-high monument.

Professor Charles F. Johnson of Trinity College read a poem he had written for the occasion, and 55-year-old Henry C. Robinson, a former mayor of Hartford delivered the memorial address.

In attendance were the statue's sculptor Karl Gerhardt, countless local citizens, and the last surviving grandson of General Putnam, 78-year-old William H. Putnam of Brooklyn, Connecticut, along with his son, John D. Putnam of Wisconsin, who conducted the statue's unveiling.[43]

Robinson's memorial address included this often quoted passage:

Ninety-eight years ago the wasted form of an old soldier, scarred by tomahawk and bullet, was laid to rest in yonder graveyard. The sacred acres were filled with mourners. He was consigned to sleep in the echoes of artillery and of musketry, and under the glories of the flag, the fibres of whose folds his own brave hands had so conspicuously helped to weave. His epitaph was written by the foremost scholar of our State. The fret of time, the frost of winter, and the selfish hand of the relic-hunter wasted the stone slab on which it was written. And here, above a handful of ashes, all that remains of that stalwart frame, which, in life, was the inspiration of Colonists, the hate of Frenchmen, the fear of Englishmen, and the awe of Indians, to day, late, but not too late, a grateful State has built a seemly and enduring pedestal, has placed upon it his war-horse, and called again to his saddle, with his bronzed features saluting the morning, the Connecticut hero of the revolution.[44]

South side of Putnam's burial monument in Brooklyn, Connecticut, displays the words of Timothy Dwight's epitaph: "If a Patriot, remember the distinguished and gallant services rendered thy country by the Patriot who sleeps beneath this marble; if thou art honest, generous & worthy, render a cheerful tribute of respect to a man whose generosity was singular, whose honesty was proverbial, who raised himself to universal esteem and offices of eminent distinction by personal worth and a useful life" (photograph by author).

The activities ended with a parade of 1,500 troops passing the reviewing stand. Many visitors spent the remainder of the day walking

Putnam's field, visiting the wolf den, viewing the site of his old tavern, and seeing the house where Putnam died.[45]

In 1896, the *New York Times* carried an article on a collection of correspondence with government leaders on the subject of General Putnam's legacy. E. Stevens Henry, a banker and nine-term U.S. Congressman from Connecticut responded:

> I was taught as a boy to regard the name of Israel Putnam as second only in the galaxy of American Patriots and heroes to that of George Washington. Possibly a reason for this may be found in the fact that my paternal great-grandfather served as a scout under Putnam during two campaigns in the French and Indian War, and my grandfather was always willing to fill my boyish ears and imagination with stories of the redoubtable hero that he pleased to style "Old Put." He was preeminently a man who knew no fear, a typical son of New England, and Connecticut's titular hero.[46]

John Williams, the Presiding Bishop of the Protestant Episcopal Church in the United States of America, calling Putnam the "bravest of the brave," stated: "No true patriot and loyal citizen of the United States can ever undervalue the life, deeds, and character of Putnam, "the bravest of the brave." He gave himself to the service of the country in the later Colonial wars, as well as in the War of the Revolution, with an entireness of self-sacrifice which deserves to be, and I am sure is, held in lasting remembrance."[47]

Possibly the first public library in the Northwest Territory was organized in 1796. Known as the Putnam Library or the Belpre Library, it included the part of Israel Putnam's family library that Israel's son Israel Putnam, Jr., brought to Belpre, Ohio two years after his father's death.[48]

Eight states have Putnam Counties that are named after General Israel Putnam. Two (Georgia and New York) were founded in the early 1800s, three (Ohio, Indiana, and Illinois) in the 1820s, and three (Tennessee, Missouri, and West Virginia) in the 1840s.[49]

Putnam's home state has always honored his memory. At the intersection of the Connecticut towns of Thompson in the north, Pomfret to the west, and Killingly on the south, a new settlement arose in the 1840s. By 1849, efforts were being made to consolidate portions of the three towns into a new town recognized by the State of Connecticut. As they fought hard for six years, the promoters of the new municipality adopted the slogan "the courage of Putnam."

Finally, in 1855, with their efforts spearheaded by ex-governor Chauncey Fitch Cleveland (1799–1887), they achieved success and named their town Putnam after the General whose home was only about two miles west of the new Pomfret-Putnam town line. In the 19th century, Putnam,

Connecticut, was perhaps best known for the giant Cargill Falls Mill on the Quinebaug River, which possessed an incredible 1,200 looms.

Many museum pieces existing today are associated with Israel Putnam's life. In 1888, the National Centennial celebration of the early settlement of the territory northwest of the River Ohio was held in Marietta, Ohio. Items on display included several once owned by Israel Putnam including his 1756 powder horn, a holstered set of pistols, and a military coat given to him by Lafayette.[50] Today, the powder horn is the property of the Memorial Hall Museum in Deerfield, Massachusetts.

A gavel prepared for the 1884 Democratic National Convention held what was believed to be a piece of the torch used by Putnam to enter the Wolf Den, as well as a fragment of George Washington's tomb.[51]

An auction in New York City in 1896 featured a treasure trove of unique items related to Israel Putnam. At its heart was a collection of portraits, sketches, and physical objects owned by artist John Trumbull. Included were sketches of Israel Putnam, Putnam's saddle pistol, and a lock of his hair. Also included among the hundreds of items, were locks of hair of some of the most important figures of the American Revolution: Franklin, Lafayette, Benedict Arnold, and Anthony Wayne. There were also locks of George Washington's hair, his mother's hair, and two locks of Martha Washington's hair: one at age 68 and one from childhood.[52]

An article in the *Boston Evening Transcript* issue of February 23, 1904, states that an A.E. Brooks agreed to transfer to the Putnam Phalanx of Hartford, Israel Putnam's saddle and "the plough which General Israel Putnam left in the field when he went to war." Today, these two items are exhibited in a display case in the lobby of the Governor William A. O'Neill State Armory, which sits to the west of the Connecticut state capitol building in Hartford.[53]

A second Putnam plow is on display in the visitor center of Putnam Memorial State Park in Redding Connecticut. The center also has the bridle that was supposedly worn by Putnam's horse as he plunged over the precipice in Horseneck (Greenwich) Connecticut in 1779. Established in 1887, Putnam Memorial State Park, which is located on the site of General Putnam's December 1778 through May 1779 encampment, is the oldest state park in Connecticut.

The west side of a granite obelisk at the park reads: "Erected to commemorate the Winter Quarters of Putnam's Division of the Continental Army November 7th 1778. May 25th 1779." The east side contains words spoken by Putnam when he put down the attempted mutiny: "The World is full of their praises Posterity stands astonished at their Deeds."[54]

Eight. The Legacy

Looking back at the opinion of 18th and 19th century Americans, historian Bruce C. Daniels has stated: "With the exception of Washington, Putnam was the most celebrated hero of the revolutionary war."[55] William Swinton's 1874 history textbook taught students:

> General ISRAEL PUTNAM was one of the dashing officers of the Revolution. He was a farmer in Connecticut, and was ploughing the field when the news of Lexington came to him. He did not stay even to unyoke his oxen, but, mounting his horse, rode rapidly to Boston. Putnam was one of the leading officers at Bunker Hill. As the British advanced, he told his men not to fire until they could see the whites of the enemies' eyes. He was not a great general, but he was very brave, and his soldiers called him "Old Put."[56]

This book may be taken as an example of what 19th century school children were taught about Putnam, but should not be considered totally accurate. For example, the author mistakenly identifies Rufus Putnam as Israel's son.

As the 20th century dawned, memories of Israel Putnam seem to have faded little. Within the first few years of the century major biographies of Putnam were published.[57] Other Revolutionary War military leaders were also honored with published life stories: Philip Schuyler in 1903 and Seth Pomeroy in 1906.

Burton Stevenson's 1913 *American Men of Action*, which summarizes the exploits of great figures of the country's history, states this of Putnam: "For sheer, extravagant daring, which paused at no obstacle and trembled at no peril, he has, perhaps, never had his equal among American soldiers."[58]

An article in the *Hartford Courant* in 1903, gives some indication of Israel Putnam's fame at the time. It details the sad state of affairs of the reputation of Cassius M. Clay, a Kentucky abolitionist who had twice been sent as a minister to Russia by President Lincoln. The ending of the column includes the statement: "If he [Clay] had died then [at the height of his anti-slavery work], his fame would have been as secure as Israel Putnam's."[59]

When in 1910, Charles H.L. Johnston decided to write his book *Famous Scouts* for his *Famous Leaders Series*, he included as "Trappers, Pioneers, and Soldiers of the Frontier" Boone, Crockett, Houston, Cody and other American Legends. But he started off the book with an 18th century "Pioneer, Soldier, and Heroic Adventurer"—General Israel Putnam.[60]

Sadly, over the last 100 years since Johnston's book, the retellings of the Putnam story have, with few exceptions, been confined to children's books. Perhaps that is because our society places more importance on the intricate financial policies of an Alexander Hamilton or the refined diplomatic skills of a Jefferson over the rough-and-tumble physical heroism of "Old Wolf" Putnam.

Conclusion

Looking back from the 21st Century, it appears that an accumulation of new heroes, real and fictional, have replaced the Francis Marions, "Mad" Anthony Waynes, and Israel Putnams of 18th century America. Each new war has added its own heroes to the pantheon, the 19th century American West alone has provided material for an incredible number of books, motion pictures and TV shows. Today we have even made heroes of the actors and actresses who have played "heroes" in movies and television shows.

After the United States' decisive role in the defeat of Nazi Germany and Imperial Japan in World War II, there was a resurgence of patriotism and a reemergence of interest in the heroes of America's past. In May 1961, the *American Legion Magazine* ran an article on the American patriot leaders at Bunker Hill. Millions of the Legion's members at the time were veterans of the war in Europe and knew what it meant for someone to be compared with George Patton. The article stated: "Commanding the American flank was another unique character, Israel Putnam. A rotund, roaring, cursing veteran of a hundred battles against the French, Spaniards and Indians. 'Old Put' was the Gen. Patton of the early days of the Revolution."[61]

Surprisingly, the most popular and complete Internet database of movie information lists only three actors as having played Israel Putnam.[62] The most popular use of Israel Putnam as a character was not in a movie, a television show, or even a book—it was in the 2012 action video game *Assassin's Creed III*. Developed by Ubisoft Montreal, the game features a highly-fictionalized account of Revolutionary War events, including the Battle of Bunker Hill. Actor Andreas Apergis provides Putnam's voice.

The story of Israel Putnam brings us back to a time when an individual had to earn his or her hero status. There were no publicists putting out press releases with Photoshopped images. There were no scheduled appearances on talk shows or featured articles in celebrity magazines. For someone in 18th century America to have their fame spread throughout the 13 colonies, like occurred with Israel Putnam, was something special, something nearly unique. Yet, even before the American Revolution and his rise to the rank of general officer, Putnam's name was a household word far beyond his home region of New England.

Eight. The Legacy

The tradition of fearless American hero may not have started with Israel Putnam, but he certainly was one of the primary examples. In the mold of Putnam, we find the defenders of the Alamo in 1836, Civil War cavalry commander Philip Sheridan riding from Winchester, Virginia to rally his troops in 1864, the World War I hero Sergeant Alvin York fighting against incredible odds on the Western Front in 1918, and the perseverance and bravery of Lieutenant Colonel Hal Moore as he personally led his courageous troops at the 1965 Battle of la Drang in the Vietnam War.

The 21st century has brought with it a plague of worldwide terrorism that shows no signs of abating soon. Perhaps today we are ready to resurrect the stories of the heroes of long ago. As Americans seek to defend their way of life, it might be advantageous to look back to the roots of the country—to draw inspiration from the great leaders who proposed a government of the people, a society where everyone believed in the goals of life, liberty, and the pursuit of happiness. It might be beneficial to study, and maybe even emulate, the men and women who fought to preserve that society.

If we are ready to mine the American past for all that was best, sooner or later we will come across the virtue of courage and the part it played in our nation's history. And there is no individual at the founding of the American republic who better demonstrated courage than Israel Thomas Putnam.

Chapter Notes

Preface

1. Given the similarities between Rickenbacker and Putnam, it's interesting to note that throughout the summer of 1918, just before Rickenbacker became America's Ace of Aces, David Endicott Putnam, General Israel Putnam's great-great-great grandson held that title. David Putnam was killed in combat over Limey, France on September 12, 1918, at age 19 after having shot down a minimum of 13 German planes while serving in the French Air Service, and later the United States Air Service. At the time of Putnam's death, no other American fighter pilot had as many victories on his record.

Introduction

1. Putnam, Eben. *A History of the Putnam Family in England and America. Recording the Ancestry and Descendants of John Putnam of Danvers, Mass., Jan Poutman of Albany, N.Y., Thomas Putnam of Hartford, Conn.* Salem, MA: Salem pub. and Print., 1891. Of Israel Putnam's siblings whose dates of death are known, only his younger sister Mehitable survived him. The others were between 2 and 28 years older than Israel.

Mary Putnam 2/2/1691 (or 1690)–4/4/1713
Elizabeth Putnam 4/12/1695–11/4/1735
Sarah Putnam 9/26/1697–March 1750
William Putnam 2/8/1700–5/19/1729
Rachel Putnam 8/7/1702–12/28/1781
Ann Putnam 4/26/1705–1751
David Putnam 10/25/1707–1768
Eunice Putnam 4/13/1710–2/2/1787
Rufus Putnam 4/14/1713–4/4/1718
Huldah Putnam 11/29/1716–Unknown
Mehitable Putnam 3/12/1720–9/2/1801
Lydia Putnam 1723–unknown

2. Humphreys, David, and Rosemarie Zagarri. *Life of General Washington: With George Washington's "Remarks."* Athens: University of Georgia, 1991. Humphreys's biography of Washington was the only one authorized by George Washington himself.

3. David Humphreys was born in Derby, Connecticut (now part of Ansonia, Connecticut) in 1752. He was the son of a Congregational Church minister who served his congregation for 54 years (1733–1787). David Humphreys died in New Haven in 1818.

4. Humphreys, Frank Landon. *Life and times of David Humphreys, Soldier—Statesman—Poet, "Belov'd of Washington,"* New York and London: G.P. Putnam's Sons, 1917. 305. On June 2, 1784, George Washington sent a letter of introduction to Benjamin Franklin in which he said of Humphreys, "This Gentleman was several years in my family as an Aid de Camp. His zeal in the cause of his Country, his good sense, prudence, and attachment to me, rendered him dear to me; and I persuade myself you will find no confidence wch [sic] you may think proper to repose in him, misplaced. He possesses an excellent heart, good natural and acquired abilities and sterling integrity—to which may be added sobriety, & an obliging disposition."

5. Sletcher, Michael. *New Haven: From Puritanism to the Age of Terrorism.* Charleston, SC: Arcadia, 2004. 54. It appears from the records that the black soldiers received the same pay and provisions as the white soldiers.

6. These include New England theologian Increase Tarbox's biography. Tarbox, Increase Niles, *Life of Israel Putnam*. Boston: 1876.
7. Livingston, William Farrand. *Israel Putnam; Pioneer, Ranger, and Major-general, 1718–1790*. New York: G.P. Putnam's Sons, 1901.
8. Hatch, Louis Clinton. *Maine; a History*. New York: American Historical Society, 1919. 166.
9. Lockhart, Paul Douglas. *The Whites of Their Eyes: Bunker Hill, the First American Army, and the Emergence of George Washington*. New York: Harper, 2011.

Chapter One

1. Livingston, *Israel Putnam*, 126–127.
2. *History of Connecticut: Its People and Institutions*. George Larkin Clark. G.P. Putnam's Sons, 1914. Connecticut. 157.
3. Livingston, *Israel Putnam*, 408–409.
4. *Ibid.*, 127.
5. John Putnam (?–1662) was born in Buckinghamshire, which is northwest of London, England.
6. Hawthorne, Nathaniel. *The Scarlet Letter, a Romance*. London: David Bogue, 1851. 13.
7. Bridge, Horatio. *Personal Recollections of Nathaniel Hawthorne*. New York: Harper & Bros., 1893. 50.
8. Hanson, J.W. *History of the Town of Danvers from Its Early Settlement to the Year 1848*. Danvers: Author, 1848. 290.
9. The day Israel Putnam was born, the old Julian calendar was using the year "1717," with the New Year not starting until March. In most countries of Europe, the Gregorian calendar was in use and they were already using "1718," since for them the New Year started on January 1. In 1752, the British colonies in North America went to the Gregorian calendar and, in retrospect, looked upon January 1717 as being in the year 1718. This has little bearing on calculations of Putnam's age at different points in his life, since, for example, in July 1718 he was six months old whether you use the old or the new calendar.
10. *Harper's New Monthly Magazine*. New York: Harper & Bros., Vol. XII. 1856, 578. The house in Salem Village (now Danvers) in which Israel was born, is still in existence. It remained in Putnam family hands from the 17th century up until 1991, when it was donated to the local historical society. The house is now surrounded by a web of asphalt roads and highways. According to an 1855 article, the house contained some furnishings that resided in its parlor at the time of his birth 137 years earlier: a high-backed chair, a small table, a mirror and "one or two other pieces of furniture."
11. Livingston, *Israel Putnam*, 6.
12. Humphreys, David, Col. *An Essay on the Life of the Honourable Major-General Israel Putnam, addressed to the State Society of the Cincinnati in Connecticut*. Hartford: 1788. 19.
13. Hanson, J.W. *History of the Town of Danvers from Its Early Settlement to the Year 1848*. Danvers: Author, 1848. 179–180.
14. Livingston, *Israel Putnam*, 8.
15. *Ibid.*, 9–11.
16. Putnam, *A History*, 90. Some foundation stones, a well, and a pear tree from the Putnam's first house are mentioned as existing as late as 1891.
17. Livingston, *Israel Putnam*, 9–11.
18. Humphreys, *An Essay on the Life, 1788 Ed.* 26. To assist the modern reader, in excerpts from Humphreys 1788 biography, as well as other 18th century works, I have converted each Long S (which appears very much like a "f"), to what today is a normal "s".
19. Grosvenor, L. *The Life and Character of Maj. General Putnam: An Address Delivered at a Meeting of the Descendants of Maj. General Israel Putnam at Putnam, Conn., Oct. 25, 1855*. Boston: Farwell &, Printers and Stereotypers, 1855. 11.
20. Iden, Jay B. "The Arkansaw Traveler in Connecticut." *The Country Gentleman* Aug. 2, 1919: 10.
21. *Ibid.*
22. Grosvenor, *The Life and Character*, 11–12.
23. Three sons and four daughters lived to be at least 20 years old. Of those seven, four lived to be over 70 years old. The children, in order of birth, were: (1) Israel, Jr. born January 28, 1740, in Danvers, Essex, Massachusetts. Died at Belpre, Ohio March 2, 1812, aged 72. Moved to Ohio with his family; (2) Daniel born March 10, 1742, in Pomfret, Connecticut. Died August 8, 1758, in Pomfret, aged 16; (3) Hannah, born August 25, 1744, in Pomfret, Connecticut. Died April 3, 1821, in Pomfret, aged 76. Moved to Vermont with her family; (4) Elizabeth, born March 20, 1747, in Pomfret, Connecticut. Died January 24, 1765, in Pomfret, aged 17; (5) Mehitable, born October 21, 1749, in Pomfret, Connecticut. Died November 28, 1789, in Brooklyn, aged 40; (6) Mary born May 10, 1753, in Pomfret, Connecticut. Died November 18, 1825, in Conway, New Hampshire, aged 72; (7) Eunice born January

10, 1756, in Pomfret, Connecticut. Died June 27, 1799, in Pomfret, aged 43; (8) Daniel born November 18, 1759, in Pomfret, Connecticut. Died April 30, 1831, in Brooklyn, aged 71; (9) David Putnam born October 14? 1761, in Pomfret, Connecticut. Died November 21, 1761, aged 1 month; (10) Peter Schuyler born December 31, 1764, in Pomfret, Connecticut. Died September 1827 in Williamstown, Massachusetts, aged 62.

24. Griggs, Susan Jewett. *Early Homesteads of Pomfret and Hampton.* Abington Conn.: n.p., 1950. 84, 101.

25. Grosvenor. *The Life and Character,* 10.

26. Hurd, D. Hamilton. *History of New London County, Connecticut with Biographical Sketches of Many of Its Pioneers and Prominent Men.* Philadelphia: J.W. Lewis, 1882.

27. Bayles, Richard M. *History of Windham County, Connecticut.* New York: W.W. Preston, 1889. 574.

28. Islands with pastures were prized by colonial sheep owners of the 18th century. The water barrier provided an effective and inexpensive means by which the animals were prevented from straying and protected from their predators. Some small islands in Boston Harbor were noted for their abundance of sheep. Unfortunately, the island solution was not available to most New England farmers like Putnam whose property was located far inland.

29. Larned, Ellen D. *History of Windham County, Connecticut.* Thompson, CT: Author, 1874. 360.

30. *Ibid.,* 362.

31. Humphreys, *An Essay on the Life, 1788 Ed.* 24–25.

32. *Ibid.,* 25.

33. This was perhaps the first occurrence of an "animal" nickname being applied to a famous American military leader. Later, in the War of Independence, American generals Thomas Sumter and Francis Marion would earn the sobriquets, respectively, "the Carolina Gamecock" and "The Swamp Fox." In the 20th century, U.S. Army general Norman Schwarzkopf, Jr. acquired the nickname, "The Bear."

34. Putnam. *A History,* 348.

35. United States. U.S. Department of the Interior. National Park Service. *National Register of Historic Places Inventory-Nomination Form for the Israel Putnam Wolf Den.* Washington: GPO, 1985. In 1985 the Connecticut Historical Commission nominated the Israel Putnam Wolf Den in Pomfret for inclusion in the National Register of Historic Places. Describing it as a "small cave formed from a natural fissure in an outcropping of grey gneiss ledge overlooking a branch of Wolf Den Brook," the nomination form notes that early accounts of the cave's description (including John Warner Barber's Connecticut Historical Collections, which includes a 1838 engraving) closely match its appearance in the late 20th century. It also states that the killing of the wolf was "a deed which earned the future Revolutionary War hero the respect of his fellow farmers and townspeople."

Chapter Two

1. Griggs. *Early Homesteads,* 99.

2. Clark, George Larkin. *History of Connecticut: Its People and Institutions.* Connecticut: G.P. Putnam's Sons, 1914. Connecticut. 157; Bayles. *History of Windham,* 58. The other towns of Windham county reported the following numbers in 1756: Ashford, 1,245 white; Canterbury, 1,240 white, 20 black; Killingly, 2,100 white; Plainfield, 1,751 white, 49 black; Voluntown, 1,029 white, 19 black; Windham, 2,406 white, 40 black; Woodstock, 1,336 white, 30 black; Coventry, 1,617 white, 18 black; Lebanon, 3,171 white, 103 black; Mansfield, 1,598 white, 16 black; Union, 500 white.

3. Ford, Paul Leicester. *The True George Washington.* Philadelphia: J.B. Lippincott, 1896. 38–39. George Mercer (1733–1784), who was an aide to George Washington during the French and Indian War, wrote this description of a 28-year old Washington in 1760: "He may be described as being as straight as an Indian, measuring six feet two inches in his stockings, and weighing 175 pounds when he took his seat in the House of Burgesses in 1759. His frame is padded with well-developed muscles, indicating great strength. His bones and joints are large, as are his feet and hands. He is wide shouldered, but has not a deep or round chest; is neat waisted, but is broad across the hips, and has rather long legs and arms ... blue-gray penetrating eyes, which are widely separated and overhung by a heavy brow. His face is long rather than broad, with high round cheek bones, and terminates in a good firm chin. He has a clear though rather a colorless pale skin, which burns with the sun.... His mouth is large and generally firmly closed, but which from time to time discloses some defective teeth.... In conversation he looks you full in the face, is deliberate, deferential and engaging. His voice is agreeable rather than strong...."

4. Bayles. *History of Windham,* 53–54. The meetings were held on September 9.

5. Sawyer, Charles Winthrop. *Firearms in*

American History. Boston: Author, 1910. 101. The heavy infantry muskets of the British troops during the French and Indian War weighted about 10½ pounds, or 11½ with a bayonet, and were almost five feet long. The light infantry muskets weighed about a pound less and were around three inches shorter.

6. Early, Eleanor. *New England Cookbook*. New York: Random House, 1954. Little is known today of Hannah and no portraits of her exist. However, two centuries after her death, her recipe for apple pandowdy was given by her great-great-great-great-grandson to writer Eleanor Early for inclusion in her *New England Cookbook*. Apparently the baked dessert, made with sliced apples, cider, brown sugar and spices had been continually eaten by the family since Hannah's time. Hannah's dessert was the subject of a 1940s song, "Shoo-Fly Pie and Apple Pan Dowdy" which became a huge hit for American singer Dinah Shore.

7. Forty-six years later another intrepid adventurer, Moses Austin, would be born in Durham. Austin's dream to found an American settlement Texas would end with his death, but be picked up again by his son Stephen Austin, who became known as the "Father of Texas."

8. Sabine, Lorenzo. *Biographical Sketches of Loyalists of the American Revolution with an Historical Essay*. Boston: Little, Brown, 1864. 36.

9. Humphreys, *An Essay, 1788 Ed.*

10. Parkman, Francis. *Historic Handbook of the Northern Tour: Lakes George and Champlain, Niagara, Montreal, Quebec*. Boston: Little, Brown, 1885. 21.

11. Walker, Joseph Burbeen. *Life and Exploits of Robert Rogers, the Ranger. A Paper Read before the Members of the New England Historic Genealogical Society, at Their Monthly Meeting in Boston, November 5, 1884*. Boston: J.N. McClintock, 1885. 1.

12. Rogers, Robert. *Journals of Major Robert Rogers Containing an Account of the Several Excursions He Made under the Generals Who Commanded upon the Continent of North America, during the Late War; from Which May by Collected the Most Material Circumstances of Every Campaign upon That Continent, from the Commencement to the Conclusion of the War*. Albany: Joel Munsell's Sons, 1883. 82–85.

13. Humphreys, *An Essay 1788 Ed.*, 28.

14. Livingston, *Israel Putnam; Pioneer, Ranger, and Major-general, 1718–1790*, 37–39. Much of this chapter and the succeeding ones that cover incidents in Putnam's life during the French and Indian War are taken from Humphreys's biography, especially the first edition, which was published in 1788. That book can be divided into two major parts: the French and Indian War and the American Revolutionary War. While the former consists mostly of action stories probably related by Putnam himself, the Revolutionary War chapters are more detailed with dates and names, and even contain some first person stories by Humphreys himself.

15. Humphreys, *An Essay on the Life, 1788 Ed.*

16. *Ibid.*

17. *Ibid.*

18. Johnston, Henry Phelps. *Record of Service of Connecticut Men in the I. War of the Revolution, II. War of 1812, III. Mexican War*. Hartford: Case, Lockwood & Brainard, 1889. Ninety years after the massacre, the U.S. Congress saw that the name Wyoming was not forgotten: it gave the name to a territory 1,500 miles west of Pennsylvania's Wyoming Valley to the surprise of its residents. Twenty-two years later it became the 44th state of the United States.

19. Humphreys, *An Essay on the Life, 1788 Ed.*, 50.

20. *Ibid.*, 29–30.

21. Wells, Frederic P. *History of Newbury, Vermont, from the Discovery of the Coös Country to Present Time. With Genealogical Records of Many Families*. St. Johnsbury, VT: Caledonian, 1902. 487. New Hampshire-born Jonathan Butterfield served under Putnam as a scout in the war. Later, he became a gristmill owner and, when in his 60s, served in the Revolutionary War. He died at age 91 in 1804.

22. Rogers, *Journals* 34.

23. *Ibid.*, 33–34.

24. Humphreys, *An Essay on the Life, 1850 Ed.*, 20.

25. Tucker, Spencer, James R. Arnold, and Roberta Wiener. *The Encyclopedia of North American Indian Wars, 1607–1890: A Political, Social, and Military History*. Santa Barbara, CA: ABC-CLIO, 2011. 526. *The Encyclopedia of North American Indian Wars* estimates that a French flintlock musket would misfire about once in nine shots and experience a delayed fire approximately once in 18 shots.

26. McFeely, William S. *Grant: A Biography*. N.p.: W.W. Norton, 2002. In September 1756, Noah Grant died in action. His great-grandson Ulysses S. Grant would lead Union troops to victory in the American Civil War 109 years later.

27. Livingston, *Israel Putnam* 43.

28. The fort was never rebuilt. In the War of 1812, a handful of cannon were mounted at the site by the Americans, but were easily taken by the British forces.

29. Humphreys, *An Essay on the Life 1788 Ed.*
30. Livingston, *Israel Putnam*, 61.
31. *Ibid.*, 62.
32. Humphreys, *An Essay on the Life 1788 Ed.*, 45.
33. *Ibid.*, 43–48.
34. *Ibid.*, 40.
35. *Ibid.*
36. Humphreys, *An Essay on the Life 1788 Ed.*, 39.
37. Starbuck, David R. *The Great Warpath: British Military Sites from Albany to Crown Point.* Hanover, NH: University of New England, 1999. 84.
38. *Ibid.*
39. Lossing, Benson John. *The Pictorial Field Book of the Revolution: Or, Illustrations, by Pen and Pencil, of the History, Biography, Scenery, Relics, and Traditions of the War of Independence.* New York: Harper, 1851. 111–112.
40. Starbuck, David R. *Massacre at Fort William Henry.* Hanover, NH: University of New England, 2002. 58–59. The body of Richard Rogers, brother to the Rogers Rangers' commander Robert Rogers was one of those dug up and desecrated at Fort William Henry.
41. Humphreys, *An Essay on the Life 1788 Ed.*
42. *Ibid.*, 51.
43. *Ibid.*, 52.
44. *Ibid.*, 54.
45. *Ibid.*
46. Humphreys, *An Essay on the Life 1788 Ed.* 53–55.
47. Humphreys, *An Essay on the Life* 55–56.
48. Humphreys, *An Essay on the Life* 56. Humphreys describes Howe as "Exemplary to the officer, a friend to the soldier, the model of discipline, he had not failed to encounter every hardship and hazard." Since Humphreys was only six years old in the summer of 1758, we might assume that these are the sentiments of Israel Putnam.
49. Some readers might think this sounds like the stuff of folklore—something along the lines of the apocryphal tales of Buffalo Bill Cody or Calamity Jane. Indeed this heroic action might well be embellished or even invented, but it is also the type of impulsive action for which Putnam was known.
50. Humphreys, *An Essay on the Life 1788 Ed.* 58.
51. Rose, Alexander. *Washington's Spies: The Story of America's First Spy Ring.* New York: Bantam, 2006. 19–20. Alexander Rose goes into some detail in describing the depraved actions by Robert Rogers, as does the 2014 television series *Turn: Washington's Spies*, which is based on his book.
52. Humphreys, *An Essay on the Life 1788 Ed.*, 59.
53. Starbuck, *Great Warpath* 165.
54. Humphreys, *An Essay on the Life 1788 Ed.*, 60–61.
55. *Ibid.*, 61.
56. *Ibid.*, 62.
57. *Ibid.*, 63.
58. Livingston, *Israel Putnam* 87.
59. Humphreys, *An Essay on the Life 1788 Ed.*
60. Livingston, *Israel Putnam* 88–9.
61. Ridpath, John Clark. *The New Complete History of the United States of America.* Cincinnati: Jones Bros., 1904, 2305; Burton, Clarence Monroe, William Stocking, and Gordon K. Miller. *The City of Detroit, Michigan, 1701–1922.* Detroit-Chicago: S.J. Clarke, 1922, 899.
62. Humphreys, *An Essay on the Life 1788 Ed.* 67–68.
63. *Ibid.*, 68.
64. *Ibid.*, 68–69.
65. Holmes, Abiel. *The Annals of America, from the Discovery by Columbus in the Year 1492.* Cambridge: n.p., 1829. 523. Holmes was 26-years-old when Putnam died and about 63 when this edition of his *Annals* was published. A respected graduate of Yale College, Holmes was the father of the poet Oliver Wendell Holmes, Sr. and the grandfather of U.S. Supreme Court justice Oliver Wendell Holmes, Jr.
66. Humphreys, *An Essay on the Life 1788 Ed.* 69. Most depictions of this event show Putnam in some clothing or even in full uniform. However, in all likelihood, this is the description Humphreys received from Putnam himself.
67. Humphreys, *An Essay on the Life 1788 Ed.*, 70.
68. *Ibid.*, 94.
69. *Ibid.*, 71.
70. Tapley, Harriet Silvester. *Historical Collections of the Danvers Historical Society.* Vol. 10. Danvers, Massachusetts: Danvers Historical Society, 1922. 32.
71. Dwight, Timothy. *Travels in New-England and New-York: In Four Volumes.* London: Baynes, 1823. 131.
72. Humphreys, *An Essay on the Life 1788 Ed.*
73. *Ibid.*
74. *Ibid.*, 74–76.
75. Schuyler died in 1762 at age 52.
76. Humphreys, *An Essay on the Life 1788 Ed.* 76–82; Drake, Samuel G. Indian Captivities Or Life in the Wigwam: Being True Narratives of Captives Who Have Been Carried

Away by the Indians, from the Frontier Settlements of the U.S., from the Earliest Period to the Present Time. Auburn: Derby and Miller, 1850. 156–165.

77. This was the same General Thomas Gage who would be on the opposite side from Putnam during the American Revolutionary War 15 years later.

78. Livingston, *Israel Putnam* 108–109.

79. *Ibid.*

80. A defensive barrier consisting of downed trees with pointed ends facing the enemy forces. In recent times, abattis have been replaced by wire obstacles.

81. Humphreys, *An Essay on the Life 1788 Ed.* 82–86.

Chapter Three

1. Admiral Pocock (1706–1792) received his first command in the British Navy in 1733. Eventually rising to admiral after service in India, his greatest moment came at the Spanish surrender of Havana. He is remembered by an impressive white marble statue in Westminster Abbey, although he is buried 12 miles to the west, at St Mary's church in Twickenham. William Tryon who was the British Governor of New York during the time Israel Putnam commanded Continental Army troops in the Hudson Highlands, is buried in St. Mary's churchyard.

2. Much of the following sections are indebted to Humphreys, *An Essay on the Life 1788 Ed.* 86–88 and Livingston, *Israel Putnam* 117–128.

3. Humphreys, An Essay on the Life 1818 Ed. 77.

4. *Dictionary of Canadian Biography.* Vol. IV. Toronto: University of Toronto, 2015. During the American Revolutionary War, William Haviland was on General Amherst's staff and in 1779 commanded the Western District. Haviland died in 1784, a year after his promotion to general.

5. George Keppel, the 3rd Earl of Albemarle (1724–1772), was commander of the 1762 Havana invasion.

6. *Society of Colonial Wars in the Commonwealth of Massachusetts: Publication No. 5.* Boston, MA: Printed for the Society, 1899. 133; Shea, John Gilmary. *United States Catholic Historical Magazine* 1888: 7. Years later, Washington was to take a page out of Putnam's book. In 18th century colonial America, up until the Revolutionary War, it was a custom in some parts to celebrate "Pope-Day" which expressed hatred of Catholics and their church. It was the American equivalent of the British Guy Fawkes Day, which celebrated the defeat of the Catholic Fawkes who attempted to blow up Parliament in 1605. At the beginning of the War in 1775, General Washington released the following statement: "As the Commander-in-Chief has been apprised of a design formed for the observance of that ridiculous and childish custom of burning the effigy of the Pope, he cannot help expressing his surprise that there should be officers and soldiers in this army so void of common sense as not to see the impropriety of such a step at this juncture; at a time when we are soliciting, and have really obtained the friendship and alliance of the people of Canada, whom we ought to consider as brethren embarked in the same cause,—the defence of the Liberty of America. At this juncture and under such circumstances, to be insulting their religion, is so monstrous as not to be suffered or excused; indeed, instead of offering the most remote insult, it is our duty to address public thanks to these our brethren, as to them we are indebted for every late happy success over the common enemy in Canada." This statement by Washington, almost by itself, resulted in the ending of "Pope-Day" celebrations.

7. Livingston, *Israel Putnam* 125.

8. French Canadians also were guaranteed the right to freely practice their Roman Catholic religion, an important consideration when one considers Great Britain's notorious anti–Catholic laws back home.

9. The term "Sons of liberty" was coined by the Ireland-born member of the British Parliament, Isaac Barré (1726–1802) in one of his speeches. A colonel in the French and Indian War, Barré was one of the strongest supporters of American colonist rights in Parliament.

10. In 1926, General Motors Corporation used Chief Pontiac's name as the brand name of a line of automobiles, which were produced in Pontiac. Michigan, a city which is named after Chief Pontiac. General Motors terminated Pontiac production in 2009.

11. Parkman, Francis. *The Conspiracy of Pontiac and the Indian War after the Conquest of Canada; Vol. 1.* Boston: Little, Brown, 1870.

12. In May 1763, three forts between the south ends of Lakes Michigan and Erie were captured by Pontiac allies: Sandusky, St. Joseph and Miami. At the beginning of June 1763, Fort Ouitenon (south of Lake Michigan) and Fort Michilimackinac (north of Lake Michigan) fell. At the end of June, three forts southeast of Lake Erie fell: Venango, Le Boeuf and Presque Isle.

13. Livingston, *Israel Putnam* 129.

14. Tarbox, *Life* 45.
15. Hunt, Daniel. *History of Pomfret: A Discourse Delivered on the Day of Annual Thanksgiving, in the First Church in Pomfret, Nov. 19th, 1840.* Hartford: J. Holbrook, Printer, 1841. 25. Old tenor was an issue of paper money by the Connecticut colony in the early to middle 18th century.
16. Dwight, *Travels* 131.
17. *Ibid.*
18. "Founders Online: From George Washington to Major General Israel Putnam, 19 October 1777." *Founders Online.* National Archives, n.d. Web. 29 June 2016.
19. The land had been purchased years earlier by his father, Newport trader Godfrey Malbone. It was a portion of the original land grant and was even larger than the part Israel Putnam had purchased from Governor Jonathan Belcher.
20. Livingston, *Israel Putnam* 148–9, 159, 160; Mallary, Peter T., and Tim Imrie. *New England Churches & Meetinghouses 1680–1830.* New York: Vendome, 1985. 83–87.
21. Livingston, *Israel Putnam* 159.
22. Today, the building is a Unitarian Universalist Church.
23. Root, Mary Philotheta. *Chapter Sketches, Connecticut Daughters of the American Revolution; Patron Saints.* New Haven: Connecticut Chapters, Daughters of the American Revolution, 1901. 136–148.
24. She would ultimately outlive her daughter Deborah by 13 years and her son-in-law Israel by five years.
25. *Daughters of the American Revolution Magazine* Volumes 46–47 1915: 257.
26. In the 21st century, five-square-mile Gardiner's Island, is one of the largest privately owned islands in the United States. It is still owned by descendants of Lion Gardiner.
27. Totten, John Reynolds. *The New York Genealogical and Biographical Record.* Vol. 27–28. New York: N.Y. Genealogical and Biographical Society, 1898. 15.
28. Abbott, Katharine M. *Old Paths and Legends of the New England Border; Connecticut, Deerfield, Berkshire.* New York and London: G.P. Putnam's Sons, 1907. 84–85. Captain Kidd was executed in England in 1701.
29. Payne, Robert. *The Island: The Story of the Fortunes & Vicissitudes & Triumphs of the Island, Once Known as Monchonake ... Now Known as Gardiner's Island ... Now Faithfully Related from Original Documents and Presented to the Public.* New York: Harcourt, Brace, 1958. 161.
30. Gardiner, Curtiss C. *Lion Gardiner and His Descendants.* St. Louis: A. Whipple, 1890. 116–117.
31. Green, Harry Clinton., and Mary Wolcott Green. *The Pioneer Mothers of America: A Record of the More Notable Women of the Early Days of the Country, and Particularly of the Colonial and Revolutionary Periods.* New York: G.P. Putnam's Sons, 1912. 124–130. At this time, Israel daughter, Hannah, was married and living with her husband.
32. "Sign of General Wolfe." EMuseum. Connecticut Historical Society Museum & Library, n.d. Web. 08 Dec. 2015. Sometimes newspaper articles and books have mistakenly referred to it as the "General Wolf Inn" and claimed that it was named after Israel himself and referred his killing of the sheep herd-ravaging wolf. The actual sign, now on display at the Connecticut Historical Society Museum & Library in Hartford, is imprinted with the name Wolfe, not Wolf, and includes the image of a red-coated British officer, not a wolf-hunting Pomfret farmer.
33. Larned, *History* 6.
34. Larned, *History* 6.
35. Grosvenor, *The Life and Character* 31.
36. "Unveil Tablet for Gen. Putnam: Memorial to Revolutionary War Hero Erected in Brooklyn." *The Hartford Courant* 10 Aug. 1918: 10.
37. "Founders Online: Thomas Jefferson to Walter Jones, 2 January 1814." *Founders Online.* National Archives, n.d. Web. June 29, 2016.
38. Tarbox, *Life* 284.
39. *Ibid.*, 284–285.
40. *Ibid.*
41. Frothingham, Richard. *History of the Siege of Boston: And of the Battles of Lexington, Concord, and Bunker Hill: Also an Account of the Bunker Hill Monument.* Boston: Little, Brown, 1890. 165.
42. *Ibid.*
43. Amory, Thomas C. *Old Cambridge and New.* Boston: James R. Osgood, 1871. 19.
44. Humphreys, *An Essay on the Life 1788 Ed.* 100–101.
45. Root, *Chapter Sketches* 141.
46. McCullough, David 1776, 2005. 34–5.
47. Sanguine temperament was one of the four personality types of ancient Greek medicine. It denoted a warmhearted, cheerful person. The other types were: choleric (fiery and highly reactive), melancholic (sad and fearful), and phlegmatic (slow and sluggish).
48. Grosvenor, *The Life and Character* 30–31.
49. At age 19, Knox was present at the Boston Massacre and served as a witness at the trial of the British soldiers. In 1775, in perhaps the most incredible feat of his career, Knox transported cannon captured at New York's Fort Ticonderoga to Boston. The 300-

mile-long trip in December down the Hudson and across Massachusetts on wooden sledges took 56 days, but the cannon allowed Washington to force the British out of Boston. By the end of the Revolutionary War, Knox had advanced to the position of major general, the youngest one of the war at age 31. In 1785 Knox became the new nation's Secretary of War. He died in 1806.

50. *Founding Families: Digital Editions of the Papers of the Winthrops and the Adamses,* ed. C. James Taylor. Boston: Massachusetts Historical Society, 2016.

51. Snowden, William W. *The Ladies' Companion* 1837: 260.

52. *Winthrops and the Adamses.*

53. Putnam, *A History* 302. Judah Dana was the son of Israel's daughter Hannah and John Dana. Born in Pomfret, Judah was eight months old when his famous grandfather, and his 13-year-old uncle Daniel, left for their Mississippi expedition. He was 18 years old when the Israel Putnam died. Judah graduated from Dartmouth College, became an attorney, and served in various capacities in government until in 1836, when he became one of Maine's U.S. Senators. He died at age 73 in 1845.

54. Tarbox, *Life* 322.

55. *Ibid.*

56. Head Quarters, Peeks Kill, 14 July 1777. Putnam, Israel, and Worthington Chauncey Ford. *General Orders Issued by Major-General Israel Putnam, When in Command of the Highlands, in the Summer and Fall of 1777. Edited by W.C. Ford.* Historical Printing Club: Brooklyn, N.Y., 1893. 27.

57. Parton, James. *Life and Times of Benjamin Franklin.* New York: Mason Brothers, 1864. 522.

58. Castle, Egerton. *Schools and Masters of Fence: From the Middle Ages to the Eighteenth Century.* London: G. Bell and Sons, 1885.

59. Cutter, William, *Life of Israel Putnam.* New York: 1847, 362–3.

60. *Ibid.,* 363–4.

61. Livingston, *Israel Putnam* 157.

62. Cutter, William, *Life of Israel Putnam,* 133.

63. Chernow, Ron. *Washington: A Life.* New York: Penguin, 2010, 191.

64. Patrick, Bethanne Kelly., and John M. Thompson. *An Uncommon History of Common Things.* Washington, D.C.: National Geographic, 2015. 75.

65. Deseret News 14 June 1851: 279.

66. Cutter, *Life,* 133.

67. Crawford, Mary Caroline. *Among Old New England Inns: Being an Account of Little Journeys to Various Quaint Inns and Hostelries of Colonial New England.* Boston: L.C. Page, 1907. 236. Putnam's establishment wasn't the only post–French and Indian War tavern named after General Wolfe. Boston could boast of a downtown Wolfe tavern and a Wolfe Tavern opened in the 1760s in Newburyport (in the far northeastern tip of Massachusetts) with a wooden sign depicting Wolfe's image.

68. "Sign of General Wolfe." *CHS Museum and Library.* Connecticut Historical Society, n.d. Web. June 26, 2016.

69. Livingston, *Israel Putnam,* 157–8.

70. *Winthrops and the Adamses.*

71. Livingston, *Israel Putnam,* 158.

72. Salem, F.W. *Beer, Its History and Its Economic Value as a National Beverage.* Hartford: F.W. Salem & Co., 1880. 27–28.

73. Israel Putnam Warner died at age 93 in 1862, the week before the launch of the Civil War ironclad warship, the *USS Monitor.*

74. Livingston, *Israel Putnam* 151; *Collections of the New York Historical Society.* New York: New York Historical Society, 1881. 355.

75. Tarbox, *Life,* 72.

76. Larned, *History,* 4–5.

77. Livingston, *Israel Putnam,* 162.

78. *Ibid.,* 167–172.

79. Putnam, Israel, Rufus Putnam, and Albert Carlos Bates. *The Two Putnams, Israel and Rufus: In the Havana Expedition, 1762, and in the Mississippi River Exploration, 1772–73, with Some Account of the Company of Military Adventurers.* Hartford: Connecticut Historical Society, 1931, 125–126.

80. Born the same year as Israel Putnam, Haldimand was part of Amherst's 1760 expedition to Montreal in the French and Indian War. Several years later he commanded at Pensacola, Florida, where Putnam saw him during his Mississippi journey. During the Revolutionary War and for a few years after it, Haldimand served as governor of Quebec province (1778–1786). In Canada he was known as an administrator who concentrated on resettling refugees from the 13 colonies: Tories and Native Americans who had been British allies. Haldimand was knighted by King George III in 1785 and lived one year longer than Putnam.

81. This is the same Small whose life Putnam would save years later at the Battle of Bunker Hill.

82. Britain controlled West Florida (which included the southern half of the present day state of Mississippi) from the end of the French and Indian War in 1763 until 1781. Peter Chester was the last and longest-serving of the West Florida British governors (1770–1781).

83. Livingston, *Israel Putnam*,169.
84. Putnam, *The Two* Putnams, 252–253.
85. *Ibid.*, 208.
86. Decades later, in 1830, the Choctaw were the first Native People to be forcefully moved from their ancestral homelands to the Oklahoma Indian territory under President Andrew Jackson's Indian Removal Act. Despite opposition by Christian missionaries and such notables as Congressman Davy Crockett, thousands of men, women, and children died on the forced march, which was aptly named the "Trail of Tears."
87. Putnam, *The Two Putnams* 260–261.

Chapter Four

1. *Colonial Williamsburg: The Journal of the Colonial Williamsburg Foundation.* Williamsburg, VA: The Colonial Williamsburg Foundation. Vol. 26–27 (2004): 84. Web.
2. The others were the Quartering Act, the Administration of Justice Act and the Massachusetts Government Act.
3. Daniel Tyler (1750–1832) married Israel Putnam's daughter Mehitable in 1771. She died on November 28, 1789. Six months later, Israel Putnam died. Twelve days after the General's death, Daniel Tyler married Sarah Edwards. One of their great-grandchildren was President Theodore Roosevelt's wife, Edith Kermit Carow.
4. Livingston, *Israel Putnam*, 175.
5. *Ibid.*, 176.
6. Frothingham, Richard. *Life and Times of Joseph Warren.* Boston: Little, Brown, 1865. 340.
7. It's said that Dr. Young coined the name of the state of Vermont, combining the French words for green and mountain. He died in 1777 while serving as a physician in the Continental Army.
8. Frothingham, *Life*, 341.
9. *The Boston Gazette*, founded in 1719, was one of the leading newspapers in the colonies at this time that supported the grievances of the colonists against the British government.
10. Larned, *History*, 128.
11. *Annual Report of the Registry Department of the City of Boston of Boston.* Boston: The City of Boston, 1905. 323. In the decade before the Revolutionary War, and throughout the war, the population of Boston was only about 15,000.
12. This is less than 1 percent of the United States' 2010 population.
13. Revere, who was born in 1735, became one of the top silver craftsmen in the colonies. His ride on April 18, 1775, made him a legend. He died at age 83 in 1818.
14. William Dawes died in 1799 age 44.
15. Samuel Prescott, born in 1751, later served the Patriot cause on a privateer. When he was captured, he was sent to a British prison camp in Nova Scotia, where he died in 1777.
16. Humphreys, *An Essay on the Life 1788 Ed.*, 103.
17. Tarbox, *Life*, 83.
18. Livingston, *Israel Putnam*, 193–194.
19. Williams, Stephen W. *The Genealogy and History of the Family of Williams in America.* Greenfield: Merriam & Mirick, 1847. 129–130. Born in 1723, Ebenezer Williams, like Israel Putnam, had served at Fort Edward in 1757 during the French and Indian War. When he died in 1780, he was a colonel with the colonial forces.
20. "The Regiment of the Hon. Artemas Ward, Esq. Orderly Book." *Proceedings of the Massachusetts Historical Society* (1878): 89. Web. July 3, 2016.
21. Livingston, *Israel Putnam*, 194.
22. Humphreys, *An Essay on the Life 1788 Ed.*, 103.
23. Livingston, *Israel Putnam* 196–213.
24. *Connecticut Courant* 19 June 1775: 4.
25. Livingston, *Israel Putnam*, 192.
26. Sawyer, Charles Winthrop. *Firearms in American History*, 183–188.
27. Livingston, *Israel Putnam*, 196–213.
28. "House History." *Adams House.* N.p., n.d. Web. 26 June 2016. This is the same house where, two years later, British General John Burgoyne would be held as a prisoner following his defeat at the Battle of Saratoga.
29. Livingston, *Israel Putnam* 198.
30. *Ibid.*, 198–199.
31. *Ibid.*, 199.
32. *Ibid.*, 199.
33. *Ibid.*, 199–200.
34. *Ibid.*, 200.
35. Humphreys, *An Essay on the Life 1788 Ed.*, 104–105.
36. Livingston, *Israel Putnam* 203.
37. Humphreys, *An Essay on the Life 1788 Ed.*, 107.
38. Tarbox, *Life*, 95–96.
39. Livingston, *Israel Putnam*, 204.
40. Humphreys, *An Essay on the Life 1818 Ed.*, 185.
41. Burnett, Edmund Cody. *Letters of Members of the Continental Congress.* Washington: Carnegie Institution, 1921. 142.
42. Sherman, like Putnam has been born in Massachusetts and lived there for two decades before permanently moving to Connecticut. While Putnam was undoubtedly Connecticut's foremost military leader of the time,

Sherman is often considered its preeminent politician. As a long-term member of the Continental Congress, he worked on some of its most important committees, including the one that drafted the Declaration of Independence.

43. Ibid.
44. Frothingham, Richard. *The Centennial: Battle of Bunker Hill*. Boston: Little, Brown, 1875, 18.
45. John Trumbull the painter was born in 1756 and died in 1843. The Detroit Institute of Arts' collection includes a 1793 oil painting of poet John Trumbull by painter John Trumbull.
46. Trumbull, John. *M'Fingal, a Modern Epic Poem*. Hartford: S. Andrus and Son, 1856, 77.
47. Ibid., 52.
48. Chase, Ellen. *The Beginnings of the American Revolution: Based on Contemporary Letters, Diaries and Other Documents*. London: Pitman, 1911, 367.
49. Brooks was born in 1752 and died in 1825. He was governor of Massachusetts from 1816 to 1823 and the political adversary of Putnam detractor Henry Dearborn.
50. Livingston, *Israel Putnam*, 207.
51. "Putnam Lodge No. 46." *The Hartford Courant*, Aug. 22, 1901.
52. Chase, Ellen. *The Beginnings of the American Revolution: Based on Contemporary Letters, Diaries and Other Documents*, 367.
53. Livingston, *Israel Putnam*, 208.
54. Ibid., 208.
55. Ibid., 209.
56. Ibid., 209.
57. Ibid., 209.
58. Wright, John D. *The Routledge Encyclopedia of Civil War Era Biographies*. New York: Routledge, 2012, 537; Hettle, Wallace. *Inventing Stonewall Jackson: A Civil War Hero in History and Memory*. Baton Rouge: Louisiana State University Press, 2011, 60.
59. Gardiner was mortally wounded at the Battle of Bunker Hill. When he died two weeks later, Washington attended his funeral service.
60. Fleming, Thomas J. *The Story of Bunker Hill*. New York: Collier, 1962.
61. Livingston, *Israel Putnam* 210–211.
62. Ibid., 211–212. Had Thomas Knowlton been an advisor to the British high command, it is likely the Battle of Bunker Hill would have gone far better for the King's forces, and quite possible that the American revolt would have been nipped in the bud.
63. Livingston, *Israel Putnam*, 212.
64. Ibid.
65. Ibid., 213.

66. Ibid., 214.
67. *The Journals of Each Provincial Congress of Massachusetts in 1774 and 1775, and of the Committee of Safety, with an Appendix, Containing the Proceedings of the County Conventions-narratives of the Events of the Nineteenth of April, 1775-papers Relating to Ticonderoga and Crown Point, and Other Documents, Illustrative of the Early History of the American Revolution*. Boston: Dutton and Wentworth, Printers to the State, 1838. 157. In April, only a few days after Lexington and Concord, the Congress "Resolved, That Richard Gridley, Esq., be and hereby is appointed chief engineer of the forces now raising in the colony for the defence of the rights and liberties of the American continent; and that there be paid to the said Richard Gridley, out of the public treasury of this colony, during his continuance in that service, at the rate of one hundred and seventy pounds, lawful money, per annum. And it is further Resolved, that from and after the time when the said forces shall be disbanded, during the life of said Gridley, there shall be paid to him, out of the said treasury, the sum of one hundred and twenty-three pounds, lawful money, per annum."
68. Livingston, *Israel Putnam*, 214.
69. Ibid.
70. Ibid., 216.
71. Samuel Langdon (1723–1797), a Congregational minister in Portsmouth, New Hampshire from 1774 to 1780, was the 13th president of Harvard College.
72. Livingston, *Israel Putnam*, 217.
73. Ibid., 217.
74. One of the few commanders at Bunker Hill who was older than Israel Putnam, the sixty-four-year-old John Whitcomb, had served with distinction as a colonel in the French and Indian War and was commissioned a major general by Massachusetts in early 1775. In 1776, he was appointed a brigadier general by the Continental Congress. He resigned soon after.
75. Livingston, *Israel Putnam*, 221.
76. Ibid., 227–8.
77. Ibid., 227–8.
78. Ibid., 220.
79. Wright, Robert. *The Life of Major-General James Wolfe: Founded on Original Documents and Illustrated by His Correspondence, including Numerous Unpublished Letters Contributed from the Family Papers of Noblemen and Gentlemen, Descendants of His Companions*. London: Chapman & Hall, 1864, 468.
80. Waters, Wilson, and Henry Spaulding Perham. *History of Chelmsford, Massachusetts*. Lowell, MA: Printed for the Town by

Courier-Citizen, 1917, 232. Spaulding died on July 31, 1820, and was buried in his hometown of Chelmsford, Massachusetts.
81. *Ibid.*, 226.
82. Barber, John Warner. *United States Book, Or, Interesting Events in the History of the United States.* New Haven: L.H. Young, 1833, 125.
83. Brown, A.E. *Beside Old Hearthstones.* Boston: Lee & Shepard, 1897, 329–333.
84. Wethersfield's John Chester was 26 years old at the time of the battle. He and his company didn't arrive at the scene of the fighting until late afternoon. They were delayed when he argued with another officer whose men were retreating. Chester threatened to order his men to shoot the other troops if they did not return to the fight. The other officer relented and his men returned. In 1776, Chester was commissioned a colonel. He passed away at age 60 in 1809.
85. Webb, J. Watson, Silas Deane, and John Austin Stevens. *Reminiscences of Gen'l Samuel B. Webb of the Revolutionary Army.* New York: Globe Stationery and Print., 1882, 12.
86. Humphreys, *An Essay on the Life, 1850 Ed.*, 80–2.
87. The spot in Quincy where the Adamses stood is today marked by the Abigail Adams Cairn on Penn's Hill. Constructed in 1896, the stone monument is composed of stones gathered by children and adults from historic sites as well as their own properties.
88. Livingston, *Israel Putnam* 228–230.
89. *Ibid.*, 228.
90. *Ibid.*, 228–229.
91. Swett, Samuel, *History of the Battle of Bunker Hill, with Information Derived from the Surviving Soldiers Present at the Celebration, June 17, 1825.* Boston: 1826, 30.
92. Livingston, *Israel Putnam* 229.
93. Waters, *History* 250–252. After the war, Ford became a farmer and lumberman. He died on November 6, 1822, at age 84.
94. Livingston, *Israel Putnam*, 229.
95. *Ibid.*
96. Livingston, *Israel Putnam*, 229–230.
97. "Drumming out" involved the humiliation of being publicly dismissed from the army while drums beat. In the Revolutionary War, it was often preceded by a flogging.
98. *The Free Lance-Star* [Fredericksburg, Virginia] 14 Oct. 1946: 4.
99. *Peter Force's American Archives* 4th ser. 4 (n.d.): 1438. Web.
100. *Ibid.*
101. Tarbox, *Life*, 158.
102. Humphreys, *An Essay on the Life 1788 Ed.*, 109–110.

103. *The North American Review* 7 (1818): 244. Ebenezer Bean stated: "When we arrived at the redoubt, General Putnam was there and very active; was urging the men on, giving orders, riding from one end of the line to the other, as far as I could observe, and continued active through the action."
104. *Ibid.*; Grosvenor, *The Life and Character*, 22. Amos Barns said: "When we got to the top of Bunker Hill, I saw two field pieces which had ceased firing; General Putnam was on his horse near them, and when we passed him he requested Colonel Stark to press on as fast as possible."
105. *Ibid.*, 22.
106. *Ibid.*, 22.
107. Humphreys, *An Essay on the Life 1788 Ed.*, 109–110.
108. Frothingham, *The Centennial*, 184.
109. Gridley died in Massachusetts in 1796 at age 86 from blood poisoning incurred from cutting dogwood bushes. In 1876, Gridley bones were exhumed and reburied under a large granite monument in a Canton cemetery, all except his grey braided queue, which was retained by the Canton Historical Society. Huntoon, Daniel T.V. *History of the Town of Canton, Norfolk County, Massachusetts.* Cambridge: J. Wilson and Son, 1893. 377–378.
110. Hichborn (1745–1817) was a colonel in the Massachusetts militia.
111. "To John Adams from Benjamin Hichborn, 25 November 1775," *Founders Online.* National Archives, n.d. Web. June 29, 2016.
112. "Resolved: Advances in Forensic Identification of U.S War Dead." *National Museum of Health and Medicine (NMHM): Case Study: Paul Revere.* N.p., n.d. Web. June 26, 2016.
113. Johnson, William. *Sketches of the Life and Correspondence of Nathanael Greene, Major General of the Armies of the United States, in the War of the Revolution.* Charleston: Printed for the Author, by A.E. Miller, 1822. 32.
114. Wheildon, William W. *New History of the Battle of Bunker Hill, June 17, 1775, Its Purpose, Conduct, and Result.* Boston: Lee & Shepard, 1875, 41. Of the Naval force of 1,000 men with 168 guns that participated, only one officer, a lieutenant, was wounded.
115. *Ibid.*, 33.
116. Niven, John. *Connecticut Hero, Israel Putnam.* Hartford: American Revolution Bicentennial Commission of Connecticut, 1977. 63. John Niven (1921–1997) was editor of the Salmon P. Chase Papers.
117. *Ibid.*, 62.
118. "The Decisive Day Is Come | Letter

from Lt. John Waller to a Friend, 21 June 1775." *Massachusetts Historical Society.*, n.d. Web. June 29, 2016.

119. *Ibid.*

120. Howe, William Howe., Edward Everett. Hale, and Benjamin Franklin. Stevens. *General Sir William Howe's Orderly Book at Charleston, Boston and Halifax, June 17, 1775 to 1776, 26 May: To Which Is Added the Official Abridgement of General Howe's Correspondence with the English Government during the Siege of Boston, and Some Military Returns and Now First Printed from the Original Manuscripts.* London: B.F. Stevens, 1890, 3.

121. Bailyn, Bernard. "'The Decisive day is Come...': The Battle of Bunker Hill." The Massachusetts Historical Society, 2003. https://www.masshist.org/bh/essay.html.

122. Tuchman, Barbara Wertheim. "General Israel Putnam." 200th Anniversary of Putnam's Horseneck Ride (February 24, 1979). Greenwich Historical Society, Greenwich, Connecticut. Address. Paper in the archives of the Connecticut Historical Society in Hartford.

123. *Founding Families: Digital Editions of the Papers of the Winthrops and the Adamses,* ed. C. James Taylor. Boston: Massachusetts Historical Society, 2016.

124. In addition to being one of the most influential anti-slavery figures of his time, Sturge (1793–1859) was a noted activist for peace, worker rights and the right to vote.

125. "The Decisive Day Is Come: Letter from John Quincy Adams to Joseph Sturge, Page 3." Massachusetts Historical Society, n.d. Web. June 27, 2016.

126. Rogers, J.A. *Africa's Gift to America: The Afro-American in the Making and Saving of the United States.* Middletown, Connecticut: Wesleyan UP, 2014. 108. One Hessian officer wrote in a letter on October 23, 1777, "No [American] regiment is to be seen in which there are not Negroes in abundance and among them there are able-bodied, strong, and brave fellows."

127. *Ibid.*

128. Barlow, Joel. *The Vision of Columbus: A Poem in Nine Books with Explanatory Notes.* Hagers-Town: Printed and Published by W.D. Bell, 1820.

129. Trumbull is best known for his paintings of the Revolutionary War including four large paintings in the rotunda of the U.S. Capitol building. One of these, depicting the Declaration of Independence, is arguably the most famous painting of an American Revolution scene. Since the Bicentennial year of 1976, it has been featured on the reverse of the U.S. two dollar bill, while his painting of Alexander Hamilton has appeared on the front of the ten-dollar bill since 1929. Painter John Trumbull came from arguably the most prominent 18th century family of Eastern Connecticut. His father, Jonathan Trumbull, Sr., was the only royal governor to side with independence at the beginning of the American Revolution, his brother Jonathan Trumbull, Jr. was military secretary to George Washington and became governor of Connecticut in 1797. Another brother, Joseph Trumbull was the first commissary general of the Continental Army. After Benedict Arnold's treason, the British arrested and imprisoned John Trumbull, the painter, in England as a possible American spy. He was released after seven months. He died at age 87, a decade after donating over 100 of his Revolution-era works to Yale College in exchange for an annuity. Joel Barlow later became a supporter of the French Revolution and in 1812, on a quest to interview Napoleon, died of exposure with the French Army as it retreated from Russia. He was 58.

130. Cutter, *Life,* 375.

131. Clarence, C.W. *A Biographical Sketch of the Life of Ralph Farnham, of Acton, Maine, Now in the One Hundred and Fifth Year of His Age, and the Sole Survivor of the Glorious Battle of Bunker Hill.* Boston: n.p., 1860; "The Sole Survivor of the Battle of Bunker Hill." *New York Times,* Sep. 11 1860." Acton-Shapleigh Historical Society; "Ralph Farnham." Acton Shapleigh Historical Society, n.d. Web. June 27, 2016; Friedel, Megan. "Object of the Month Archive About." *Massachusetts Historical Society: Ralph Farnham, the Last Survivor of the Battle of Bunker Hill?* Massachusetts Historical Society, Oct. 2005. Web. June 27, 2016.

132. In addition to her work to honor the patriots at the Battle of Bunker Hill, Hale was instrumental in leading efforts to preserve Washington's Mt. Vernon home, was a driving force in getting Thanksgiving declared a national holiday, and was one of the first Americans to write a novel on the subject of slavery. After Thomas Edison invented the phonograph, lines from "Mary Had a Little Lamb" in 1877 became the first human speech ever recorded.

133. Kohler, Max J. *Judah Touro, Merchant and Philanthropist.* Baltimore?: n.p., 1905, 97. Judah Touro was born in Newport, Rhode Island, on June 16, 1775, the very day that colonial troops were building fortifications that would serve them at the following day's Battle of Bunker Hill. Touro moved to Boston and then to New Orleans, where his connections with Massachusetts associates helped him grow a successful business in dry goods

and food items. A staunch patriot, Touro volunteered to serve his country during the War of 1812 and was struck down by "a twelve-pound shot" and left for dead.

134. Warren, George Washington. *The History of the Bunker Hill Monument Association during the First Century of the United States of America*. Boston: J.R. Osgood, 1877, 284; Kohler, *Judah Touro* 101. George Washington Warren's *The History of the Bunker Hill Monument*, includes this description of Touro: "He was one of that smallest of all the classes into which mankind can be divided—of men who accumulate wealth without even doing a wrong, taking an advantage, or making an enemy; who become rich without being avaricious; who deny themselves the comforts and enjoyments of life, that they may acquire the means of promoting the comfort and elevating the condition of their fellow-men." Although Touro gave generously to found synagogues and Hebrew schools, his gifts to all charities were legendary. When a friend suggested that he might make more money by use of a building he was letting a Christian congregation use rent-free, Touro replied: "I am a friend to religion and I will not pull down the church to increase my means!" Kohler, *Judah Touro* 101.

135. Lawrence, Amos, and William Richards Lawrence. *Extracts from the Diary and Correspondence of the Late Amos Lawrence: With a Brief Account of Some Incidents in His Life*. Boston: Gould and Lincoln, 1855. 174.

136. "Battle of Bunker Hill cannon found in cellar." Nashua Telegraph 3 Mar. 1989: 4.

137. Tarbox, *Life* 332–340.

138. The New York 7th was nicknamed the "Silk Stocking Regiment" because it included so many members of the wealthiest New York families. Created in 1806, it served in the Civil War, the Spanish American War and World War I.

139. *Ibid.*, 334.

140. Previously, General Grant's most important commander during the American Civil War, General Sherman held the position of Commanding General of the United States Army for a full 14 years: 1869–1883, during which he was in overall command of U.S. forces during the Indian Wars of the American West.

141. Winsor, Justin. *Celebration of the Centennial Anniversary of the Battle of Bunker Hill. With an Appendix Containing a Survey of the Literature of the Battle, Its Antecedents and Results*. Boston: Printed by Order of the City Council, 1875, 131–132.

142. *Ibid.*, 339–340.

143. TITLE I, THE STATE AND ITS GOVERNMENT, CHAPTER 3, STATE EMBLEMS, FLAG, ETC. Section 3:8. May 10, 1945. When invited to attend a veteran's reunion on the 32nd anniversary of the Battle of Bennington in Vermont, Stark was too ill to attend but instead wrote a toast for the occasion which included the phrase, "Live Free Or Die; Death Is Not The Worst of Evils." In 1945, "Live Free or Die" was adopted as the official state motto of the State of New Hampshire. The motto and Stark's name as its author appear in the state statutes: "3:8 State Motto.—The words 'Live Free or Die,' written by General John Stark, July 31, 1809, shall be the official motto of the state." For decades, every New Hampshire motor vehicle marker plate has carried Stark's four words.

144. "Founders Online: Thomas Jefferson to Walter Jones, 2 January 1814." *Founders Online*. National Archives, n.d. Web. June 29, 2016.

145. Rush, Benjamin, and Lyman Henry. Butterfield. *Letters of Benjamin Rush*. Philadelphia: American Philosophical Society, 1951. Letter of Benjamin Rush to Thomas Ruston on October 29, 1775.

146. "JONES, Walter (1745–1815)." Congressional Biographical Directory (CLERKWEB). N.p., n.d. Web. June 26, 2016.Virginia medical doctor Walter Jones was born in 1745, studied medicine in Scotland, and between 1797 and 1810 served as a member of the U.S. Congress. He died in 1815.

147. Founders Online: Thomas Jefferson to Walter Jones, January 2, 1814.

148. *Ibid.*

149. *Ibid.*, 185–186.

150. Todd, Charles B. *Guide to Putnam Memorial Camp: With a Complete History of the Encampment, Incidents, Organization of the Brigades, Itinerary, &c*. Washington: Byron S. Adams, 1890, 19–20.

151. *The United States Army and Navy Journal, and Gazette of the Regular and Volunteer Forces*, Vol. XV. New York: Army and Navy Journal Incorporated, 1878, 505. The *Army, Navy, Air Force Journal & Register* of 1878 carries the pay scales of officer ranks from 1815, 1825, 1835, 1845, and 1875. Comparing officers' pay scales of the Continental Army with the U.S. Army 50 years later (1825) and a century later (1875), we find that the pay difference between Revolutionary War major generals and brigadier generals was relatively small (85 percent) as compared with 1825 and 1875 (67 percent in both years). In the Revolutionary War, a colonel's pay was 75 percent that of a major general, while in 1825 it was only 35 percent and in 1875 it was 47 percent. Majors in the Revolution made one-half what a major general did (120 versus 240 pounds), while in 1825 that dropped to

one-quarter and in 1875, one-third. In the Revolution and in 1875, first lieutenants made 20 percent of a major general's pay; in 1825 that percentage was 13 percent.

152. "Founders Online: From George Washington to John Augustine Washington, June 20, 1775." *Founders Online*. National Archives, n.d. Web. 29 June 2016.

153. John Adams diary, September 15 and 24, 1775 [electronic edition]. *Adams Family Papers: An Electronic Archive*. Massachusetts Historical Society. A Lieutenant Colonel in the Connecticut militia in the French and Indian War, Dyer (1721–1807) was on the 1755 Crown Point expedition with Putnam. He served as a delegate to the Continental Congress several times during the War. Joseph Trumbull (1737–1778), the receiver of this letter (who would be appointed commissary general of the Continental Army a month later), was the son of Connecticut's governor and the husband of Dyer's daughter, Amelia. John Adams, in his diary, described Dyer as: "...long winded and roundabout, obscure and cloudy. Very talkative and very tedious, yet an honest, worthy man, means and judges well."

154. Burnett, Edmund Cody. *Letters of Members of the Continental Congress*. Washington: Carnegie Institution, 1921, 137.

155. Founders Online, George Washington to John Augustine Washington, 20 June 1775. http://founders.archives.gov/documents/Washington/03-01-02-0115.

156. Burnett, Edmund Cody. *Letters of Members of the Continental Congress*, 143–144.

157. Deming, Henry Champion. *An Oration upon the Life and Services of Gen. David Wooster: Delivered at Danbury, April 27th, 1854, When a Monument Was Erected to His Memory*. Hartford: Press of Case, Tiffany, 1854, 35.

158. *Ibid.*, 35–36.

159. Force, Peter. *American Archives: Consisting of A Collection Of Authentick Records, State Papers, Debates, And Letters And Other Notices Of Publick Affairs, The Whole Forming A Documentary History Of The Origin And Progress Of The North American Colonies, Of The Causes And Accomplishment Of The American Revolution, And of The Constitution Of Government For The United States To The Final Ratification Thereof; In Six Series*. Washington: n.p., 1846, 1586.

160. *Ibid*.

161. Congressional Series of United States Public Documents, Vol. 2513. Washington: Government Printing Office, 1888.

162. Livingston, *Israel Putnam*, 247–248.

163. *The Deane Papers*. Vol. XIX. New York: Printed for The New York Historical Society, 1886.

164. Livingston, *Israel Putnam* 248–249; Webb, Samuel Blachley, and Worthington Chauncey Ford. *Correspondence and Journals of Samuel Blachley Webb*. New York: Wickersham, 1893.

165. Martyn, Charles. *The Life of Artemas Ward, the First Commander-in-Chief of the American Revolution*. New York: Artemas Ward, 1921, 91.

166. *Biographical Directory of the United States Congress 1774–1989: The Continental Congress, September 5, 1774, to October 21, 1788 and the Congress of the United States from the First through the One Hundredth Congresses, Marsh 4, 1789, to January 3, 1989, Inclusive*. Washington, D.C.: U.S. Government Printing Office, 1989.

167. Lossing, Benson John. *The Life and times of Philip Schuyler*. New York: Mason Brothers, 1860.

168. *Biographical Directory of the United States Congress 1774–1989*, 1989.

169. Tuckerman, Bayard. *Life of General Philip Schuyler: 1733–1804*. New York: Dodd, Mead, 1903, 245–246.

170. "From George Washington to Major General Charles Lee, 30 June 1778," *Founders Online*. National Archives, n.d. Web. June 29, 2016.

171. The Revolutionary war fortification, Fort Lee, was named after General Charles Lee. The fort, in turn, lent its name to the city which stands at the site today: Fort Lee, New Jersey.

172. Ellis, George Edward. *March 17th, 1876: Celebration of the Centennial Anniversary of the Evacuation of Boston by the British Army, March 17th, 1776: Reception of the Washington Medal: Oration Delivered in Music Hall, and a Chronicle of the Siege of Boston*. Boston: Printed by Order of the City Council, 1876, 152.

173. One additional brigadier general's commission was offered—to John Cadwalader of Pennsylvania—but he refused to accept it.

174. Leiter, Mary Theresa. *Biographical Sketches of the Generals of the Continental Army of the Revolution*. Cambridge, MA: J. Wilson and Son, 1889, 3–5.

175. "Founders Online: To John Adams from Daniel Putnam, 21 May 1818." *Founders Online*. National Archives, n.d. Web. June 29, 2016.

176. *Ibid*.

177. *Ibid*.

178. Samuel Webb was born on December 13, 1753, thus making him 21 years old when he wrote this letter. Like Putnam, after

hearing of the Battle of Lexington, he immediately went into action, joining a Connecticut infantry regiment as a lieutenant. During the war, Webb was wounded at the battles of Bunker Hill, White Plains, and Trenton. In 1777, he was captured by the British and held as a prisoner. When Washington was inaugurated President of the United States, it was Webb who held the Bible on which he took the oath. On April 21, 1776, Washington appointed Samuel Webb his aide-de-camp with the rank of Lieutenant Colonel. He had been aide-de-camp to Israel Putnam until Aaron Burr replaced him. After Burr, David Humphreys became Putnam's aide-de-camp. One thing these three ambitious young men (when selected as aide-de-camp, Webb was 22, Humphreys 25, and Burr only 20) had in common: they respected Putnam and believed that were improving themselves under his tutelage.

179. Webb, J. Watson, Silas Deane, and John Austin Stevens. *Reminiscences of Gen'l Samuel B. Webb of the Revolutionary Army.* New York: Globe Stationery and Print, 1882.

180. Livingston, *Israel Putnam* 251–252. Qui transtulit sustinet had been the Connecticut state motto since the 1600s.

181. Moore, Frank. *Diary of the American Revolution from Newspapers and Original Documents; a Centennial Volume Embracing the Current Events in Our Country's History from 1775 to 1781.* Hartford: Publisher Not Identified, 1875, 142.

182. Greene, George Washington. *The Life of Nathanael Greene: Major-general in the Army of the Revolution.* New York: G.P. Putnam and Son, 1867, 119–121; Livingston, *Israel Putnam*, 258–259; Tarbox, *Life*, 285–286.

183. Nagy, John A. *Dr. Benjamin Church, Spy: A Case of Espionage on the Eve of the American Revolution.* N.p.: n.p., n.d. After his death, Benjamin Church's wife was given an annual pension of 150 pounds by the British government on the grounds that "her husband was a spy."

Chapter Five

1. Jones, Thomas, and Edward Floyd De. Lancey. *History of New York during the Revolutionary War and of the Leading Events in the Other Colonies at That Period.* New York: New York Historical Society, 1879, 101.

2. *Ibid.*, 102–103.

3. *Biographical Directory of the United States Congress 1774–1989. 1989.* Thomas Mifflin was 32 years old at this time, but had already served as a member of the Continental Congress (during 1774 and 1775), as Washington's chief aide-de-camp (1775), and, starting in 1775, Quartermaster General of the Continental Army. He was appointed a major general in 1777. After the war, he became a signer of the U.S. Constitution and a Governor of Pennsylvania. He died in 1800 at age 56.

4. Flick, Alexander Clarence. "Loyalism in New York During the American Revolution." Studies in History, Economics and Public Law 14.1 (1901): 73–74.

5. Force, 1398.

6. Putnam, Israel, and Worthington Chauncey Ford, *General Orders*, 29.

7. *Ibid.*

8. *Ibid.*, 23.

9. General William Howe (1729–1814).

10. Admiral Richard Howe (1726–1799). General George Howe (1725–1758), the older brother of Richard and William, was the general who Israel Putnam had cautioned before the 1758 Battle of Carillon about risking his own life. He was killed shortly thereafter.

11. "Founders Online: Orders and Instructions for Major General Israel Putnam, 29 March 1776." *Founders Online.* National Archives, n.d. Web. June 29, 2016.

12. William Heath (1737–1814).

13. John Sullivan (1740–1795).

14. "Founders Online: Orders and Instructions for Major General Israel Putnam, 29 March 1776." *Founders Online.* National Archives, n.d. Web. June 29, 2016.

15. Nelson, Paul David. *Anthony Wayne, Soldier of the Early Republic.* Bloomington: Indiana UP, 1985, 20.

16. *Liberty! The American Revolution*, 1997, television production.

17. Starbuck, Great Warpath 172. Despite Gates mentioning 17 years later that the logs cut by Putnam's men in building Crown Point "are now rotten as dirt, and tumbled in the dust," in the 21st century, the ruins were "the biggest and best-preserved fortress" between Albany and Canada. Archeologist David R. Starbuck states that the remnants give him "the truest sense of what it is like to enter into a genuine eighteenth-century fort."

18. Livingston, *Israel Putnam* 290–291; Peter Force's American Archives 5th ser. 1 (n.d.): 900. Web.

19. McCullough, *1776*, 21.

20. Johnson, *Nathanael Greene*, 56.

21. During the Revolution, the British employed about 30,000 professional soldiers from German states, especially Hessians from the state of Hesse-Cassel. The story of the Battle of Trenton relates that the Americans surprised the Hessians who were unprepared because they had been partying the evening

before. However, the average Hessian was usually the exact opposite: a professional soldier who could be relied on under any circumstance.

22. Whittemore, Henry. *The Heroes of the American Revolution and Their Descendants: Battle of Long Island*. New York: Heroes of the Revolution, 1897, 11.

23. "Founders Online: Orders to Major General Israel Putnam, 25 August 1776." Founders Online. National Archives, n.d. Web. July 25, 2016.

24. *Baltimore Sun Almanac*. N.p.: A.S. Abell, 1899. 92; "William Smallwood, MSA SC 3520-1134." *William Smallwood, MSA SC 3520-1134*. Maryland State Archives, n.d. Web. June 27, 2016.William Smallwood, a graduate of England's Eton College, served in the French and Indian War and held a seat in the Maryland assembly for 13 years. Days after the Battle of Lexington, he brought 1400 Marylanders to Boston to join the Continental Army. After distinguished service in the Army's southern campaign, Smallwood was promoted to major general. After the war, he became the governor of Maryland and died in 1792. As the story goes, his expressed wish was that a monument not be erected over his remains. However, a neighbor planted a nut on his grave, it grew into a large chestnut tree, and served to mark his grave for 106 years. The grave was provided with an appropriate grave marker in 1898.

25. Whittemore, Henry. *The Heroes of the American Revolution and Their Descendants: Battle of Long Island*, 11.

26. Parton, James. *The Life and times of Aaron Burr, Lieutenant-colonel in the Army of the Revolution, United States Senator, Vice-president of the United States, Etc.* New York: Mason Bros., 1858. Perhaps the most popular and prolific biographer of his time, James Parton went on to write biographies of Franklin, Jefferson, Jackson, and Voltaire.

27. Commander of all Hessians fighting in the American colonies, Heister led his troops in the Battle of White Plains and was later recalled after the Battle of Trenton. He died in 1777.

28. Polk, Ryan. "Holding the Line: The Origin of the 'the Old Line State'" *Archives of Maryland Online*. N.p., 2005. Web. June 29, 2016.

29. Caldwell, Charles. *Memoirs of the Life and Campaigns of the Hon. Nathaniel Greene*. Philadelphia: Robert Desilver and Thomas Desilver, 1819, 50.

30. Stirling was later freed in a prisoner exchange and went on to provide valuable service to the Colonial Army until his death in the last year of the war.

31. Richman, Jeff. "Commemorating the Battle of Brooklyn | Green-Wood." *Green-Wood*. Green-Wood Cemetery, 27 Aug. 2013. Web. 27 June 2016; Bielinski, Stefan. "Robert Troup." *The People of Colonial Albany*. New York State Museum, 20 July 2010. Web. June 27, 2016. One of the thousands of soldiers buried at the cemetery is Robert Troup, friend and roommate of both Alexander Hamilton, and (later) Aaron Burr. Twenty-year-old Troup was captured at the Battle of Long Island, placed on a prison ship for a short period, and exchanged in 1777. Later he served as an aide to General Horatio Gates. Troup's body was moved to Green-Wood in 1872, which was 40 years after his death.

32. Whittemore, Henry. *The Heroes of the American Revolution and Their Descendants: Battle of Long Island*, 25.

33. Humphreys, *An Essay on the Life 1788 Ed.* 122–8.

34. "Founders Online: To George Washington from Major General Israel Putnam, 7 May 1779." *Founders Online*. National Archives, n.d. Web. June 29, 2016.

35. "Founders Online: To George Washington from Thomas Jefferson, 4 January 1786." *Founders Online*. National Archives, n.d. Web. June 29, 2016. On September 26, 1785, George Washington wrote Thomas Jefferson about Bushnell, describing him as "a man of great Mechanical powers, fertile of invention, and master in execution." Washington remembers: "He [Bushnell] came to me in 1776 recommended by Governor Trumbull (now dead) and other respectable characters.... Although I wanted faith myself, I furnished him with money, and other aids to carry it into execution ... he never did succeed ... he had a Machine which was so contrived as to carry a man under water at any depth he chose, and for a considerable time and distance, with an apparatus charged with Powder which he could fasten to a Ships bottom or side and give fire to in any given time (Sufft. for him to retire) by means whereof a ship could be blown up, or sunk...." After a career late in life as a medical doctor, Bushnell died in Georgia at age 84.

36. Senator Moynihan spoke before the U.S. Senate Subcommittee on National Parks, Committee on Energy and Natural Resources, on Tuesday, July 31, 2001. United States. Cong. Senate. SUBCOMMITTEE ON NATIONAL PARKS. Hearing on S. 689, TO CONVEY CERTAIN FEDERAL PROPERTIES ON GOVERNORS ISLAND, NEW YORK. 107th Cong., 1st sess. S S. 689. Washington: U.S. Government Printing Office, 2002.

37. *Ibid.*

38. Johnson, *Nathanael Greene*, 56. Letter of August 30, 1776.
39. Jones, Thomas, and Edward Floyd De Lancey. *History of New York during the Revolutionary War and of the Leading Events in the Other Colonies at That Period*. New York: New York Historical Society, 1879. 119–120.
40. Livingston, *Israel Putnam* 308–322.
41. It was also approximately at the end of 34th Street. Today, the Empire State Building stands about seven blocks west of there, on the corner of Fifth Avenue and 34th. Between 1931 and 1972 the 102-story Empire State Building was the tallest building in the world. No trace of Kip's Bay exists today—it was totally filled in.
42. The Morris-Jumel Mansion (as it's known today) was built in 1765 and is the oldest surviving house in Manhattan.
43. Livingston, *Israel Putnam* 308.
44. Silliman (1732–1790) was later to play an important part in the 1777 Battle of Ridgefield, and in 1779 he and his son were captured by Tories at their Connecticut home. Imprisoned by the British, they were exchanged the following year.
45. Stiles, Henry Reed. *History of Ancient Windsor, Connecticut: Including East Windsor, South Windsor, and Ellington, Prior to 1768, the Date of Their Separation from the Old Town; and Windsor, Bloomfield and Windsor Locks, to the Present Time*. New York: C.B. Norton, 1859. 715. Born in 1753, Munsell died in 1844 at age 91.
46. Livingston, *Israel Putnam* 310.
47. Eastman, Clarence Willis. An Account of Some of the Ancestors of Harry Thompson and Myra Hull. Amherst, Ma.: Priv. Printed, 1916. 3–6. A lieutenant colonel from Derby, Connecticut, Thompson was 49 years old. It is said that his body was buried with honor by the British officers who he had served with in the French and Indian War.
48. Humphreys, David. The miscellaneous works of Colonel Humphreys. New York: 1804. 304.
49. Livingston, *Israel Putnam; Pioneer, Ranger, and Major-general, 1718–1790*, 311. Livingston details the approximate route taken: "The line of Putnam's successful retreat seems to have been from Bayard's Hill Fort on Grand Street across the country to Monument Lane (Greenwich Avenue), which led to the obelisk erected in honour of General Wolfe and others, at a point on Fifteenth Street a little west of Eighth Avenue. The lane there joined with an irregular road running on the line of Eighth Avenue, known afterwards as the Abingdon or Fitz-Roy Road, as far as Forty-second or -third Street. From here Putnam's troops kept west of the Bloomingdale road, and finally, taking the road at some point above Seventieth Street, pushed on to Harlem Heights."
50. Today, Park Avenue and 36th Street is six blocks south of Grand Central Station, which is at Park Avenue and 42nd Street.
51. Rutkow, Ira M. "James Thacher and His Military Journal During the American Revolutionary War." *Arch Surg Archives of Surgery* 136.7 (2001): 837. Web. After leaving military service at the end of the war, Thacher would go on to become one of Massachusetts' most respected medical doctors and historians. He died in 1844 at age 90.
52. Thacher, James, and Samuel X. Radbill. *Military Journal of the American Revolution: From the Commencement to the Disbanding of the American Army: Comprising a Detailed Account of the Principal Events and Battles of the Revolution with Their Exact Dates, and a Biographical Sketch of the Most Prominent Generals*. Hartford, CT: Hurlbut, Williams, 1862. 58–59; Jay, John, 1817–1894. *The Battle of Harlem Plains: Oration Before the New York Historical Society, September 16, 1876*. New York: The Society, 1876. 19. At the time of the British officers' visit, Putnam's division was passing by less than a mile west of the Murray house. Since Mary Lindley Murray's husband was away, she was in charge of entertaining the British with the help of her daughters. Mary Lindley Murray died in 1782 at age 56. Her son, Lindley Murray (1745–1826), through his textbooks, especially *English Grammar*, became one of the world's best-selling authors of the 19th century.
53. Tarbox, *Life*, 309.
54. The legend of Mary Lindley Murray was developed into two Broadway plays: 1925's highly acclaimed *Dearest Enemy*, a musical with songs by Richard Rodgers and Lorenz Hart, and 1957's *A Small War on Murray Hill*, a comedy which starred Academy Award nominee Jan Sterling (1921–2004) as Mary Murray. Appropriately, Sterling was a descendent of Presidents John Adams and John Quincy Adams. Although *Small War* was written by Robert E. Sherwood and directed by Garson Kanin, it was unsuccessful.
55. Humphreys, *An Essay on the Life 1788 Ed.*, 133.
56. *Ibid.*, 132.
57. George Weedon (1734–1793) was commissioned a brigadier general five months later. In addition to later crossing the Delaware with Washington and serving at the Battle of Trenton, he was at Valley Forge, and, most significant of all, with his Virginia militia played a critical part in preventing the escape of Cornwallis's troops at Yorktown,

thus effectively ending the war. Like his fellow general, Israel Putnam, Weedon was a tavern owner (in Fredericksburg, Virginia).

58. Leitch died on October 1, 1776.

59. Colonel Charles Greenberry Griffith was born in 1744 and died in 1792. A former Maryland assemblyman, Colonel William Richardson (1735–1825) was responsible for moving the Continental Congress's treasury from Philadelphia to Baltimore in 1777.

60. "Founders Online: From George Washington to John Hancock, 18 September 1776." *Founders Online.* National Archives, n.d. Web. June 29, 2016.

61. Chasseurs were Loyalists who were fighting alongside the British troops.

62. Humphreys, *An Essay on the Life 1788 Ed.* 138–140.

63. "Founders Online: General Orders, 17 September 1776." *Founders Online.* National Archives, n.d. Web. June 29, 2016.

64. *Statue of Colonel Thomas Knowlton Ceremonies at the Unveiling.* Hartford, CT: Press of Case, Lockwood & Brainard, 1895. 6. In 1895 a 16-foot-high bronze statue of Thomas Knowlton was erected on the ground of the Connecticut State Capitol in Hartford about 600 feet south of J.Q.A. Ward's statue of Israel Putnam. The only source for the artist's image of Knowlton was Trumbull's famous Bunker Hill painting in which Knowlton is a prominent figure. Knowlton's widow Anna died in 1808 at age 64.

65. Hutson, James. "Nathan Hale Revisited A Tory's Account of the Arrest of the First American Spy." *Nathan Hale Revisited (July/August 2003).* N.p., n.d. Web. June 26, 2016.

66. Ibid.

67. "Battle of Harlem Heights Marker." *Monuments.* New York City Department of Parks & Recreation, n.d. Web. 26 June 2016. The 1961 marker reads: "Battle of Harlem Heights/September 16–1776/In grateful remembrance of the brave soldiers of New York, New Jersey, Connecticut, Massachusetts, Rhode Island, Pennsylvania, Maryland and Virginia who under General George Washington fought and died on this site for liberty in their country's struggle against British tyranny. Dedicated By The Daughters Of The Defenders Of The Republic, U.S.A."

68. "Harlem Heights First Line of Defense Marker." *Monuments.* New York City Department of Parks & Recreation, n.d. Web. June 26, 2016. The current 2001 plaque (as well as the 1909 original that it replaced) reads: "This Stone Marks The Position Of The First Line Of Defence Constructed Across These Heights And Bravely Defended By The American Army 1776."

69. Martin, Joseph Plumb. *A Narrative of Some of the Adventures, Dangers and Sufferings of a Revolutionary Soldier; Interspersed with Anecdotes of Incidents That Occurred within His Own Observation.* Hallowell: Printed by Glazier, Masters, 1830. 37–38. Surviving through seven years of the war, Martin died in Maine in 1850 at age 89. His account of his military service lay unnoticed by historians until a century later when it was recognized as an important primary source for information on the Revolutionary War. It has become known to the general public through the reading of Martin's words in such historical documentaries as PBS's 1997 television series *Liberty! The American Revolution.*

70. Today it is the location of the Throg's Neck Bridge, which since its construction in 1961, has linked the New York City boroughs of the Bronx and Queens.

71. Today the eastern end of the George Washington Bridge (opened in 1931) lies just south of the site of Fort Washington.

72. *The Memoirs of Rufus Putnam and Certain Official Papers and Correspondence,* Published by the National Society of the Colonial Dames of America in the State of Ohio. Boston: Houghton, Mifflin, 1903, 64–65. This paragraph has been edited for spelling and punctuation, since Rufus' mistakes in this regard are about equivalent to those of his cousin, Israel.

73. Ibid.

74. Humphreys, *An Essay on the Life 1850 Ed.*, 131.

75. Bolton, Reginald Pelham. *Fort Washington: An Account of the Identification of the Site of Fort Washington with a History of the Defence and Reduction of Mount Washington.* New York: Empire State Society of the Sons of the American Revolution, 1902, 28.

76. Himes, Charles Francis. *Col. Robert Magaw, the Defender of Fort Washington: Major in Colonel William Thompson's "Battalion of Pennsylvania Riflemen," the First Troops from the South to Reach Boston; Colonel of the Fifth Pennsylvania Regiment, Assigned by Washington to Defend Fort Washington. Paper Read before the Hamilton Library Association, Carlisle, Pa.—The Historical Society of Cumberland County, Pennsylvania.* Carlisle, PA: Hamilton Library Association, 1915, 41.

77. Knyphausen (1716–1800) became commander of Hessian troops in America after his immediate superior, General Leopold Philip von Heister returned to Europe in 1777. Knyphausen greatest success in the war was his part in the Battle of Fort Washington. Although 60 years old and suffering from

cataracts, he personally led his troops to victory.

78. Bolton, Reginald Pelham. *Fort Washington: An Account of the Identification of the Site of Fort Washington*, 80. Later, during the British occupation of Philadelphia, Demont was put in charge of overseeing Colonial prisoners of war. In January 1792, burdened by debt in London, England, Demont sent a letter to a Rev. Dr. Peters, in which he admitted his traitorous role and lamented his plight by paraphrasing one of King Henry VIII's closest associates, who died in 1530 after being charged with high treason: "in the language of Cardinal Wolsey had I have served my God as I have done my King he would not Thus have Forsaken Me."

79. Performing well at the Battles of Lexington and Concord and the Battle of Bunker Hill, Percy resigned his command in 1777. It was the donation of Percy's illegitimate half-brother scientist James Smithson that led to the founding of America's Smithsonian Institution 70 years later.

80. Corbin (1751–1800) later became the first woman to receive a pension for U.S. military service. She is buried at the West Point Cemetery at the United States Military Academy.

81. As a captive, Colonel Magaw was sent to New York City. He wasn't exchanged until almost four years later (October 25, 1780), when he returned to his previous profession, the practice of law. Born in 1738, Magaw died in 1790.

82. Hall, Edward, and Walter Benjamin. *Fort Washington, November 16th, 1776: A Memorial from the Empire State Society of the Sons of the American Revolution to the Honorable Mayor and Municipal Assembly of the City of New York, Praying for the Erection of a Suitable Monument to Mark the Site of Fort Washington; Presented to the Municipal Authorities May 3, 1898*. New York: Empire State Society of the Sons of the American Revolution, 1898, 25.

Chapter Six

1. Hancock was president of the Continental Congress for almost two and one-half years. During that span (May 24, 1775, through October 30, 1777), every major battle of the Revolutionary War in the northern colonies occurred, except for the 1778 Battle of Monmouth, New Jersey. Hancock's name is a household word today primarily because he signed it so large on the Declaration of Independence. Legend has it that Hancock wanted to make certain that King George III could read it without his reading glasses. Hancock died in 1793 at age 56.

2. "Founders Online: From George Washington to John Hancock, 9 December 1776." *Founders Online*. National Archives, n.d. Web. June 29, 2016.

3. Ford, Worthington Chauncey. *Journals of the Continental Congress, 1774–1789*. Washington: Government Printing Office, 1906.

4. *Ibid.*

5. *Ibid.*

6. "The United States Navy Memorial." *Welcome to*. N.p., n.d. Web. June 26, 2016. *United States Naval Institute Proceedings*. Vol. 43. N.p.: United States Naval Institute, 1917. 7–12. When he returned to the scene of the explosion five days later, Captain Vincent of the Yarmouth found these four men standing on floating wreckage. They had survived on rainwater collected on a piece of blanket.

7. Humphreys, *An Essay on the Life 1788 Ed.*, 145–146.

8. *Ibid.*, 146.

9. *Force's American Archives* 5th ser. 1180.

10. *Ibid.*, 1181.

11. Livingston, *Israel Putnam*, 330.

12. "Founders Online: From George Washington to the Society of Quakers, 13 October 1789." *Founders Online*. National Archives, n.d. Web. June 29, 2016.

13. Young, John Russell, Howard M. Jenkins, and George O. Seilhamer. *Memorial History of the City of Philadelphia from Its First Settlement to the Year 1895*. New York: New-York History, 1898, Vol. 2, 48.

14. *Ibid.*

15. Livingston, *Israel Putnam* 330–331.

16. *Ibid.*, 332.

17. *Ibid.*, 334.

18. Pennsylvania's Joseph Reed had been elected adjutant-general after serving as one of Washington's aides-de-camp. After his service, he was a delegate to the Continental Congress, and signed the Articles of Confederation. He died in 1785 at age 43.

19. Livingston, *Israel Putnam*, 332.

20. *Ibid.*, 334.

21. Monroe would serve two terms as president of the United States before dying on July 4, 1831, the 55th anniversary of the Declaration of Independence.

22. Livingston, *Israel Putnam* 336. From the Journal of the Regiment von Lossberg.

23. *Ibid.*, 335–336.

24. Forman died of the effects of a stroke in 1797 at age 51.

25. Humphreys, *An Essay on the Life 1788 Ed.* 146–147.

26. Nelson, William, Peter Ross, and Fen-

wick Y. Hedley. *The New Jersey Coast in Three Centuries; History of the New Jersey Coast with Genealogical and Historic-biographical Appendix*. New York: Lewis pub., 1902. 184.

27. Quaker Betsy Ross fell in love with and married fellow upholsterer, John Ross in 1772. Since Ross was not a Quaker, Betsy was expelled from the society. In 1776, after Ross was killed in a gunpowder explosion while on military duty, Betsy took over operation of their upholstery business. One of her specialties was making flags. A year later she married a sailor, but he was captured in 1781 and died a prisoner of the British. Two years afterward, she married one of his fellow prisoners and this third husband died in 1817. Betsy Ross carried on the family business almost her entire life, passing away on January 30, 1836, at age 84.

28. It wasn't until 1870, that Betsy Ross's grandson, William Canby, in a presentation to the Historical Society of Pennsylvania, revealed a family story that Betsy had, at the bequest of Washington in 1776, sewn the first stars and stripes flag. This is the first known mention of Ross's role in the creation of the official flag of the new nation. Whether the family history that he related was true is a matter of dispute. No corroborating testimony has been found, although no evidence to disprove his claims has been found either.

29. "Founders Online: From George Washington to Major General Israel Putnam, 28 May 1776." *Founders Online*. National Archives, n.d. Web. June 29, 2016.

30. *Princeton Alumni Weekly* Vol. 79 1978: 28.

31. Hamilton, John Church. *The Life of Alexander Hamilton Vol. 1*. New York: Halsted Et Voorhies, 1834. 57.

32. Humphreys, *An Essay on the Life 1788 Ed.* 151–153. Later, McPherson's care was handed over to Dr. Benjamin Rush (1745–1813), surgeon-general of the Continental Army and a signer of the Declaration of Independence.

33. *Ibid.*

34. *Ibid.*

35. *Putnam's Monthly Historical Magazine* Vol. 1 (1893): 47.

36. Force, *American Archives* 636. After the war, Betts lived out the rest of his life in Canada.

37. Johnston, Elizabeth Bryant. *George Washington Day by Day*. New York: Cycle, 1895. 168. Washington himself was immune to smallpox, having acquired it on the island of Barbados in 1751 at age 19. He was bedridden for three weeks and suffered no disfigurement except for some barely noticeable marks.

38. Adams, John, and Charles Francis Adams. *Letters of John Adams, Addressed to His Wife*. Boston: C.C. Little and J. Brown, 1841. 212–213.

39. Putnam, Israel, and Worthington Chauncey, Ford. *General Orders*, 21.

40. *Ibid.*, 69.

41. *Ibid.*, 58.

42. *Ibid.*, 23.

43. *Ibid.*, 28–9.

44. *Ibid.*, 31.

45. *Ibid.*, 38.

46. Humphreys, *An Essay on the Life 1788 Ed.*, 166–167.

47. *Ibid.*, 167.

48. *Ibid.*, 33–5.

49. Proceedings on the Occasion of the Dedication of the Monument on the One Hundredth Anniversary of the Paoli Massacre, in Chester County, Pa., September 20, 1877. West Chester, PA: F.S. Hickman, Printer, 1877. 39.

50. Lossing, Benson John. *The Pictorial Field Book of the Revolution: Or, Illustrations, by Pen and Pencil, of the History, Biography, Scenery, Relics, and Traditions of the War of Independence*. New York: Harper, 1859. 164.

51. Lt. Col. George Baylor's 3rd Regiment of Continental Dragoons took quarters for the night on several nearby farms. Tories betrayed their presence to a British force, who surrounded the Dragoons during the night. A number of Americans were killed or wounded after they surrendered. After the remains of six of the American soldiers were found in 1967, a plaque was erected at the site which reads: "In memory of American soldiers killed during the Revolutionary War in the 'Baylor Massacre' on September 28, 1778."

52. Grey died in 1807 at age 78. In 1830, his son, Charles Grey, 2nd Earl Grey became British prime minister and oversaw the abolition of slavery in the British Empire. Earl Grey tea is named after this second Earl Grey.

53. Washington, George, and Jared Sparks. *The Writings of George Washington; Being His Correspondence, Addresses, Messages, and Other Papers, Official and Private*. New York: Harper & Bros., 1847, 29.

54. Graham, James. *The Life of General Daniel Morgan, of the Virginia Line of the Army of the United States, with Portions of His Correspondence*. New York: Derby & Jackson, 1858, 29.

55. *Ibid.*, 448. Morgan was one of the heroes of the 1777 Battle of Saratoga. In October 1780, he was appointed a brigadier gen-

eral, and three months later confronted British Lieutenant Colonel Banastre Tarleton at Cowpens, South Carolina. Tarleton was a highly successful cavalry officer, but a brutal man who didn't hesitate to burn civilian homes or kill prisoners of war. In quite possibly the most brilliant and successful maneuver of the war, Morgan had his militia tempt the British troops into the clutches of the seasoned Continentals. The result was a total victory for the Americans, leading directly to the British surrender at Yorktown, Virginia nine months later. Like Israel Putnam, Morgan became very religious in his adult life. James Graham, in his biography, states: "When the battle at the Cowpens was over, and all the enemy and prisoners were flying, Morgan rode across the fields offering to the Almighty thanks, which were audible to many of his men as he passed." Daniel Morgan died in 1802 at age 66.

56. Humphreys, *An Essay on the Life 1788 Ed.*, 167–168.

57. Henry Clinton in 1780 was responsible for blockading and capturing Charlestown, South Carolina.

58. At the time of the Forts Montgomery and Clinton battle, British William Tyron was considered governor of New York by the British. American general George Clinton ultimately was elected New York State governor for a total of 21 years in two nonconsecutive terms, the longest any person has been the governor of a U.S. state. He later served as vice-president of the United States under both Thomas Jefferson and James Madison.

59. Carrington, Henry Beebee. *Battle Maps and Charts of the American Revolution: With Explanatory Notes and School History References.* New York: A.S. Barnes, 1881.

60. Adams, Arthur G. *The Hudson River Guidebook.* New York: Fordham UP, 1996, 167.

61. Lossing, Benson J. Lossing's *History of the United States: From the Aboriginal times to the Present Day.* New York: Lamb, 1909, 951.

62. Hubbard, Robert, and Kathleen Hubbard. *Legendary Locals of Middletown, Connecticut.* N.p.: n.p., n.d. 82. In May 1777, Return Jonathan Meigs, Sr., led a heroic raid against the British forces in Sag Harbor, New York.

63. Humphreys, *An Essay on the Life 1788 Ed.*, 170–171.

64. Colonel Samuel Wyllys served as Secretary of the State of Connecticut from 1796 until 1810. It was apparently a "family" position, since for 98 consecutive years only Samuel, his father George or his grandfather Hezekiah held the position. (George Wyllys was secretary from 1735 to 1796 and Hezekiah from 1712 to 1735.) Thus, Hezekiah's and George's tenures included the entire lifespan of Israel Putnam.

65. Humphreys, *An Essay on the Life 1788 Ed.* 169.

66. Ober, Frederick A. *"Old Put" the Patriot.* New York: D. Appleton, 1904, 233.

67. Livingston, *Israel Putnam* 367.

68. Humphreys, *An Essay on the Life 1788 Ed.*, 177–9.

69. Except for the fact that both had been active in the Connecticut Sons of Liberty and joined the army days after the battle of Lexington, Jedidiah Huntington and Israel Putnam could hardly have been different. Physically Putnam was described as "corpulent." Huntington on the other hand weighed about 130 pounds. (A memorandum of the weighing of several revolutionary officers at West Point on August 19, 1788, showed George Washington weighing 209 pounds, Gen. Benjamin Lincoln, 224, Gen. Henry Knox, 280, and Gen. Huntington, 132.) Also, throughout his entire life, Putnam was a notoriously poor writer, while Huntington was a graduate of Harvard with a Master's degree from Yale.

70. Ober, *Old Put*, 233.

71. Cutter, *Life*, 314.

72. Dwight, *Travels*, 435–6.

73. Knight, Erastus C., and Frederic Gregory Mather. *New York in the Revolution as Colony and State, Supplement.* Albany, NY: O.A. Quayle, 1901, 49.

74. "The Van Wyck Homestead Museum." The Fishkill Historical Society. N.p., n.d. Web. June 26, 2016.

75. Livingston, *Israel Putnam* 357.

76. After the Revolutionary War, Robinson moved to England where he lived for the remainder of his life.

77. Gardiner, Curtiss C. *Lion Gardiner and His Descendants.* St. Louis: A. Whipple, 1890. 118.

78. "Founders Online: From George Washington to Major General Israel Putnam, 19 October 1777." *Founders Online.* National Archives, n.d. Web. June 29, 2016.

79. *Ibid.*

80. "Founders Online: To Alexander Hamilton from George Washington, 30 October 1777." *Founders Online.* National Archives, n.d. Web. June 29, 2016.

81. *Ibid.*

82. Livingston, *Israel Putnam*, 363.

83. "Founders Online: From George Washington to Major General Israel Putnam, 19 November 1777." *Founders Online.* National Archives, n.d. Web. June 29, 2016.

84. Riethmüller, Christopher James. *Alexander Hamilton and His Contemporaries; Or,*

The Rise of the American Constitution. London: Bell & Daldy, 1864, 37–38.

85. Hill, George Canning, and Henry Ketchum. *The Life of Israel Putnam*. New York: A.L. Burt, 1903, 231–2.

86. It might be noted that Fish would have been interested in the St. Philip's Church graveyard since the most famous members of his family were buried there. He and his wife, Marion "Mamie" Fish, would eventually be entombed there (in 1923 and 1915 respectively).

87. Samuel P. Hyman and Levi Morris against Jacob Kapp and Charles H. Dyett. 53. Supreme Court, Appellate Court, First Judicial Department. 1887. When mechanical engineer and industrialist Henry R. Worthington died in 1880, he left $500 to Michael Lee. It was quite a sum in those days, especially when one considers that he left his widow only $5,000.

88. Bondeson, Jan. *Buried Alive: The Terrifying History of Our Most Primal Fear*. New York: Norton, 2001. 8.

89. "Grave of Mrs. Putnam Found." *New York Times* Jan. 10, 1904: 9.

90. Chorley, E. Clowes. *History of St. Philip's Church in the Highlands, Garrison, New York: Including, up to 1840, St. Peter's Church on the Manor of Cortlandt*. New York: E.S. Gorham, 1912, 345–346.

91. "The Works of the Late Edgar Allan Poe (1850–1856)." *Edgar Allan Poe Society of Baltimore*. N.p., n.d. Web. June 22, 2016, 325.

92. Brighton, Ray. *The Checkered Career of Tobias Lear*. Portsmouth, NH: Portsmouth Marine Society, 1985.

93. Madison, James, and William C. Rives. *Letters and Other Writings of James Madison Fourth President of the United States; in Four Volumes; Published by Order of Congress*. Philadelphia: J.B. Lippincott, 1865. 168–169; Vile, John R. *The Constitutional Convention of 1787: A Comprehensive Encyclopedia of America's Founding*. Santa Barbara, CA: ABC-CLIO, 2005. 108; Wright, Robert K., and Morris J. MacGregor. *Soldier-statesmen of the Constitution*. Washington, D.C.: Center of Military History, U.S. Army, 1987. A few months earlier, Gouverneur Morris [Gouverneur, not Governor—his mother was Sarah Gouverneur], a signer of the Articles of Confederation, had helped prevent senior military and government leaders from removing Washington from his position in what has become known as the Conway Cabal. At the time Washington wrote this letter to him, Gouverneur Morris was only 26, but with a long career ahead of him: as Minister Plenipotentiary to France (1792–1794), a U.S. senator (1800–1803), and a signer of the U.S. Constitution. In fact, he more than anyone was responsible for the final wording of the Constitution, with James Madison saying in a April 8, 1831, letter to Jared Sparks: "the finish given to the style and arrangement of the Constitution fairly belongs to the pen of Mr. Morris." During the French Revolution's Reign of Terror, Morris was the only diplomat who refused to escape from Paris. Morris died in 1816 at age 64.

94. Washington, George, and Worthington Chauncey Ford. *The Writings of George Washington*. New York: Putnam's Sons, 1890. 31–32.

95. Thacher, James. *A Military Journal during the American Revolutionary War, from 1775 to 1783 Describing Interesting Events and Transactions of This Period; with Numerous Historical Facts and Anecdotes, from the Original Manuscript*. Boston: Richardson & Lord, 1823, 145–146.

96. *Ibid.*

97. *Ibid.*, 184.

98. John Peter Muhlenberg (1746–1807) was an ordained Lutheran minister.

99. Thacher, *Military Journal*, 151–152.

100. Livingston, *Israel Putnam*, 381.

101. *Ibid.*, 380–1.

102. Nelson, Paul David. "Charles Lee." *American National Biography Online: Lee, Charles*. N.p., Feb. 2000. Web. June 26, 2016. Lee spoke Greek, Latin, French, Spanish, Italian and German.

103. Livingston, *Israel Putnam*, 381–2. The words in square brackets are Livingstons.

104. Niven, *Connecticut Hero*, 8.

105. John Adams and John Hancock graduated from Harvard, Alexander Hamilton and John Jay went to Columbia University (when it was called King's College), and Thomas Jefferson graduated from William and Mary.

106. Letter to Dr. Walter Jones from Monticello on January 2, 1814. Simpson, Stephen. *The Lives of George Washington and Thomas Jefferson: With a Parallel ...* Philadelphia: H. Young, 1833. 185–186.

107. *Ibid.*

108. Livingston, *Israel Putnam*, 56.

109. *Ibid.* According to Livingston, Rufus did try. Despite the fact that his "step-father had little sympathy with the boy's ambition to study and denied him all school advantages. But Rufus devoted his spare time to text-books, which he bought with the money earned by serving guests at the tavern and by selling small game which he had shot. By his own unaided efforts, he made considerable progress in the way of education."

110. "McDougall, Alexander (1731–1786)."

Congressional Biographical Directory (CLERK-WEB). N.p., n.d. Web. June 26, 2016. Alexander McDougall (1731/1732–1786) was born on island of Islay off the west coast of Scotland and immigrated to the colonies when he was eight years old. During the French and Indian War, he commanded privateers, and made a significant amount of money from the sale of captured French ships and their cargoes. In the Revolution, he was promoted to colonel in 1775, brigadier general in 1776, and major general on October 20, 1777. He was trusted with command of West Point after Benedict Arnold's plot was discovered in 1780. Later McDougall became the first president of the Bank of New York.
111. *Frank Leslie's Popular Monthly*, Vol. 19 1885: 662.
112. Humphreys, *Miscellaneous Works*, 34.
113. Todd, *Putnam Memorial Camp*, 20.
114. *Ibid.*, 20–21.
115. *Ibid.*, 21.
116. Livingston, *Israel Putnam; Pioneer, Ranger, and Major-general, 1718–1790*, 199–200.
117. *Ibid.*, 384.
118. Livingston, *Israel Putnam* 384. Livingston mentions Huntington's brigade.
119. Humphreys, *An Essay on the Life 1788 Ed.*, 179–180.
120. *Ibid.*, 180.
121. Todd, Charles B. *Guide to Putnam Memorial Camp: With a Complete History of the Encampment, Incidents, Organization of the Brigades, Itinerary, &c.* Washington: Byron S. Adams, 1890, 20–21.
122. "Founders Online: To George Washington from Major General Israel Putnam, 5 January 1779." Founders Online. National Archives, n.d. Web. June 29, 2016.
123. *Ibid.*
124. "Founders Online: From George Washington to Major General Israel Putnam, 18 January 1779." Founders Online. National Archives, n.d. Web. June 29, 2016.
125. *Ibid.*
126. Born in Beverly, Massachusetts, only a few miles from Israel Putnam's birthplace, Frederick A. Ober was a prolific writer of biographies, and books on travel and natural history. He died in 1913 at age 64.
127. Ober, *Old Put*, 238.
128. Livingston, *Israel Putnam*, 386.
129. Todd, Charles Burr. *The History of Redding, Conn., from Its First Settlement to the Present Time. With Notes on the Adams, Banks ... Stow Families.* New York: J.A. Gray, 1880, 65–66.
130. Cruson, Daniel. *Putnam's Revolutionary War Winter Encampment: The History and Archaeology of Putnam Memorial State Park.* Charleston, SC: History, 2011. 63; Smith, Joel. *Orderly book. 3rd Connecticut Regiment, 1st Brigade of Connecticut Infantry, 1779.* Original in the collection of the Connecticut Historical Society.
131. Cruson, *Winter Encampment*, 88.
132. *Ibid.*, 90.
133. *Ibid.*, 94.
134. Ives (1874–1954) received a 1947 Pulitzer Prize for his Symphony No. 3.
135. It's not surprising that the famous modernist composer would refer to the park, as he was born in Danbury and was the son of a bandleader who specialized in patriotic music.
136. Minks, Louise, and Benton Minks. *The Revolutionary War.* New York: Infobase Publishing, 2009, 126. Salt was an extremely valuable commodity during the war because it was needed to preserve meats and fish, including that earmarked for the troops. Many woman and children were enlisted in the effort to extract salt from seawater.
137. Mead, Spencer P., and Daniel M. Mead. *Ye Historie of Ye Town of Greenwich County of Fairfield and State of Connecticut, with Genealogical Notes ...* New York: Knickerbocker, 1911. 193. A militia soldier, who had survived a musket ball through one of his lungs, the 30-year-old Mead witnessed Putnam's ride down the steep hill in Horseneck. As the story goes, he was standing in the doorway of his house at the base of the hill when Putnam came down, escaping from the British troops. Mead was close enough to hear Putnam cry out to the soldiers who were firing at him from the top of the hill.
138. Almon, John, and Thomas Pownall. *The Remembrancer, or Impartial Repository of Public Events.* London: Printed for J. Almon, 1775, 268.
139. *Ibid.*
140. "Revolutionary Figure—Redding Unveils Putnam Statue." Norwalk Hour [Norwalk, Connecticut] 23 Sept. 1969: 1. This moment was captured by one of America's finest sculptors of equestrian statues, Anna Hyatt Huntington (José Martí in New York's Central Park, El Cid in San Diego's Balboa Park, and Revolutionary War hero, Sybil Ludington, in Carmel, New York). Her bronze equestrian statue of Putnam, entitled "Putnam's Escape at Horse Neck," stands near the entrance of Putnam Memorial State Park in Redding, Connecticut. After completing the statue in her 90s, Huntington donated it to the people.
141. Livingston, *Israel Putnam*, 393.
142. William Tryon was governor of North Carolina from 1765 to 1771, and governor of New York from 1771 to 1780. Simultaneous

with the New York posting, he was made a British major general (but only while serving in the North American colonies). Primarily conducting raids of Continental supply positions in the Connecticut area, Tryon performed admirably at the Battle of Ridgefield, defeating troops of Generals Benedict Arnold (while Arnold was still a loyal American) and David Wooster. Less admirable was his insistence, even against the orders of General Clinton, of making war on civilians. Health reasons (primarily gout) led to Tryon's return to England in 1780 where he died eight years later.

143. Huntington, E.B. *History of Stamford, Connecticut from Its Settlement in 1641, to the Present Time, including Darien, Which Was One of Its Parishes until 1820.* Stamford: Author, 1868, 239.

144. Root, *Patron Saints*, 456.

145. After the war, General Howard, who lost his right arm at the Battle of Seven Pines, led the Freedmen's Bureau, which was charged with the task of integrating freed slaves into American society. He was also founder and third president of Howard University, which was named after him. It is historically the most prestigious African American University in the United States. On June 14, 1906, General Howard would come back to Greenwich to attend the dedication of the Putnam Cottage, which is a stone's throw from the Putnam steps. The other veteran who made the trip to honor Israel Putnam was General Miles who the previous year had served as the Commanding General of the U.S. Army during the Spanish-American War. After a Civil War battlefield promotion to Major General of volunteers at age 26, he went on to command the troops that defeated, in succession: Sitting Bull, Chief Joseph, and Geronimo. Perhaps General Miles pondered the similarities between his own life and that of Putnam. Both had little education and no formal military training (Putnam was a farmer and Miles a store clerk), yet both had risen through the ranks to become major generals and legends in their own times. "Putnam Cottage is Dedicated." *Hartford Courant*, June 15, 1906: 17.

146. Tuchman, *General Israel Putnam*. Address notes are in the archives of the Connecticut Historical Society.

147. "Anecdote of General Putnam." *Hartford Daily Courant* 24 Nov. 1854: 2.

Chapter Seven

1. Humphreys, *An Essay on the Life 1788 Ed.* 182. Henry Lee (1756–1818) earned the nickname "Light-Horse Harry Lee" because of his success in using cavalry for quick raids. After the war he served in the Continental Congress, as governor of Virginia, and in the U.S. House of Representatives. In his 50s, he was twice sent to debtor's prison. Lee was the father of Civil War general Robert E. Lee.

2. Humphreys, *An Essay on the Life 1788 Ed.*, 182–183.

3. Smith, *Old Put*, 274–5.

4. Humphreys, *Miscellaneous Works*, 199–200.

5. Livingston, *Israel Putnam*, 401.

6. *Ibid.*, 403.

7. British Major John André was captured in Tarrytown, jailed in a local inn, and tried at Tappan on September 29, 1780. Found guilty, he was hanged three days later. Major General Nathanael Greene had headed up the board of enquiry.

8. Grosvenor, *The Life and Character* 35. Judge Payne passed away in 1842 at age 85.

9. Born in 1748, Gibbs joined General Washington's personal security staff, the Washington Guards in 1776. While head of the Guards, he served Washington until 1781. A few months later, at the Battle of Yorktown, he was wounded. Maintaining a friendship with Washington until the latter's death in 1799, Gibbs died at age 70 while serving at his post as superintendent of the Boston Navy Yard.

10. Moore, Frank. *Diary of the American Revolution from Newspapers and Original Documents; a Centennial Volume Embracing the Current Events in Our Country's History from 1775 to 1781.* Hartford: Publisher Not Identified, 1875, 254. Maggie Lauder is a traditional Scottish song written by Francis Sempill of Beltrees who lived from approximately 1616–1682. It's not difficult to imagine the battle-hardened Israel Putnam relaxing with his comrades, after a full meal and a tankard of ale, and singing the 17th century Scottish ballad. *Maggie Lauder* begins with:

Wha wadnae be in love
  Wi' bonnie Maggie Lauder!
A piper met her gaun to Fife,
  And spier'd what was't they ca'd her;
Right scornfully thus answered she,
  Begone, you hallan-shaker;
Jog on your gate, you blether-skate,
  My name is Maggie Lauder.

Maggie, quoth he, now by my bags,
  I'm fidging fain to see you
Sit down by me, my bonnie bird,
  In troth I winna steer you;
For I'm a piper to my trade,
  Men call me Rab the Ranter:
The lasses loup as they were daft,
  When I blaw up my chanter.

11. "Original Revolutionary Anecdote." *The Army and Navy Chronicle* V.1 (1837): 327.

12. Decades later, in the American Civil War (1861–1865), the Union Army was populated by many high-ranking officers who either had served in the Mexican-American War (1846–1848) or earned their promotions in the Civil War itself and did not attend a military training institution. They found themselves at a disadvantage, much like Putnam 90 years earlier.

At the outbreak of the Civil War in 1861, seven of the eight U.S. military colleges were in southern states. This translated into a Confederate leadership that was far better educated than that of the Union Army. This was an important factor that allowed the South to stretch the war out to four years, even though they had far fewer soldiers and a vastly inferior industrial power base (at the start of the Civil War almost all of the country's firearms were manufactured in Northern factories). After the Civil War it became increasing difficult for an uneducated person to achieve high rank. There were just too many well-educated competitors; many with extensive military training.

13. Dwight, *Travels*, 131.

14. Humphreys, *Soldier—Statesman—Poet*, 233–235.

15. Thirty-six-year-old Maryland native Tench Tilghman served as an aide-de-camp to Washington for over five years (1776–1781).

16. One indication of popularity is the use of a person's image on paper and hard currency. Washington and Lincoln are the only U.S. presidents to have their pictures appear both on common paper currency and coins. Jefferson's images appears on both paper currency and coins too, but his $2 bill is uncommon. (About 40 times as many Washington $1 bills are printed as Jefferson $2 bills.)

17. Leiter, Mary Theresa. *Biographical Sketches of the Generals of the Continental Army of the Revolution*. Cambridge, MA: J. Wilson and Son, 1889. These 24 generals and the dates they were commissioned to the rank of major general are:

George Washington, June 17, 1775
Israel Putnam, June 19, 1775
Horatio Gates, May 16, 1776
William Heath, August 9, 1776
Nathanael Greene, August 9, 1776
Arthur St. Clair, February 19, 1777
Benjamin Lincoln, February 19, 1777
Marquis de Lafayette, July 31, 1777
Robert Howe, October 20, 1777
Alexander McDougal, October 20, 1777
Baron Wilhelm von Steuben, May 5, 1778
William Smallwood, September 15, 1780

Henry Knox, March 22, 1782
William Moultrie, October 15, 1782
Lachlan McIntosh, September 30, 1783
James Clinton, September 30, 1783
John Paterson, September 30, 1783
Anthony Wayne, September 30, 1783
Peter Muhlenburg, September 30, 1783
George Clinton, September 30, 1783
Edward Hand, September 30, 1783
Charles Scott, September 30, 1783
Jedediah Huntington, September 30, 1783
John Stark, September 30, 1783

Of these 24 men, 14 came from the northern colonies, 8 from the southern (including Maryland) colonies, and two from foreign countries (Lafayette and Steuben). A little over half received their commissions as major generals after the war shifted to the southern colonies.

18. "The Society of the Cincinnati." *The Society of the Cincinnati*. N.p., n.d. Web. June 25, 2016.

19. Bernard, John. *Retrospections of America, 1797–1811*. New York: Harper, 1887, 110.

20. Humphreys's fellow Connecticut Wit, Joel Barlow, and Putnam's cousin, General Rufus Putnam were also members.

21. "Founders Online: To George Washington from Israel Putnam, 20 May 1783." *Founders Online*. National Archives, n.d. Web. June 29, 2016.

22. *Ibid.*

23. "Founders Online: From George Washington to Israel Putnam, 2 June 1783." *Founders Online*. National Archives, n.d. Web. June 29, 2016.

24. *Ibid.*

25. The battle casualty differences between the two wars is far greater: the Revolutionary War had a total of 4435 battle deaths (versus approximately 140,000 on the Union side and 72,000 on the Confederate side in the Civil War) and 6,188 non-mortal wounds (versus the Union's 280,000 and the Confederate's 140,000). Given the staggering benefits gained by the American colonies in the Revolution—total independence from Britain, the freedoms enshrined in the Bill of Rights, and a democratic system of government that has survived virtually intact for a quarter of a millennium, the limited losses are astounding. If it wasn't for the Civil War's elimination of slavery, that war would be considered far less significant than the American Revolutionary War.

26. Putnam, *A History*, 348.

27. Livingston, *Israel Putnam*, 410.

28. "Letter from General Israel Putnam." *Hartford Daily Courant* 20 Nov. 1845: 2. Also see Livingston, *Israel Putnam*, 407–408.

29. *Connecticut Courant and Weekly Intelligencer* [Hartford, Connecticut] 21 December 1784: 3.
30. Larned, *History*, 249.
31. Grosvenor, *The Life and Character*, 31.
32. Livingston, *Israel Putnam*, 409.
33. "General Douglas MacArthur Delivered his Farewell Address to a Joint Meeting of Congress." U.S. House of Representatives: History, Art & Archives. N.p., n.d. Web. June 26, 2016. MacArthur delivered his speech on the 176th anniversary of The Battles of Lexington and Concord.
34. Daughters of the American Revolution Magazine Volume 47 1915: 335.
35. Livingston, *Israel Putnam*, 411.
36. The 1811 edition of David Humphreys' Putnam biography ends with "Gen. Putnam died the 29th of May 1790." However the 1850 edition gives "19th of May, 1790" on page 170 and incorrectly "copies" the Putnam gravestone, giving "19th of May, A.D. 1790" (page 173). Apparently someone didn't do their fact-checking since in the original gravestone on display at the state capital building in Hartford shows: "And died On the twentyninth day of M[edge of marble chipped off] AD 1790" Peabody in his 1837 biography (page 215) states that Putnam was attacked by an inflammatory disease on the 17th of May and died two days later, i.e., May 19th. Cutter in 1850 and Tarbox in 1876 repeat the error in their copy of the grave marker inscription. Even Fellows in his 1843 pamphlet attacking Humphreys's book uses the wrong date (May 19th). Interestingly, the 1903 edition of Hill's biography had the May 19th mistake on page 257, but the correct May 29th date in the marker description on page 260. The 1904 Ober biography has the correct date in both his text and the epitaph. Livingston in 1901 (page 416–417) points out the discrepancy in the dates and attributes it to the fact that the original edition of Humphreys's biography did not include a date of death since Putnam was still alive in 1788, but the 1818 edition, published just after Humphreys's death, had a few paragraphs added relating his death and used the wrong day of the month, i.e., May 19th. Today, Putnam's death certificate is with the Pomfret town clerk (not Brooklyn) and gives his date of death as May 29, 1790. (Verified 9/28/15). The bottom line: the correct date of Israel Putnam's death was Saturday, May 29, 1790.
37. Whitney was pastor of this Congregational church for 64 years of his 93-year-long life.
38. Livingston, *Israel Putnam* 412–3.
39. "Israel Putnam." *Connecticut Courant and Weekly Intelligencer* [Hartford, Connecticut] 7 June 1790: 3.
40. Kelly, Howard A., and Walter L. Burrage. *American Medical Biographies*. Baltimore: Norman, Remington, 1920. 1184.
41. Humphreys, *Soldier—statesman—poet* 413.
42. Only a couple of years after Waldo's death, it was proven that inoculating with the relatively benign cowpox virus, could give people immunity from smallpox.
43. Humphreys, *An Essay on the Life 1850 Ed.*, 171–2.
44. In this will he left approximately 1,000 acres of land in Pomfret, Brooklyn, and Canterbury, Connecticut to his sons, Israel, Daniel, and Peter Schuyler Putnam. Peter Schuyler was also to receive his father's livestock, husbandry tools, and provisions. Israel left his daughters Hannah, Mehitable, and Mary 300 pounds each and daughter Eunice 150 pounds. Eunice's son Elisha Avery received 300 pounds. Elisha Avery was the only child of Eunice and her first husband, Elisha Avery. Thus, Israel's grandson through his daughter Eunice was also his stepgrandson though his second wife Deborah. Elisha had just been born at the time of this will. With her second husband, Lemuel Grosvenor (1752–1833), Eunice had five sons: Lemuel, Guy, Ebenezer, Clark, and Lewis. On February 3, 1786, Putnam added a codicil to his will: Eunice's inheritance was increased from 150 to 300 pounds, making it equal to her sisters, and her son's allotment was reduced from 300 to 150 pounds.
45. Lee, Charles. *Memoirs of the Life of the Late Charles Lee*. London: Jordan, 1792, 192. Lee died eight years before Putnam.

Chapter Eight

1. Today, while Israel Putnam's remains rest under a 25-foot-high equestrian statue in Brooklyn, Connecticut, Robert Rogers' pauper grave probably lies under the pavement of London's St. Mary's Churchyard public park, which was built on top of a churchyard. The church building was demolished in 1876. Source: Outdoor information tablet at St. Mary's Churchyard Park in Newington Butts in the London Borough of Southwark.
2. *Lives of John Stark, Charles Brockden Brown, Richard Montgomery, and Ethan Allen*. Boston: Hilliard, Gray & Co., 1834. 7–11. One of the great military commanders of the Revolutionary War, New Hampshire's John Stark served in Rogers Rangers during the French and Indian War (from 1754 to 1759), where like Israel Putnam he learned much from Na-

tive Americans on the tactics of warfare; knowledge that would serve him well when fighting the British Army 20 years later. Actually, Stark begin his informal education a couple of years before the war, when at age 23 he was held captive for several months by Native American warriors. At the start of the Revolutionary War, Stark was made a colonel in the New Hampshire militia and served with honor and great success at the Battle of Bunker Hill. He also fought in Canada, New Jersey, and the Battle of Bennington (near Walloomsac, NY). Most notably his actions helped defeat British General Burgoyne at the 1777 Battle of Saratoga, which, in turn, led to French entry into the war as an American ally. At the end of the Revolutionary War, on September 30, 1783, John Stark was one of ten key leaders promoted to the rank of Major General, joining Washington, Lafayette, Greene, Knox, Putnam and nine others who were already on the active list of major generals. When Stark died in New Hampshire in 1822 at age 93, he and Lafayette were the only living members of this list of 24 major generals.

3. Society, Massachusetts Historical. *Proceedings of the Massachusetts Historical Society*. Vol. III. Boston: Society, 1888. Second. 320; Green, Samuel A. *Groton Historical Series. A Collection of Papers Relating to the History of the Town of Groton, Massachusetts*. Groton: n.p., 1890. 436. Eight men from William Prescott's hometown of Pepperell, Massachusetts were killed at Bunker Hill. One of them, Nathaniel Parker, had a story similar to farmer Israel Putnam: he too was plowing a field two months earlier when he was informed that the colonial militia was being attacked by the British Army at Concord. He abandoned the plow and went off to aid his fellow Massachusetts patriots. Today, Parker's plow rests in the museum of the Lawrence Library in Pepperell. Interestingly, the wooden cultivator made and used by Prescott is also on display in the Lawrence library. After Bunker Hill, William Prescott was given command of the 7th Continental Regiment, which fought in New York in 1776. Prescott is pictured in John Trumbull's famous painting of the British General Burgoyne's 1777 surrender at Saratoga. In 1786 Prescott led militia that helped put down the armed uprising in Massachusetts known as Shays' Rebellion. In 1795, Prescott died at his home in Pepperell, Massachusetts on the New Hampshire border, leaving his wife Abigail who survived him by 26 years. In the late 1880s, William Prescott's grand-niece Sarah Rockwood (born 1785) was the last surviving person to have known him. She related her memory of the elderly Colonel, who died when she was almost 10 years old: "a tall, well-proportioned man, with blue eyes and a large head. He usually wore a skull cap; and he parted his hair in the middle, wearing it long behind, braided loosely and tied in a club with a black ribbon, as was common in those days. He had a pleasant countenance, and was remarkably social and full of fun and anecdote. He was dignified in his manners, and had the bearing of a soldier." Sarah Rockwood died on November 26, 1889, at age 104. Green states: "It was a frequent saying of Mrs. Rockwood that she belonged to a generation taught to preserve life as long as possible. She certainly put in use the precepts of extreme carefulness in the way of diet, exercise, and methodical habits."

4. "Burr, Aaron (1756–1836)." Congressional Biographical Directory (CLERKWEB). N.p., n.d. Web. June 26, 2016; "Aaron Burr (1801–1805)." Senate Historical Office. GPO: 1997) 31–44. Web. June 26, 2016.

5. *Daughters of the American Revolution* 47 1915: 335.

6. Lossing, *Philip Schuyler*, 65.

7. "Ward, Artemas (1727–1800)." Congressional Biographical Directory (CLERKWEB). N.p., n.d. Web. 26 June 2016; Martyn, Charles. *The Life of Artemas Ward, The First Commander-in-Chief of the American Revolution*. 1921. Reprint, Port Washington, N.Y.: Kennikat, 1970. Today, Harvard University maintains Artemas Ward's house in Shrewsbury, Massachusetts as a museum.

8. Deming, Henry Champion. *An Oration upon the Life and Services of Gen. David Wooster: Delivered at Danbury, April 27th, 1854, When a Monument Was Erected to His Memory*, 57.

9. Campbell, John W., and Eleanor W. Campbell. *Biographical Sketches with Other Literary Remains of the Late John W. Campbell*. Columbus, OH: Printed by Scott & Gallagher, 1838, 32.

10. Washington, George, John Clement Fitzpatrick, and David Maydole Matteson. *The Writings of George Washington from the Original Manuscript Sources, 1745–1799*. Washington: U.S. Govt. Print. Off., 1931.

11. Campbell, *Biographical Sketches*, 33.

12. He became the 5th Viscount Howe when his brother died in 1799.

13. The lives of both Napoleon and George III ended poorly. At age 51, Napoleon died in exile on St Helena, an island off the west coast of Africa, which was (and is) one of the loneliest places on earth. George lived to be 30 years older, but spent his last years blind and mentally ill.

14. Trautsch, Jaspar M. "Atrocity and Rec-

iprocity: The Burnings of Toronto and Washington D.C. and the Challenges to the Laws of War in the War of 1812." *The Routledge Handbook of American Military and Diplomatic History: The Colonial Period to 1877.* New York: Routledge, 2005. 190. One of the major actions of the War of 1812 was the 1814 British burning of Washington, D.C., including the White House and Capitol buildings. Little known is the fact that the actions were taken in retaliation for the burning and looting of Toronto (then called York) the year before by General Dearborn's out-of-control soldiers.

15. After the rejection vote, the senate allowed Monroe to withdraw the Dearborn nomination. Therefore the initial vote does not appear in the official record.

16. As we have seen, Israel's son Daniel also accompanied his father on the Mississippi expedition of 1772–1773.

17. It's also instructive to note that the publication of Dearborn's accusation against the long-dead general was made only one month after the death of Putnam biographer David Humphreys. Did Dearborn hold his tongue until the one man who could best refute him was in his grave? Not only was Humphreys the only man alive who had systematically interviewed Putnam and other people important to his life, but he could quote George Washington himself should the occasion arise. After all, he had written his Putnam biography under the great general's watchful eye when he was a year-long houseguest at Mt. Vernon.

18. "Founders Online: From Abigail Smith Adams to John Quincy Adams, 30 May 1818." *Founders Online.* National Archives, n.d. Web. June 29, 2016.

19. This was written eight years before the death of John Adams. He and Thomas Jefferson passed away within hours of each other on July 4, 1826. It was the 50th anniversary of the Declaration of Independence, which they had both signed.

20. Tarbox, *Life* 350–351. After Daniel Putnam read Dearborn's attack on the character of his father, he lost no time in seeking out evidence to the contrary. One of those who responded was John Trumbull, who was a Harvard College graduate, an aide of General Washington, a Revolutionary War Colonel, a long-term diplomat in Europe, and, most important of all, the "Artist of the Revolution," whose pictorial history of the American Revolution was unequaled. Trumbull personally knew well Putnam and almost every other key figure of the American Revolution. In a March 30, 1818, letter, he tells Daniel Putnam that Dearborn's Bunker Hill account "appears to have been written for the mere purpose of introducing a most unjustifiable attack upon the memory of your excellent father. It is strange that men cannot be contented with their own honest share of fame, without attempting to detract from that of others—but, after the attempts which have been made to diminish the immortal reputation of Washington, who shall be surprized [sic] or who repine at this enviable attendant on human greatness." Trumbull relates a conversation he had in 1786 with British Colonel John Small, who had served with Putnam during the French and Indian War. As Small was looking at the nearly finished Trumbull painting of the Battle of Bunker Hill, he commented: "I don't like the situation in which you have placed my old friend Putnam; you have not done him justice.... I glanced my eye to the enemy, and saw several young men levelling their pieces at me; I knew their excellence as marksmen, and considered myself gone. At that moment my old friend Putnam rushed forward, and striking up the muzzles of their pieces with his sword, cried out, "For God's sake, my lads, don't fire at that man—I love him as I do my brother." We were so near each other, that I heard his words distinctly. He was obeyed; I bowed, thanked him, and walked away unmolested." Trumbull continued: "You remember, my dear sir, the viper biting the file [from Aesop's tale of a snake biting a metal file]. The character of your father for courage, humanity, generosity and integrity is too firmly established by the testimony of those who did know him, to be tarnished by the breath of one who confesses that he did not. Accept, my dear Sir, this feeble tribute to your father's memory, from one who knew him, respected him, loved him—and who wishes health and prosperity to you and all the good man's posterity."

21. Soon after Dearborn made his assertions, Daniel Webster, one of the most famous men in 19th Century American government, came to the General's defense. In a long and illustrious career as a statesman and orator, Webster (1782–1852) would represented New Hampshire, and later Massachusetts in the U.S. Congress, and also served as Secretary of State in the cabinets of Presidents Harrison, Tyler, and Fillmore.

22. Putnam, A.P. *A Sketch of General Israel Putnam.* Salem, MA: Eben Putnam, 1893, 29.

23. Dwight, *Travels,* 131.

24. Franklin, Wayne. *James Fenimore Cooper: The Early Years.* New Haven: Yale UP, 2007, 654.

25. Cooper, James Fenimore. *Lionel Lin-*

Notes—Chapter Eight

coln, Or, The Leaguer of Boston ... in Three Volumes. London: John Miller, 1825.
26. Ibid.
27. Ibid.
28. "Letter from General Israel Putnam." Hartford Daily Courant 20 Nov. 1845: 2. Also Livingston, Israel Putnam, 407–408.
29. Marsh, John. Putnam and the Wolf, Or, The Monster Destroyed: An Address, Delivered at Pomfret, Con., October 26, 1829, before the Windham Co. Temperance Society, by Rev. John Marsh ... Published by Request of the Society. Hartford: D.F. Robinson, 1830. 4.
30. Griggs, Early Homesteads, 53.
31. Ireland, Joseph Norton. Records of the New York Stage, from 1750 to 1860. Vol. II. New York: T.H. Morrell, 1867, 417.
32. Ibid., 578.
33. Irving, Washington, and Washington Irving. Life of George Washington: Vol. 2. New York: G.P. Putnam, 1856. 2: 440–441.
34. Excursion of the Putnam Phalanx to Boston, Charlestown and Providence, October 4th, 5th, 6th and 7th, in the Year of Our Lord 1859. Hartford, CT: Published by the Phalanx, 1859. 5.
35. Daniel Chester French (1850–1931), sculptor of the Lincoln Memorial in Washington D.C., was one of Ward's students.
36. "Founders Online: [Notes on a Tour of English Country Seats, &c., with Thomas Jefferson, 4–10? April 1786.]" Founders Online. National Archives, n.d. Web. 29 June 2016. Apparently, taking pieces of an historical object was a common occurrence at the time. Even John Adams and Thomas Jefferson resorted to the practice when they together visited the home of William Shakespeare in April 1786. In his, Notes on a Tour of English Country Seats, &c., with Thomas Jefferson, Adams writes: "Stratford upon Avon is interesting as it is the Scaene of the Birth, Death and Sepulture of Shakespear. Three Doors from the Inn, is the House where he was born, as small and mean, as you can conceive. They shew Us an old Wooden Chair in the Chimney Corner, where He sat. We cutt off a Chip according to the Custom."
37. Livingston, Israel Putnam, 416.
38. Beach, Randall. "Leatherman mystery lives on; no body found in New York grave of 19th century wanderer." The Register Citizen, May 25, 2011. The Connecticut soil is noted for its acidity, which causes a body, including its bones, to disintegrate rapidly. In 2011, across the Connecticut–New York border in Ossining, New York, the Connecticut State archaeologist attempted to exhume the body of a 19th century wanderer known as the Old Leatherman. (For over 30 years, he dressed entirely in leather and walked a set route though Connecticut and New York State.) After a burial of 122 years, all that was found were coffin nails and discolored soil that was presumably all that remained of the coffin and the Leatherman's body. Before exhumation, Israel Putnam's body had been buried for 98 years.
39. Bayles, History of Windham, 578.
40. "Found On Old Tombstones: Curious Specimens of Connecticut Graveyard Literature." New York Times, Dec. 26, 1894: 6.
41. "Early Settler Memorials VIII. Memorials to Major-General Anthony Wayne." American Architect and Building News Apr. 2, 1887: 159.
42. "Israel Putnam." Boston Evening Transcript, June 14, 1888: 8.
43. Seymour, M.W. A History of the Equestrian Statue of Israel Putnam, at Brooklyn, Conn.: Reported to the General Assembly, 1889. Hartford, CT: Press of The Case, Lockwood & Brainard, 1888, 61–2.
44. Robinson, Henry Cornelius. Address of Henry C. Robinson: At the Dedication, by the State of Connecticut, of Gen. Putnam's Statue, at Brooklyn, June 14, 1888. Hartford, CT: Press of the Case, Lockwood & Brainard, 1888. 3; Seymour, History of the Equestrian Statue 33.
45. Boston Evening Transcript 14 June 1888: 8.
46. "How the Moderns Esteem Old Put; Several Prominent Men Express Their Ideas of Israel Putnam." New York Times, May 10, 1896.
47. Israel Putnam's grave markers were not limited to the two in Connecticut. The monument erected in the Putnam Cemetery in Devola, Ohio, over the grave of General Putnam's son, Col. Israel Putnam, by Maj. L.J.P. Putnam (who was one of General Putnam's great-grandsons) also lists the General and his grandson Israel Putnam, who is buried at Rockland Cemetery, Belpre, Ohio.
48. Howe, Henry. Historical Collections of Ohio ... an Encyclopedia of the State: History Both General and Local, Geography ... Sketches of Eminent and Interesting Characters, Etc., with Notes of a Tour over It in 1886 ... Norwalk OH: Published by the State of Ohio, 1896, 802.
49. The states with counties named for General Israel Putnam with the date of founding/establishment are: Putnam County, Georgia (1807); Putnam County, New York (1812); Putnam County, Ohio (1820); Putnam County, Indiana (1821); Putnam County, Illinois (1825); Putnam County, Tennessee (1842); Putnam County, Missouri (1845); Putnam County, West Virginia (1848). Putnam County, Florida

is named for Benjamin Alexander Putnam (1801–1869), an officer in the Second Seminole War.

50. *Report of the Commissioners of the National Centennial Celebration: Of the Early Settlement of the "territory Northwest of the River Ohio," and of the Establishment of Civil Government Therein, Held at Marietta, Ohio, July 15 to 19 Inclusive, 1888: Including Verbatim Reports and Speeches and Transactions of the Occasion.* Columbus, OH: Westbote, State Printers, 1889; *List of Relics Exhibited at Centennial Celebration of the Establishment of Civil Government, at Marietta, Ohio, July 15–19, 1889.* Columbus, OH: Publisher Not Identified, 1889, 22–23.

51. The Milwaukee Journal 17 June 1884: 2. Governor Grover Cleveland of New York was nominated at this convention. He went on to win the general election, and he was sworn in as the 22nd president of the United States in 1885.

52. Trumbull Revolutionary Gallery Comprising Portraits, Miniatures, Groups, Sketches, Studies, Arms, Battle-field Relics, Mementoes of General George Washington. New York: American Art Association, Anderson Art Galleries, 1896.

53. *Boston Evening Transcript* 23 Feb. 1904: 415.

54. On February 27, 1889, a special committee appointed by the Connecticut General Assembly inspected the grounds and the obelisk, and listed the inscriptions, including the mistaken dates of "November 9, 1777— May 25, 1778."
Report of the Commissioners of the Israel Putnam Memorial Camp Ground ... for the Fifteen Months Ending September 30, 1902 (for the Two Years Ending September 30, 1904- nineteen Months Ending January 31, 1915). Vol. 4. Hartford: n.p., 1903.

55. Specializing in colonial and Revolutionary America, Dr. Daniels served for many years as professor of history at the University of Winnipeg and at Texas Tech University.

56. Swinton, William. *Swinton's Primary United States. First Lessons in Our Country's History: Bringing out Its Salient Points, and Aiming to Combine Simplicity with Sense.* New York and Chicago: Ivison, Blakeman, Taylor & Co., 1874, 177.

57. Livingston's in 1901 and Ober's in 1904.

58. Stevenson, Burton Egbert. *American Men of Action.* Garden City: Doubleday, 1913, 265.

59. "A Tragic Contrast." *Hartford Courant* 10 July 1903: 10. Cassius Clay, Jr., was the name of heavyweight boxing champion Muhammad Ali, before he converted to Islam. Ali's father, Cassius Clay, Sr. was named after the abolitionist by Ali's grandfather.

60. Johnston, Charles H.L. *Famous Scouts, including Trappers, Pioneers, and Soldiers of the Frontier; Their Hazardous and Exciting Adventures in the Mighty Drama of the White Conquest of the American Continent.* Boston: L.C. Page, 1910.

61. Fleming, Thomas J. "History Can be Fun." *American Legion Magazine* May 1961: 43.

62. Robert Brower (1850–1934) appeared as the General in two short films that were released in 1911 as part of the Edison Company's "United States History Series" of movies. The titles were: *How Mrs. Murray Saved the American Army* and *The Death of Nathan Hale.* Seven years later, British actor Lionel Belmore (1867–1953) played Putnam in *The Beautiful Mrs. Reynolds.* It was 96 years later that Mark Bean played Israel Putnam in the 2014 TV movie, *Samuel Adams.*

Bibliography

Abbott, Katharine M. *Old Paths and Legends of the New England Border; Connecticut, Deerfield, Berkshire.* New York and London: G.P. Putnam's Sons, 1907.

Adams, John, Margaret A. Hogan, and C. James Taylor. *My Dearest Friend: Letters of Abigail and John Adams.* Cambridge, MA: Belknap of Harvard UP, 2007.

Almon's Remembrancer or Impartial Repository of Public Events for 1775. London.

Amory, Thomas C. *Old Cambridge and New.* Boston: James R. Osgood, 1871.

The Baltimore Sun Almanac for 1899, A.S. Abell Co., 1899.

Barber, John Warner. *United States Book, Or, Interesting Events in the History of the United States.* New Haven: L.H. Young, 1833.

Bayles, Richard M. *History of Windham County, Connecticut.* New York: W.W. Preston, 1889.

Bolton, Reginald Pelham. *Fort Washington: An Account of the Identification of the Site of Fort Washington with a History of the Defence and Reduction of Mount Washington.* New York: Empire State Society of the Sons of the American Revolution, 1902.

Caldwell, Charles. *Memoirs of the Life and Campaigns of the Hon. Nathaniel Greene.* Philadelphia: Robert & Thomas Desilver, 1819.

Campbell, John W., and Eleanor W. Campbell. *Biographical Sketches with Other Literary Remains of the Late John W. Campbell.* Columbus, OH: Printed by Scott & Gallagher, 1838.

Castle, Egerton. *Schools and Masters of Fence from the Middle Ages to the End of the Eighteenth Century.* London: G. Bell, 1885.

Chase, Ellen. *The Beginnings of the American Revolution: Based on Contemporary Letters, Diaries and Other Documents.* London: Pitman, 1911.

Chernow, Ron. *Alexander Hamilton.* New York: Penguin, 2004.

_____. *Washington: A Life.* New York: Penguin, 2010.

Chorley, E. Clowes. *History of St. Philip's Church in the Highlands, Garrison, New York: Including, up to 1840, St. Peter's Church on the Manor of Cortlandt.* New York: E.S. Gorham, 1912.

Clinton, George. *Public Papers of George Clinton.* Albany: Quayle, 1900.

Cruson, Daniel. *Putnam's Revolutionary War Winter Encampment: The History and Archaeology of Putnam Memorial State Park.* Charleston, SC: History, 2011.

Cutter, William, *Life of Israel Putnam.* New York: 1847.

Deming, Henry Champion. *An Oration upon the Life and Services of Gen. David Wooster: Delivered at Danbury, April 27th, 1854, When a Monument Was Erected to His Memory.* Hartford: Press of Case, Tiffany, 1854.

Disturnell, John. *A Trip through the Lakes of North America Embracing a Full Description of the St. Lawrence River, Together with All the Principal Places on Its Banks, from Its Source to Its Mouth: Commerce of the Lakes, Etc., Forming Altogether a Complete Guide for the Pleasure Traveler and Emigrant*. New York: J. Disturnell, 1857.

Drake, Samuel G. *Indian Captivities Or Life in the Wigwam: Being True Narratives of Captives Who Have Been Carried Away by the Indians, from the Frontier Settlements of the U.S., from the Earliest Period to the Present Time*. Auburn: Derby & Miller, 1850.

Dwight, Timothy. *Travels in New-England and New-York: In Four Volumes*. London: Baynes, 1823.

Early, Eleanor. *New England Cookbook*. New York: Random House, 1954.

Everett, William. *Oration in Honor of Col. William Prescott: Delivered in Boston, 14 October, 1895 by Invitation of the Bunker Hill Monument Association*. Boston: Bunker Hill Monument Association, 1896.

Excursion of the Putnam Phalanx to Boston, Charlestown and Providence, October 4th, 5th, 6th and 7th, in the Year of Our Lord 1859. Hartford, CT: Published by the Phalanx, 1859.

Fellows, John. *The Veil Removed: Or, Reflections on David Humphrey's Essay on the Life of Israel Putnam: Also, Notices of Oliver W.B. Peabody's Life of the Same, S. Swett's Sketch of Bunker Hill Battle, Etc., Etc*. New York: James D. Lockwood, 1843.

Force, Peter. *American Archives: Consisting of A Collection Of Authentick Records, State Papers, Debates, And Letters And Other Notices Of Publick Affairs, The Whole Forming A Documentary History Of The Origin And Progress Of The North American Colonies, Of The Causes And Accomplishment Of The American Revolution, And Of The Constitution Of Government For The United States To The Final Ratification Thereof; In Six Series*. Washington: n.p., 1846.

Ford, Paul Leicester. *The True George Washington*. Philadelphia: J.B. Lippincott, 1896.

Ford, Worthington Chauncey. *Journals of the Continental Congress: 1774–1789*. Washington: Government Print. Office, 1907.

Founding Families: Digital Editions of the Papers of the Winthrops and the Adamses, ed. C. James Taylor. Boston: Massachusetts Historical Society, 2016.

Franklin, Wayne. *James Fenimore Cooper: The Early Years*. New Haven: Yale UP, 2007.

Freeman, Douglas Southall, John Alexander. Carroll, and Mary Wells. Ashworth. *George Washington: A Biography*. New York: Scribner, 1948.

Frothingham, Richard. *The Centennial: Battle of Bunker Hill*. Boston: Little, Brown, 1875.

———. *History of the Siege of Boston: And of the Battles of Lexington, Concord, and Bunker Hill: Also an Account of the Bunker Hill Monument*. Boston: Little, Brown, 1890.

———. *Life and times of Joseph Warren*. Boston: Little, Brown, 1865.

Gardiner, Curtiss C. *Lion Gardiner and His Descendants*. St. Louis: A. Whipple, 1890.

General Orders Issued by Major-General Israel Putnam, When in Command of the Highlands, in the Summer and Fall of 1777. Brooklyn: Historical Prtg. Club, 1892.

Golway, Terry. *Washington's General: Nathanael Greene and the Triumph of the American Revolution*. New York: H. Holt, 2005.

Governors Island, New York. 107th Cong., 1st sess. S S. 689. Washington: U.S. Government Printing Office, 2002. Web. Nov. 26, 2015. http://www.gpo.gov/fdsys/pkg/CHRG-107shrg77015/html/CHRG-107shrg77015.htm.

Graham, James. *The Life of General Daniel Morgan, of the Virginia Line of the Army of the United States, with Portions of His Correspondence*. New York: Derby & Jackson, 1858.

Green, Harry Clinton, and Mary Wolcott Green. *The Pioneer Mothers of America: A Record of the More Notable Women of the Early Days of the Country, and Particularly of the Colonial and Revolutionary Periods*. New York: G.P. Putnam's Sons, 1912.

Griggs, Susan Jewett. *Early Homesteads of Pomfret and Hampton*. Abington? Conn.: n.p., 1950.

Griswold, Rufus W., William Gilmore Simms, and Edward D. Ingraham. *Washington and the Generals of the American Revolution ... With Sixteen Portraits on Steel*. Philadelphia: Carey and Hart, 1848.

Hanson, J.W. *History of the Town of Danvers, from Its Early Settlement to the Year 1848*. Danvers: Author, 1848.

Hatch, Louis Clinton. *Maine; a History*. New York: American Historical Society, 1919. 166.

Hawthorne, Nathaniel. *The Scarlet Letter, a Romance*. London: David Bogue, 1851.

Hibbert, Christopher. *George III: A Personal History*. New York: Basic, 1998.

Hill, George Canning. *Benedict Arnold. A Biography*. Boston: E.O. Libby, 1858.

_____. *Life of Gen. Israel Putnam*. Boston: 1858.

Himes, Charles Francis. *Col. Robert Magaw, the Defender of Fort Washington: Major in Colonel William Thompson's "Battalion of Pennsylvania Riflemen," the First Troops from the South to Reach Boston; Colonel of the Fifth Pennsylvania Regiment, Assigned by Washington to Defend Fort Washington. Paper Read before the Hamilton Library Association, Carlisle, Pa. The Historical Society of Cumberland County, Pennsylvania*. Carlisle, PA: Hamilton Library Association, 1915.

Howe, Henry. *Historical Collections of Ohio ... an Encyclopedia of the State: History Both General and Local, Geography ... Sketches of Eminent and Interesting Characters, Etc., with Notes of a Tour over It in 1886 ...* Norwalk OH: Published by the State of Ohio, 1896.

Howe, William Howe, Edward Everett Hale, and Benjamin Franklin. Stevens. *General Sir William Howe's Orderly Book at Charleston, Boston and Halifax, June 17, 1775 to 1776, 26 May: To Which Is Added the Official Abridgement of General Howe's Correspondence with the English Government during the Siege of Boston, and Some Military Returns and Now First Printed from the Original Manuscripts*. London: B.F. Stevens, 1890.

Hubbard, Robert Ernest. *The Last Survivors of Historical Events, Movies, Disasters, and More*. Lincolnwood, IL: West Side Pub., 2009.

Humphreys, David, Col., *An Essay on the Life of the Honourable Major-General Israel Putnam, addressed to the State Society of the Cincinnati in Connecticut*. Hartford: 1788.

_____. *An Essay on the Life of the Honourable Major-General Israel Putnam. With notes and additions. With an Appendix containing an Historical and Topographical Sketch of Bunker Hill Battle by S. Swett*. Boston: 1818.

_____. *An Essay on the Life of the Honourable Major-General Israel Putnam, addressed to the State Society of the Cincinnati in Connecticut*. Hartford: 1850.

_____. *The miscellaneous works of Colonel Humphreys*. New York: 1804.

Humphreys, Frank Landon. *Life and times of David Humphreys, Soldier—Statesman—Poet, "Belov'd of Washington."* New York and London: G.P. Putnam's Sons, 1917.

Hurd, D. Hamilton. *History of New London County, Connecticut with Biographical Sketches of Many of Its Pioneers and Prominent Men*. Philadelphia: J.W. Lewis, 1882.

Iden, Jay B. *The Arkansas Traveler in Connecticut*. Philadelphia, 2 August 1919. The Country Gentleman, 84 (1919): 10.

Irving, Washington. Life of George Washington: Vol. 2. New York: G.P. Putnam, 1856.

Johnson, Clifton. *Highways and Byways of New England, including the States of Massachusetts, New Hampshire, Rhode Island, Connecticut, Vermont and Maine*. New York: Macmillan, 1915.

Johnson, William. *Sketches of the Life and Correspondence of Nathanael Greene, Major General of the Armies of the United States, in the War of the Revolution*. Charleston: Printed for the Author, by A.E. Miller, 1822.

Johnston, Charles H.L. *Famous Scouts, including Trappers, Pioneers, and Soldiers of the Frontier; Their Hazardous and Exciting Adventures in the Mighty Drama of the White Conquest of the American Continent*. Boston: L.C. Page, 1910.

Jones, Thomas, and De Lancey Edward F. *History of New York During the Revolutionary War.* New York: Printed for the New York Historical Society, 1879.

Kelly, Howard A., and Walter L. Burrage. *American Medical Biographies.* Baltimore: Norman, Remington, 1920. 1184.

Ketchum, Richard M. *The Battle for Bunker Hill.* Garden City, NY: Doubleday, 1962.

Kohler, Max J. *Judah Touro, Merchant and Philanthropist.* Baltimore (?): n.p., 1905.

Langguth, A.J. *Patriots: The Men Who Started the American Revolution.* New York: Simon & Schuster, 1988.

Lee, Charles. *Memoirs of the Life of the Late Charles Lee.* London: Jordan, 1792.

Longacre, James B., and James Herring. *The National Portrait Gallery of Distinguished Americans.* Philadelphia, PA: Henry Perkins, 1834.

Lossing, Benson J. *The Life and times of Philip Schuyler.* New York: n.p., 1860.

_____. *History of the United States: From the Aboriginal times to the Present Day.* New York: Lamb, 1909.

_____. *The Pictorial Field Book of the Revolution: Or, Illustrations, by Pen and Pencil, of the History, Biography, Scenery, Relics, and Traditions of the War of Independence.* New York: Harper, 1851.

_____. *The Pictorial Field Book of the Revolution: Or, Illustrations, by Pen and Pencil, of the History, Biography, Scenery, Relics, and Traditions of the War of Independence.* New York: Harper, 1859.

Mallary, Peter T., and Tim Imrie. *New England Churches & Meetinghouses 1680–1830.* New York: Vendome, 1985.

Marsh, John. *Putnam and the Wolf, Or, The Monster Destroyed: An Address, Delivered at Pomfret, Con., October 26, 1829, before the Windham Co. Temperance Society, by Rev. John Marsh.* Published by Request of the Society. Hartford: D.F. Robinson, 1830.

Marshall, John. *The Life of George Washington: Commander in Chief of the American Forces, during the War Which Established the Independence of His Country, and First President of the United States: Compiled under the Inspection of the Honourable Bushrod Washington, from Original Papers ... to Which Is Prefixed, an Introduction, Containing a Compendious View of the Colonies Planted by the English on the Continent of North America, from Their Settlement to the Commencement of That War Which Terminated in Their Independence.* Fredericksburg, VA: Citizens' Guild of Washington's Boyhood Home, 1926.

Martin, Joseph Plumb. *A Narrative of Some of the Adventures, Dangers and Sufferings of a Revolutionary Soldier; Interspersed with Anecdotes of Incidents That Occurred within His Own Observation.* Hallowell: Printed by Glazier, Masters, 1830.

Martyn, Charles. *The Life of Artemas Ward, the First Commander-in-Chief of the American Revolution.* New York: Artemas Ward, 1921.

McCullough, David. *1776.* New York: Simon & Schuster, 2005.

_____. *John Adams.* New York: Simon & Schuster, 2001.

Middlekauff, Robert. *The Glorious Cause: The American Revolution, 1763–1789.* New York: Oxford UP, 2005.

Minks, Louise, and Benton Minks. *Revolutionary War, Updated Edition.* New York: Infobase Publishing, 2009.

Moore, Frank. *Diary of the American Revolution from Newspapers and Original Documents; a Centennial Volume Embracing the Current Events in Our Country's History from 1775 to 1781.* Hartford: publisher not identified, 1875.

Nelson, James L. *With Fire & Sword: The Battle of Bunker Hill and the Beginning of the American Revolution.* New York: Thomas Dunne/St. Martin's, 2011.

Nelson, William, Peter Ross, and Fenwick Y. Hedley. *The New Jersey Coast in Three Centuries; History of the New Jersey Coast with Genealogical and Historic-biographical Appendix.* New York: Lewis Pub., 1902.

Niven, John. *Connecticut Hero, Israel Putnam.* Hartford: American Revolution Bicentennial Commission of Connecticut, 1977.

Ober, Frederick A. *"Old Put" the Patriot.* New York: D. Appleton, 1904.

Ohio Archaeological and Historical Quarterly. Columbus. Ohio: Ohio Archaeological and Historical Publications Society, XVI.1 (1907).

BIBLIOGRAPHY

Parkman, Francis. *Historic Handbook of the Northern Tour: Lakes George and Champlain, Niagara, Montreal, Quebec.* Boston: Little, Brown, 1885.

Parton, James. *Life and times of Benjamin Franklin.* New York: Mason Brothers, 1864.

Peabody, Oliver W.B., *Life of Israel Putnam. In Sparks's Library of American Biography.* Vol. VII. Boston: 1837.

Pomeroy, George Eltweed. *An Address on the Character of General Seth Pomeroy.* Toledo: Franklin, 1906.

Putnam, A.P. *A Sketch of General Israel Putnam.* Salem, MA: Eben Putnam, 1893.

Putnam, Eben. *A History of the Putnam Family in England and America. Recording the Ancestry and Descendants of John Putnam of Danvers, Mass., Jan Poutman of Albany, N.Y., Thomas Putnam of Hartford, Conn.* Salem, MA: Salem Pub. and Print., 1891.

Putnam, Elizabeth Cabot, and Harriet Silvester Tapley. *The Hon. Samuel Putnam and Sarah (Gooll) Putnam: With a Genealogical Record of Their Descendants.* Danvers, MA: Danvers Historical Society, 1922.

Putnam, Israel, Rufus Putnam, and Albert Carlos Bates. *The Two Putnams, Israel and Rufus: In the Havana Expedition, 1762, and in the Mississippi River Exploration, 1772–73, with Some Account of the Company of Military Adventurers.* Hartford: Connecticut Historical Society, 1931.

Putnam, Rufus, and Rowena Buell. *The Memoirs of Rufus Putnam and Certain Official Papers and Correspondence,* Published by the National Society of the Colonial Dames of America in the State of Ohio. Boston: Houghton, Mifflin, 1903.

"Revolutionary Figure—Redding Unveils Putnam Statue." *Norwalk Hour* 23 Sept. 1969: 1.

Ridpath, John Clark. *The New Complete History of the United States of America.* Washington, D.C.: Ridpath History, 1905.

Robinson, Henry Cornelius. *Address of Henry C. Robinson: At the Dedication, by the State of Connecticut, of Gen. Putnam's Statue, at Brooklyn, June 14, 1888.* Hartford, CT: Press of the Case, Lockwood & Brainard, 1888.

Rogers, Robert. *Journals of Major Robert Rogers Containing an Account of the Several Excursions He Made under the Generals Who Commanded upon the Continent of North America, during the Late War ; from Which May by Collected the Most Material Circumstances of Every Campaign upon That Continent, from the Commencement to the Conclusion of the War.* Albany: Joel Munsell's Sons, 1883.

Root, Mary Philotheta. *Chapter Sketches, Connecticut Daughters of the American Revolution; Patron Saints.* New Haven: Connecticut Chapters, Daughters of the American Revolution, 1901.

Rose, Alexander. *Washington's Spies: The Story of America's First Spy Ring.* New York: Bantam, 2006.

Rutkow, Ira M. "James Thacher and His Military Journal During the American Revolutionary War." *Arch Surg Archives of Surgery* 136.7 (2001): 837. Web.

Seymour, M.W. *A History of the Equestrian Statue of Israel Putnam, at Brooklyn, Conn.: Reported to the General Assembly, 1889.* Hartford, CT: Press of The Case, Lockwood & Brainard, 1888.

Shaara, Jeff. *The Glorious Cause: A Novel of the American Revolution.* New York: Ballantine, 2002.

"Sign of General Wolfe." EMuseum. Connecticut Historical Society Museum & Library, n.d. Web. 08 Dec. 2015. http://emuseum.chs.org/emuseum/view/objects/asitem/People$00401247/1;jsessionid=18CE2DAC665FBCD69D450C3B0DD9452C?t%3Astate%3Aflow=964c5221-7373-43fb-a904-03836b647847.

Smith, Fredrika Shumway. *Old Put: The Story of Major General Israel Putnam.* Chicago: Rand McNally, 1967.

Starbuck, David R. *The Great Warpath: British Military Sites from Albany to Crown Point.* Hanover, NH: U of New England, 1999.

———. *Massacre at Fort William Henry.* Hanover, NH: U of New England, 2002.

Statue of Colonel Thomas Knowlton Ceremonies at the Unveiling. Hartford, CT: Press of Case, Lockwood & Brainard, 1895.

Stevenson, Burton Egbert. *American Men of Action.* Garden City: Doubleday, 1913.

Stiles, Henry Reed. *History of Ancient Windsor, Connecticut: Including East Windsor, South Windsor, and Ellington, Prior to 1768, the Date of Their Separation from the Old Town ; and Windsor, Bloomfield and Windsor Locks, to the Present Time.* New York: C.B. Norton, 1859.

Sumner, Samuel B., and G.H. Hollister. *1779–1879: Centennial Commemoration of the Ride of General Israel Putnam, at Greenwich, Conn., February 26, 1779: Observed February 22, 1879.* Greenwich, CT: Greenwich Observer Book and Job Print, 1880.

Symonds, Craig L., and William J. Clipson. *A Battlefield Atlas of the American Revolution.* Annapolis, MD: Nautical & Aviation Pub. of America, 1986.

Tarbox, Increase Niles, *Life of Israel Putnam.* Boston: 1876.

Thacher, James, and Samuel X. Radbill. *Military Journal of the American Revolution: From the Commencement to the Disbanding of the American Army: Comprising a Detailed Account of the Principal Events and Battles of the Revolution with Their Exact Dates, and a Biographical Sketch of the Most Prominent Generals.* Hartford, CT: Hurlbut, Williams, 1862.

Todd, Charles Burr. *Guide to Putnam Memorial Camp: With a Complete History of the Encampment, Incidents, Organization of the Brigades, Itinerary, &c.* Washington: Byron S. Adams, 1890.

_____. *The History of Redding, Conn., from Its First Settlement to the Present Time. With Notes on the Adams, Banks ... Stow Families.* New York: J.A. Gray, 1880.

Trumbull, John. *Autobiography, Reminiscences and Letters of John Trumbull, from 1756 to 1841.* New York & London: Wiley & Putnam, 1841.

_____. *M'Fingal, a Modern Epic Poem.* Hartford: S. Andrus and Son, 1856.

Tuchman, Barbara Wertheim. "General Israel Putnam." 200th Anniversary of Putnam's Horseneck Ride (February 24, 1979). Greenwich Historical Society, Greenwich, Connecticut. Address.

Tucker, Spencer, James R. Arnold, and Roberta Wiener. *The Encyclopedia of North American Indian Wars, 1607–1890: A Political, Social, and Military History.* Santa Barbara, CA: ABC-CLIO, 2011.

Tuckerman, Bayard. *Life of General Philip Schuyler: 1733–1804.* New York: Dodd, Mead, 1903.

The United States Army and Navy Journal and Gazette of the Regular and Volunteer Forces. Vol. XV. 1877–1878. New York: Army and Navy Journal Inc., March 16, 1878, 505.

United States. Cong. Senate. Subcommittee on National Parks. Hearing on S. 689, To Convey Certain Federal Properties on Wheildon, William W. *New History of the Battle of Bunker Hill, June 17, 1775, Its Purpose, Conduct, and Result.* Boston: Lee & Shepard, 1875.

Warren, George Washington. *The History of the Bunker Hill Monument Association during the First Century of the United States of America.* Boston: J.R. Osgood, 1877. 284.

Washington, George. *The Writings of George Washington Being His Correspondence, ...* Boston: American Stationers, 1834.

Waters, Wilson, and Henry Spaulding Perham. *History of Chelmsford, Massachusetts.* Lowell, MA: Printed for the Town by Courier-Citizen, 1917.

Webb, J. Watson, Silas Deane, and John Austin Stevens. *Reminiscences of Gen'l Samuel B. Webb of the Revolutionary Army.* New York: Globe Stationery and Print., 1882.

Webster, Daniel. *The Orations on Bunker Hill Monument: The Character of Washington and the Landing at Plymouth.* New York: American Book, 1894.

Whittemore, Henry. *The Heroes of the American Revolution and Their Descendants: Battle of Long Island.* New York: Heroes of the Revolution, 1897.

Winsor, Justin. *Celebration of the Centennial Anniversary of the Battle of Bunker Hill. With an Appendix Containing a Survey of the Literature of the Battle, Its Antecedents and Results.* Boston: Printed by Order of the City Council, 1875.

Woodward, P.H., and Ashbel Woodward. *Statue of Colonel Thomas Knowlton: Ceremonies at the Unveiling.* Hartford,

CT: Press of the Case, Lockwood & Brainard, 1895.

Wright, Robert. *The Life of Major-General James Wolfe; Founded on Original Documents and Illustrated by His Correspondence, including Numerous Unpublished Letters Contributed from the Family Papers of Noblemen and Gentlemen, Descendants of His Companions.* London: Chapman & Hall, 1864.

Young, John Russell, Howard M. Jenkins, and George O. Seilhamer. *Memorial History of the City of Philadelphia from Its First Settlement to the Year 1895.* New York: New-York History, 1898.

Index

Numbers in **_bold italics_** indicate pages with photographs

Abercrombie, Gen. James 31, 33–35, 37
Adams, Abigail 57, 90, 97, 140, 192
Adams, John 4, 62, 88, 90, 94, 97, 140, 174, 188–189, 192, 215, 218, 221, 224, 226, 232–233, 235, 238
Adams, John Quincy 4, 90, 97, 216, 221n54
Adams, Samuel 63, 70–71, 88, 101, 234n62
African Americans 4, 7, 11, 30, 98, 205n5, 228n145
Alexander, William (Lord Stirling) 118, 155, 220n30
Allen, Ethan 62
Almon's Remembrance 43, 77, 235
American Legion Magazine 202
Amherst, Jeffrey 33, 35, 36, 43, 62, 210n4, 212n80
Ansonia, Connecticut 205n3
Apergis, Andreas 202
Armstrong, Gen. John 109
Articles of Confederation 223, 226
Ashbow, John 98
Ashbow, Samuel 98
Assassin's Creed III 202

Bannister, Nathaniel 194
Barber, John Warner 207n35
Barlow, Joel 99, 216n129, 229n20
Baylor Massacre 143, 224n51
Bernard, John 177
Betts, Azor 139, 224n36
Biddle, Capt. Nicholas 133
Blackbeard (Edward Teach) 3
Boston (city) 10–11, 52, 54, 69–103, 109–112, 115, 158, 172, 190, 200–210, 207n28, 211n49, 212n67, 213n9, 213n11, 215n114, 220n24, 228n9

Boston Evening Transcript 200
Boston National Historical Park 66, **_86_**
Boston Tea Party 69
Braintree (Massachusetts) 90
Breed's Hill 77, 85–88, 90, 92–93, 95–96, 98, 102, 119, 190
Brooklyn, battle of *see* Long Island, battle of
Brooklyn (Connecticut) Congregational Church 19, 50–**_51_**, 52, 56, 179
Brooks, A.E. 200
Bunker Hill, battle of 22, 55, 74–75, 77, 80–**_86_**, 87–102, 108–111, 119, 124, 129, 153, 179, 182, 188, 190–191, 194–195, 201–202, 212n81, 214n59, 214n62, 214n74, 215n104, 216n132–133, 219n178, 222n64, 223n79, 231n2, 231n3, 232n20
Bunker Hill Monument **_86_**, 100–102, 217n134
Burbeck, Henry 88
Burgoyne, Gen. John 83, 100, 135, 144–146, 149, 190, 213n28, 231n2, 231n3
Burr, Aaron 59, 75, 118, 123, 149, 151, 176, 188, 219n178, 220n31
Bushnell, David 119–120, 220n35
Bushnell Park (Hartford, Connecticut) **_193_**, 195

Cambridge, Massachusetts 7, 54–56, 72–73, 75–77, 80–81, 83–85, 88, 92, 93, 98, 102–103, 106–107, 110–111
Cargill Falls Mill 200
Chappel, Alonzo **_122_**
Charlestown (Massachusetts) 76–77, 80–88, 97, 100, 109, 129
Chatterton Hill 129

243

244 INDEX

Chester, Capt. John 74, 79, 90, 93, 215
Choctaw People 67, 213*n*86
Church, Benjamin 111–112 219*n*183
Clay, Cassius M. 201, 234*n*59
Cleveland, Chauncey Fitch 199
Cleveland, Josiah 85, 87
Clinton, Gen. George 145, 148, 225*n*58, 229*n*17
Clinton, Gen. Henry 83, 145–6, 150, 225*n*57, 228*n*42
Clinton, Gen. James 145–146, 229*n*17
Colonial Williamsburg 69
Conant, Sylvanus 99–100
Concord, Massachusetts 71–72, 74–75, 79–80, 89, 197, 214*n*67, 223*n*79, 230*n*33, 231*n*3
Congregational Church 19, 50, *51*, 52, 56, 179, 205*n*3, 230*n*37
Connecticut Courant 74, 213*n*; see also *Connecticut Courant and Weekly Intelligencer*; *Hartford Courant*; *Hartford Daily Courant*
Connecticut Courant and Weekly Intelligencer 180, 183, 230*n*; see also *Connecticut Courant*; *Hartford Courant*; *Hartford Daily Courant*
Connecticut Historical Society Museum 61, 211*n*32
Connecticut National Guard 196
Connecticut State Capitol *73*, *193*, 196, 200, 222
Connecticut Wits 99
Continental Army 79, 94–95, 103–104, 107, 109, 111, 115, 118–119, 125, 127–129, 134, 136–137, 149, 154–155, 158–159, 161, 164, 174, 179, 183, 189 200, 210*n*1, 213*n*7, 216*n*129, 217*n*151, 219*n*3, 220*n*24, 224*n*32, 225*n*55, 228*n*142, 228*n*1, 229*n*17
Continental Congress 78, 105–108, 111, 114, 117, 122–123, 135, 137, 147, 154, 176, 178, 189 213*n*42, 214*n*74, 218*n*153, 219*n*3, 222*n*59, 223*n*1, 223*n*18
Cooper, James Fenimore 31, 149, 192–193, 194
Copp's Hill 85, 87
Corbin, Margaret 131, 223
Cornwallis, Gen. Charles 137 194 221*n*57
court martials 92, 141
Craigie House 111
Crown Point (New York) 20, 21, 23, 26, 28, 33, *35*, 36, 40, 116, 218*n*153, 219*n*17
Cuba 7 45–47, 65–66, 68, 80, 89, 127
Cutter, William 59–61, 99, 147, 230*n*36

Dalzell, Capt. James 34, 37–38
Danbury News 163
Daniels, Bruce C. 201, 234*n*55
Danvers (Massachusetts) *see* Salem Village
Dawes, William 71, 88, 213*n*13
Deane, Silas 74, 106, 110

Dearborn, Henry 191–192, 232*n*14, 232*n*15, 232*n*17, 232*n*20, 232n21
DeKalb, Gen. Johan 155
Deseret News 61
"Don't fire until you see the whites of their eyes" 90, 97, 201
dueling 58–60, 188–189
Durkee, Robert 22–23, 31, 63, 98, 118
Dwight, Timothy IV 5, 41, 49, 50, 147, 157, 175, 192, 197, ***198***
Dwight, Timothy V 197

HMS *Eagle* 119
Enos, Roger 65

farming 13, 177, 12 21, 94, 96 148
Farnham, Ralph 100
fear 40–41, 100, 118, 151, 199
Fish, Stuyvesant 152
Fishkill, New York 144, 148–150, 155, 164
Fitch, Thomas 63–64
flogging 140–142, 144, 215*n*97
Forbes, Gen. John 33, 35
Ford, Capt. John 91
Forman, David 137, 223*n*
Fort Carillon (Fort Ticonderoga) 28, 33, 36, 219*n*10
Fort Clinton 146–149, 225*n*58
Fort Detroit 48–49
Fort Duquesne 33, 35
Fort Frontenac 35
Fort Lee 130–131, 218*n*171
Fort Miller 36
Fort Montgomery 144–149
Fort Oswego 26
Fort Presque Isle 197
Fort Ticonderoga 25, 28, 33–36, 40–41, 108, 112, 116, 211*n*49
Fort Washington 129–131, 222*n*71, 222*n*77
Fort William Henry 26, 28–***29***, 30–31, 209*n*40
Franklin, Benjamin 58, 188, 200, 205*n*4, 220*n*26
Franklin, Wayne 192
Freemasonry 39, 80, 157, 184
French, Daniel Chester 233*n*35
French and Indian War 7, 17, 19–44, 46–48, 59–64, 66, 71, 76–78, 80, 89, 96, 104, 107–108, 110, 116, 127, 144, 153, 157–158, 166, 173, 175, 187, 191, 199, 207*n*3, 208*n*5 208*n*14, 210*n*9, 212*n*67, 212*n*82, 214*n*74, 218*n*153, 220*n*24, 221*n*47, 227*n*110, 230*n*2, 232*n*20
Frye, Col. James 83, 98
Frye, Gen. Joseph 109

Gage, Gen. Thomas 43, 48, 71, 76–80, 102, 110–112, 210*n*77
Gardiner, John 52–54, 56, 65, 74
Gardiner, Lion 52, 211*n*26
Gardiner, Septimus 52–53, 65, 74, 149

Index

Gates, Gen. Horatio 104, 111, 116, 144, 150–151, 154–155, 178, 220n31, 229n17
General Wolfe Tavern 53, 61, 221n32
Gerhardt, Karl *183*, 196, 198
Goodrich, Capt. 66
Governor William A. O'Neill State Armory 200
Governors Island 116, 120–121
Grant's Tomb 128
Green Berets 21
Green Mountain Boys 62
Greene, Nathanael 95, 104, 111, 115–118, 121, 129–130, 135, 160, 173, 178, 188, 194, 228n7, 229n17
Grey, Charles 143, 224n52
Gridley, Col. Richard 83, 87, 91, 94, 214n67, 215n109
Gridley, Capt. Samuel 83, 91
Griffith, Charles 126, 222n59
Griggs, Susan Jewett 194
Grosvenor, Lemuel (brother-in-law) 172, 230n44
Grosvenor, Lemuel (grandson) 14, 230n44
Grosvenor, Rev. Lemuel (great-grandson) 13, 54, 57, 93, 172, 180

Hale, Nathan 127–128, 196
Hale, Sarah Josepha 100 216n132
Hamilton, Alexander 41, 59, 138, 150–152, 177, 188–189, 201, 220n31, 234n62
Hamilton, Col. J.S.C. 153
Hancock, John 71, 88; cannon 101, 126, 132, 223n1, 226n105
Harlem Heights 122–123, 125, 221n49
Harlem Heights (battle of) 125–128, 222n67, 222n68
Hartford Courant 201, 211n, 214n, 228n; see also *Connecticut Courant*; *Connecticut Courant and Weekly Intelligencer*; *Hartford Daily Courant*
Hartford Daily Courant 169, 229n, 233n; see also *Connecticut Courant*; *Connecticut Courant and Weekly Intelligencer*; *Hartford Courant*
Hathorne, John 8
Hathorne, William 8
Haviland, William 32–33, 43, 46, 210n4
Hawthorne, Nathaniel 8
Hazen, Col. Moses 158, 160, 164
Heath, Gen. William 104, 115, 132, 219n12, 229n17
Hessians 117–118, 136, 219n21, 220n27
Hill, George Canning 151, 230n36
Hinman, Col. Benjamin 74
Hobby, Capt. John 165
Holland, Joseph 70
Horseneck 164–*165*, *167*, *168*–169, 200, 227n137
Howard, Gen. O.O. 169, 228n145
Howe, Gen. George 33–34 209n48 219n9
Howe, Jemima 41–42 219n10

Howe, Adm. Richard 115–116 119
Howe, Gen. William 83, 89–90 96 115–116 119 121 122 123–126 128 129–131 135 150 190 231n12
Humphreys, David 3–4, 10, 15, 17, 21, 23–24, 26–27, 29, 32–34, 36–40, 43–44, 72, 76–78, 90, 93, 99, 119–120, 123, 124, 126, 129, 133, 138, 142, 144, 146, 147, 151, 160–162, 171–172, 176, 178, 184, 188–189, 193, 205n2, 205n3, 205n4, 206n18, 208n14, 209n48, 209n66, 219n178, 229n20, 230n36, 232n17
Huntington, Anna Hyatt *168*, 227n140
Huntington, Jedediah 118, 141, 147, 160, 162, 225n69, 229n17

Ingersoll, Jared, Sr. 63
Irving, Washington 5, 192, 194–195

Jamaica 65–66, 68
James, Thomas 67
Jefferson, Thomas 4, 17, 54, 58, 102–103, 156–157, 188–189, 202, 220n26, 220n35, 225n58, 226n105, 229n16, 232n19, 233n36
Johnson, Charles F. 197–198
Johnston, Charles H.L. 201

Kemp, Reuben 88, 93
Kidd, Capt. William 52
Kip's Bay (battle) 121–123, 126, 221n41
Knapp Tavern 169
Knowlton, Thomas 82–83, 88, 93, 118, 125–127, 222n64
Knowlton's Rangers 127
Knox, Henry 57, 112, 123, 177, 192, 211n49, 225n69, 229n17, 231n2
Knyphausen, Gen. Wilhelm von 117, 130–131, 222n77

Lafayette, Marquis de 41, 80, 178, 192, 200, 229n17
Lake George 24–25, 28–29, 31, 33, 37
Larned, Ellen 16, 53, 54, 64, 70, 207, 211–213, 230
The Last of the Mohicans 31, 192
Lawrence, Amos 100
Lee, Charles 103–104, 106–109, 154, 156, 176, 185, 189, 218n6, 226n, 230n
Lee, Henry 171
Lee, Michael 152, 226n87
Leitch, Andrew 126, 222n58
Leonard, Rev. Abiel 111
Lexington, Massachusetts 70–71, 74–75, 79, 81, 195–197, 201, 214n67, 219n178, 220n24, 223n79, 225n69, 230n33
Library of Congress 127
Lincoln, Benjamin 190, 192, 225n69, 229n17
Lionel Lincoln 193
Lively (ship) 80, 87
Livingston, William Farrand 4, *11*, 24, *27*,

39–**40**, 60–61, 63, 66, 72, 80, 87–88, 91, **110**, 116, **122**, 136, 147, 163, 167, 174, 196, 208*n*14, 221*n*49, 226*n*109, 227*n*118, 230*n*36
Long Island, Battle of 92, 99, 115–121, 126, 128, 190, 220*n*31
Lossing, Benson 143
Louisbourg (Cape Breton Island) 33
Lounsbury, Phineas C. 197
Lyman, Phineas 21, 26–27, 32–33, 45
Lyman, Thaddeus 65, 67

MacArthur, Douglas 177, 181, 230*n*33
Machin, Thomas 145, 148
Madison, Dolly 189
Magaw, Robert 130–131, 223*n*81
"Maggie Lauder" 174, 228*n*10
Manhattan 116–118, 121–125, 128–129, 221*n*42
Marion, Francis 173, 202, 207*n*33
Marsh, John 194
Martin, Joseph Plumb 128, 222*n*69
"Mary Had a Little Lamb" 100
Massachusetts Committee of Safety 72, 92
massacre 23, 28, 30–31, 48, 143, 208*n*18, 209*n*40, 211*n*49, 224*n*51
McCullough, David 57, 117
McDougall, Alexander 129, 147, 154, 158, 226*n*110
McPherson, John 138–139 224*n*32
Meade, Gen. Ebenezer 165
Meigs, Return Jonathan 105, 146–147, 225*n*62
Memorial Hall Museum (Deerfield, Massachusetts) **27**, 200
Mifflin, Thomas 113–116, 132, 134–135, 219*n*3
Miles, Gen. Nelson A. 169
Mississippi (boat) 65
Mississippi (river) 31, 47, 51, 64, 66–68, 158, 181, 190, 212*n*53, 212*n*80, 212*n*82, 232*n*16
Molang 39
Monmouth, Battle of 98, 109, 154, 184, 223*n*1
Monro, Lt. Col. George 28
Monroe, James 128, 136, 191, 223, 232
Montcalm 28–30, 34, 36, 41
Montgomery, Gen. Richard 104, 192
Montreal 41–43, 68, 89, 170, 212*n*80
Moore, Col. Hal 203
Morgan, Daniel 143–144, 173, 178, 224*n*55
Morris, Gouverneur 154, 226*n*93
Morris, Roger 122, 126 221*n*42
Morristown, New Jersey 139, 171
Morro Castle 46
Moulton's Hill 85
Moynihan, Sen. Daniel Patrick 120–121
Muhlenberg, Peter 154–155, 226*n*98
Munsell, Hezekiah 123, 221*n*45
Murray, Mary 124–125, 221, 234

muskets 161, 208*n*5
mutiny 161–163, 200

Nassau Hall 138; *see also* Princeton University
Native Americans 15, 19, 23, 28, 30–31, 36–37, 38–40, 42, 49, 66, 71, 96, 98, 129, 143, 144, 164, 197, 213*n*86, 231*n*2
Nelson, Adm. Horatio 41
New England Cookbook 208*n*6
New Haven, Connecticut 73, 172, 189, 205*n*3
New Orleans 47, 66, 100, 216*n*133
New York (city) 47, 65, 68, 71, 87, 115, 117, 119, 123, 125, 128, 131, 143–144 146, 150, 155, 157, 190, 194–195, 200, 222*n*67, 222*n*68, 222*n*70, 223*n*81, 227*n*140
New York (state) 14, 20–21, 23, 26, 28–29, 35–36, 40–41, 43, 45–46, 48, 64, 96, 104, 107–108, 112–113, 120, 127, 129, 141, 145, 148–149, 152–153, 155–156, 158, 160, 164, 169, 171, 173–174, 181, 188, 199, 210*n*1, 211*n*49, 217*n*138, 227*n*142, 228*n*142, 231*n*3, 233*n*38, 233*n*49, 234*n*51
New York Times 152, 196–197, 199, Newport, Rhode Island 111, 181, 211*n*19, 216*n*133
nicknames 18, 101, 137, 197, 207*n*33, 217*n*138, 228*n*1
Niven, John 95, 156
Noddle's Island 77–79, 105

Occum, Jonathan 98

Paine, Judge Elijah
Palmer, Edmund 141–142
Paoli Massacre 143
Parsons, Samuel H. 105, 114, 145–147, 160
Patton, Gen. George 186, 202
pay scales 103–104, 162, 217*n*151
Pell's Point (in Bronx, New York) 128
Philadelphia 71, 104, 106, 117, 130–137, 139–140, 143, 147, 150, 154, 157, 162, 176, 197, 222*n*59, 223*n*78
piracy 3, 52, 66, 211*n*28
Plains of Abraham, battle of 36, 61
Poe, Edgar Allan 153
Pollard, Asa 89
Pomeroy, Seth 104, 109, 201
Pontiac's War 48
Poor, Salem 98
Prescott, Samuel 71, 213*n*
Prescott, Col. William 81–85, 87–90, 92–93, 95–98, 101–108, 188, 191, 231*n*3
Princeton 137–139
prison ships 131, 220*n*31
Putnam, Albert D. **168**
Putnam, Alfred P. 192
Putnam, Ann 9
Putnam, Catherine Hutchinson 181, 188
Putnam, Daniel 14, 20, 49, 53–55, 65, 72,

74–76, 78, 80–84, 110, 160, 171, 181–182, 188, 191–192, 207n23, 212n53, 230n44, 232n16, 232n20
Putnam, David Endicott 157, 205n
Putnam, Deborah Lothrop Avery Gardiner (second wife) 50, 52–56, 61, 65, 74, 149, 152–153, 173, 211n24, 230n44
Putnam, Eben 205n1
Putnam, Eunice (daughter) 14, 26, 49, 53, 65, 74, 172, 182, 205n1, 206n23, 230n44
Putnam, Hannah (daughter) 49, 53, 65, 74, 182, 206n23, 211n31, 212n53, 230n44
Putnam, Hannah Pope (first wife) 11, 12, 14, 19–20, 42, 49–50, 52, 208n6
Putnam, Israel: bamboo cane 7–8; birth 3, 10, *11*; captain 26; childhood 10–11; courage 40–41, 95, 100, 151, 157; death 182–185; education 156, 158, 176; family involvement with the Salem Witch Trials 3, 8–10; farmer 11–18, 49, 53–54, 100, 127, 169, 177, 201, 207n28, 228n145, 231n3; first Pomfret house 12–13, 206n16; freemason 39–40, 80, 157, 184; Horseneck escape 164–*165*, *167*, *168*–169, 200, 227n137; humor 59–60, 155, 169–170, 173–174, 180–181, 228n10; inventiveness 170; major general appointment 104; marriages 11–12, 52–54; opposition to additional public houses 179–180, 194; paralytic stroke 18, 172–174, 179, 188; plow 72, *73*, 196–197, 200; physical appearance 57–58; portraits *110*, *122*, *174*; powder horn *27*, 200; promoted to major 26; religion 19, 49–51, 179, 183–185; saddle 200; saves Rogers's life 23–24; second Pomfret house *14*; set on fire 38–*40*; shipwreck at Cuba; 45–46, 65; shoots wolf 14–15, *16*–19, 179–180, 194, 199–200, 207n35, 211n32; statues *168*, *183*, *193*, *198*; tomb (1790) 182, 196; tomb (1888) 182, 197–198; torch 16, 17, 200; West Point 148, 154–155, 171; wounds 39, 41, 174, 198
Putnam, Israel, Jr. (son) 14, 20, 65, 74, 172, 181–182, 206n23
Putnam, John 8
Putnam, John D. 198
Putnam, Joseph (father) 3, 8, 9
Putnam, Mary (daughter) 49, 53, 65, 74, 172, 182, 205n1, 206n23, 230n44
Putnam, Mehitable (daughter) 14, 49, 53, 65, 74, 172, 182, 205n1, 206n23, 213n3, 230n44
Putnam, Peter Schuyler (son) 14, 42, 49, 53, 65, 74, 181–182, 207n23, 230n44
Putnam, Rufus 65–68, 129–130, 157–158, 181, 190, 201, 222n72, 226n109, 229n20
Putnam, Samuel (Judge) 7, 18, 40, 151, 157, 179
Putnam, Sarah Waldo (daughter-in-law) 53
Putnam, Thomas (grandfather) 8–9, *11*
Putnam, William H. 198

Putnam (Connecticut) 1, 172, 199–200
Putnam counties 199, 233n49
Putnam Cottage (also Knapp Tavern) *165*, 169 228
helpPutnam, or the Iron Son of '76" (play) 194
Putnam Library or the Belpre Library 199
Putnam Memorial State Park (Redding, Connecticut) *159*, 160, 164, 169, 200, 227n140
Putnam Phalanx 196, 200

Quakers 135, 223n
Quebec 36, 42–43, 53, 89, 212n80
Queen's Rangers 127–128

railing 113–114
Randolph (frigate) 133
Revere, Paul 71, 88, 94, 213n13
Richardson, William 126, 222n59
Rickenbacker, Eddie 1, 205n
Robinson, Beverly 149
Robinson, Henry C. *183*, 198
Rogers, Robert 21–26, 34, 37–38, 78, 89, 110, 119, 127–128, 133, 166, 187–188, 208–209n, 230, 239
Rogers Rangers 21–22, 25, 34, 37, 78, 89, *110*, 119, 127, 133, 187–188, 209n40, 230n2
Roman Catholicism 47–48, 58, 69, 210n6, 210n8
Ross, Betsy 137, 224
Runnels, Ezra 91

St. Philip's Church (Garrison, New York) 149, 153, 226n86
Salem Village (now Danvers) 7, 8, 9, 10, *11*, 12, 13, 40, 80, 101, 157, 179, 206n10, 206n23
Salem witch trials 3, 8–9, 157
Saratoga, New York 98, 100, 144, 146, 149, 158, 213n28, 224n55, 231n2, 231n3
The Scarlet Letter, a Romance 8
Schuyler, Elizabeth 189
Schuyler, Col. Peter 41–42, 209n75
Schuyler, Philip 104, 107–108, 178, 189, 201, 234n62
Scott, Charles 154, 229n17
Scott, John 75
Shays' Rebellion 190, 231n3
sheep 12, 15, 16, 70, 77, 207n28, 211n32
Sheridan, Philip 163, 203
Sherman, Roger 78, 79, 105, 213n42
Sherman, William Tecumseh 81, 101–102, 217n140
shipwreck (Cuba) 45–46, 65
Sigourney, Lydia Huntley 195
Silliman, Gold Selleck 123, 221n44
Small, John 66, 70, 110, 212n81, 232n20
smallpox 31, 139–140, 184, 224n37, 230n42

Smallwood's Maryland regiment 118, 220*n*24, 229*n*17
Society of the Cincinnati 177–178
Somerset (ship) 89
Sons of Liberty 48, 63–64, 69–71, 93, 158, 210*n*9, 225*n*69
South Cemetery (Brooklyn, Connecticut) 196
Spaulding, Joseph 89, 214*n*80–81
Spencer, Gen. Joseph 73, 104–107, 109, 154
The Spy 149
Stamp Act 62–64
Stanislaus, King of Poland 108
Stark, John 77, 88, 93, 96, 102, 188, 215*n*104, 217*n*143, 229*n*17, 230*n*2
Stevens, Henry, E. (Connecticut member of Congress) 199
Stevenson, Burton 201
Stony Point, New York 145, 171
submarines 119–120, 170
Sullivan, John 104, 115, 117–118, 138, 219*n*13
Sumter, Gen. Thomas 173, 207*n*33
Swett, Samuel 91–92
Swinton, William 201

Taft, Royal C. 197
Tarbox, Increase N. 49, 54, 57, 64, 72, 101–102, 124, 232*n*20
temperance 179–180, 194
Thacher, James 124, 155, 221*n*51
Thomas, Gen. John 104
Throg's Neck (Bronx, New York) 128, 222*n*70
Tilghman, Tench 176, 229*n*15
Tories 47, 79, 108, 113–114, 135–136, 212*n*80, 221*n*44, 224*n*51
Touro, Judah 100, 216–217, 238
Tracy, Spencer 188
Treaty of Paris 47, 178
Trenton 136–137, 144, 219*n*178, 219*n*21, 221*n*57, 220*n*27
Trumbull, John (painter) 79, 93, 99, ***174***, 192, 200, 214, 216, 222, 231–232, 240
Trumbull, John (poet) 79, 214
Trumbull, Jonathan 72, 104, 121, 166
Trumbull, Joseph 104, 218
Tryon, William 124, 142, 164, 168–169, 210*n*1, 227*n*142
Tuchman, Barbara Wertheim 97, 169, 216*n*122
"Turtle" 119–120
Tyler, Daniel 70, 172, 180, 213*n*

United States Constitution 4, 178, 182, 219*n*3, 226*n*93

Valley Forge 23, 100, 139, 152, 154, 160, 184, 190, 221*n*57
Van Wyck, Cornelius 148–149
Van Wyck Homestead 148–149

Vaughan, John 146
Verplanck, New York 145
Veterans Administration 179
Vision of Columbus, The 99
Von Heister, Gen. Leopold Philip 117–118, 220*n*27, 222*n*77

Wadsworth, Jeremiah 171, 178
Waldo, Albigence 38, 184 230*n*42
Waller, Lt. John 96
Ward, Artemas 72, 75, 78, 82–84, 88, 95, 103–104, 107–108, 189, 213*n*, 218*n*, 231, 238
Ward, J.Q.A. (John Quincy Adams) ***193***, 195
Warner, Israel Putnam 62, 212
Warner, Seth 62
Warren, Joseph 70, 75–76, 78–80, 82, 88, 90, 93–95, 97–99, 191–192
Warrups, Tom 164
Washington, George 4, 17, 19–20, 50, 54–55, 57–59, 75, 78, 80, 92–94, 99, 102–113, 115, 117–118, 120–127, 129–132, 135–140, 143–145, 147, 149–158, 160, 162–164, 171, 173–174, 176–179, 181, 186–190, 192, 194–195, 197, 199–201, 205*n*2, 205*n*4, 207*n*3, 209*n*51, 210*n*6, 212*n*49, 214*n*59, 216*n*129, 216*n*132, 219*n*178, 228*n*9, 229*n*15, 229*n*16, 229*n*17, 231*n*2, 232*n*17, 232*n*20
Washington, John Augustine 104
Washington, Martha 54, 200
Washington D.C. 232*n*14
Wayne, Anthony 115–116, 143, 171, 178, 189, 197, 200, 202, 229*n*17
Webb, Gen. Daniel 25, 28, 29
Webb, Samuel B. 74, 90, 106, 110, 142–143, 151, 176, 188, 218*n*178
Webster, Daniel 192, 232*n*21
White Plains, battle of 128–131, 219*n*178, 220*n*27
Whitney, Rev. Josiah 51, 182–184, 230*n*37
Wigglesworth, Edward 147
Williams, John 199
Wilson, Henry 101
Wolcott, Oliver 135
wolf 14–19, 179–180, 194, 199–200, 207*n*35, 211*n*32
Wolfe, Gen. James 35–36, 61, 212*n*67, 221*n*49
Woodford, William 154
Wooster, David 73, 78, 104, 105, 109, 189, 228n142

Yale College 21, 41, 49, 52, 99, 105, 119, 147, 157, 175, 192, 197, 209*n*65, 216*n*129, 225*n*69
HMS Yarmouth 133, 223*n*6
York, Alvin 203
Young, Thomas 70

www.ingramcontent.com/pod-product-compliance
Ingram Content Group UK Ltd.
Pitfield, Milton Keynes, MK11 3LW, UK
UKHW041937140426
5217IPUK00014B/520